INTERNAL INVESTIGATIONS

ABOUT THE AUTHOR

Dr. Frank A. Colaprete is the owner and lead consultant for Justice Systems Solutions, LLC as well as a faculty member for Keuka College, Roger Williams University's Justice and Training Research Institute, the Civic Institute at Mercyhurst College, and Norwich University. With respect to his law enforcement background, he was a police lieutenant who served in the law enforcement field from 1985 to 2005. He was assigned to patrol, research, training, administration, internal affairs, and investigative support.

INTERNAL INVESTIGATIONS

A Practitioner's Approach

By

FRANK A. COLAPRETE, ED.D.

Justice Systems Solutions, LLC

With a Foreword by

Dr. Richard C. Lumb

CHARLES C THOMAS • PUBLISHER, LTD.
Springfield • Illinois • U.S.A.

Published and Distributed Throughout the World by

CHARLES C THOMAS • PUBLISHER, LTD.
2600 South First Street
Springfield, Illinois 62704

ISBN 978-0-398-07713-6 (hard)
ISBN 978-0-398-07714-3 (paper)

Library of Congress Catalog Card Number: 2006049248

With THOMAS BOOKS *careful attention is given to all details of manufacturing and design. It is the Publisher's desire to present books that are satisfactory as to their physical qualities and artistic possibilities and appropriate for their particular use.* THOMAS BOOKS *will be true to those laws of quality that assure a good name and good will.*

Printed in the United States of America
SR-R-3

Library of Congress Cataloging-in-Publication Data

Colaprete, Frank A.
Internal investigations : a practitioner's approach / by Frank A. Colaprete, with a foreword by Richard C. Lumb.
p. cm.
Includes bibliographical references and index.
ISBN 978-0-398-07713-6 (hard) -- ISBN 978-0-398-07714-3 (paper)
1. Police--Supervision of. 2. Investigations. I. Title.

HV7936.S8C63 2007
363.2'2--dc22

2006049248

Frank Louis Colaprete
Military Police Officer
WWII
1925 to 1989

For you dad. Your memory will always live on in your loving son.

DISCLAIMER

In regards to federal, state, and local statutes, case laws, court rulings, labor laws, and agreements, it should be noted that different jurisdictions must abide by all applicable legal and procedural requirements. Readers and users should examine their own requirements as well as seek legal counsel if needed.

This book is designed to provide information in regards to the subject matter covered. It should not be interpreted as legal advice. The author assumes no responsibility or liability to any person or entity with respect to any loss or damage caused or alleged to be caused, directly, or indirectly by the information and illustrations in this book.

FOREWORD

Competing demands for social justice, police ethics, and police community service often meet in conflict at the door of a police Internal Affairs unit. Policing, by its very nature, is controversial and can evoke deep emotion. Police officers are tasked with an often impossible expectation that demands they keep us safe, provide top quality service, follow the rules, do no harm, and remove undesirable people from causing social mischief or committing a crime. Executing these duties, the officer frequently encounters people who have little regard for the law, social norms, the outcome, or impact of committing a crime, or the plight of victims. When dealing with a person who is agitated, fleeing from the police, or willing to resist being arrested, even to the extent of killing, police officers are in a very traumatic and difficult situation.

People who disagree with police action or behavior have the right to file a complaint against the officer and expect that justice will prevail. When a complaint is filed it initiates an internal police activity that seeks the truth of events leading to a decision of the appropriate outcome. All parties to this action are apprehensive, defensive, and there is anticipation that they will be vindicated. At the end of the day, one or more parties will be unhappy and experience feelings they were judged unfairly. The complexity of the investigative process, the absolute demand for impartial and thorough investigation of all complaints against a police officer is the foundation of trust by citizens of our police.

For many years, Frank Colaprete practiced the police profession, rising to the rank of Lieutenant. He served in a number of capacities and those experiences provide a wealth of knowledge and examples that he applies to the practice and performance of police officers in today's society. This book combines common sense approaches to policing that are grounded in both empirical research and proven practice.

In his book, Dr. Colaprete explores the issues and process of conducting proper and thorough internal investigations. He carefully examines the intricacies of this important police function and throughout the book illustrates the importance of knowing how and understanding why it is important to be complete, respect all parties to the complaint, represent the police organization with the utmost integrity of purpose, and remain sensitive to the individuals involved.

Dr. Colaprete has combined his education, experience, and practical wisdom in writing this book. If we accept the underlying organizational philosophy and guiding principles of conducting an internal investigation, then this book will serve as an invaluable source of information. Dr. Colaprete's approach emphasizes common sense, best practices, the need for unyielding ethical behavior, and a depth of empathy for both the complainant and the officer.

This text is a valuable contribution to policing and community justice. The final product is a book that should be read by every police executive, internal affairs officer, and others in the criminal justice system that have responsibility for maintaining social cohesiveness. It is a book of immense value with immediate and future application.

Dr. Richard C. Lumb

PREFACE

Throughout the history of law enforcement, the internal investigation process has held the most negative connotation of any investigation conducted by law enforcement personnel. Formalized procedural edicts were formed in many large organizations during the late sixties and early seventies. They were the result of horror stories such as Serpico and the like that had cast an imposing as well as everlasting shadow upon the law enforcement community's ability to police its' own. Questionable and criminal activities within police organizations have given rise to such investigative bodies as the Knapp Commission, the Mollen Commission, and the Christopher Commission, just to name a few. Despite the venerable history of law enforcement in the United States, it pales in comparison to the actions of an insignificant number of officers who engage in misconduct that sadly, has a negative impact on the entire institution.

The insertion of independent civilian review boards has been identified by many police administrators, politicians, and communities as a means of checks and balances in the system. Even though these quasi-investigatory and judicial bodies have proven effective in maintaining the delicate balance needed to police a free society, most review boards are perceived by special interest groups as being a "rubber stamp" of vindication for eons of perceived and real police injustice.

The mission of this book is to demonstrate the need for proper and complete internal investigations as well as to teach the entry level and tenured police supervisor the form and function of the internal investigations process. Throughout the text you will find a model for conducting internal investigations of police personnel that will allow you as a police supervisor or commander to conduct investigations in a thorough, legal, and equitable manner. This book is also designed to meet the needs of attorneys who litigate cases involving allegations of police misconduct as well as representatives of collective bargaining groups who represent police personnel in similar actions. Those who are involved as members of investigative groups such as a civilian review board will also find this text helpful in understanding the unique and complex nature of the task of investigating law enforcement personnel complaints.

As we progress through the new millennium, the task of efficient and effective law enforcement services and practices grows ever more critical. As law enforcement officials, the job becomes evermore complex as new and more demanding restrictions are placed on our ability to police an even more complex society than when most first entered the police service. Sensitivity to civil rights as well as media exploitation of newsworthy events further adds to the insurmountable task of effectively policing a free society. This book is designed to foster and engender an understanding of effective tactics and practices of internal investigation that protects the rights of the complainant, the organization, and the involved personnel realizing that each entity's interests are tantamount to the others. The internal investigator does not have to be "pro-cop," "pro-administration," or "pro-community" to complete the internal investigation properly. The internal investigator must however, be "pro-investigation" to achieve this noble outcome.

The leadership and change management begins with you!

Dr. Frank A. Colaprete

ACKNOWLEDGMENTS

Throughout developing this project, I was faced with the fascination of discovering new and varied methodologies in the internal affairs process that was ultimately balanced against the agony of such a monumental writing project. Amidst all of these painful efforts I found the motivation from those who were supporters of this work. A work that I am hoping adds value and positive change to the concept and practice of internal investigations. I would be remiss though, if I didn't acknowledge those who have been such an integral part of this worthy process.

My first gratitude goes to Michael P. Thomas of Charles C Thomas • Publishers Ltd. as without his encouragement and trust, this project would not have been as meaningful or successful development in a critical area of law enforcement. His staff and his personal professionalism have added much to the final product.

As for the people behind the scenes, I credit much of my success in life and my profession to those who have so graciously given me the gifts of knowledge and wisdom as I have navigated life's path. They are most likely humbled by my comments, however they deserve the highest recognition for their generosity and their deeply felt love of true friendship: Dr. Richard C. Lumb, Professor Rand Gee, Captain Joseph J. Davis, Lieutenant Michael VanRoo, Officer Jonathan Northrup, and last, but certainly not least, Officer Emre Arican, who is not only a close and trusted friend, but also worked diligently and tirelessly in editing the manuscript and assisting in the photography. I am eternally grateful to those who have contributed to my professional and personal development throughout the years.

A special thanks also is afforded to Chief Dan Varrenti and Sergeant Mark Philippy of the Brockport Police Department for their assistance in the illustrations for this book. In line with this, several media groups and companies provided materials and copyrights that made this text a comprehensive and contemporary review of the discipline. In addition, Diann Henry of CNN provided invaluable assistance in her research and advocacy for the use of many of the photographs of high profile cases that added depth and reality to this review of the topic.

And finally, to my dearly departed father, Frank Louis Colaprete, who has been my guiding light throughout my life. Even in death, he is still there for me lighting the path. To my wife Katherine, there are no words that will ever compensate her for the sacrifices she has made for me throughout our lives together. Her patience, understanding, and unselfish love for me allow me to produce these works that may benefit the field and save the lives and careers of those who serve in the most noble of professions.

Dr. Frank A. Colaprete
Justice Systems Solutions, LLC

CONTENTS

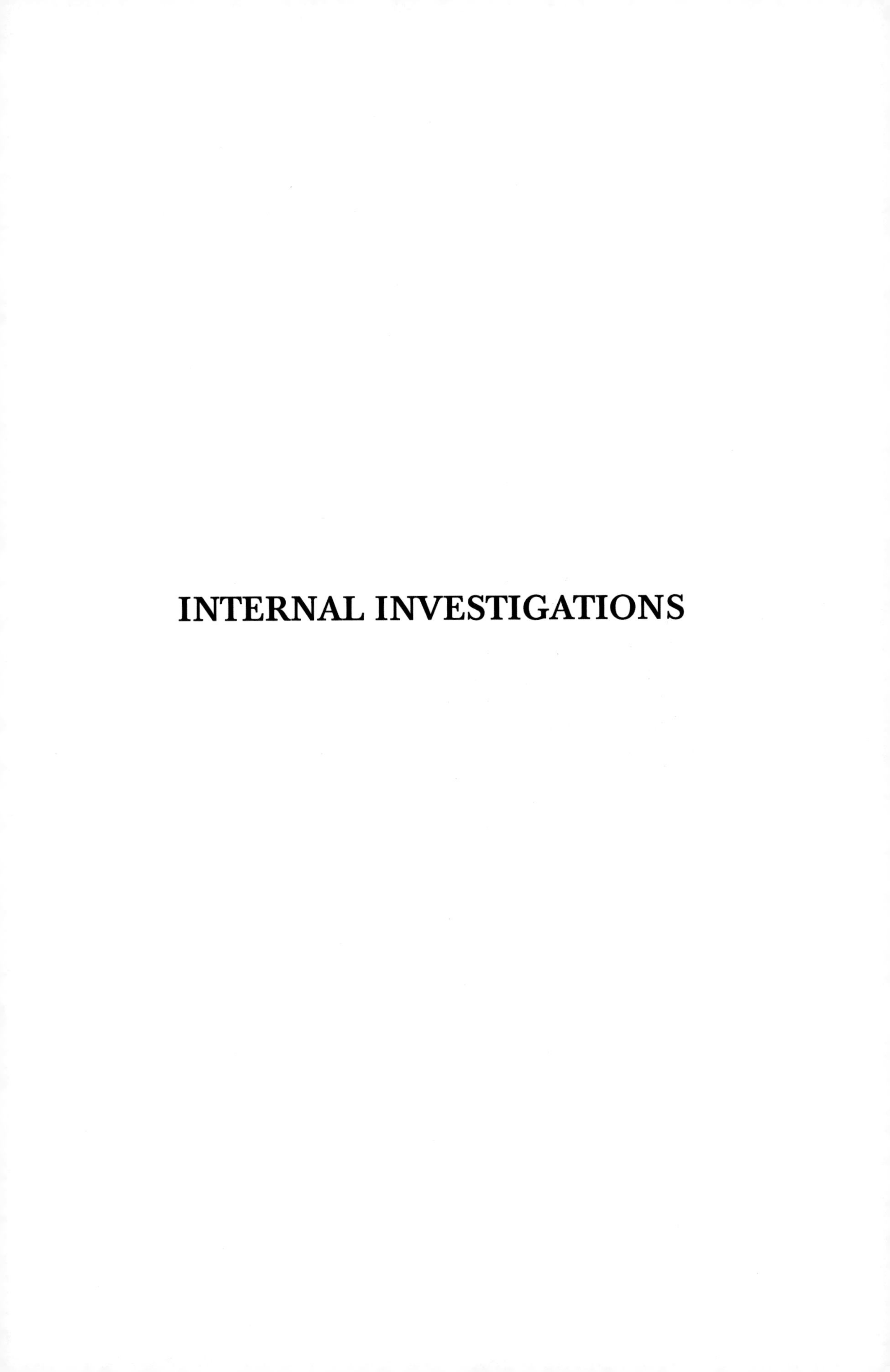

INTERNAL INVESTIGATIONS

Chapter 1

THE PURPOSES AND PRACTICAL IMPLICATIONS OF INTERNAL INVESTIGATION

INTRODUCTION

The purposes and practical implications of the internal investigation process must be understood at the outset for the internal investigator and law enforcement administrator to appreciate the need. While the text addresses the legal and procedural issues, the reader must also understand the reasons why the internal investigation is an integral part of the entire context of law enforcement service delivery.

THE PURPOSES OF INTERNAL INVESTIGATION

The purposes of the internal investigation are multitudinous. While perceived by most as only for the purpose of discipline, the process must evolve into an orientation of continuous improvement activities. From this orientation, police administrators, the community, collective bargaining units, and most importantly, the officers themselves may understand why the process is critical to progressive law enforcement services. Absent this orientation, as a profession, we forego our ability to police ourselves and the opportunity to continue to improve on the quality of services that we offer our respective communities.

The internal investigation process in many organizations has led to the identification of not only misconduct, but criminal behavior on behalf of law enforcement personnel. In addition, these outcomes have served the purpose of protecting the community from rogue officers while demonstrating the image that an organization can effectively rectify its own mistakes in hiring, retention, and monitoring practices. The investigation of personnel complaints can also lead to several positive outcomes, for example, the need for new, modified, or improved and innovative training. Because of emerging case law and technology, the process can lead to the development of new and innovative policies, procedures, and practices that meet the needs of contemporary society. The internal investigation can also lead to the identification of several other issues such as problem employees and the initial steps to remedial or disciplinary action, as well as the potential for civil liability claims that can be abated or at least mitigated. Of paramount importance is the identification of personnel who are justified in their actions and supported by a credible and unbiased process of inquiry and review. There are numerous advantages to the internal investigation process that are lost in the reflection of media frenzy, politics, poor leadership, and inadequate investigative process. The most crucial point of this text is to affirm that the driving forces of the process should not taint the process.

One final point is the need for law enforcement administrators to grasp a lucid understanding that they must always manage for the rule and not the exception. A parody in many law enforcement organizations is the attachment of a single officer's name to a new rule, policy, or procedure. Police administrators must always avoid the alarmist approach to policy development. When personnel make legitimate mistakes, the best route to take to the high road is to understand a concept based in the legal realm; that of the "totality of the circumstances" of an event. As such, objective review of an incident must include this concept and a measure of the true need for reinventing policy. Care must always be taken in changing a rule in place subsequent to an incident as the question will then be, "Why wasn't the rule changed before the incident, thus the incident may have been avoided?" The courts of this land recognize and wholly embrace the fact that policing is an inexact science and as such, measure an incident not so much by strict rules, but by the reasonableness of the law enforcement officer's actions. This orientation is critical to delivering a fair finding to any case investigated.

Internal or administrative investigations serve numerous purposes. Many are obvious, some are not so obvious, and many are misunderstood. An honest and fair investigative process should be viewed as an opportunity to: (1) reestablish credibility in a department's internal investigation process, (2) defend officers who are the subject of false allegations, and (3) allow the chief executive officer to evaluate the current level of training and equipment available to the officers in the department (Stine, 2001). In addition, internal investigations serve several other purposes such as:

1. *Protection of the Involved Officer:* Only a small percentage of all complaints filed result in a sustained finding, therefore, the overwhelming majority of complaints filed are either baseless, emanate from a misunderstanding of police procedure, or are false and initiated by individuals who are seeking retribution for some negatively perceived police actions.
2. *Protect the Community:* Although infrequent, occasions present themselves when an officer has violated policy, procedure, or engaged in police misconduct.
3. *Protect the Department:* Protect against baseless or unfounded complaints and the subsequent civil claims filed against the organization and its members (e.g., vicarious liability, poor press, etc.).
4. *Removal of Unfit Personnel:* Infrequently, unfit personnel enter the ranks and are discovered because of aberrant behavior, criminal behavior, corruption, misconduct, and the like. These situations mandate that the department take appropriate remedial or even disciplinary action to correct behavior and prevent future complaints and exposure to liability.
5. *Correction of Procedural Problems:* Occasionally, a policy is discovered to be outdated or personnel have not received adequate training in the policy in question. The discovery during the internal investigation provides the department the opportunity to review and revise the policy to meet contemporary needs. (Garmire, 1982, p. 281)

The Driving Forces

The internal investigation process involves several driving forces. These forces will have a significant impact on a case dependent upon the influence or amount of force applied. Politics and community outcry have had a profoundly negative impact on the internal investigation process. The subsequent damage caused to law enforcement organizations because of incomplete or biased investigations, have led to unjust actions taken against law enforcement personnel. In addition, communities that lose confidence in a department's administrative investigation process may redirect their complaints to municipal administrators and civilian review boards (Thurnauer, 2002).

ALLCOP = Quality Customer Service

A conceptual argument for the driving forces of the process can be made from the most prominent entities that influence the process. They can be considered as part of the acronym ALLCOP, which means:

Administrative requirements
Legal requirements
Liability risks
Community expectations
Organizational expectations
Personnel/employee satisfaction

ALLCOP = Quality Customer Service and is discussed as follows:

Administrative, Legal, and Liability Requirements: These three considerations must overcome the politics, community, and other subsequent forces. If politics or community pressure forces unjust or premature disciplinary actions, the case may be lost, and the process, the administration, and the community will all suffer the consequences. Legal and procedural requirements must be followed without deviation along with the adherence to collective bargaining agreements and administrative law. Failure to provide these most basic due process rights will leave the rank and file with the validated opinion that their rights are less important than the hardened criminals they arrest. Civil liability is inexorably linked to these issues as litigation often follows such violations of legal or administrative requirements.

Community Expectations: The community is the customer and as such has the right to efficient, effective, and ethical law enforcement services. However, this is lost when the rank and file believes that a law enforcement officer was disciplined unjustly and they themselves respond by failing to provide the highest quality service possible because of numerous reasons. In addition, the return of an unethical officer to the service because of illegal investigative practices of the law enforcement organization also impacts the quality of service to the customer. While many organizations laud a "customer service first" mission statement, absent the first two components in priority order, quality customer service will be rendered impossible.

Organizational Expectations: This will be the most difficult concept for the administrator to grasp. Organizational expectations in this equation are last in line. This concept emerges from the premise that supported and satisfied law enforcement personnel will act ethically and legally and thus satisfy the community. The byproduct is that the organization's expectations will be met at the conclusion of the process, not the beginning. Many law enforcement organizations have adopted an inverse relationship with customer service; the chief and not the community being the customer. Organizational members move quickly to satisfy the chief at the exclusion of all other factors. This exclusion unfortunately leads to significant gaps in real quality customer service.

Personnel/Employee Satisfaction: Personnel need to believe that they are contributing to the organization, are appreciated, and are growing within their positions. They are the first and not subsequent, or last link in the customer chain. Ensuring that they are subjected to a fair investigative process is the highest priority in the process. Absent this consideration, all others will ultimately fail.

Legal precedents exist for the liability of agencies who fail to investigate complaints that are brought to their attention. For example, in *Vinyard v. Wilson* (2002), the Eleventh Circuit Court ruled that a claim of a right to a use-of-force investigation had no basis as a substantive or due process right in the law. However, the case also revealed that individual states may grant procedural due process rights to individuals who make such a claim (Makholm, 2003a).

However, other case law exists where the courts denied summary judgment to a police department when an agency places a custom or practice in place that discourages the filing of complaints. As such, in "discouraging, ignoring, and not tracking complaints" constructively results in constitutional deprivations. This may then lead to a cause for a Section 1983 claim as this practice of inadequate complaint investigation resulted in unpunished police malpractice and a subsequent deliberate indifference to the rights of citizens (Martinelli, 2002). In addition, under Title VII, employers have a legal duty to investigate serious complaints such as those of rape or sexual harassment (Americans for Effective Law Enforcement, 2005).

The issue of a complaint investigation process hinges on the level of service a department desires to give a community, augmented by state and federal laws, any existing local, state, or federal oversight, as well as the requirements of accreditation.

THE PRACTICAL IMPLICATIONS OF INTERNAL INVESTIGATION

A certain pragmatism is involved in understanding the implications of the internal investigations process. That pragmatism emerges from an understanding that the process involves a delicate balancing act in order for all stakeholders to be served not only in proper fashion, but also with a measure of equity. Absent this balance, one or more entities will suffer. From a historical perspective, Sir Robert Peel in the Nineteenth Century employed the concept of the "Iron Discipline" in maintaining a productive police force. However, that discipline is tantamount to credibility and that credibility is both hard earned and extremely fragile when subjected to even the most isolated of police misconduct incidents (J. Anderson, 2001).

The foundation of discipline emanates from both an internal locus of control, where officers rely on beliefs, values, social mores, and personal experiences to guide their actions as well as the external controls such as laws, regulations, and policies. The conflict arises when the officers, who enter the service with the notion of the nobility of policing, through an evolutionary process, place themselves in precarious positions in order to make an arrest or do the proverbial right thing (Aveni, 2002a). The practical implications are that the arrest is lost, the criminal is set free, and the officer may face criminal, civil, and departmental sanctions for their misguided attempt to make the community a safer place to live.

And, while the question still looms, "Can the police be trusted to police themselves?" (McCarthy, 2000), the practical implication of an internal investigator who violates the rules is much more damaging than the former. These problems result in a breakdown of community trust. When misconduct is featured in the media, often a rise in unsubstantiated civilian complaints is realized by the agency, and a sympathetic response is felt across the country dependent upon the level of the media attention (Meissner, 1998).

The reality is that the process must exist, must function to serve many masters, and must be equitable and objective in order to be practical. Serving one master over others results in an impractical approach that will most likely damage the remaining entities that were not served equitably in the process.

Corruption v. Misconduct

This is one of the most difficult arguments in the internal investigation process at present. Police administrators, the public, and the media seem to have blended these two concepts as one. While this may appear to be a fine line of demarcation, the reality is that these are starkly different concepts. The media, the public, and sadly, police administrators paint this picture with a broad brush. Corruption is intended conduct and most often of a criminal nature. Corruption has been discovered in agencies large and small and can involve crimes at all levels. Studies have suggested that police officer corruption may be linked to the nature of policing immoral members of society (Stevens, 1999). While corruption is not unique to policing, no other profession seems to be more adversely affected by its presence (Monahan, 2000).

Misconduct is officer actions that are intentional, but do not rise to the level of criminal activity. This is an important distinction, as an officer who is intentionally discourteous, is not in effect, corrupt, nor a criminal. However, this is not specifically defined in some internal investigation processes.

Then too, is the officer who is neither corrupt, nor has committed misconduct, but has made a mistake in judgment. This can emerge from not being properly trained, the knowledge of a procedure has changed, or memory has lapsed because of the infrequency of use. For example, a penal or criminal law example can be offered as there are varying levels of culpability within the meaning of varied acts. This construct can be applied to police actions such as in building the definitional acts into the allegations themselves. Such a thought process allows for the appropriate and accurate measurement of the conduct as when an officer may not have knowingly been discourteous, may have acted recklessly when using a flashlight as a defensive tool and causing an injury, or unintentionally applying a defensive tactics technique incorrectly. These officers, while technically guilty, do not rise to the level of corruption or misconduct, and should be treated appropriately. Lieutenant Kevin Costello of the Rochester Police Department adeptly noted that these types of incidents can be categorized under several headings, like corruption, misconduct, or even "wisdomless ignorance."

In completing the internal investigation, the investigator must draw these clear distinctions in their conclusions and recommendations for penalty such as termination, disciplinary action, or remedial training. This distinction will have a significant impact on criminal and civil liability as well as department morale issues.

Living the Company Line

The edicts of a law enforcement organization can be found in rules, regulations, policies, and mission statements. These organizations will laud the respect for the community as well as their own employees. As a matter of course, organizations have worked diligently throughout history to be part and parcel to the community. These partnership and service ideas date back to the days of Sir Robert Peel and have been recurring themes in police organizations throughout the modern world. The problem in the internal investigations realm is that law enforcement organizations many times see that the needs of external entities far outweigh the needs of their internal staffs. As such, the mission, vision, and value statements that include the fair and equitable treatment of employees along with the affirmation that the human resources of a law enforcement organization are the most precious resource are constructively a fallacy. Therefore, law enforcement organizations that espouse this orientation must follow through with stated promises and edicts.

Company lines also include the need for officers to be aggressive and to protect the innocent in the community. As such, organizations need to recognize how the internal investigation impacts this motivational attitude in officers who are the subject of these administrative investigations. Issues that affect how officers approach their jobs are varied, such as: (1) the front page of the local newspaper, or the six-o'clock news, (2) lawsuits, (3) Federal consent decrees, (4) peer pressure to be less proactive, and (5) administrative pressure to avoid adverse incidents (Meyer, 2001). A supervisor, manager, or administrator must take great care in making promises to support the rank and file in aggressive police actions. History has revealed that this is a promise that is ill-advised and, more importantly, ill-kept.

To reiterate, the practice seems to lose something in the translation. Law enforcement organizations many times will treat all other entities far better than their own employees. That results in resentment and poor performance standards by employees who believe they are treated worse than the criminals they arrest. Therefore, the internal investigation should be as fair, objective, and respectful to all parties involved. The internal investigation should also be a fact-finding process and be "as interested in establishing innocence as in establishing guilt" (Garmire, 1982).

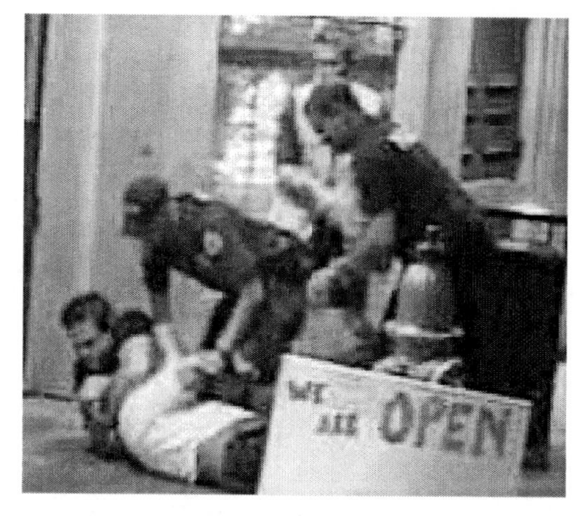

Figure 1-1. Media attention such as in the arrest of Robert Davis during the Katrina aftermath in New Orleans may have an adverse affect on the investigative process (CNN).

Contemporary Issues

Law enforcement and in particular, the policing environment, is in effect, a paradox. The practitioner, scholar, and layman consistently observe the venerable nature of policing fraught with controversy on an almost daily basis. With the advent of real-time media coverage and an extreme sensitivity to civil rights, the American public is exposed to the majority of controversial incidents that occur across the country in an unprecedented manner. This sad, but real fact seems to overcome much of the quality and service that is offered on a daily basis to the same constituents.

The contemporary nature of internal investigations is self-evident. The field is one that is dynamic and evolving as society's needs change. Historically, some of the first police scandals were revealed during the nineteenth century. Reformists like former President Theodore Roosevelt were appointed by agencies like the New York Police

Figure 1-2. Judge Milton Mollen of the Mollen Commission (CNN).

Figure 1-3. Officer Rafael Perez of the L.A.P.D. Rampart Division corruption scandal (CNN).

Department to eradicate corruption and make positive change. During the 1930s, the Wickersham Commission was empowered to investigate police corruption, uncovering bribery and corruption across the country during the Great Depression. The Knapp Commission and Mollen Commission both examined corruption in the New York City Police Department. The Christopher Commission examined civil rights violations in the Los Angeles Police Department. This list is not all inclusive, but representative of the issues identified in policing that have had significant impacts on how investigations and oversight are administered. However, the problem seems to remain the same.

Of significance is that many investigative commissions have dealt with widespread corruption in police departments. Many have also dealt with allegations of civil rights violations and excessive force. The United States Department of Justice was given reign over such investigations and in pattern and practice allegations, the Justice Department and Federal Bureau of Investigation will intercede and determine if their involvement and oversight is needed.

One of the more noted investigations took place in the Los Angeles Police Department Rampart Division scandal which was one of the most devastating in police history. The subsequent Board of Inquiry investigation and report addressed the issues of brutal misconduct and accusations of negligence and abuse in the ranks of the organization. The investigation revealed that officers in the anti-gang unit of the Rampart Division believed that they were in a life-or-death struggle that entitled them to break the established rules. The unit had also developed its own culture and operated as an entity unto itself. The Board of Inquiry also blamed the scandal on individual officers and supervisors rather than problems with the rules (*Law and Order*, 2000a). These types of investigations are devastating to not only the agency, but the profession as a whole.

Police organizations have responded by employing methods to discover and deter corruption. One example is found in the Los Angeles Police Department which has taken additional measures in attempting to fight corruption by exploring the possibility of tracking officers' personal finances by the use of a narrowly tailored financial disclosure requirement balancing the public's right to a corruption-free police force against the officers' right to privacy protection (*Law and Order,* 2000f). This type of methodology may have a significant impact on personnel who engage in corruption when the records can provide a trail for the investigation to follow in the efforts of the discovery of corrupt activities.

Allegations of excessive use-of-force seem to be more pervasive than allegations of corruption. Agencies like the New York Police Department have developed a program entitled Force Related Integrity Testing in which undercover officers pose as angry citizens. The program is designed to test the integrity of officers who have a history of abuse complaints. While the intent is to weed out corrupt and brutal officers, concerns have been voiced that the tactic of baiting can provoke a violent response from an armed officer, and could result in the serious injury or death of the undercover officer (*Law and Order,* 1999).

Concerns of privacy issues such as in the Los Angeles Police Department and safety issues in the New York Police Department are legitimate concerns. While problems have always existed in pervasive and episodic events, contemporary police administrators must consider all possible outcomes of a plan prior to implementing a strategy that is ineffective, exposes the agency to civil liability, or worse yet, is a danger to department personnel and the public at large.

To this point, the discussion has centered on the historical and contemporary nature of police misconduct and corruption. In addition, the examples provided have been the most egregious in context. Care must also be taken in examining incidents in the light of politics or contemporary community concerns reflected in the actions of other agencies and officers. History is also replete with examples of police administrators that have overreacted to recent events in the field and have caused more damage than good in their own departments and respective communities. Worse yet is the devastating effect that such actions have on the personnel of the agency as well as the law enforcement field as a whole.

A prime example of this is noted in the responses of the public to videotaped use-of-force incidents. Numerous high profile incidents across the country have spurred intense emotions and exaggerated reactions from police administrators. These emotions and reactions are a direct result of the public's lack of understanding of the methodology in the use-of-force. The majority of the public has no frame of reference of the proper or accepted methods in the use-of-force, which are compounded by inaccurate media accounts, lack of exposure, and stereotypes that create an unrealistic expectation of police officers by the community (Meyer, 1999). As such, police administrators must exercise a great amount of discretion in how they respond to emerging incidents that occur in their own or other law enforcement agencies.

Complaint Statistics

The issue of personnel complaint statistics is one of the most complex that a police administrator and internal investigator will face. In general, police organizations measure their effectiveness at customer service by the number of complaints received as well as the number of complaints that are actually sustained or result in some type of evidence that misconduct or corruption has occurred. From this, many agencies report to federal, state, and local administrators and the public the results of this analysis which is usually on an annual basis. The complexities in this process are numerous though and need consideration before a process is put in place.

That process must also be managed and reported accurately.

For the most part, despite inequities in the systems, politics, and flawed reporting processes, the average number of sustained complaints for police misconduct and corruption is approximately five percent to 10 percent of all complaints filed. Complaints also run the gamut and are not all corruption type or based in criminal activity. For example, many complaints received by a law enforcement agency are related to basic traffic stops where a ticket is issued and no use-of-force is involved (Onder, 2001).

With respect to founded allegations of police misconduct and corruption, from 1994 to 1997, a total of 508 persons were convicted in law enforcement corruption cases investigated by the FBI. These figures exclude those officers who are incarcerated in state and local correctional facilities. During this same period, the FBI also identified that 45 percent of these cases involved illicit narcotics. Speculation suggests that the lowering of hiring standards of the 1970s and 1980s have led to these problems (Hall, 1998). These figures suggest that much deeper issues exist in not only training, policy, practice, and monitoring systems, but in the candidate pools that law enforcement agencies have to choose from in the hiring phases.

In examining the statistics surrounding the use of deadly physical force, prosecutions of officer-involved shootings where criminal liability is involved averages one in 500 shootings (Gundy, 2003). Taken in context, most police-involved uses of deadly force involve three separate and distinct investigations (e.g., criminal many times involving local, state, and federal authorities, administrative within the organizations internal investigation process, and criminal and civil court review). The merits of this encompassing review process certainly would suggest that the overwhelming majority of police use of deadly force in the United States is justified based upon legal, departmental, and most importantly, moral standards.

In considering use-of-force complaints relative to the internal investigations process, research conducted by the International Association of Chiefs of Police in the use-of-force revealed that of the 3,972 incidents studied, only 20 complaints resulted. Of those 20, only one of them (5%) was sustained for violating policy (International Association of Chiefs of Police, 1998b). The IACP use-of-force study also indicated a trend in the decline in both the rate of use-of-force and the number of calls for service answered by police (Neubauer, 1999). However, this needs to also be placed in context to the total service picture offered to a community by a law enforcement agency.

One final issue with respect to complaint statistics deals with the issue of false complaints. While no research was located that indicated a percentage of total complaints that were false or baseless, this is a very real issue. Police and municipal administrators most often point to statistics as being the foundation for validating service levels, or showcasing the anti-corruption strategies employed in keeping an organization disciplined and free from corruption. However, false or baseless complaints should not be included in this statistical analysis. A salient opinion is offered by Jess Gundy (2003) as he states with respect to complaint statistics that:

> The situation is further exacerbated by law enforcement opponents that rely upon counting the frequency of complaints and civil suits brought against a police agency, and then using the data as an indicator of excessive force. This process is inherently flawed due to the nature of the complaints, which are more often than not extremely frivolous in nature. This perception of rampant excessive force used by officers is not entirely accurate. (p. 61)

While the issue of operationalizing the handling of false complaints is addressed later in the text, it is critical that they are also addressed from a systems or process perspective in order to ensure proper disposition in the reporting process.

Complaint statistics can polarize a department and a community. Such a response can result in lawsuits, civil unrest, federal oversight, and decreased morale and performance. In developing a system of reporting, organizations must study the parameters of complaint reporting that are unique to the organization aligned with accepted standard operating practices in the field. In addition, the reporting process should demonstrate the highest caliber of honesty as "adjusting" the statistics to meet the needs most often results in unintended outcomes. An example of this is the onslaught of agencies across the country that have modified crime statistics in order to offer the appearance of safer communities. Many of these agencies have been discovered and called to task, not only by their own municipal administrators, but also by the federal government and the media.

The studies conducted through the International Association of Chiefs of Police have laid a solid foundation for demonstrating confidence levels in the statistics reported in use-of-force in the country. For example, the International Association of Chiefs of Police study on police use-of-force revealed that well over 99 percent of the calls for service involved no use-of-force at all (Sanow, 2001a). This validated research on use-of-force to date refutes the claims by the media and the public that police abuse and misconduct are running rampant (Neubauer, 1999). Therefore, in building on internal studies of use-of-force and complaint reporting procedures, they must emanate from data-driven and accurate statistical reporting processes for them to be valid, useful, and beneficial rather than detrimental to the organization and possibly the field as a whole.

SUMMARY

This chapter has discussed the purposes and practical implications of the investigative process, which have been discussed in terms of the impact at the individual, organizational, community, and political levels. The purpose of internal investigations has been discussed from the perspective of legal, administrative, organizational, community, and personnel expectations. These perspectives were offered in order to develop an understanding of the internal investigation process from a systems perspective. The issues of corruption v. misconduct have also been reviewed and the fact that each concept must be reviewed in context as opposed to blending them together much like a mosaic, where the definitions become interlaced. The chapter then discussed the contemporary issues of internal investigations, the development and reporting of statistics, and the need to maintain an internal investigation process that is apolitical and motivated only by the discovery of the truth.

Chapter 2

PITFALLS OF CONDUCTING INTERNAL INVESTIGATIONS

INTRODUCTION

The internal investigation is the most difficult investigation that will be conducted by an investigator. The criminal investigator faces issues of resources, time, and criminal procedure laws, but for the most part is cast as an ingenious and almost mythical character in both fiction and in real life. Criminal investigators, and especially those in specialized assignments such as homicide, hold the highest esteem among the ranks of the profession. In contrast, the internal investigator is considered the pariah of fictional as well as real law enforcement agencies (Arnold, 1999). This image derives in part from media hype and Hollywood's characterizations of the burdens faced by the good, aggressive cop who altruistically fights the bureaucracy in order to protect the public.

The majority of this image problem actually is derived from several areas that include: (1) undue and unwarranted political influence, (2) poor and mismanaged internal investigation processes, (3) police administrators who find that the path of least resistance is to discipline rather than critically examine conduct from a perspective of the totality of the circumstances and understanding that policing is an inexact science at best, (4) internal investigators who take the assignment through a belief that the work will lead to promotion in the organization, (5) collective bargaining units that will block legitimate as well as illegitimate attempts to maintain discipline in an organization, and (6) the problem officers who are constantly exposed to the system and spread false propaganda concerning their innocence. These issues may seem collectively as well as individually insurmountable at times. Despite these pitfalls, the internal investigator must always adapt and overcome in order to ensure that the most comprehensive and objective investigation bears his or her name at the end. With this in mind, Jon Arnold (1999) states that, "Internal affairs investigators should hold places of honor not contempt. Law enforcement professionals should regard internal affairs functions as an integral part of their agencies" (p. 43). Changing the current mindset and developing a level of respect for the process begins with the internal investigator.

THE FUNCTION OF THE INTERNAL INVESTIGATOR

Simply stated, the function of the internal investigator is to determine the facts of the case (Arnold, 1999). From the perspective of a criminal investigator, the function is to collect facts that establish whether probable cause exists to make an arrest in a criminal case. While the orientation is for the most part objectively based in theory, the criminal investigator works for the victim of the crime and the prosecutor of the case. This characterization, may seemingly be overly simplistic, however, it is the basic function that is served in the criminal investigation process.

The function of the internal investigator is quite different than that of the role of a criminal investigator. The internal investigator must be prepared to perform numerous functions, analysis, and balance the process in consideration of the rights of all involved entities. The following is a list of the considerations that an internal investigator must consider in case investigation:

1. *The Complainant:* The internal investigator must be an advocate for the complainant, protecting their right to quality police service, right against unjust actions, violations of civil rights, and their rights to seek redress when they have been treated unjustly or unfairly by a law enforcement officer.
2. *The Community:* The internal investigator must be an advocate for the community that the target officer works in as if the conduct is sustained, the community must be protected from further unprofessional, unjust, corrupt actions.
3. *The Department:* The internal investigator must be an advocate for the department or organization as failing to correct unjust actions, failure to discipline or terminate, failure to exonerate the target officer's actions when justified, failure to identify training needs, and failure to protect the organization can all lead to such sanctions as civil and criminal liability as well as a loss of respect from the community they serve.
4. *The Municipal Administration:* The internal investigator must be an advocate for the federal, state, or local government entity served. The internal investigator must determine the facts, present the case, and in many incidents, be a witness to protect the entity from false allegations, civil liability, and negative opinions from the public and the media.
5. *The Court System:* The internal investigator must be an advocate for the legal aspects and the court system itself. Some investigations lead to the charging of criminal conduct. Some may also lead to internal sanctions and civil liability. The internal investigator must protect the rights of all entities involved from the legal, procedural, and civil edicts of this process.
6. *The Collective Bargaining Unit:* The internal investigator must be an advocate for the collective bargaining unit as required by legislative act, case law, and union agreement. The internal investigator must understand that violating contractual agreements is akin to violating the criminal laws.
7. *The Law Enforcement Personnel Involved in the Investigation:* The internal investigator must be an advocate for all other law enforcement personnel involved in the investigation who are not the target. Personnel who witness and have knowledge of incidents also have certain rights that need to be protected.
8. *The Target of the Investigation:* The internal investigator must be an advocate for the target of the investigation. The target must be provided all of the rights afforded through federal and state legislation, as well as any existing collective bargaining agreement. Those rights must transcend both the letter and spirit of the law.

The question is often raised concerning advocacy for the complainant. The expectation is that the internal investigator must be an advocate for the complainant and de facto advocate for the organization. The problem arises in the concept of advocacy. If the internal investigator is responsible to be fair, unbiased, and objective, then he or she must be an advocate for all entities involved, including the officer who is the target of the investigation. The aforementioned list delineates the need for such an orientation in the process. An internal investigator exercises an immense amount of power in the process that must be aligned perfectly with the rights of the complainant, organization, and involved officer, otherwise there will exist an irreparable injustice to all parties involved, not just the target officer.

COMMON ASSUMPTIONS AND MYTHS

In any process there will exist common assumptions and myths. The internal investigator must overcome such notions in order to conduct the fair and unbiased investigation that the complainant, organization, and target officer deserve. The following set of examples discusses the common myths and issues that arise when they are encountered.

The first common assumption or myth is that the officer is always wrong. The foundation of this archaic mindset can be found in the adage, "Round up the usual suspects!" This orientation is likely the most dangerous of the four cited. Sadly, the public, law enforcement administrators, and many supervisors believe that by virtue of the filing of a complaint, the officer has committed some wrongdoing. Given that statistically officers are only found guilty of some type of misconduct or error in approximately five percent to 10 percent of all complaints filed, this is a statistical impossibility, as well as an impractical mindset to work from. Even considering that the complaint is of similar conduct that may have been sustained in the past does not justify this assumption without the benefit of a complete investigation. Worse yet is that the investigator may attempt to influence the investigation by failing to uncover relevant facts that may exonerate the officer's actions or unfound the case.

The officer is always right is the second assumption that can have dangerous and long-reaching affects to all of the involved entities. This assumption is usually fostered by supervisors and managers who have actually been practitioners, or "worked in the trenches." As such, they are far more forgiving of their personnel. These people also assign more weight to an officer's statement than they do a complainant. Care must be taken in this assumption as the process is based upon a preponderance of evidence. As discussed later, involved witnesses usually carry equal weight in measuring the evidence, while independent witnesses and physical evidence are higher on the scale of evaluation.

The citizen is always wrong (or right) is the third assumption. This assumption also evolves from a supervisor's or administrator's belief that the citizen can either do no right or no wrong. This is different than the previous two assumptions, as the conclusion is drawn from the relationship held with the officer as opposed to this orientation where the relationship and assumption is born from the citizen complainant.

The administration is always right (or wrong) is the final assumption. This orientation is probably the second most damaging or treacherous of the four assumptions. The supervisor or administrator who functions from this perspective will do almost anything to prove their point in the process. If the administration is always right, the supervisor will engage in measures that at the behest of all involved will bend with the prevailing administrative winds in order to satisfy the chief administrator. If the administration is always wrong, then the supervisor will take risks in covering up or masking complaints and discovered misconduct. This may emanate from a desire to advance in the organization without having to travel the traditional route, political pressure applied in high profile cases or those that involve unpopular personnel, or just a matter of failing to defend a thorough and proper investigation as a means of making the path easier to travel.

In all of these assumptions, the fact remains that the process cannot attain or regain credibility unless the credibility can be first demonstrated and inculcated as a matter of course. The internal investigator must be devoid of these faults in order to provide for the needs of all involved in an impartial and objective manner. The complainant, organization, and target officer deserve nothing less in the process.

Figure 2-1. L.A.P.D. Officer Roby was considered an outcast because she had broken the "Code of Silence" (CNN).

THE "RAT" AND "WITCH HUNT" MENTALITY

The internal investigation process has always been plagued by two malevolent mentalities; the "Rat" mentality and the "Witch Hunt" mentality. Albeit, unwarranted in many cases, it is still a "reality of perception" in the process. When you examine the foundation of these terms, they emerge from such negative images as the days of the height of organized crime and how those who informed were referred to as "Rats." Worse yet is the visualization of the fear people demonstrated in seventeenth century Salem, Massachusetts of innocent women who were accused of possessing evil powers. In both times in our history, those accused were executed because of a "reality of perception." That metaphor can be applied as an indictment or "execution" of the legitimate process of the internal investigation.

Usually the rat mentality stems from a deep-rooted distrust of the internal affairs division or the internal investigation process which is seen as biased and harsh (Martinelli & Pollock, 2000). Officers who are identified in the strictest sense as informants offer information concerning crimes that they have witnessed or are complicit in. These individuals usually have something to gain from offering their observations, usually in an attempt to minimize their involvement or bargain for reduced discipline or sanction. Officers are also involved in offering testimony of basic observations, or components of an incident that may seem innocuous or unimportant at the time, but later result in discipline or sanction to a target officer. However, in both cases, these individuals are painted with a very broad brush. The problem is exacerbated when officers who admit to egregious acts are allowed to maintain employment while officers who may commit minor acts seem to be exacted the harshest discipline allowed. That mentality will not change absent the infusion of equity in the process. Officers must be convinced, through action and not rhetoric, that the law enforcement administration is fair to all involved. More importantly, officers who offer information must not be ostracized in the organization by other officers, supervisors, and the administration.

In addition, most internal investigations are perceived to be witch hunts. There seems to be empirical and anecdotal evidence that supports this theory. There have been several publicized examples of law enforcement organizations that have sacrificed their own personnel for less than legitimate or immoral reasons. These usually evolve from a complaint against an unpopular or troublesome employee, or worse yet, an event that is politically charged or evokes public outcry. In these cases, no matter the merits of the case, someone must be held accountable to, in effect, restore the organization to its previous state. These efforts are extremely transparent and cause far more damage with the rank and file; damage that most often is pervasive, hidden, and cannot be accurately calculated. The damage from this can be direct, resulting in the loss of quality personnel through varied attrition means, to indirect wherein officers can engage in work slowdowns and sabotage. The resounding theme through this text is that a balance must be created in order for the system to be effective. That balance must transcend these types of situations to reach a viable outcome.

Overcoming these perceptions requires honesty, the highest credibility, fair investigations that are of the highest quality, and explicit candor when possible so the investigation can be perceived as fair and impartial to all stakeholders in the process. There is no substitute for honesty with all of the involved entities, especially the officer who is the subject of the investigation. There is no magic formula other than these tried and true methods. The process should emerge from several maxims:

1. Set clear expectations at the outset of assignment whether as a first-line supervisor, chief, or internal affairs investigator.
2. Be honest with the personnel of the organization and have an expectation that they will respond in kind until you are proven wrong.
3. Trust and loyalty are reciprocal agreements.
4. If department personnel are expected to march into Hell with the supervisor or chief, then the supervisor or chief must be willing to march into Hell for their personnel.

THE POLITICAL BACKLASH

The political machine runs in all aspects of work and life. As a democracy, the political machine is acknowledged as the vehicle for freedom of choice and voice. The politics however, do not stop at the foot of Capital Hill. In an examination of the policing environment, politics have been inserted into every aspect of the field at varying degrees throughout the history of the profession. The political machine can have positive impacts, such as in enacting laws and legislative acts that afford the police the ability to effectively police a free society. The political machine can also act as a deterrent to police corruption and misconduct through the levying of political pressure against agencies that are unresponsive to the needs of a public that is subjected to police abuse.

The threshold is crossed though when politics interfere with proper investigative process. This line should never be crossed in the internal investigations process. Sadly, politics are seen as the only component of the process by some police supervisors and administrators. This fallacy should not supersede the understanding that politics are only a small component of the internal investigation process. Neither external nor internal political influence should guide or influence the process. The process is a system that includes the complainant, the community, the department, the human resources of the department, the legal issues, the procedural guidelines, and the target of the investigation. This entire group must be served before the politics of an issue can be addressed.

Research has indicated that political interference is prompted by intentional self-serving political motivation in which an official receives a concealed benefit, which by definition is corruption (Trautman, 2003b). Politicians, through intent or ignorance, will insert themselves into the internal investigations process usually through high profile incidents in a community. With intent, they see these as opportunities to gain votes. With ignorance, despite their lack of understanding of the procedural and legal issues, they will interfere with the purpose of championing the rights of the complainant and the community at large. Both are equally damaging to the process. Police administrators may follow because of pressure to conform in order to maintain their positions. Managers and supervisors may also feel the wrath of these situations. The internal investigator may be exposed to the most pressure by virtue of being the last line of defense or voice of reason.

The police administrator, manager, or supervisor, and most importantly, the internal investigator must consider that no justice is served when a corrupt officer wins their case because of investigative flaws, or worse yet, an innocent officer is found guilty in order to relieve the political pressure. In addition, collective bargaining groups use these cases as proof of allegations of how their membership is treated unfairly by the organization. The final consideration is that when the internal investigator is presented with the occasion to testify in a departmental, civil, or criminal proceeding, arbitrators and judges are not interested in the politics of the case, only evidence that is submitted that meets the standards of due process.

While political interference is most often inevitable, it is also most often episodic in nature. The proverbial "heat of the moment" must not fester into long-term or irreparable damage to a case. Despite this, the investigator must operate from the perspective that true evidence is free from political interference. The internal investigator must conduct a thorough investigation and then weigh all of the evidence in an apolitical environment before the case is sent forward. The recommended finding should be based only upon the facts of the case and the prevailing procedural and legal issues involved. While the politics may be inevitable, the investigative finding and recommendation from the internal investigator should not. Again, there is no magic formula other than these tried and true methods. The process should emerge from several maxims as follows:

1. Politics are inevitable.
2. Your boss is quick to remind you that being a supervisor is not a popularity contest. This concept is necessary for your boss to embrace as well.
3. It's your investigation so you need to do what's legal, proper, justified, and moral.
4. You will be judged and respected on your fairness, not your political prowess.

THE MEDIA

The media is another force to be reckoned with in the internal investigation process. Most states have privacy laws that protect personnel records. However, when an investigation makes it into the public arena, the media will clamor for the facts in order to report to their readership. These cases most often involve very sensitive issues. While the facts of a criminal case involving the arrest or prosecution of an officer can be released, any information discovered during the internal investigation should remain private. The internal investigator must never lose sight of the fact that the media is a business; a business of information development and dissemination. The media is a business that depends on its lifeblood in providing to a defined market, information that is interesting, of individual and community interest, and evokes emotion and controversy. Advertising dollars are not based upon altruism, but upon viewership.

The media can be credited for creating some of the most devastating manmade disasters in our history as a nation. Several high profile cases have made this point self-evident. Events such as the Rodney King incident and the Philadelphia "beating" were offered as distorted, rather than evidential perspectives. The media capitalized on these controversial incidents and then played them to infinitum spurring civil unrest and massive property damage (Nowicki, 2000a). Another profound observation concerning the media also comes from Ed Nowicki (2000b) who states that, "The media may be practicing more media brutality than there is police brutality" (p. 76). The media often reports only limited known facts, or distorted facts in order to create controversy and draw advertising dollars. Along these lines, Ed Buice (2003a) adds that, "Reality is that perception upon which we are willing to act" (p. 24). The media subsequently creates an alternate reality wherein the public will act upon misinformation and respond in a manner that will force the need for a perceived change.

This does not however, relegate the responsibility of a law enforcement agency to report the evidentially-based facts that can be legally released to the community through the media. In addition, the media must be acknowledged and managed in the process in order to maintain good relations (Close, 2001; Meyer, 2001).

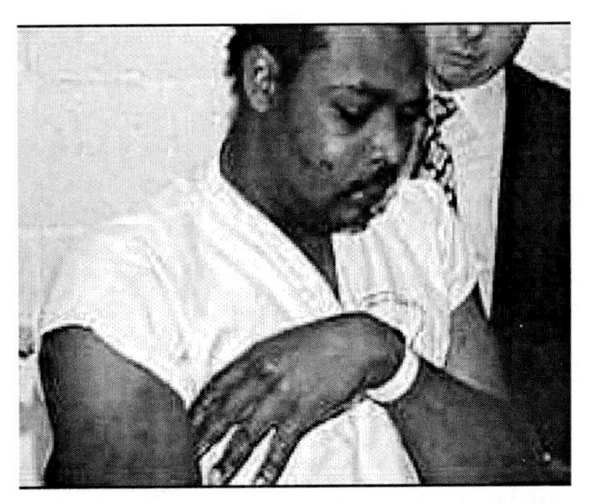

Figure 2-2. The media's portrayal of Rodney King after his stop and arrest (CNN).

Information the Media Needs

The media requires information on a daily basis to survive. They depend on world events and local stories of interest, but mostly upon crime issues. One cannot pickup a newspaper or watch a news broadcast without the lead story being some local, state, or national crime issue. This requires the constant search for the lead story. As such, journalistic ethics is many times compromised to meet the business needs of selling advertising space (Nowicki, 2000a). Keeping this in mind, law enforcement must take great care in what is released to the media, how it is released, and when it is released.

The media needs information that is contemporary and thought-provoking. Ed Buice (2002a) describes the needs of the media as the Seven I's and Big C: Importance, Impact,

Immediacy, Imminence, Illumination, Interest, Images, and Conflict (p. 8). Another view of the needs of the media is presented through the Public Information Officer (PIO) Triangle. The PIO Triangle consists of Action, Reaction, and Impact (Buice, 2003c; Rosenthal, 2001c). In understanding these concepts though, the primary determinant in a press release concerning an investigation or arrest of a law enforcement officer is not what the media needs, but what can be legally released.

Cases of police misconduct and corruption are devastating to a community. They are also fodder for the media. The media and community however, are not an overarching force with respect to the rights of the individual officer. This is the challenge in satisfying the needs of the media in these types of incidents. Therefore, communication with the media emanates more from a position of a strategy that delivers both information and reassurance and restores confidence in the law enforcement organization (Buice, 2002c; Buice, 2003a).

Developing a Protocol

First and foremost in the development of a media protocol is a keen understanding of the Freedom of Information Law, civil rights, rights to privacy, personnel and personal protections, and contractual agreements (Rosenthal, 2001a). The PIO must know what can and cannot be legally released. This crosses the boundaries of basic crime scene information and public service announcements. In these situations, great care must be taken in what information the media is allowed to have.

At the outset, internal investigations unit personnel should not be providing press releases if at all possible. Those personnel assigned should be a separate police administrator or PIO. This will prevent the IA representative from inadvertently releasing confidential information. The police administrator must designate a department spokesperson or contact who will be used as the department media contact for incidents of this type. In addition, a public information specialist and subject matter expert should be available to the spokesperson to guide and educate them in media tactics, employee rights, and the circumstances of the incident involved, such as a defensive tactics expert in use-of-force cases (Rosenthal, 2001b).

The spokesperson is responsible for not only releasing the proper information, but also controlling the media during the press release. The loss of control can result in unexpected and disastrous outcomes. For example, Dr. Vince Covello of Columbia University suggests that there are five significant media interview failures: (1) failing to take charge, (2) failing to anticipate questions, (3) failing to develop key questions, (4) failing to stick to the facts, and (5) failing to keep calm (Buice, 2003c). The spokesperson must develop a plan of action prior to any contact with the media in these types of incidents. A media management plan can be used to establish the proper "rules of engagement" in handling the media (Rosenthal, 2001b).

The protocol should also be extremely restrictive on offering the community empty promises. Chief executives across the country have made a practice of affirmatively stating their individual responsibility for their organizations. However, stating that they are personally responsible with no sanction attached is for all intents and purposes, a nonexistent responsibility. Chiefs who proclaim this and then discipline or terminate an officer lose immense credibility with their departments and communities. This should not be confused with an apology to the community. We must always be sympathetic and empathetic to community injustices that have been precipitated by members of a law enforcement agency, however, police administrators must not engage in games of semantics in an attempt to placate the community.

The news conference can be one of the most demanding and precarious positions a police administrator or department spokes_ person can be placed in. In conducting a press release or news conference, a plan of action should be in place and communicated to the media prior to any on-camera statements. Several strategies are recommended for a news conference:

1. Take a proactive role in developing the ground rules and parameters of the interview ahead of time.
2. Allow no questions from the media until all speakers at the briefings have finished.
3. Allow no interruptions. Stress the basics of good behavior to media representatives prior to the briefing.
4. Allow no mini news conferences after the main news conference.
5. Do not make threats or promises you cannot keep.
6. Understand that media leaks are inevitable. Realize this ahead of time and prepare for this when it happens. Expect the unexpected and stay on message.
7. Deliver the news message and do not hope that the media will take it easy on you. Develop messages and not answers and realize there is a difference.
8. Do not say "No comment." Use terminology like, "It would be inappropriate to comment at this time."
9. Make every attempt to redirect the media's negative energy into a positive outcome.
10. When using a PIO to conduct a news release, police commanders need to anticipate the information the PIO will need for the press release/conference.
11. PIOs must learn to anticipate both the questions and answers, and must also think about not only what to say but how to say it.
12. End the interview when agreed-upon points have been covered. Do not let the interview become a fishing expedition. (Buice, 2002b; Buice, 2003a; Buice, 2003b; Buice, 2003c)

Other recommended strategies involve the use of e-mails to media representatives to release information as opposed to face-to-face contact (Buice, 2003c). This will allow the spokesperson time to prepare the release as opposed to being caught unprepared. Another recommendation is to record the press release in order to defend against the release of inaccurate information and provide a method for self-critique for future press releases (Buice, 2002d).

Finally, these types of press releases should also include positive statistics. A police-involved use of deadly force should include department statistics on justified shootings on a national and local level. Complaint statistics, positive characteristics of the officer if applicable, and offender conduct. An example is an offender who is shot while attempting to run down a police officer. While press releases have been conducted where the police administrator has stated that the offender was "unarmed," the reality is that the offender was armed with, and aggressively using a deadly weapon/dangerous instrument, the vehicle. In this scenario, the use of deadly force may not have occurred had the offender not taken aggressive action with such a deadly weapon/dangerous instrument. Positive statistics can also include the workload of the department, levels of violence, and methods employed to avoid the use-of-force.

Negotiated Media Agreements

One suggestion is to develop negotiated agreements with the media ahead of time in critical incidents to ensure officer, community, and suspect safety (Rosenthal, 2000). Negotiated media agreements may prove to be extremely valuable in these types of incidents. During the negotiated media agreement, the law enforcement agency can take steps to educate the media on the legal issues involved in information release of such items as personnel records and also develop the boundaries of the interview prior to the press release. Negotiated media agreements also allow the law enforcement agency an opportunity to take a proactive step towards media relations as opposed to a reactive response that may prove to be too late to present a properly considered response.

THE COMMUNITY

Another pitfall of the internal investigation process is dealing with the community. In crime issues and community policing efforts, police administrators and supervisors can offer solutions in a collaborative partnership. In quality of life complaints, the administrator or supervisor can offer assistance by increased patrols and enforcement activities. In the case of internal investigations, the issues become far more complex. The administrator and supervisor must weigh the safety and trust of the community against the administrative investigation process and the rights of the involved officer.

The administrator and supervisor can gain much in the way of community cooperation and trust when an honest and forthright position is taken with the community at the outset. An administrator and supervisor should release as much information as legally possible in order to keep the community informed on the incident at hand. Likened to a press release, the administrator or supervisor should develop a synopsis of the incident, be well-versed in the circumstances, develop an outline of the incident, and anticipate any questions that the community may have. In general, the circumstances of criminal investigations can be released, while the internal investigations process is most often confidential. In the case of a police-involved shooting, the administrator should conduct the information release to the community using the information garnered from the criminal investigation only. This will work to prevent allegations of a scandal or cover-up in the incident.

With respect to family members, some police administrators have chosen to have closed-door sessions with family members of an incident in an attempt to allay their fears and provide information on the incident not appropriate for general dissemination. These meetings should be avoided at all costs. These one-on-one sessions can lead to greater animosities in the community when confidential information is released, inaccurate information is later brought back to the public that cannot be verified when the release was conducted in an open forum, and increased scrutiny and liability of the administrator, agency, and the investigation.

BREAKING THE NEWS TO THE BOSS

A significant part of case presentation is advising the supervisor and/or administrator of the outcome. This may prove to be difficult in investigations that are sensitive, politically charged, or have an outcome that was in contrast to that which was anticipated by the administrator or supervisor. There are a few strategies that can overcome these issues.

The internal investigator must understand basic communication skills such as how to effectively convey the salient points of the case and the rationale for the findings. Thoroughly supporting the case findings in an objective manner builds the internal investigator's credibility and increases the chances for supervisor and administrator consensus. The case quality will be measured by thoroughness first which will naturally lead to the findings. The thoroughness will work to support the recommended findings of the internal investigator. The investigator must leave the supervisor or administrator with no other logical choice.

In contrast, if the internal investigator has conducted a thorough investigation and has constructively supported their findings, the supervisor and administrator must not force the investigator to change their findings if any disagreement is presented. This does not preclude the supervisor or administrator from invoking command or executive privilege in changing the recommended findings in their own documentation. The internal investigator should be allowed to conduct their investigation based upon discovering the facts and making a recommendation based upon their knowledge of the totality of the circumstances of the case.

SUMMARY

This chapter has discussed the function of the internal investigator as it relates to the entire investigative process. This chapter has also discussed the common assumptions and myths of the internal investigation process as well as the "Rat" and "Witch Hunt" mentalities as to how they adversely affect those involved in the investigation and subsequently the entire investigative process. Further discussion examined the politics of the internal investigation process and the role of the internal investigator in divesting their investigation of political influences. An extensive review of the media was conducted with a series of recommended strategies in handling the media in information releases of this nature. Additionally, such controversial issues of dealing with the community and reviewing command staff are all pitfalls to the internal investigations process. In order to be effective, the internal investigator must acknowledge that these issues exist and take the most appropriate steps to address problems before they occur.

Chapter 3

ETHICS AND LEADERSHIP

INTRODUCTION

Ken Adcox (2000) states that, "Nothing is more important to police administrators than maintaining the public's confidence in their organization's honesty, truthfulness and integrity" (p. 16). An example of efforts to maintain high standards of ethics in a police organization comes from Cincinnati Police Chief Thomas Streicher Jr., who in response to the results of a critical internal investigation, issued a memo to the entire department that stated, "Dishonesty cannot and will not be tolerated in our organization and that police officers who lie to investigators can expect to be terminated" (Korte, 2002). A particularly tragic case in Monroe County New York involved a sheriff's supervisor who was convicted of downloading and distributing child pornography. In response to Sergeant Ron Sheffer's arrest, Monroe County Sheriff Patrick O'Flynn stated, "This case is especially offensive because a public servant has betrayed the public trust" (Morrell, 2004). The perspective of ethics and leadership in this chapter is brought from the role of the internal investigator, supervisor, and administrator. The ethics and leadership of an internal affairs unit can also be institutionalized throughout an organization as most answer directly to the chief administrator and are influential in policy formation and enforcement. Therefore, the ethics and leadership of the internal investigator as well as the policies and practices of the internal investigations unit must rise above all else in the organization.

Ross E. Swope (2002) offered the following definitions: "Integrity is the adherence to professional standards; ethics are the rules of conduct governing a particular class of human actions; accountability is defined as answering for one's conduct; and responsibility is upholding the obligations of performance of duty." Dr. Frank L. Perry (2001) added that:

> Three organizational failures can foster a resentful, cynical, and demoralized work force leading to individual and collective acts of corruption. These failures are: little or ineffective discipline and deselection of trainees (a commitment to fairly but firmly graduate only those individuals who truly demonstrate performance and integrity standards); ignorance of the nature and effects of the goal-gradient phenomenon (the farther away individuals remain from their goal, the less the tendency to remain passionately interested in its attainment); and the allowance of a double standard within the organization, thereby decreasing moral accountability as professional responsibility increases. (p. 23)

Figure 3-1. Former Sergeant Ronald Sheffer of the Monroe County Sheriff's Office (Courtesy of WHEC-TV Channel 10 News, Rochester, New York).

Sadly, these issues seem to be timeless in law enforcement organizations.

Furthermore, according to the research, "ethics is our greatest training and leadership need today and into the next century" (International Association of Chiefs of Police, 1998a). Current ethics training does not address the stress created by "conflicting organizational values, professional subcultures, individual morals, and public expectations" (Martinelli & Pollock, 2000). Ethics training is also a thing to be desired and is usually conducted by the force of an external mandate as opposed to an internal need. Internal affairs units, for the most part, do not receive a separate and distinct training program that is tailored to the needs of such a function.

From a historical perspective, internal investigators and internal affairs units have been looked upon as outsiders who are ready to second-guess the noble actions of those who actually do the job. This leads to a troubling perception that internal investigators and internal investigations units are biased, unfair, and corrupt (Martinelli & Pollock, 2000). Most internal investigations units are highly supervised and regulated which seems to work against this perception, however, problems do exist. Like any organizational unit, an internal investigations unit must report on its activities. Several of these measures are the ability to correct substandard behavior, service the community, and uncover corruption. Statistically speaking though, these events are episodic in most law enforcement organizations. Unit commanders may feel obliged to justify their existence by finding problems where none may exist. This only adds to the poor perceptions of an internal investigations unit and its staff. In keeping with this thought, Richard E. Lober (2002) states that, "A police department should not measure the effectiveness of its internal affairs unit by the number of sustained cases but by the conformance of the department's officers to its standards of conduct" (p. 57).

Two questions must then be considered when a unit functions: (1) Is the unit and its staff aggressively taking a posture of finding misconduct and corruption as opposed to conducting fair and impartial internal investigations? And (2) Are the issues being addressed of consequence and meaning or are they inconsequential in the scheme of the overall service provided by the rank and file of the organization? All involved in the process, from the internal investigator to the chief executive of the agency must answer these questions in order to determine if the personnel, process, and organization are ethically driven in the internal investigation process.

ACCOUNTABILITY AND OWNERSHIP

The term accountability has been bantered about since the inception of policing. While most parents endeavored to instill this noble quality in their offspring, culture teaches us something different. Accountability has been defined as "to be liable or to be called on account, or answerable" (Arnold, 2002). Accountability has become the watchword but not the practice in society. Because we have been failed by some of our highest and most respected leaders who transfer blame in all possible cases, we assume that this is acceptable in all walks of life. Subsequently serious crimes such as income tax fraud, cable theft, and CD pirating just to name a few, have been embraced as not only acceptable, but expected.

In policing, the concept is not only more complex, but more divisive. In addition, the concept of accountability is one of the most misused and misunderstood terms of policing (Arnold, 2002). The concept of accountability to many police administrators and supervisors seems to only apply to everyone else. When line personnel observe these behaviors, it is only natural that they will mimic them. Consequently, the problem becomes so pervasive and ingrained in the culture to the point where there seems to be no viable remedy.

Research has also laid the blame on supervision and management for omissions or failure to take appropriate actions when dealing with acts of unethical conduct (International Association of Chiefs of Police, 1998a). This speaks to turning a blind eye rather than corrupt actions. In addition, police trainers should train law enforcement personnel concerning the pitfalls associated with wearing the symbol of public trust on their uniforms and the duties associated with policing (Martinelli, 2002). While many issues impact accountability in policing, what is comforting is the opinion of Dr. Paul A. Pommerville (1999) who states that, "In American democracy, the constitutional checks are in place–police accountability is a reality and incidents of police misconduct are the exception rather than the rule" (p. 128).

In the internal investigation realm, accountability should be stressed in the process. Accountability should be practiced from the perspective of investigative thoroughness and integrity in case findings. Another concept that should be considered is that of Ownership Theory. Fostering Ownership Theory in the law enforcement process breeds pride, professionalism, and productivity (Scanlon, 2004). The internal investigator must feel a sense of ownership in every investigation conducted. Ownership must emanate from the pride that is taken in conducting the most complete and objective review as humanly possible of the incident in question. Ownership Theory then comes from adherence to a set of guidelines and principles, not politics or situations. Breeding this belief system throughout the process changes the mindset and accomplishes the ultimate objective of investigations of this type being fact-finding inquiries that are not motivated by politics, personality, or expediency.

ENDS V. MEANS AND RESULTS-BASED APPROACHES

The ends v. means and results-based approaches are used in law enforcement when conventional methods are ineffective. This mindset is easy to understand given the pressure from police administrators to produce results for the community no matter what the approach or tactic used. Ken Adcox (2000) states that:

> History has shown that some police officers have come to value results over duty and principle, and the standard measurement of good police work has become goal achievement, with all else secondary. In results-based teleological reasoning, ethical actions are weighted by comparing net benefits with potential harm. (p. 19)

As this occurs, police officers become willing to go outside of the law to achieve their objectives in the name of justice or the noble cause defense (Adcox, 2000; Lober, 2002). This mindset also transcends the management orientation in many agencies that are under pressure to make their respective communities safer. Examples of this have been observed in many large, midsize, and small agencies in strict enforcement efforts that have led to scandals and civil rights violations. The Los Angeles Police Department Rampart Division scandal speaks to this as officers believed that they were under siege and had to step well beyond the normal bounds of proper procedural and legal convention in order to get results.

This mindset also connotes a certain amount of discretionary power given to the officer, supervisor, and administrator. Discretion is making a decision based on individual choice or judgment and is influenced by a number of factors. The factors include not only the law and established organizational guidelines, but also individualized personal values and beliefs, as well as the values, beliefs and norms of one's peers and work group (Adcox, 2000, p. 16). Discretionary powers in law enforcement can be positive and negative in results. Care must be taken to not empower personnel to resolve issues at all costs. These efforts experience short-term gains that are lost in long-term damages. A significant consideration in this mindset is the potential harm that it may cause others such as organizational morale (Adcox, 2000). Liability is also created by exaggerated enforcement efforts to satisfy the community instead of proper problem-solving techniques to resolve issues when statistics become the measure of success rather than actually solving the problem (Soto, 1998).

Figure 3-2. Aggressive policing tactics come under scrutiny when incidents occur such as the tragic death of Amadou Diallo in New York City (CNN).

In the internal investigations process, the investigator and administrator may be faced with these same issues. Legal and contractual protections compounded by uncooperative witnesses, and the lack of physical evidence in most internal investigations may exacerbate the problems faced by the investigator and administrator. The internal investigator may then be tempted to bolster inculpatory evidence or exclude exculpatory evidence in an effort to solve the problem. The difference in a poor investigation and a results-based approach is that the investigator fully intends to use whatever means that are necessary to convict the officer of the alleged violation. This is probably the most insidious of situations. This is brought on by several reasons that include political pressure, the desire to advance by a belief that these types of actions will bring favor to the internal investigator, and the problem officer that consistently beats the system. This should be avoided at all costs. Internal investigators should not succumb to political or personal pressures, administrators should not foster or encourage such a mindset as the results can be devastating to morale, image, and in civil litigation against the organization and its administration.

CULTURAL INDOCTRINATION

Cultural indoctrination in law enforcement begins with most even before entry into the service. The media and Hollywood have a great impact on the perceptions of those who enter the field. Slowly, as the inductee evolves, they realize that the discipline is not all it is depicted as in the movies and the media. When the academy experience begins, officers are exposed to such concepts as community policing and that only a small portion of the community is the foundation for the actual crime problems they will face on a daily basis. The inductee soon finds that they are only exposed to this anomaly in the population, however, all of their opinions become based in this stereotyping orientation. A metamorphosis then occurs so that officers can cope with the realities through the process of internal adaptation (Adcox, 2000). This phenomenon is not limited to the line level as this can be observed in all ranks and assignments. Examples of this are the supervisor who has a few substandard employees but paints every officer with the same broad brush; the vice officer that sees all their community contacts as drug dealers, and so on.

While cultural indoctrination occurs at the officer levels (Adcox, 2000), the same phenomenon can occur with internal investigators, separate from the ranks and expected to perform a function and find evil on a daily basis. Not only will new members tacitly accept the existing norms of the group, but will adopt the behaviors of their peers in order to be accepted and survive in the environment (Adcox, 2000). This occurs in internal investigations units where all the investigator hears is complaints against officers. While the complaints are usually lodged against a small portion of the organization's staff, they become the norm for the internal investigator. The investigator may then allow these attitudes towards the few substandard employees to impact every investigation conducted. This introduces an unacceptable level of bias and discriminatory practices to the internal investigations process.

Internal affairs can however, impact the cultural and core values of a department in several ways by: (1) opening cases for investigation that are legitimate, (2) maintaining a fair process that has respect for all employees, (3) conducting quality and thorough investigations of allegations of employee misconduct, (4) by dropping unfounded investigations against officers, (5) by severely limiting satellite issues in cases where the primary allegations are unfounded or exonerated, and (6) consistently and fairly applying discipline and preventing the perception of discriminatory treatment (Lober, 2002).

INVESTIGATOR INTEGRITY

Investigator integrity seems to be a timeless issue. Cases have been brought to light wherein criminal investigators have been convicted of false testimony and planting evidence in order to secure convictions against those who were alleged to have committed crimes. This orientation comes from not only corruption, but more importantly, a belief that the end justifies the means in protecting the community from a suspect who may be

Figure 3-3. Corruption takes place not only when an officer steals money, but when they violate their oath of office by not treating everyone fairly. This edict needs to translate to how not only the community is treated, by how organizations treat their own personnel.

acquitted in a case given the evidence available. Corruption also extends beyond monetary gains to the exacting of personal vendettas in the prosecutorial process. In the internal investigation process, it is difficult at best to pursue a disciplinary action when the integrity or credibility of the investigator or investigation is not at question. Adding the element of false accusations and prosecution only intensifies the problem.

Adding to the problem of investigator integrity is the argument of loyalty v. integrity. Dr. Kevin M. Gilmartin and John J. Harris (1998) identify the loyalty v. integrity argument in policing as they state, "Most officers would like to be known for their loyalty and integrity. A problem occurs, however, when a sense of victimization and overidentification with the job sets into motion the dilemma of loyalty versus integrity" (p. 26). Same phenomenon exists with internal investigators who overidentify with the cause as opposed to the proper procedural and legal conduct of the investigation.

The problem is compounded when a double standard exists in the organization. Ken Adcox (2000) states that, "Few things are as obvious as hypocrisy, and contradictions are very clear when officers on the street are being disciplined for behavior that is unpunished when displayed by managers" (p. 24). While necessity is sometimes the mother of invention, a true disservice to the organization, community, and involved officer is done when those who have questionable integrity are either placed in the role of internal investigator or charged with the responsibility for their review and subsequent levying of findings and discipline. In this environment, impropriety is as pernicious as the appearance of impropriety.

Personal agendas and politics must be set aside for the internal investigator to bring an unparalleled level of integrity to the process. As Dr. Paul A. Pommerville (1999) so eloquently states, "Police are the vanguard for human rights in a democratic society. They are responsible for protecting and securing civil and human rights for every citizen" (p. 127). Internal investigators must live to a higher standard to not only protect the rights of complainants, but also the rights of accused officers.

Every police officer is a representative of the occupation itself (Martinelli & Pollock, 2000). As such, that role only grows more critical as one rises through the ranks or assumes such responsibilities as investigating the conduct of other officers. While the internal investigator may not have control over the particular case, evidence, or other barriers, the internal investigator does have absolute control over their own integrity and professionalism (Gilmartin & Harris, 1998). This concept must be taught and practiced to all those who are connected to the internal investigation process.

THE STEPPING STONE TO PROMOTION

This is such an insidious concept that those who actually believe this is possible, or worse yet, use this as a means to advance for any means other than the development of personal acumen or merit, do not belong in the law enforcement field to begin with. This type of orientation emerges from both an ethical and psychological character flaw. Assignments to internal investigations should be not so much based upon skill, but upon intent. Administrators must closely screen those who express an interest in working in internal investigations for such ethical and psychological character flaws and exclude their assignment within their investigative staff.

The administrator should interview and test for the motivational factors for assignment to internal investigations as the subsequent knowledge, skills, and abilities to be successful in the position of internal investigator can be developed through training, experience, and leadership. These psychological and behavioral constructs are extremely transparent to the rank and file and do irreparable damage to the image of the internal investigations unit, the investigative process, and to the chief executive's reputation in the organization. There exists no higher area of scrutiny than with the staff assigned to an internal investigations unit. If the staff is credible then the process will gain credibility.

AN IA CODE OF ETHICS

While mission and vision statements are at the vanguard of organizational development because they give guidance and direction, an IA Code of Ethics should also be developed for the very same reasons. Ethics specifies the type of conduct that is expected from personnel (Forsyth, 2003; International Association of Chiefs of Police, 1998a). An IA Code of Ethics provides the internal investigations unit direction beyond that required for the organization in general. Because their role is beyond that expected of the general employee population, such a standard needs to be developed in order to demonstrate this to the organization and community.

Figure 3-4. Frank Serpico is the icon for the ideology that ethics is more what a person believes and what they practice rather than what is a department philosophy (CNN).

With respect to ethics in general, Ross E. Swope (1998) states that:

> To be truly worthy of the public trust, we must maintain an environment in which it makes sense to behave with prudence, justice, courage, intellectual honesty, responsibility, self-effacement of interests and trustworthiness, and where these core virtues can be continuously exercised as standard operating procedures.

Since the internal investigations unit must rise above all others in the organization with respect to values, the use of such a definition or statement to emphasize the nature of the role of the internal investigator may help to build credibility and improve the function of the internal investigations unit.

In the development of an IA Code of Ethics, the internal investigations unit must identify the stakeholders in the process. They should include, but not be limited to: (1) department command, (2) internal investigation unit command and investigators, (3) patrol and specialized unit representatives, (4) legal and municipal counsel, (5) collective bargaining units, (6) representatives from the governmental entity under which the organization falls, and (7) the community serviced. This group should be involved in developing an organization-specific ethos statement that meets the needs of the collective group. The use of the IA Code of Ethics should then be directed at monitoring the internal investigation process in rewarding successes and sanctioning unwarranted deviations from the intent of the ideology.

LEADERSHIP

Leadership has been at the forefront of police issues for quite some time. Leadership transcends an organization in many different manners, from the very top to the very bottom. As such, leadership must be demonstrated on behalf of all members. The internal investigation process is not immune to these needs. The leadership role in this environment is critical in defending the rights of those officers who have been wrongly accused as well as having the courage and fortitude to challenge those personnel who have committed some wrongdoing.

All too often, the feedback from an internal investigations unit is negative, citing the number of complaints filed and the number of sustained findings. This can create its own set of unique problems. Leadership driven by constant negative feedback creates an organization in which wrongdoing should be expected (Trautman, 2003a). A leader in an internal investigations unit must have the drive to also acknowledge the quality work that is being conducted on a daily basis by organizational personnel. This information compares and contrasts the negative information and gives perspective to the problems, rather than inflate the problems in an organization.

The internal investigator must take a leadership role in relentless case investigation that uncovers all of the available facts and demonstrate their objectivity and fairness by supporting the findings of the case only with facts, not supposition or conjecture. The internal investigator must then be a leader by presenting the case to the proper authorities by supporting the findings, whether they exonerate or find the officer culpable of some error in judgment, misconduct, or corruption. The organizational leader must also lead by example, by not allowing hypocrisy and double standards that divide an organization and act like a cancer. The essence of leadership in the internal investigations process is doing what is legal, proper, justified, and fair to all involved without consideration for entities that, if given the opportunity, will negatively impact the outcome of the investigation.

SUMMARY

This chapter discussed the issues of ethics and leadership in the internal investigation process. The concepts of accountability and ownership were discussed with respect to developing the proper orientation in case responsibility. Other concepts discussed were the flaws in the use of an ends v. means/results-based approach in case investigation. The chapter also discussed such topics as investigator integrity, an IA Code of Ethics, and leadership in the internal investigations process at all levels. All of these ethical and leadership issues impact the proper outcome of the case. In addition, each case is an individual examination based upon the evidence uncovered, not a blanket indictment of the officer, unit, or organization in general. With respect to the conduct of each individual case, Craig E. Ferrell (1997) states that, "The police administrator must conduct each investigation without infringing upon the employee's civil rights–perhaps the most harrowing of tightropes to walk toward a just resolution" (p. 10). Therefore, the internal investigator and administrator cannot violate the law, policy, or collective bargaining agreement in order to make the case, otherwise the standards that are being enforced are rendered meaningless.

The progression of the process should always emerge from an ethical orientation. As such, the investigator and administrator will always be able to defend their actions in those cases where personnel are found culpable for their actions. Therefore, a systematic approach to organizational ethics needs to be employed as, while a well-regulated internal affairs unit is an effective tool, it is only one component of the process to be a comprehensive approach (McCarthy, 2000). Other components of the system include a proactive, human development, problem-solving approach to controlling the behavior of their employees (Adcox, 2000).

Richard Forsyth (2003) profoundly states that:

> One sure way to develop an ethical atmosphere is through meaningful relationships with personnel. Care for people, treat them as valued assets of the organization, develop a bond of trust, and have open communication channels within the agency. As people find enjoyment and meaning in their working relationships, they will take pride in themselves, their organization, and their profession. (p. 105)

Chapter 4

POLICE OFFICER STRESS

INTRODUCTION

The police profession brings with it the exposure to unparalleled levels of violence and acts that have severe impacts on the health of the individual officer on a daily basis. Police administrators need to acknowledge that these experiences have varying effects on the personal and professional lives of these same officers (Atkinson-Tovar, 2003; Kinchin, 2000). In addition, a primary cause of stress in law enforcement is unfair disciplinary practices (Kirschman, 1998). This chapter discusses those issues and the considerations necessary for the internal investigator and police administrator.

Jonathan L. Anderson (2001) opined that:

> Police are continually immersed in an unforgiving virulent world that breeds disillusionment, frustration, cynicism, and burnout and exposes one to the tempting seductions of self destructive behavior. It is a profession that continually places the limits and vulnerability of human frailty in the view of a scrutinizing public eye. Yet, it is a profession that perpetually demands the highest morale and ethical standard. (p. 78)

The policing environment creates some of the highest stress levels of any given discipline. This is compounded by a mantra of doing more with less, which is the eternal law enforcement idiom. Additional stressors involve most officers who feel more stress from their own supervision than they do from simply doing their job (Trautman, 2001). This does not come without the cost of increasing levels of stress in the rank and file (Atkinson-Tovar, 2003). High levels of stress can cause physical, emotional, and interpersonal changes in the officer (Smotzer, 2003). Such stressors are also not limited to law enforcement work as Ed Brown (2000) states that, "Many of the challenges that officers face are psychological in nature within and outside of the department" (p. 90). The cumulative affect on officer health and performance can be disastrous if not identified and treated.

The aforementioned issues address the daily trauma an officer faces in the normal course of duties. With the commencement of an internal investigation, the officer will experience significantly higher levels of stress. This is emphasized by Dr. Ellen Kirschman (1998) who states that:

> What is important for everyone–families, officers, administrators, and supervisors–to understand in advance is that organizational stress will hurt and agitate a cop more deeply than the crooks on the street. They need to know that cops who go through an Internal Affairs (IA) or a disciplinary action are often symptomatic–unable to sleep, preoccupied, anxious, feeling helpless, out of control, depressed and inconsolable. They may act out, go in search of villains, find

Figure 4-1. Police work brings stress from critical and even routine incidents. Stress can be manifested in some of the simplest tasks that have the potential for danger such as basic field interview that could turn into a dangerous situation without any notice or overt signs (Photo courtesy of the Brockport, New York Police Department).

> people to blame, seek revenge, or simply shut down and refuse to do any work. (p. 129)

In addition, officers under internal or criminal investigation will suffer significant stress that may even lead to suicidal thoughts or attempts. Whether they are guilty or innocent does not affect the critical issue of the profound effects of stress on the officer. Even minor charges may be very damaging and cause for suicide as a suicidal person's problems are very important to him or her even if they don't seem as important to the internal investigator (Czarnecki, Kasanof, & Trautman, 2002). Officer Emre Arican's insightful comments in this area include the realization that the process must be timely to reduce these types of stressors in the officer's life. Anecdotally, he believes that a case that is unresolved for two years may take a decade off of the officer's natural life span.

Sadly, police organizations have seldom attended to their employees' emotional well-being (Harris & Gilmartin, 2000). While some organizations have recognized the need for posttraumatic stress counseling in police shootings and critical incidents, stress counseling has been all but ignored in other aspects of policing. In the stress caused during the internal investigation process, many organizations have chosen to totally disregard the adverse affects, much to the detriment of their human resources as well as the disservice to the profession as a whole.

STRESS DISORDERS AND TRAUMATIZATION

There are two concepts that should be considered in developing an understanding of the affects on officers that are involved in traumatic incidents. An understanding must also be developed in the affects of stress on those who surround the officer such as other officers, supervisors, family, and friends.

The concept of Vicarious Traumatization refers to a "transformation in the officer's inner experience resulting from empathetic engagement with victim's trauma material" (Atkinson-Tovar, 2003). This concept is applicable to the emotions a fellow officer may experience after being involved in a traumatic incident. Vicarious Traumatization can result in core changes in an officer's psychological foundations. Such changes can be marked by symptoms of repression (forcing painful thoughts from the memory), denial (refusing to acknowledge painful experiences), isolation (creating distance to painful experiences), and dissociation (a disruption in consciousness, memory, identity or perception of the environment and functions as a defense against pain, fear, helplessness, and panic (Atkinson-Tovar, 2003; Herman, 2002; Zelig, 1998).

Another important concept in the area of stress disorders and traumatization is that of a condition known as Secondary Traumatic Stress Disorder (STSD). Lynn Atkinson-Tovar (2003) defines Secondary Traumatic Stress Disorder (STSD) as, "The natural consequent behavior and emotions resulting from knowing about a traumatizing event experienced by a significant other–The stress result from helping or wanting to help a traumatized or suffering person" (p. 119). As such, the officer will perceive a role conflict when they themselves are in need of counseling services (Atkinson-Tovar, 2003).

While much needs to be done in the area of the counseling of officers who are personally involved in traumatic incidents, the need for counseling services for secondary victims must not go unnoticed. Law enforcement often overlooks the secondary victims of traumatic incidents, such as the families of the officers (Zelig, 1998). The internal investigator must, through policy or practice work to meet the needs of these people as well.

PHYSIOLOGICAL RESPONSES TO STRESS

From an investigative perspective, the internal investigator and administrator should have a working knowledge of the physiological responses to stress and how they affect an officer's health, cognitive abilities, and demeanor in the investigative process. The detrimental effects to the body during a traumatic incident have been well documented. Research has indicated that the body experiences several responses in highly stressful situations such as: (1) increased heart rate, (2) effects to the visual system, (3) effects to the auditory system, (4) effects to the brain, and (5) effects to motor skills (Laur, 2002). This is also supported in part by studies that have revealed physiological and emotional problems such as perception of time, visual, and auditory distortions (Parent, 1999). Further correlative research has identified the Survival Stress Reaction (SSR), which is an automatic response that happens without conscious thought and there is a direct correlation between SSR and increased heart rate (Laur, 2002). All of these responses can severely affect the ability of an officer to respond to a threat as well as recall it accurately after the incident.

The affects of stress on the body can be extensive, hindering, and in many cases, debilitating. Rick Baratta (1998) cites the effects on the body when stress is induced by a critical incident as follows: (1) increased heart rate and blood pressure, (2) dilation of blood vessels in major muscle groups, (3) loss of fine and complex motor skills, (4) constriction of the blood vessels to the brain and viscera, (5) loss of peripheral vision (tunnel vision), (6) increased visual dependency, (7) pupil dilation, (8) focus on visual stimulus and exclude other senses, (9) hypervigilance (panic/irrational behavior), brain stall, (10) constriction of surface level blood vessels, (11) decreased sensory perception to pain, (12) mental confusion following the incident, (13) heightened adrenaline release, (14) glycogenolysis (increased blood sugar with increased energy), and (15) crouching for balance, bracing, muscle tension, reduced target (p. 189).

Additionally, Rick Baratta (1999) also states that, "When the brain perceives that there is no time to prevent the perceived action it may freeze or stall, and the officer may remain immobile, awaiting the execution" (p. 67). Some officer's also may perceive the lethal threat incident as it occurs in slow motion. Often, the officer's vision is focused upon the perceived threat with minimal awareness of the events taking place around them (Parent, 1999). Another study by Dr. Alexis Artwohl (1997) of 157 police officers involved in deadly force incidents revealed the specific diminished capacity conditions experienced by the officers as:

1. 84% experienced diminished sound (auditory exclusion).
2. 79% experienced tunnel vision (peripheral narrowing).
3. 74% experienced "automatic pilot" with little or no conscious thought.
4. 71% experienced visual clarity.
5. 62% experienced slow motion time.
6. 52% experienced memory loss for part of the event.
7. 46% experienced memory loss for some of their own behavior.
8. 39% experienced dissociation; sense of detachment or unreality.
9. 26% experienced intrusive distracting thoughts.
10. 21% saw, heard, or experienced memory distortion.
11. 17% experienced fast motion time.
12. 7% experienced temporary paralysis. (Byrnes, 2003, p. 24)

This is only a partial list of the possible affects of stress on officers involved in traumatic events. The internal investigator should be aware of these possible responses to a stressful incident and consider their affect on the investigation, specifically, all dealings with the involved officer.

Diminished Capacity

Diminished capacity is an accepted and legitimate legal foundation for mitigating criminal culpability. In the legal sense, diminished capacity is due to emotional distress, physical condition, or other factors that prevent the individual from fully comprehending the nature of the act he or she is accused of committing. It is not solely attributable to psychological disease, but is rather, impacted by many other variables that include emotional and physical distress as well.

Even normal actions by an individual may not produce full awareness and control of one's actions let alone when a law enforcement officer is faced with moderate to severely stressful situations. Therefore, a law enforcement officer may be unconsciously or unwittingly committing acts that may be in violation of a policy or procedure, but may be mitigated by the concept of diminished capacity. In a noted case involving the murder of a law enforcement officer, a back-up officer is observed on videotape clearly using profanity towards the murder suspect who is a passive resister and failing to follow the officer's clear directions. While attending to the fatally wounded officer, monitoring the uncooperative murder suspect who has not yet been handcuffed and searched and therefore representing an extremely high level of immediate threat, and keeping a vigil on other motorists who were in close proximity and approaching the scene, the officer used what would be construed to be highly abusive language. This is a clear case for the consideration of the psychological construct of diminished capacity. The officer should not be held strictly accountable for these actions given the totality of the circumstances of the evolving event.

Memory Loss and Distortions

Stressful events frequently have an impact on the ability to recall specific information about a traumatic event. This too, extends to lower level incidents of use-of-force, hectic, or chaotic scenes, and stress induced through heightened emotions when dealing with others. As previously identified, 52 percent of officers who suffered stress from a traumatic event had experienced diminished memory capacity (Byrnes, 2003). The levels of stress and release of chemicals in the body are believed to be, in part, the cause of this frailty. Research has identified the negative effects of how stress produces Cortisol in the system, enough of which can block memory of basics–like training and remembering to perform (Mulroy, 2000). In addition, research has also revealed that Critical Stress Amnesia occurs after a critical incident where it is not uncommon for a person to have difficulty recalling as much as 70 percent of the incident in the first 24 hours, 50 percent in 48 hours, and 72 percent to 95 percent in 72–100 hours (Laur, 2002). These times should be considered when the internal investigator attempts to minimize the stress on the involved officer as well as maximize the ability to accurately and effectively conduct a probing and complete interview.

Those who are involved in an incident who assert that they do not recall certain aspects, may constructively be conveying the truth as they know it. Certain aspects of the incident may be recalled later or never recalled based upon the individual capacity to overcome the stressful incident trauma over time. Therefore, even when independent evidence refutes a claim that an officer is not completely accurate, or may not be completely candid in their statement, the totality of the circumstances must be weighed against the officer's ability to recall the event and the importance of the aspect of the event in question.

This issue also extends to an interview that is removed in time from the event. The setting of the internal investigation can create immense stress in the officer to be interviewed. The scale of the event, scrutiny the officer has been exposed to up to the point of the interview, poor supervisory and management practices, experience of the officer, and the strict formality of the interview under threat of termination are all aggravating factors to the ability to accurately recall information. Physical problems compounded by a psychological overlay can unduly cast the officer as untruthful when it is the totality of the circumstances that have led to the condition.

Post-Traumatic Stress Disorder

Post-Traumatic Stress Disorder (PTSD) is a medically and psychologically recognized ailment. Suffered primarily by military personnel involved in highly traumatizing events, there has been an immense amount of subsequent research in the area. The research has also been extended to include those involved in public service who have been subjected to similarly violent or tragic events. In the case of law enforcement personnel, the danger comes from exposure by not only witnessing a tragic event, but being directly involved such as in the case of the use of deadly force. PTSD has both short- and long-term affects on the officer involved as well as those who may have had some part in the incident.

In lethal threats, research has revealed that involved officers experience: (1) loss of fine motor skills, uncontrollable spasms, (2) loss in appetite, (3) sleep pattern changes, (4) marked decrease in sex drive, (5) depression, (6) guilt, (7) nightmares, (8) flashbacks, (9) a heightened sense of danger and fear, (10) marital or relationship breakdowns, and (11) substance and alcohol abuse (Parent, 1999). The internal investigator should remain vigilant in recognizing the signs of such problems and making the appropriate professional referrals of personnel involved in these types of incidents.

Internal investigators, direct supervisors, and administrators should also be aware of the use of humor as a stress reliever. This humor, sometimes termed "Gallows Humor," is common, however, extremely inappropriate in these types of incidents. The officer's peers may add to the stress through isolation of the officer or through the use of inappropriate jokes or comments (Parent, 1999). These activities should be avoided at all costs.

A final note in this area is the recognition of other personnel involved in the incident who may also suffer from PTSD because of their observations and actions. Consideration for officers who were present but did not use deadly physical force is important as research has also revealed they, too, may suffer similar effects of stress (Parent, 1999). The internal investigator, immediate supervisor, and administrator should also monitor the behavior of these individuals with the same thought in mind, to provide appropriate assistance and counseling services in order to minimize the effects of PTSD.

Fatigue and Lack of Sleep

Dr. William C. Dement states that: "It is totally reprehensible that the cops we expect to protect us, come to our aid, and respond to our needs when victimized should be allowed to have the worst fatigue and sleep conditions of any profession in our society" (Vila & Kenney, 2002, p. 20).

Fatigue and lack of sleep are universal problems facing workers. A review of the reasons for traffic accidents lists fatigue and lack of sleep as a major causal factor. Most industrial accidents occur during midnight shifts and 90,000 deaths each year are attributed to fatigue errors (Pedersen, 2001). As a 24/7 operation, law enforcement officers suffer with these same problems on a daily basis. This is another consideration for internal investigators and administrators when officers are involved in critical incidents, motor vehicle accidents, and the like when working night time hours.

The human biological clock is not designed to function appropriately during the night time hours. As the circadian clock works in humans, the normal rhythm is that sleep occurs during the night so as the body can properly rejuvenate. Lack of sleep and fatigue can detrimentally affect patience, mood, aggressiveness and irritability. Fatigue also influences how an officer interacts with citizens, spouses, and colleagues, and may lead to gastrointestinal problems (heartburn), depression, and insomnia (Pedersen, 2001).

The affects of lack of sleep and fatigue can also lead to some unique problems in body chemistry. Australian research into fatigue compared the affects of fatigue to the affects of alcohol. A comparative analysis was conducted concerning the number of hours a person is awake as a measure of the affects of certain amounts of alcohol in the body. The lack of sleep for 18 hours equates to a blood alcohol content level of .05 to .06 percent. The lack of sleep for 24 hours proved equivalent to a 0.10 percent blood alcohol content level which in most states is at or beyond the level of legally intoxication (Pedersen, 2001).

The internal investigator should ascertain these facts if the incident occurred at night or during non-working hours, when the officer would be normally sleeping such as in the case of an overtime situation or off-duty incident involving the exercise of police powers. The level or lack of sleep should be determined in the investigation no matter the shift assigned or time of the incident. Even officers assigned to days may moonlight in overnight security positions in order to make some extra money. This will often result in the lack of proper sleep and recuperation of the human body. The lack of sleep and fatigue may prove to be a mitigating circumstance for the involved officer when measured against all of the circumstances of the incident being investigated.

Correlating Stress and Questionable Behavior

Atypical and questionable conduct on behalf of an officer can be attributed to intentional as well as unintentional acts. Therefore, officer conduct is not always related to malice and may be a cry for help when conduct becomes unprofessional or questionable. The internal investigator should consider these factors when conducting the inquiry into allegations of questionable conduct.

Organizational stressors created through politics and bureaucracy can far exceed the stressors created by the normal course of police duties (Kirschman, 1998). Organizational stressors are credited with being some of the lead causes for lost time and sick leave in most organizations. Organizational stressors can lead to serious physical and psychological problems in employees. Organizational stress can also manifest itself in behavioral misconduct such as anger and frustration and the misconduct that can be proportional to the level of anger, frustration, and low morale in an organization (*Law and Order,* 2001c).

The research has also revealed that the everyday policing activity produces stress levels that may lead to negative conduct. As critical incident stressors are compounded by general work stressors the health and welfare of the officer and community may be placed at risk. The nature of police work produces pain and frustration for officers and ultimately, the community at large (Stevens, 1999). The concept of "cumulative interactive stress" speaks to those factors of organizational, routine and personal stressors that come to bear when taken collectively. This cumulative effect may also be responsible for atypical or unprofessional conduct on behalf of law enforcement employees (Stevens, 1999).

A salient concern is that of an officer's conduct going beyond unprofessional acts to acts of excessive force and violence towards others, both on and off the job. Police psychologists have studied excessive force incidents in which deadly force was used, however, no substantive attention has been directed towards cases of physically abusive officers in non-lethal force incidents wherein patterns of behavior that determine an officer unfit for duty can be identified and acted upon (Brown, 2000). While the research base is minimal, an organization's responsibility for identifying and correcting these types of behaviors is self-evident. Tantamount to the organization's responsibility is the responsibility of peers and supervisors to monitor and intervene when such behaviors begin to surface at the earliest stages.

Organizational stressors can create these types of conduct. Ironically, these same organizations hold personnel accountable for the very actions they have created. While organizational stressors may not be reduced in any significant form, they must be considered during the internal investigation process and review as a mitigating factor if substandard conduct is discovered. Dr. Ellen Kirschman (1998) states with respect to law enforcement officers that:

> Much of the time they experience the terrible dilemma of being both powerful and powerless at the same time – powerful because their every action has potentially critical consequences and powerless because they are constantly scrutinized, supervised, and reined in by their department and the community. There is no question that cops must be held accountable for their actions and their time, but to hold them accountable without simultaneously providing them with support creates resentment and rebelliousness. (p. 129)

CRITICAL INCIDENT STRESS DEBRIEFING

The concept of critical incident stress debriefing (CISD) has been recognized as the first step in identifying the psychological trauma suffered by public safety personnel involved in tragic and large scale incidents. Many who are involved in such incidents may suffer short and long-term psychological and physical ailments that are directly related to witnessing or assisting in the resolution of such incidents. Debriefing is not counseling. It is a cognitive-emotive restructuring of the event in the mind of the debriefee based on crisis intervention theory and methods of helping. The purpose is to encourage integration and understanding within the victim of the traumatic event (Kinchin, 2002). One of the main goals of critical incident stress debriefing is to restore the employee to his pre-incident level of functioning (Zelig, 1998).

Critical Incident Defined

A critical incident is any event, on or off the job that is outside the realm of an individual's coping mechanisms and has the potential to result in significant emotional and/or physical reactions. Such an incident could have serious effects for those who are directly or indirectly involved (Smotzer, 2003). These incidents have serious and long term affects on the involved officers as well as their families. It is estimated that as many as three fourths of all officers involved in a critical incident leave the force within five years (Berger, 2002).

Law enforcement personnel have the highest potential for being exposed to such incidents and consequently suffering the negative affects. A critical incident can be a homicide, fatal car accident, a case of severe child abuse, or involvement in a police use of deadly force. Other types of incidents that may fall into this category are an officer involved in a significant use-of-force in taking a violent suspect into custody or an in-custody death. These types of incidents would necessitate an internal investigation and the trauma suffered is no less than that of the trauma suffered in the previously mentioned incidents. Therefore, the internal investigator must recognize that a balance between conducting the investigation and the officer's health must be maintained.

Symptomatic Responses to Critical Incident Trauma

The impact of a trauma ecology has on the psyche of an officer involved in a traumatic incident should not be understated. Those responses should be monitored in the officer's post incident behaviors, both on and off the job. The immediate supervisor, internal investigator, and administrator should be aware of the warning signs and monitor officer behavior so as early intervention can be employed when such signs are demonstrated by the exposed officer. Officers involved in a critical incident, such as a suicide-by-cop may experience one or more of the following CISD symptoms: (1) anger, (2) resentment, (3) disbelief, (4) a preoccupation with the incident, (5) nightmares, (6) anxiety, (7) hypervigilence, (8) diminished self-confidence, (9) social avoidance, (10) changes in eating and/or sleeping patterns, (11) hypersensitivity, (12) depression, (13) ambivalence, (14) perceived loss of control, and (15) memory difficulties (Burke & Rigsby, 1999, p. 100).

These responses may be episodic, which increases the necessity for closely monitoring officer behaviors. The immediate supervisor and administrator must consider post traumatic stress when reviewing subsequent incidents of reported officer misconduct or aberrant behavior observed beyond the officer's normal affect. The internal investigator should also review any previous incidents or investigations involving the officer in order to develop a clear picture of the history and possible causes of the behavior. This review should occur after the case is investigated and not before so as not to taint the investigation of the reported incident.

The Value of Critical Incident Stress Debriefing

One method of reducing the effects of critical incident trauma is the use of Critical Incident Stress Debriefing (CISD). CISD has gained immense popularity in many disciplines including fire, EMS, and policing. The value of CISD has been proven countless times. The simple act of expressing, venting, and discussing traumatic events can greatly reduce the negative effects of the event. A survey conducted of those involved in traumatic events revealed that 90 percent of the respondents considered debriefings valuable (Honig & Roland, 1998).

CISD is a trained and professional model of therapeutic value. CISD is beyond the kind ear of a friend or confidante, yet does not rise to the level of professional psychological or psychiatric counseling services. The use of CISD in the law enforcement realm is a more palatable means of offering professional services to those who have experienced a traumatic incident while maintaining a level of expertise that goes beyond a basic catharsis with a friend or supervisor that may be more damaging if not handled correctly.

Some additional valuable insight is offered by Officer Emre Arican who believes that when appropriate, such incidents should be discussed in depth during in-service trainings in order to develop a healthy awareness in the organization of the events and their real circumstances. Additional measures could be the use of training bulletins to reach officers in departments that cannot afford the time or commitment for an in-service training of this type. Critical to these sessions is the involved officer's input so as an intrinsic value can be enjoyed. The officer may feel that they are instrumental in teaching others by their mistakes or actions. These types of actions can lead to a therapeutic affect on the entire organization by abating the "rumor mill" effect in dissemination of true and accurate information as opposed to damaging supposition.

Legal and Procedural Issues

The use of CISD does not come without some controversial opinions and issues. The first and foremost issue is that of confidentiality in the sessions. When the CISD is performed by those who are not licensed counselors or professionals, then most likely the information disclosed may not be protected under any law. If an agency decides to utilize such a model, then the officer should be advised at the outset of the session what information is and isn't protected by statute. Otherwise, the officer and process can be irreparably damaged because of the disclosure of information elicited during the CISD that may not have been intended for disclosure. Worse yet is information that is disclosed that may be taken out of context or used inappropriately in any subsequent proceeding (see *Jaffee v. Redmond,* 1996). Since the CISD is intended to heal the involved officer then all policy and procedure should emerge from this perspective. A method to overcome this issue is the use of licensed and credentialed professionals who can guarantee confidentiality and thus bring credibility to the process and maximize use by those who need it most.

There has also been a move in the law enforcement field to mandate such practices as counseling subsequent to a traumatic incident like a police involved shooting. One thought process is that if the counseling is mandated it removes the stigma attached to the use of counseling services that is attached in the law enforcement environment. While this thought process has merit, some argue against the practice. Some agencies require a full psychological evaluation subsequent to a police-involved shooting for the purpose of mitigating liability issues. Advocates for choice in the issue believe that incumbent upon the officer's authority to use force is their self-awareness for the need for counseling services as well as the damage a mandatory counseling policy may cause (Paynter, 2000). This will be a difficult policy call in an organization that is intent on protecting the employee's physical and emotional well being as well as the liability implications involved. CISD advocates argue that the benefits outweigh the losses or disadvantages. From this perspective, the officer's health supersedes all other factors and the organization should not only offer professional services, either voluntarily or involuntarily, but ensure that these services are used to maintain the health and welfare of the work force in these most trying of circumstances.

The Steps in Critical Incident Stress Debriefing

A process must be developed in the CISD process for it to be administered uniformly and effectively. The immediate supervisor, internal investigator, and administrator should be aware of the steps in the process when developing the policy and procedure for CISD or when a request for a contract in professional services is drafted. Dr. Daniel A. Goldfarb (1998) reports the steps of CISD as: (1) introduction, (2) fact phase, (3) thoughts phase, (4) reactions phase, (5) symptoms phase, (6) teaching phase, and (7) re-entry phase (p. 121). If the CISD counselors are professionally trained in-house employees or contractors, the process should be standardized and include the methodology for consistent administration and follow-up activities for personnel involved in traumatic incidents.

CISD debriefings and follow-up should also include: (1) key people in the employee's life such as spouse, children, extended family, and close friends, (2) allowing the officer to have a spouse/significant other accompany him or her during the CISD, (3) CISD sessions for family members only, (4) special care for children, (5) providing coping instructions for the family, (6) follow-up with the family, and (7) identification of all secondary victims of trauma (Zelig, 1998).

CISD briefings are also time sensitive. In order for the intervention to be effective, it must be somewhat contemporaneous to the incident so that the trauma can be minimized and the therapeutic value can be maximized. The CISD should occur between 24 to 48 hours after the incident (Paynter, 2000).

POLICE SUICIDE

Police involved suicide seems to be one of the most ignored issues of the profession. Commonly referred to as the silent killer, the response is just as ominous. While police administrators, community activists, and the media take pleasure in the chance to expose and address police abuse of power and corruption, minimal attention is afforded by the same groups to acknowledge the devastatingly adverse affects of stress on law enforcement personnel. The rate of police suicide has overtaken the rate of police personnel killed in the line of duty by intentional and accidental means. For example, in NYPD, there have been years when more officers have died at their own hands than in the line of duty (Czarnecki, Fabrice, Kasanof, Adam, & Trautman, 2002). For every woman who completes suicide, four men do so, and the total deaths by suicide in the United States outnumber the homicide deaths by three to two (Hoofnagle, 2002; IACP, 1998a). This problem is pandemic in law enforcement and must be treated as any other acutely fatal disease.

Policy Considerations

Policy must be developed that mandates procedures and training for the organization's supervisory and command personnel in recognizing the behaviors as well as intervention strategies and services that can be offered. A training program should be provided for immediate supervisors and peers, and if necessary, a discrete reporting policy should be employed in order to provide help to those in need of intervention and counseling services. Internal investigations personnel should also be trained in recognizing indicators of depression and suicide in police personnel. Mood swings that include five or more of the following symptoms should be considered serious enough for further investigation of possible depression: (1) significant changes in appetite and sleep patterns, (2) irritability, anger, worry, agitation, anxiety, (3) loss of energy, persistent lethargy, (4) unexplained aches and pains, (5) feelings of guilt, worthlessness, and/or hopelessness, (6) inability to concentrate, indecisiveness, (7) inability to take pleasure in former interests, social withdrawal, (8) pessimism, indifference, (9) prolonged sadness or unexplained crying spells, (10) excessive consumption of alcohol or use of chemical substances, and (11) recurring thoughts of death or suicide (Hoofnagle, 2002).

The organization must understand the need for services for intervention and develop guidelines and contacts that can be offered to the officer for assistance such as: (1) professional counseling, (2) internal counseling units or peer counselors, (3) police chaplains, (4) organizations such as Samaritans, Alcoholics Anonymous, Alanon, Cocaine Anonymous Hotline, (5) doctors, (6) priests, ministers, rabbis, etc., (7) Union or PBA, and (8) lawyers (Czarnecki, Fabrice, Kasanof, Adam, & Trautman, 2002).

Policy development should be an in-depth research process that involves the collective opinions of mental health and counseling professionals as well as key law enforcement personnel. Policy should also be agency specific addressing the needs of the officer, the officer's family, the administration, and possibly need alignment with any restrictions assigned to these matters through the prevailing collective bargaining agreement. A three-pronged approach should be considered for developing policy: (1) consider mandatory counseling after traumatic events, (2) consider in-service training on depression and manic-depression, and (3) review department policies on leave and disability (Hoofnagle, 2002).

Investigative Considerations

The internal investigations unit should be involved in any incident of police suicide. Most internal investigations are protected by personnel records laws and thus the use of an internal in this type of investigation may protect the officer's privacy while uncovering salient issues that may be used to prevent future acts in the organization, other personnel who may also be suffering from such deep depressive episodes, and protection from any liability that may be incurred by the agency.

Symptoms of depression are often manifested in the officer's daily actions and through investigation may be detected and prevented. In a police suicide investigation, it is important to determine the issues that led to the suicide for use as a prevention tool. Signals of suicidal behavior are: (1) depression, (2) talking about or threatening suicide, (3) making plans for the care of the children, (4) giving away valued possessions or pets, (5) saying goodbye, (6) sudden interest in insurance, wills, burial plots, etc., (7) sudden calmness or the calm before the storm, (8) hopelessness, (9) alcohol, (10) drugs, (11) divorces, break-ups, etc., (12) being investigated on charges of crime or serious misconduct, and (13) separation from family or friends (Czarnecki, Fabrice, Kasanof, Adam, & Trautman, 2002). The internal investigation should establish if any of these factors were present.

The instrument of many police suicides is the service weapon because of its accessibility. If the signs of suicidal behavior are detected, the agency must take action. Firearms removal in an agency should be supported by policy and procedure and be non-disciplinary in nature: (1) supervisors should be able to remove an officer's firearm discreetly, without bringing disciplinary action against the officer and (2) officers themselves should be able to surrender their firearms voluntarily, without disciplinary consequences. Officers should also be able to surrender their personally owned firearms (both handguns and long guns) for safekeeping, as well as surrendering department-owned firearms or duty weapons (Czarnecki, Fabrice, Kasanof, Adam, & Trautman, 2002).

In a suicide investigation, the method should be investigated as thoroughly as any other unattended death investigation. The investigation should be thorough with respect to the events and actions leading to the act as well as any information that could have indicated the individual was in a depressive state. The investigation should also document any methods of prevention that were taken or not taken as a result of any information known to the organization. When possible, this information should then be used to develop new suicide prevention programs or enhance existing programs in order to address this problem.

EMPLOYEE ASSISTANCE PROGRAMS

Employee Assistance Programs (EAP's) have been long recognized as a method to maintain a healthy and productive workforce. As human beings, employees have frailties that rise to the surface and disrupt productivity. Some rise to the level where employees can enter into patterns of self-destructive behavior and become not only a liability to the organization, but in public service, a danger to other employees, and the community at large. This makes EAP's in law enforcement a critical component to any human resource initiative.

EAP's are important due to the stress that law enforcement work creates, individual coping strategies may not be enough to overcome the damage done to the officer. Coping strategies fall into two categories: (1) personal and (2) professional. Personal strategies include time off, personal attention to oneself, critical reflection and self-exploration, while professional strategies include peer supervision and consultation, working in a professional setting with others rather than isolation, and diversifying professional contacts. These coping strategies can be stabilizing factors in the life of an officer who has experienced such traumatization (Atkinson-Tovar, 2003).

There are two factors that impact the use of EAP's that are made available to law enforcement personnel: (1) the failure to recognize the warning signs as serious enough to seek counseling and treatment and (2) the stigma attached to the use of counseling services by law enforcement personnel. With respect to the first issues, the inability to recognize the symptoms of depression and the reluctance to seek treatment caused by the stigma are two main barriers to treatment and recovery (Hoofnagle, 2002). Many personnel will write-off or disregard the symptoms believing they are related to other inane issues rather than the true causes such as stress and the like. The second issue involves that of the stigma involved in seeking treatment. Many factors such as embarrassment, concern over change in status or loss of employment, and the police culture of secrecy which in effect protects officers from the attacks of the outside world prevent officers from seeking assistance (Atkinson-Tovar, 2003).

Unfortunately, EAP's are not utilized to their fullest potential. Police psychologists confirm that counseling is more likely to take place as a response to excessive-force incidents than as a means of prevention (Stevens, 1999). A need to develop confidence in EAP's and the fact that programs are confidential must be instilled in officers in order to avoid transgressions that can have devastating outcomes (Trautman, 2003a). In order to overcome some of these issues, a strategy must be employed so that personnel believe in the value of the system as outweighing any negatively perceived consequence. Departments should also consider a four-phase program for stress education: (1) education, (2) prevention, (3) support, and (4) research (Atkinson-Tovar, 2003). Another unique strategy is used by the Los Angeles Police Department with their bureau psychologists. Bureau psychologists are infused into daily activities such as roll calls and ride-alongs in order to develop rapport with police personnel and have a declared mission of providing outreach, education, and consultation to local division commanding officers and their personnel (Gelber, 2003). The development of an EAP is a significant step toward the maintenance of a healthy and productive work environment.

Inset 1

Psychosis: A state of mind where one loses touch with reality. Subjects hallucinate and lose their sense of self. Subjects hallucinate and lose their sense of self. Symptoms include disorganized thought, disorganized speech and behaviors and hearing voices or seeing things and delusions (Fixed false beliefs). Psychosis can accompany many medical and psychiatric diseases. Among adult psychiatric diseases, psychosis is most commonly associated with Schizophrenia (SCZ), Depression and Manic-Depression, Post-Traumatic Stress Disorder (PTSD) and substance abuse. Such medical conditions as delirium and high blood sugar can also cause psychosis. The term psychosis is used to describe the presence of the symptoms above. Persons suffering from psychosis may be more likely to be violent and symptoms associated with the violence may include delusions of paranoia, a belief that one's own mind is controlled by external forces, and command hallucinations (voices telling the subject to do something). A person with psychotic depression may be out of touch with reality but they believe what they think. (Clede, 1998)

Inset 2

Schizophrenia: SCZ is a mental illness characterized by disturbances in thinking and perceptions that result in obvious and not so obvious behaviors. The perceptual experience of someone experiencing paranoia is distorted. It appears in persons between their late teens to mid-30s. It crosses all boundaries of social, economic, and cultural groups and is a lifelong disorder with intermittent periods of normalcy and psychosis. The five subtypes of SCZ are the most associated with violence and are: (1) Paranoid Schizophrenia: Involves psychotic symptoms and in most associated with violence, (2) Antisocial Personality Disorder: APD is a pervasive pattern of disregard for, and violation of, the rights of others and are also referred to as sociopaths of psychopaths, (3) Depression: The most common mental illness, it is a mood disorder that can begin at any age. An episode must last at least two weeks and represent a change from a person's previous attitude. The violence can be directed towards one's self or others, as in the case of a murder suicide, (4) Suicide: Is a significant symptom of depression and one that every police officer is likely to face unexpectedly. Self-directed violence and suicide by cop are symptoms of this disorder, (5) Post-Traumatic Stress Disorder: PTSD is a group of symptoms that include recurrent and intrusive recollections or dreams of the event and distress at exposure to cues that symbolize the event. One suffering PTSD may have difficulty falling asleep, be irritable, and have a hard time concentrating, be overly vigilant or respond in an exaggerated manner to being startled. Violence is rare, but possible. (Clede, 1998)

SUMMARY

This chapter discussed the issues of police officer stress as a result of work responsibilities as well as those created during critical incidents and internal investigations. The chapter also discussed investigative considerations for the internal investigator and administrator when investigating and reviewing the completed internal investigation. Several issues were discussed with respect to the physiological responses that affect cognitive skills, incident recollection, and health concerns. The chapter then discussed methodologies for the remedy of these conditions such as CISD and EAPs. The internal investigator and police administrator must recognize that many police officers, while dealing with the pain and trauma of others do not appreciate the affects that these observations will have on them personally. Police administrators need to recognize these problems and provide adequate services for officers to lead healthy and productive careers and lives (Atkinson-Tovar, 2003).

Chapter 5

DEFINITIONS AND TERMINOLOGY

INTRODUCTION

Definitions and terminology in all of the investigative types are unique. For example, in a criminal case, defendant, prosecutor, defense, and the like are the proper terms used. In a civil suit, it's the plaintiff who sues the defendant as contrasted in a criminal case where the entity bringing the allegation is the people of that particular state or government. In an internal investigation, the terminology is distinctive with respect to the involved parties and the evidence needed to support a case disposition. This chapter discusses those differences and their uses in the internal investigation process.

CIVIL SERVICE TERMINOLOGY

Civil Service terminology defines the entities and actions from a human resource perspective. These terms must be used as they relate to the type of action levied against the employee. For example, if a person is the victim of a wrongful death, different states have different definitions of homicide and murder as well as varying degrees of the act. Filing an accusatory instrument that does not meet statutory requirements will most likely result in the case being dismissed. Therefore, the internal investigator must know the laws of their respective state in order to properly address the issue.

In general, a public employer would be identified as a state, county, or municipal entity. In taking disciplinary actions, the public employer is usually not the entity bringing the action; rather it is the agency head who acts as the complainant. A public employee would be any person, whether through appointment or employment, who holds a position with a public employer. A governmental body is the appointed authority or the agency itself identified in taking personnel actions which are actions that may adversely affect a public employee's property or liberty interest in a position, such as compensation, promotion, demotion, transfer, or performance evaluation.

When perfecting complaints against personnel of the organization, proper terminology and legal review are essential. The internal investigator should not be sensitive to constructive criticism in this area as personnel law is a complex body of law and qualified advice should be welcomed in the development of a case.

TYPES OF COMPLAINTS

The designation of complaints can be confusing as in the designation of witness types as discussed later in the text. For the purposes of this discussion, complaint types can be divided into three main categories: (1) Primary (Direct) or those that are filed directly by those who believe they have been the subject of police misconduct, (2) Secondary (Indirect), from a person who has witnessed or has knowledge of alleged misconduct by the police, and (3) Third Party from a person or persons acting on behalf of a complainant or organization such as an attorney or advocacy group.

In the primary or direct complaint scenario, the subject of the alleged misconduct such as the arrestee files a complaint directly with the law enforcement organization through means made available through the organization either by telephone, formal complaint in person, mail, alternative complaint sites, and the Internet.

In the secondary or indirect complaint, the allegation is made by a person who witnesses or has knowledge of the alleged misconduct. This type of complaint can be filed in the same manner as previously mentioned and by anyone who has knowledge of the incident. These types of complaints emanate from a person who witnesses a use-of-force during an arrest and the arrestee has not filed a complaint. Concerned citizens who believe they also have witnessed or have knowledge of law enforcement personnel engaged in criminal acts where the officer and other party are complicit are also included in this complaint type. A final party included in this category is other law enforcement personnel. A partner or witnessing officer may also come forward and file a complaint with the agency upon witnessing some alleged transgression of another officer.

The complaint process can also be delineated more from a categorical rather than conceptual framework when identifying the need to track complaints through statistical analysis. Complaint types can be defined as complaint sources and be classified as:

Citizen Complaints:

1. Citizen complainant
2. Citizen witness
4. Citizen advocate
5. Anonymous

Internal Complaints:

1. Peer/co-worker/department employee
2. Supervisor/command officer
3. Chief of Police/Sheriff
4. Anonymous

Satellite and Ancillary Issues:

1. Internal Investigation Unit staff during the investigation

TYPES OF INTERNAL INVESTIGATIONS

Internal investigations can be divided into seven categories: (1) Procedural, (2) Use-of-force, (3) Missing Property, (4) Criminal, (5) Civil, (6) Fleet Vehicle Accidents, and (7) Police Pursuits. The categories are delineated as follows:

Procedural: In the internal investigation, all complaints in essence are procedural. Even in a criminal case, the internal investigation addresses how department procedures were violated in the commission of the alleged criminal act. The procedural investigation usually is the category for all investigations that do not fall under the aforementioned categories.

Use-of-Force: Use-of-force investigations are all investigations that involve some allegation of excessive, unnecessary, or improper force. As with the remainder of the categories, these should be isolated in the investigative process because of the serious nature of these complaints as well as the potential liability involved.

Missing Property: Missing property investigations may have procedural or criminal implications. Missing property such as a license plate not turned into a property office may be a procedural violation while missing currency confiscated from a suspect may be criminal in nature. These investigations carry importance due to the responsibility of law enforcement to safeguard confiscated property.

Criminal: Criminal investigations are the most serious of cases investigated. However, they are investigated from an administrative and not criminal prosecution perspective. While the conduct may violate criminal laws, the internal investigation addresses how the criminal act violates departmental rules, regulations, and procedures. The sanction in criminal court may be conviction and incarceration while in the departmental setting the highest sanction may only be termination.

Civil: Civil suits are filed on a daily basis against law enforcement agencies. These investigations differ from an internal investigation that has the intent of determining whether or not departmental violations of conduct occurred. The civil investigation concentrates only on the allegations of the lawsuit and actions of the officers or defendants in the litigation. While an internal investigation must be thorough with respect to investigation and review, the civil investigation should be limited to the acts alleged in the lawsuit. The civil suit may also trigger the internal investigation process after the initial review.

Fleet Vehicle Accidents: Fleet vehicle accidents involve the investigation of any accident involving a law enforcement vehicle, whether directly or indirectly involved.

Police Pursuits: Police pursuit investigations involve the actions of the pursuing and assisting officers as well as monitoring supervisors and command officers as they relate to policy and legal statute. This is an area of high controversy and liability. Even in pursuits where no accident occurs as a result, a review should be conducted of the circumstances and justification by higher departmental authority.

Sometimes, there is confusion in the different classifications. For example, an officer may be accused of applying a set of handcuffs too tightly. Is this a use-of-force or procedural complaint? The answer is in the analysis of the intent after the investigation is completed. In this scenario, the complainant initially states that the officer applied the handcuffs during the arrest and as a result the complainant experienced some pain from the application. The investigation reveals that the complainant did not experience the pain until being placed in the rear of a police vehicle and as a result of leaning backwards in the seat, the complainant applied pressure to the handcuffs and thus experienced the pain subsequent to the application. This would then be an unfounded procedural complaint as the intent was correct in applying the handcuffs and the conduct alleged did not occur.

Changing the scenario slightly, the officer is actively involved in a use-of-force and applying handcuffs to the complainant who is resisting arrest. The officer struggles to apply the handcuffs which are later determined to be "tight" on the complainant's wrists. After the complainant calms down, the officer immediately loosens the handcuffs for the complainant. This then becomes a use-of-force investigation wherein the officer's actions are exonerated. The officer took reasonable measures to secure the complainant's custody and then remedied the condition when the situation was safe.

The internal investigator must also consider the need for changing the classification of the investigation after the case is completed. The aforementioned scenario is an appropriate example for this type of situation. The original complaint may be filed as a use-of-force, when in reality it is later determined to be a procedural complaint. The internal investigator must change the classification if appropriate so as the investigation, officer's record, and departmental statistics all accurately reflect the allegation. In consideration of changing the classification of the investigation, as the investigation unfolds, the wording in the allegation may also require such appropriate change as is necessary to reflect the information developed in the process.

TYPES OF RESPONSES

The types of responses to a personnel complaint refer to the manner and depth of the investigation completed. There are numerous factors that impact the proper response to a complaint. The level of severity, cooperation, available evidence, as well as many other factors will determine the level of response to a personnel complaint. The level of response in an internal investigation can be divided into four categories: (1) Field Conciliation or Mediation, (2) Incident/Administrative Review (Precautionary Investigation), (3) Departmental Investigation, and (4) Formal Personnel Complaint. The categories are delineated as follows:

Field Conciliation or Mediation: The field conciliation or mediation is the lowest level of complaint usually involving an explanation of departmental or legal (e.g., vehicle towing policy, ticket issuance, etc.) policy or procedure. In some cases documentation is completed. The field conciliation or mediation most often results in the complainant's satisfaction with the action or inaction of the involved officer. As a form of formal mediation, it can involve informal methods such as the use of a supervisor who acts in the role while bringing a complainant and officer together in order to attempt to resolve the issue at hand (Finn, 2000a). Care must be taken in deciding to bring both parties together too close in time to the event. Most conciliations or mediations should be handled only though direct supervisory contact and without the presence or involvement of the involved officer.

Incident/Administrative Review (Precautionary Investigation): The incident/administrative review is based upon information that has been brought to the attention of the department by a citizen that warrants further and more in-depth inquiry than a field conciliation. Cases that are classified as incident/administrative review carry much of the same documentation as a formal complaint except for the formal complaint form. The incident/administrative review most often will have a case disposition as well.

Departmental Investigation: The departmental investigation can be an intra-departmental (within the department) or inter-departmental (between departments) investigation where information is brought to the attention of the department by a member, either command or other, that warrants further and more in-depth inquiry than a section/zone/shift level review. Departmental investigations carry much of the same paperwork as a formal complaint, and sometimes include the formal complaint form.

Formal Personnel Complaint: The formal personnel complaint is the initiation of a complaint investigation against an employee or employees of a law enforcement agency.

The internal investigator must also consider the need for changing the classification of the investigation after the case is completed. For example, a field conciliation or mediation, after review may warrant follow-up with the complainant that may lead to a formal complaint or incident/administrative review. An example of this would be the complaint of an officer who was allegedly discourteous during an arrest. While the complainant may be satisfied with the explanation of the officer's conduct, further investigation may reveal that the arrest was illegal and thus warrant an incident/administrative review. In contrast, a complainant may file a formal complaint, but then refuse to cooperate further in the investigation. These cases must be closely scrutinized and a decision made to suspend or continue based upon a responsibility on the organization to police its own in an effective and efficient manner. When the decision is made to suspend the investigation, the case may be reclassified as an incident/administrative review. As in the type of internal investigation, the internal investigator must change the classification if appropriate so as the investigation, officer's record, and departmental statistics all accurately reflect the level of response to the allegation made.

CASE FINDINGS

The types of case findings in a personnel complaint refer to the final disposition of the investigation. The primary factor that impacts the proper disposition of a complaint is the level of available evidence as weighed against the applied standard of a preponderance of evidence. Internal investigation case findings can be divided into seven categories: (1) Sustained, (2) Not Sustained, (3) Exonerated, (4) Unfounded, (5) Policy and Procedure, (6) Policy Failure, (7) Training Issue, and (8) Incomplete Investigation/No Findings/Closed as Office. The categories are delineated as follows:

Sustained: The sustained finding in an internal investigation indicates that there is evidence sufficient to prove the allegations made.

Not Sustained: The not sustained finding in an internal investigation indicates that there is insufficient evidence to either prove or disprove the allegations made.

Exonerated: The exonerated finding in an internal investigation indicates that the incident occurred and was lawful, proper, and justified.

Unfounded: The unfounded finding in an internal investigation indicates that the allegation is false or not factual or the employee was not involved.

Policy and Procedure: The policy and procedure finding in an internal investigation indicates that the nature of the investigation dealt solely with a complainant's objection or criticism against an agency policy or procedure even if the complaint was against an individual officer.

Policy Failure: The policy failure finding in an internal investigation indicates that the nature of the investigation revealed that an agency policy or procedure was outdated or incorrect even if the complaint was against an individual officer.

Training Issue: The issue of inadequate, poor, or incorrect training may affect the individual officer as well as the entire department. In using this finding, the organization progressively recognizes that the issue was one that may have been beyond the control of the officer and responds by correcting the situation that created the problem. Training is also a perishable commodity and as such, must be considered a mitigating factor in case determinations. While this may in essence replace a sustained finding, it is much more palatable for the officer involved as well as the agency.

Incomplete Investigation/No Findings/Closed as Office: The incomplete investigation/no findings/closed as officer finding in an internal investigation indicates that the investigation could not be thoroughly or properly investigated. This may be caused by a lack of cooperation by the complainant and/or witnesses, or the absence of a critical interview which was necessary to proceed with the investigation, and/or the available physical evidence or witness statements are insufficient to adjudicate the complaint (International Association of Chiefs of Police, 2000b, p. 48).

At the conclusion of the internal investigation all cases require a disposition (Thurnauer, 2002). In case disposition, each allegation must also have a finding applied. Cases may involve numerous allegations and each allegation may have separate and distinct findings. For example, a complainant may allege excessive force (unfounded), discourtesy (sustained), and missing property (not sustained) all in the same case. The clustering of allegations will be discussed later as this example provides three separate categories as an example (e.g., Use-of-force, Procedural, and Missing Property).

One additional note is the internal investigator must pay attention to the wording used in the allegation and subsequent application of a finding. For example, an allegation may be worded as, "Struck with a PR24," or "Allegation of Excessive Force–Struck with a PR24." In "Struck with a PR24," if the officer admits to the use of the PR24 in a use-of-force report, there is no alternative but to find the allegation sustained, despite the fact that the use-of-force may have been wholly justified as an active countermeasure to a resisting suspect. In the, "Allegation of Excessive Force–Struck with a PR24," the issue is clarified and a proper finding can be applied as if the act was justified, the finding is exonerated. In this same scenario, if the act was unjustified or excessive, the finding applied is sustained. Another example of this is a "Courtesy" complaint. Can a person complain that the officer was courteous? Therefore, the proper terminology is an "Improper Procedure - Discourtesy" complaint. Consistent and proper wording is critical in applying appropriate case findings.

Another discussion that is appropriate to this section is the issue of evidence with respect to the order of proof and the corpus delicti. The issue of physical and testimonial evidence as well as its admissibility is discussed in-depth in chapter 12 "Evidence Identification, Evaluation, and Collection," the internal investigator must have a grasp of the specific rules of evidence in proving a case. Frank Morn (2000) discusses this salient aspect of criminal investigation which has a direct connection to the use of evidence in internal investigations. Two conceptual components of the issue are discussed as: (1) the order of proof and (2) the corpus delicti.

The order of proof involves an order to the investigation which establishes that all of the legal elements of a crime have been committed, or in the case of an internal investigation, a violation of some policy, procedure, or rule has been violated. Within the concept of the corpus deliciti, several additional components must be established. Those five elements are delineated as follows:

1. *Legality:* An alleged violation must be of a legally constituted written law, rule, or policy.
2. *Intent:* There must be an evil intent behind the act in question. This concept speaks to the *Mens rea* or guilty mind theory in the law. While accidental and unintended acts can be irresponsible and negligent, they may not rise to the level of culpability of an intentional act.
3. *Act:* The corpus delicti demands that some wrongful act or omission of an act be committed. The culpability of the act may also be negated if a justification exists for engaging in the conduct or the omission.
4. *Concurrence:* There needs to be a connection or causal relationship between the act and the harm done.
5. *Culpability:* A person may intend to carry out a criminal act or violation of a policy, rule, or code and perform the illegal act and still not be culpable. Culpability is affected by justification, self-defense, and other reasons that reduce or totally mitigate the actions. (Morn, 2000, p. 161)

Learning the definitions of particular case findings is of the same priority as learning the conceptual issues surrounding the proving of a case in the court and administrative realms. The internal investigator must use this examination every time an allegation is investigated and reviewed with the intent of applying a fair and accurate finding to the case disposition. The internal investigator may be well advised to repeat these steps in each case for each allegation so as a template for legality is mirrored in every internal investigation.

SUMMARY

This chapter discussed the issues of definitions and terminology in the internal investigation process. The use of proper and appropriate terms and titles can impact the outcome of an internal investigation if the case is submitted for such actions as discipline or termination proceedings. The chapter then discussed the types of complaints and investigations that the internal investigator may encounter in the process. The chapter then advanced through the types of responses to an internal investigation that are acceptable practices based upon the level of severity of the case as well as other salient factors. The chapter then concluded with a discussion on case findings and offered several examples in all of the above subsections to help guide the internal investigator in the process and provide clarification in the difficult positions that may be faced.

Chapter 6

LEGAL AND LABOR ISSUES

INTRODUCTION

The legal and labor issues involved in the internal investigation are extremely complex. While many federal laws and rules apply, many states have carved out additional and stricter standards for the legal redress of these types of investigations. This chapter is designed to offer general guidance in the process and a resource for the internal investigator and administrator in identifying the legal and labor issues involved. While this chapter is devoted to the general legal issues, there are several additional legal citations that are topic specific included throughout the text. In all instances where an investigation is conducted, the investigator and administrator should refer to their own state law standards, departmental collective bargaining agreements, and consult with legal counsel prior to taking any adverse employee actions.

THE PRINCIPLES OF DUE PROCESS

The principle of due process applies to the rights of the accused officer. Therefore, the onus is on management, not the unions or defense attorneys to protect these inalienable rights. Management not only has the burden of proof in a case, but more importantly, must protect the due process rights of the accused employee as well. While this seems to be an unorthodox approach, the ideology is answered in the question, "How can an organization discipline an alleged act of misconduct or corruption when the actions of the organization are just as complicit?" The internal investigator and administrator must rise above illegal and improper practices in order to ensure the same level of due process is afforded to the organization's employees as is done for any accused criminal on the street.

Some management philosophy however, is grounded in an unrealistic belief system that seems to condone the violation of the rights of its own employees in lieu of the end result in finding an officer guilty at all costs. This is supported in the following quote, "The American judicial system operates on the principles that a person is innocent until proven guilty. Unfortunately, too many managers seem to have the idea that employees lose their constitutional rights when they step onto company property" (Alexander Hamilton Institute, 1991, p. D1). Therefore, the United States Constitution is not nullified as a term and condition of employment. The Constitution ensures equal protection under the law for municipal and government employees through certain procedural safeguards. These safeguards are intended for all who are within the political boundaries of the United States. As a measure of our humanity, democracy, and freedom, we must afford these rights to all.

Due process is linked to the concepts of both a property interest and liberty interest in one's employment rights. As such, violating due process will most likely lead to the eradication of the charges and return to the state of employment enjoyed previous to the adverse action. An example is provided by Beverly A. Ginn (2003) who states that:

> The Fifth Amendment to the United States Constitution guarantees all citizens due process before the deprivation of life, liberty, or property. Public employers may trigger the due process clause in two circumstances: first, when they deprive a public employee of a property interest by terminating that person or, second, when they deprive an employee of a liberty interest in his or her 'good name, reputation, honor, or integrity' by executing an adverse employment action. (p. 10)

The concept of due process predicates even the internal investigation and disciplinary proceedings themselves as argued by Thomas J. Martinelli and Joycelyn M. Pollock (2000) who state that:

> The very foundation of due process is fair notice. If an officer can make any case at all that he or she was unaware that certain conduct was unethical or violated departmental policies, then due process is compromised and disciplinary sanctions are likely to be overturned by civil service review committees or arbitrators. (p. 61)

The Fourteenth Amendment to the United States Constitution includes the Due Process Clause. The outset of this chapter is based upon this as the foundation for all that is done in the internal investigation process. The internal investigator and administrator must adhere to this sacred principle in the investigative process not as a notion, but as an edict for progression.

Deprivation of a Property Interest

A property interest in a position can be defined as that interest enjoyed at the completion of a probationary period of employment. The Supreme Court has held that a public employee who has a property interest in their job (generally, an employee who may only be dismissed for cause) is entitled to a limited pretermination hearing in addition to a full posttermination hearing.

The pretermination hearing includes: (1) oral or written notice of the charges, (2) an explanation of the employer's evidence (e.g., allowing an employee to review the investigative files or providing a written summary of the evidence to the employee meets this requirement), and (3) an opportunity for the employee to tell his or her side of the story (Ginn, 2003).

The property interest in a position requires some type of cause for discipline or termination as opposed to the probationary period where no right is enjoyed by the employee to maintain employment. The employee thus serves at the caprice of the organization or chief administrator. The protection of a property interest usually occurs when an employee who is protected by civil service laws is suspended without pay or terminated without cause. The due process rights then apply in protecting the employee's property interest and the agency must show cause for the deprivation of those rights.

Deprivation of a Liberty Interest

The deprivation of a liberty interest in a position is a more complex issue. The liberty interest deals with one's name or reputation in the organization. A stigma that would rise to the level of a constitutional violation would involve an issue with the person's reputation for honesty or integrity (Ginn, 2003). The Circuit Court for the Tenth Circuit has set a four-part test which must be met before a claim of deprivation of liberty interests is actionable: (1) the statements at issue must impugn the good name, reputation, honor, or integrity of the employee, (2) these statements must be false, (3) these statements must occur in the course of terminating the employee or must foreclose other employment opportunities, and (4) these statements must be published. Adding such information to an employee's personnel file may be sufficient to raise such a liberty interest. The reputational injury must also coincide with some other "alteration of legal status," such as termination of employment (Unkelbach, 2003).

Providing a pretermination hearing for a member whose employment is about to be terminated based on honesty, integrity, or reputational issues is the best way for an agency to guard against any future claims that the officer was unconstitutionally deprived of his or her liberty interest (Unkelbach, 2003).

THE PRINCIPLES OF JUST CAUSE

In any disciplinary case, management must prove they had "just cause" to administer the discipline. The foundation of this rule derives from the *Enterprise Wire Company and Enterprise Independent Union* (1966) case. This case prescribes an "Arbitrator's Seven Tests for Just Cause" to administer discipline as follows:

1. *Proper Notice:* Was the employee given advance warning of the probable consequences of his or her conduct?
2. *Reasonable Rule or Order:* Was the controlling rule or order reasonably related to efficient and safe working conditions?
3. *Full Investigation:* Was the investigation fair and objective?
4. *Fair Investigation:* Was the investigation fair and objective?
5. *Substantial Proof:* Did the investigation uncover substantial proof of guilt?
6. *Equal Treatment:* Was the employer's treatment even-handed and non-discriminatory?
7. *Appropriate Penalty:* Was the disciplinary action reasonably related to the employee's record of service with the organization and the gravity of his/her offense? (Institute for Labor Studies and Research, 2005)

These components of a disciplinary action should be considered by the internal investigator when conducting the investigation, reaching the finding, and recommending any discipline in a case. The administrator should also use this list as a guide for reviewing the case, the employee record, and the discipline contemplated prior to commencing with a disciplinary action.

GENERAL DISCIPLINARY SANCTIONS AND PROGRESSIVE DISCIPLINE

Generally, disciplinary actions can be invoked for two reasons: (1) incompetency or (2) misconduct. While other rules are in place for removal of employees for cause such as for medical reasons, these are the general basic requirements. Proving and incompetence case is extremely difficult, so the majority of cases are handled under misconduct.

General disciplinary sanctions for internal investigations that result in a sustained finding for misconduct or corruption can vary from state to state. Protections can be guaranteed by state laws such as civil service and other protections such as collective bargaining agreements. Sanctions and disciplinary actions can include: (1) informal and formal counseling, (2) oral and formal reprimands, (3) documented formal disciplinary actions, (4) loss of accrued time and suspension without pay, (5) demotions or transfers of assignment, (6) termination, and (7) criminal prosecution. Also of note are specific state cases laws. An example is presented in *Fabio v. Civil Service Commission of Philadelphia* (1980), the Pennsylvania Supreme Court held that unethical behavior can be grounds for dismissal when: (1) it has created rumors in the workplace, (2) it affects co-workers, (3) it affects the officer's family, and (4) it was the subject of numerous complaints and media attention (Martinelli & Pollock, 2000). The internal investigator and administrator should review all of the listed resources prior to making a disciplinary recommendation in a case involving sustained misconduct.

Each state may vary slightly as to the sanctions allowed when a case is sustained and all due process rights have been afforded to the employee. For example, state statutes may define disciplinary limits and a progression or hierarchy, such as in New York State; discipline is defined under the *New York State Civil Service Law* as: (1) letter of reprimand, (2) a fine not to exceed $100.00, (3) suspension without pay for up to 60 days, (4) demotion in rank, or (5) dismissal from service. In addition, alternate laws also may be in place and offer the administrator flexible options for discipline. For example, the *New York State Town Law* offers variations in discipline that echo civil service law, but limits suspension time to 20 days. This law also adds an option of performing extra hours or tours of duty not to exceed 20 days. Labor agreements may offer the employee the option to choose which system he or she would like to be adjudicated under.

A caveat to the concept of discipline is the principle of progressive discipline. Progressive discipline is the application of progressively stricter disciplinary action shall be taken against employees who persist in violations of department policy. Interpreted differently by different entities, such as a department that may say that consistent violations, no matter the category equate to eligibility for the increase of disciplinary action, while a union arbitrator or state court judge may narrowly define progressive discipline to similar violations. The concept of discipline and progressive discipline should also include determinate and indeterminate sanctions. For example, violations should include minimum and maximum penalties so as the organization can justify their disciplinary actions when meting out discipline and defending it as a fair and equitable practice.

An option that must be considered in all cases is that of training and counseling. The administrator must balance the sanction with the ultimate need to prevent future behavior. In most cases, training is the proper solution. Training offers a few tangible benefits such as mitigating any future civil liability and claims of inadequate training as well as providing a remediation effort and first step in the progressive discipline process. Counseling and training are also not considered as discipline under the system, so a case can be sustained and remedial action taken that does not result in discipline as defined.

CIVIL SERVICE LAW

The foundation of civil service dates back to ancient China and progresses through most civilized nations until taking root in the United States in its present form around 1940. Civil service law exists to select the proper person for the needed job, remove the politics of the hiring process, and protect employees who have gained a property interest in their positions. Usually, state civil service laws will control the process and sanctions to discipline an employee for proven misconduct. For example, the *New York State Civil Service Law* Article 75 governs the investigative process, rules, and sanctions for such acts of commission or omission that result in misconduct. If a department falls under these regulations, the rules should be studied intimately by the internal investigator and administrator.

STATUTE OF LIMITATIONS

The concept of a statute of limitations was conceived for the purposes of limiting the government's ability to prosecute offenders for certain types of offenses. Based in the *Common Law,* a statute of limitations was designed also to ensure fairness and closure for certain types of offenses. While minor offenses are limited to prosecutorial time frames of six months to one year, crimes such as homicide have no time limits.

With respect to administrative investigations and proceedings, a statute of limitations also exists in the law. These proceedings are civil in nature and thus have many of the same rules. The specific state law should be referenced when determining the time limits on bringing a disciplinary action against an employee who has been found culpable in some type of misconduct. For example, in New York State, any departmental violation under state law has a statute of 18 months unless a crime is alleged, then it defers to the statute of limitations for the crime. Collective bargaining agreements may also limit these time frames and circumstances of the investigative process.

The internal investigator and administrator should consider the time of the offense, not the time reported as the commencement of the clock. Complaints of misconduct may surface significantly later in time than when they allegedly occurred. While there is no restriction on investigation, the restriction solely lies in when the sanction or discipline is meted out which must be prior to the time limit. The internal investigator and administrator must decide if the case is of such a serious nature that it warrants a full investigation when the report is significantly removed in time from the alleged event. In addition, while there is a restriction on discipline, there is no restriction on training and remedial training. The event may be more appropriately remedied by the use of training the involved employee. In the final analysis, the spirit of the concept should be adhered to, which the basis for the doctrine is to promote fairness and closure in the system of jurisprudence.

CIVIL RIGHTS LAW

The civil rights laws were put in place due to the injustices suffered by protected classes of persons in the United States. Legislative acts and statutes were enacted at the federal and state levels in order to prevent these injustices as well as provide a remedy for violations of the acts. Two areas of the civil rights laws need to be understood when conducting internal investigations, those acts alleged to have occurred against complainants, and the responsibilities of internal investigators, administrators, and law enforcement organizations in protecting the civil rights of their own employees.

Civil rights policy is found in Section 1983 of Title 42, *United States Code* and states that, "any person, who acting under the color of any law, deprives any other citizen of a right guaranteed by the Constitution or in law, shall be liable to the injured party" (Devanney & Summers-Devanney, 2003a). Most cases investigated by an internal investigator have civil rights implications. Cases involving allegations of excessive force, false arrest, seizure of property and the like are all prohibited in civil rights laws and are actionable in the federal system. The internal investigator and administrator must be aware of the provisions of Section 1983 and those components of the act that must be addressed in the internal investigation.

The internal investigator must also be aware of the civil rights enjoyed by departmental employees. While the restrictions may be lessened due to employment, certain acts of the employer or its agents can be actionable. For example, under the *New York State Civil Rights Law,* law enforcement personnel records are confidential and not subject to review by anyone not authorized within the agency, nor outside without written consent or court order (Section 50-a Subdivisions 1 and 2). The release of confidential records is a crime and subject to criminal and civil penalties. Cases have been made law where criminal investigators have continued to interview suspects when they have invoked their right against compulsory self-incrimination and use of counsel. While the confession cannot be used in a criminal case, civil suits have been filed against the investigators for violating these rights. In the landmark case of *Cooper v. Dupnik* (1992), a plaintiff who was repeatedly questioned in violation of his *Miranda* rights could sue for damages for a violation of his Fifth Amendment rights. In the decision of *Franklin v. City of Evanston* (2004), a worker was allowed to continue a civil rights lawsuit against the city wherein the claim was that the city failed to inform the employee that his answers to questions in a criminal investigation would be immunized from use in the criminal case. In *McKinley v. City of Mansfield* (2005), the federal court allowed the continuance of a civil rights claim filed by an officer against his superiors after a prosecutor used his *Garrity* protected statements against him in a subsequent prosecution (Americans for Effective Law Enforcement, 2005). With this protective attitude being adopted by the courts, the next logical progression may be in cases such as those of the violation of public employee civil rights where civil compensatory and punitive damages may be the remedy.

HUMAN RIGHTS LAWS

The human rights laws mirror those of civil rights laws as they are there for the protection of the employee, however, they are prosecuted at the state level as opposed to the federal level such as in a Section 1983 violation. Human rights laws preclude discriminatory practices on the basis of age, race, creed, color, national origin, sex, disability, genetic predisposition or carrier status, or marital status of any individual that results in a work place action such as adverse change in compensation, or in the terms, conditions, and privileges of employment (*New York State Executive Law–Human Rights Law* Section 296). The internal investigator and administrator should be versed in these laws so as to not violate the rights of an employee under investigation.

These types of lawsuits and complaints emerge from employees who believe that the impetus of the adverse action is attached to some protected class and hence a discriminatory practice. These may be claims that the internal investigations unit will need to investigate in employee-to-employee, supervisor-to-subordinate, or class action lawsuit that may be filed against the agency.

An example of such a claim would be a subordinate who complains that his female supervisor and male command officer are involved in an illicit affair. The female supervisor is ultimately taking disciplinary action against the subordinate, which is supported by the male command officer. The subordinate alleges that the illicit affair is the foundation of the alleged harassment. During the subsequent interview of the female supervisor and male command officer, the internal investigator asks probing and personal questions concerning the sexual relationship of the interviewees. While trying to make a connection to the case, the private lives of the supervisor and command officer are private matters unless they affect the work environment and if that relationship is the cause of the alleged harassment. These types of questions are inappropriate, just as probing such protected issues as race, religion, sexual orientation, and the like.

Questioning in this scenario should be solely and narrowly related to the acts alleged, to wit, harassing behaviors, and if the conduct of the employee was of a level to warrant disciplinary type actions. Even if information is offered during an interview of this nature, the investigator should not pursue a line of questioning in this area and should also consider redacting the information offered from review by other parties involved in the case.

CIVIL LIABILITY: DEFINITION AND LAWSUITS

Civil liability is a serious concern for law enforcement administrators as well as law enforcement officers. The internal investigator will most likely be at the front line for the investigation of these incidents in the complaint process as well as assisting corporation or municipal counsel in investigating the circumstances of a lawsuit and preparing the ultimate defense of the agency and its personnel. As such, the internal investigator and administrator should be familiar with the causes of liability and specific terminology used in this area of law.

Civil liability is born from a duty to perform a function. That duty is breached when the law enforcement officer or agency fails to perform or inadequately performs the function. Liability is defined by law as a legal obligation incurred for an injury suffered or complained of that results from a failure to conduct a specific task or activity within a given standard. A standard is defined as a recognized practice or level of competence for an occupation or task. The level of competence is ultimately set for safety reasons in most occupations (Soto, 1998). Lawsuits, however, are not indicative of wrongdoing as many lawsuits are dismissed during preliminary reviews by attorneys and the court system. However, a small percentage survives the review and motions process to reach the courts. Those that do can result in lawsuits that award plaintiffs record compensation that in many cases is in the millions of dollars.

Causes and actions of civil liability emerge from the following types of actions: (1) unlawful arrest, (2) unlawful search and seizure, (3) excessive force, (4) improper use of weapons, (5) negligent vehicle operation, (6) improper first aid, and (7) acts of omission. Understanding technical terminology for liability gives managers an idea of responsibilities being measured. Terminology such as negligent entrustment, assignment, hiring, training, etc. means the law enforcement officer or the organization has done something improper by ignoring proper precautions and standards (Soto, 1998). Civil liability actions are filed in state and federal courts by the use of Torts. Torts are in the form of a Constitutional Tort, Intentional Tort, and Negligence Tort. Within a Tort, three elements must be established to support the action: (1) existence of a legal duty between the defendant and plaintiff, (2) breach of duty, and (3) damages as a proximate result (Sullivan, 1999). The burden of proof in a civil court is a preponderance of the evidence (Nowicki, 2004).

The courts are also expanding the definitions and scope of civil liability claims, for instance, cities and public safety agencies may be held liable for deaths, injuries, and even arrests that occur during civil disorders (Beasely & Holmberg, 2000).

The United States Supreme Court has also recognized how civil liability impacts other issues, such as motivation to do law enforcement work, by stating that, "The danger that fear of being sued will dampen the ardor of all but the most resolute, or the most irresponsible public officials, in the unflinching discharge of their duties" (see *Harlow v. Fitzgerald,* 1982) (Means, 2004). This fear impacts police organizations throughout the United States. Aligned with this mindset, Ed Nowicki (2001c) profoundly states that, "Sad, but unfortunately true, it seems that most officers would rather face a criminal with a firearm than an excessive force lawsuit" (p. 29). That same fear is prevalent in officers who must appear to give a statement in an internal investigation. While the organization's administrators must be mindful of the issues of liability, effective operations, and image, they must be equally mindful of morale and motivational issues that impact line personnel on a daily basis.

The most effective preventative method is the education of the organization's personnel in the requirements for civil liability protection and avoidance. The internal investigator must also include these issues in any investigation that may have the potential for a civil suit so as these questions can be answered at the beginning of the process rather than having to reinvestigate the matter later when the actions may appear to be an initial cover-up of the facts or haphazard investigation process. Experienced officers and internal investigators should also be willing to assist and advise defense counsel in these incidents for case preparation (Nowicki, 2001c).

The Concept of Negligence

Negligence is a doctrine that holds that the police owe society a certain standard of care in the performance of their occupation and tasks. Negligence in performing functions will result in a legal obligation. Negligence occurs when through act or omission, law enforcement personnel fail to conform to behavior set standards, resulting in harm (Soto, 1998). There are four elements of negligence: (1) A duty to act with care, (2) A breach of duty occurs, (3) a link between the breach of duty and the harm caused or a proximate cause, and (4) an actual injury.

Negligence suits are usually filed in response to injuries incurred during a use-of-force, police involved shooting, or police pursuit. The courts will most often apply a "gross negligence" standard to evaluate the merits of a specific claim. The internal investigator should review the facts of each case as they measure against industry standards, the existing case law, and departmental policy. Usually, departmental policy is written to restrict law enforcement actions beyond those required by law. These can be important documents and issues when the case is presented to a court in defense of the organization. In addition, the internal investigator, in consultation with defense counsel, must also determine that if some negligence existed in the incident, that remedial actions are taken to prevent further incidents and limit future liability.

Industry Standards

Industrial standards are levels of practice for a specific "industry" (or as recommended by industry/occupation experts). For example, police trainers require general law enforcement officers to maintain a certain level of proficiency with firearms. Firearms instructors, SWAT members, and others in specialized fields, should be required to have higher levels of competence due to increased responsibilities and knowledge required by their position (Soto, 1998).

The internal investigator should include all records of training the law enforcement officer has received in the case file so as they are available for the defense attorney when preparing and presenting the case. The internal investigator should request any additional documents that are not on file with the agency from the involved personnel, such as certificates, transcripts, degrees and the like. This also necessitates that the department administrator support a system of training records retention in order to defend against and mitigate impending liability. The training records of the specialized units should also be available to the internal investigator so that this information can be introduced into the record during depositions, examinations before trial (EBT's), and the trial itself.

The internal investigator, department administrator, and defense counsel can also request copies of contemporary policy and procedure from other law enforcement organizations to compare current policy with similar policies in other law enforcement agencies. This can validate the current policy and practice of the organization as well as provide guidance for updating the department's policies, procedures, and practices.

Qualified Immunity

There are concepts in the law that provide immunity from liability in law enforcement actions. Absolute immunity means that there is no liability at all for actions taken in an official capacity while qualified immunity means that a law enforcement officer will not be held personally liable as long as the actions are reasonable in light of current American law (Sullivan, 1999). A good faith effort shown in performing functions or managing a situation (as a manager, trainer, officer, etc.) can mean some immunity for acting without malice, also referred to as qualified immunity. However, good faith requires demonstrable effort. A good faith effort will not protect anyone from a negligence claim (Soto, 1998).

Black's Law Dictionary defines Qualified Immunity as, "Immunity from civil liability for public officials who are performing discretionary functions, as long as their conduct does not violate clearly established constitutional or statutory rights" (Makholm, 2002a). In addition, the Eleventh Circuit Court also clarified that the qualified immunity defense embodies an objective reasonableness standard, giving a government agent the benefit of the doubt, provided that the conduct was not so obviously illegal in the light of then-existing law that only an official who was incompetent or who knowingly was violating the law would have committed the acts (Makholm, 2003b).

In the case of *Saucier v. Katz* (2001), the United States Supreme Court preserved the doctrine of qualified immunity in excessive force cases (Rohr, 2001). In this case, the Court established the proper way to review the issue of qualified immunity protections against claims of excessive force during arrests. The Court reinforced that the courts must take a two-step approach: (1) the first inquiry must be whether a constitutional right would have been violated on the facts alleged by the plaintiff and (2) assuming the violation is established, the question whether the right was clearly established must be considered in a more specific level than recognized by the Court of Appeals. The privilege of qualified immunity is an immunity from suit rather than a mere defense to liability (Makholm, 2001; Makholm, 2002a). In testing the concept of qualified immunity in use-of-force cases, the Courts may use the decision in *Graham v. Connor* (1989), if the use-of-force was determined to be reasonable, even if mistakes occur, the officer may still have qualified immunity as long as the mistakes were reasonable (Milazzo, 1998).

In false arrest suits, the plaintiff must establish that the police officer did not have probable cause at the time of the arrest to justify the filing of criminal charges (Stine, 2001). Arguable probable cause is distinguished from probable cause as it is based on information where reasonable officers in the same circumstances and possessing the same knowledge as the defendants could have believed that probable cause existed to arrest the plaintiff. Arguable probable cause is all that is necessary for an officer to be granted qualified immunity on a false arrest claim (Makholm, 2004).

Vicarious Liability

Respondeat superior is defined under the law as "let the master answer," as the employer may be responsible for acts of their employees when acts are committed within the scope of employment (J. J. Sullivan, 1999). Vicarious liability is based on relationship and would hold an employer liable for employee misdeeds during the course and scope of employment whether or not the employer did anything wrong (Means, 2004). Vicarious liability is then the attachment of a legal obligation to a person (e.g., supervisor, trainer, team member, etc.) for the acts/omissions of another. As a supervisor, liability may be incurred for not taking action to correct misconduct by subordinates and even other supervisors (Soto, 1998). The internal investigation should include supervisory actions or lack of actions in the incident being investigated. This tactic can be used to mitigate any liability as well as identify substandard supervisory behavior that can be corrected in future behavior.

Liability for Failure to Disclose Exculpatory Information

Leaving out exculpatory evidence may lead to liability for false arrest, malicious prosecution, and illegal search and seizure claims. To support such liability claims, a plaintiff must show that the affiant knowingly and deliberately, or with reckless disregard for the truth, omitted facts that are material or necessary to a finding of probable cause. Testing the validity of a plaintiff's complaint involves inclusion of the alleged exculpatory facts in order to determine whether their inclusion would negate the probable cause (Spector, 1998).

Many officers facing exculpatory information claims must defend against allegations that they did not conduct adequate investigations and that, if more had been done, the alleged exculpatory information would have been discovered. The majority opinion appears to be that once officers have discovered sufficient facts to establish probable cause, they have no constitutional obligation to conduct further investigation (Spector, 1998).

Liability Through a Pattern of Indemnification

Pattern and practice suits are becoming common in the realm of litigation. In these lawsuits, the plaintiff attempts to determine if the act is a pattern or practice in the organization that violates a federally protected right. This liability then extends to the organization and as such can lead to class action lawsuits. In a 1997 civil rights case filed in Los Angeles, plaintiffs utilized a legal theory to extend liability to the city council members and their attorneys that deserves careful attention. The plaintiffs' counsel alleged that city officials made it a practice to quickly approve settlements of police misconduct cases, and in so doing, implicitly encouraged officer brutality and excessive use-of-force. The court used this "policy of indemnification" to deny motions for summary judgment (see *Cunningham v. Gates,* 1997) (Martinelli & Pollock, 2000). This case demonstrates the creativity of plaintiff's counsel in applying the law to establish liability on behalf of law enforcement personnel as well as the agreement of the court.

Investigative Considerations

The internal investigator and administrator should consider several factors when investigating a personnel complaint that could lead to civil litigation or when a lawsuit is filed against the organization. The following is a list of questions that should be asked when completing the case:

1. Were the actions of the law enforcement personnel done in good faith?
2. Did the law enforcement personnel act in a reasonable manner?
3. Were the actions of the law enforcement officers justified under the law?
4. Did the injured party contribute to their own injuries?
5. Were the law enforcement personnel acting within the scope of their employment and following department policy and standards?

FEDERAL CIVIL RIGHTS VIOLATIONS

Because of the injustices that were brought upon protected classes in the United States, the federal government enacted legislation that provides federal powers to investigate and prosecute such matters when the states have failed to make appropriate redress. These powers were later extended in the law to include acts committed by agents of the government who act under color of law. The federal act that empowers federal authorities to take action is included in the *United States Code.* Section 1983 of Title 42 of the *United States Code* states in part that:

> Every person who, under color of any statute, ordinance, regulation, custom, or usage, of any State or Territory, subjects, or causes to be subjected any citizen of the United States or other persons within the jurisdiction thereof to the deprivation of any rights, privileges, or immunities secured by the Constitution and laws, shall be liable to the party injured in an action at law, suit in equity, or other proper proceeding for redress. (Sullivan, 1999, p. 29)

The internal investigator and administrator must consider a set of specific factors when investigating and reviewing internal investigations that have the potential for a Section 1983 claim. There are four elements that must be present to commence a 1983 action:

1. The defendant must be a natural person or a local government.
2. The defendant must be acting under "color of law."
3. The violation must be of a federal constitutional or federally protected right.
4. The violation must reach a constitutional level. A slight push or touching would not rise to a constitutional level, but a brief detention could. (Sullivan, 1999, p. 29)

CASE LAW: CRIMINAL

The next section discusses the various criminal case laws that are related to the internal investigations process. Specific attention is paid to admissions and confessions, integrity issues, and evidentiary requirements in

Figure 6-1. Former NYPD Officer Justin Volpe was sentenced to 30 years in prison for the torture of Abner Louima, a Haitian immigrant (CNN).

presenting cases for termination proceedings as well as criminal prosecution.

Self-Incrimination in Criminal Investigations

The *Miranda v. Arizona* (1966) case established the right against compulsory self-incrimination in the United States. This right is also included in the Fifth Amendment which entitles a suspect to the assistance of counsel during a custodial interrogation by law enforcement officers if requested by the suspect. These rights must be knowingly and voluntarily waived in order for the admission or confession to be admitted into evidence in a criminal court.

The Sixth Amendment guarantees a formally charged defendant a right to counsel, which protects him from any effort by the government to deliberately elicit from him incriminating information about the charged matter. The Sixth Amendment right to counsel attaches at the commencement of judicial proceedings whether by way of formal charge, preliminary hearing, indictment, information, or arraignment and applies even when there is no interrogation and no Fifth Amendment applicability. With respect to the Sixth Amendment rights, if a judicial proceeding has commenced, under *Patterson v. Illinois* (1988), if the defendant is advised of the proceeding and knowingly waives his *Miranda* rights, he may then be interrogated (Kruger, 2004).

In a criminal investigation, law enforcement personnel are afforded all of the same rights as other suspects are. This applies in cases where a law enforcement officer is involved in a use of deadly physical force, use-of-force, or any other matter that could lead to criminal charges and prosecution. Under the Miranda decision, if the officer is subjected to a custodial interrogation the warnings must be read. The warnings must also be knowingly and voluntarily waived for the interrogation to proceed. An extension of this rule can be found in the Eleventh Circuit ruling in the case of *Benjamin v. City of Montgomery* (1986) wherein the an officer is allowed to invoke their Fifth Amendment rights against compulsory self incrimination where they are merely a witness in a case. The Court ruled that only the department can give the *Garrity* immunity clause (Americans for Effective Law Enforcement, 2005).

The internal investigator must be aware of the possibility that if the admission or confession is precluded from use in a criminal trial due to a technical violation, the statement may also be precluded from use in the internal investigation. The internal investigator must also strongly consider taking another statement from the law enforcement officer in the case under the *Garrity* decision and during the internal or administrative investigation portion of the case. This will ensure that if the criminal statement is barred from use, the administrative investigation can still proceed to a hearing if necessary. However, in

City of Hollywood v. Washington (1980), a case involving immunity from prosecution did not bar the use of the confession in an interdepartmental disciplinary trial (Americans for Effective Law Enforcement, 2005).

Some additional considerations in self-incrimination in criminal investigations deal with additional employee rights and the loss of rights. For example, in the federal appeals court ruling of *United States Department of Justice v. Federal Labor Relations Authority* (2001) a member of a bargaining unit is entitled to a union representative during an interview even if management characterizes the investigation as criminal rather than administrative. The Massachusetts Supreme Court has also ruled that public employees who are interrogated in a disciplinary investigation are entitled to full and final immunity from prosecution. Other states limit the scope of any constitutionally protected immunity and ban the use of employer compelled statements in criminal proceedings (Americans for Effective Law Enforcement, 2005).

In *State v. Koverman* (2002), an incriminating statement given by a law enforcement officer to his superiors, after he had received *Miranda* warnings, was admissible in his criminal prosecution. At no time did his superiors advise him that he had to answer questions as a condition of continued employment. In the *United States v. Vangates* (2002), a federal appeals court allowed an officer's testimony in a prior civil lawsuit to be used against her in a criminal prosecution as she failed to claim her Fifth Amendment privilege against compulsory self-incrimination at the civil trial. In *Blackburn v. Superior Court* (Kelso) (1993), a California appellate court held that a person may not assert their Fifth Amendment rights to remain silent in a civil proceeding without showing the possibility of criminal prosecution. The self incrimination privilege is not applicable to a person's possible civil liability. A final case involving *Miranda* decided in *Reyes v. Granados* (1996), involved a failure to provide *Miranda* warnings in an investigation. The plaintiff alleged that this was a violation of civil rights. The court ruled that the failure to give *Miranda* warnings did not violate the plaintiff's rights against compulsory self incrimination as she was never formally charged with a crime (Americans for Effective Law Enforcement, 2005).

Self-Incrimination in Administrative Investigations

The decision in *Garrity v. New Jersey* (1967) was the foundation for precluding a government employer from using compelled statements in criminal proceedings. In the *Garrity* decision, the United States Supreme Court held that a state employee cannot impose substantial penalties against an employee solely because that employee invokes a Fifth Amendment privilege against compelled self-incrimination. Specifically, the Court stated that, "the protection of the individual under the Fourteenth Amendment against coerced statements prohibits use in subsequent criminal proceedings of statements obtained under threat of removal from office, and . . . it extends to all, whether they are policemen or other members of the body politic" (Ferrell, 1997) (also see *Spevack v. Klein,* 1956). This was also affirmed by the United States Supreme Court's thinking in the decision of *Gardner v. Broderick* (1968). In *Gardner,* the Court decision extends protection to an employee from being forced to waive immunity from a constitutionally protected right. In the decision of *State v. Lacaillade* (1994), the New Jersey appellate court ruled that a disciplinary interrogation is non-custodial for the purposes of Miranda, but an employee may not be required to waive his Fifth Amendment rights as a condition of employment. However, in the Idaho court decision of *State v. Connor* (1994), if the interrogation turns to a "custodial" situation, then *Miranda* rights attach (Americans for Effective Law Enforcement, 2005).

Like the *Miranda* decision, *Garrity* is the federal guideline for the delineation of self-incrimination rights between civil or employee type actions and criminal actions. Under *Garrity,* a government employee can be compelled to give a statement during an internal investigation and may be disciplined if they do not comply. This requirement has been reaffirmed in such cases as *Szmaciarz v. California State Personnel Board* (1978) wherein an employee must answer job-related questions or forfeit employment as no Fifth Amendment privileges are applicable to an internal investigation, however, the answers are not admissible in a criminal prosecution (Americans for Effective Law Enforcement, 2005). In some states, police chiefs have the legal authority to terminate a police officer who refuses to answer questions directly related to their official duties as long as the officer is not coerced into waiving a constitutional right in the process. For example, in *Plaster v. City of Houston* (1986) the Texas Court of Appeals held that the involuntary statement may not be used for any purpose, including impeachment, in a criminal trial. It is critical that police administrator's keep administrative and criminal investigations as separate and distinct entities (Ferrell, 1997). This decision is aligned with the United States Supreme Court decision in *Mincey v. Arizona* (1978) that an "involuntary" statement cannot be used against a defendant to impeach his in-court testimony (Americans for Effective Law Enforcement, 2005).

Garrity does not, however, provide for free and uncontrolled questioning measures or techniques. In the decision of *Department of Public Safety v. Shockley* (2002), an appellate court in Maryland affirmed that public employees must answer questions, if required to do so, that "specifically, directly, and narrowly relate to the performance of their official duties or their fitness for continued employment." In addition, supervisors must give a clear order and advisement of rights to interviewed employees (also see *Evangelista v. City of Rochester,* 1988) (Americans for Effective Law Enforcement, 2005).

In the *Garrity* decision, the employee subjected to a compelled interview automatically attains these rights, whether advised or not. In *Gilbert v. Nix* (1994) a federal appeals court ruled that employees who are compelled to answer their employer's questions automatically acquire use immunity for their answers. The failure to give such warnings and advise of the prevailing rights can result in the loss of the ability to discipline or have the discipline imposed overturned by the courts as decided in *Debnam v. North Carolina Department of Corrections* (1992) and *Lybarger v. City of Los Angeles* (1985) (Americans for Effective Law Enforcement, 2005).

Discovery proceedings can also impact this issue. In compelling law enforcement personnel to give statements, discovery privileges can compel the agency to afford the officer the right to review the statements of others in the investigation. In the *Pasadena Police Officers Association v. City of Pasadena* (1988), an appellate court in California interpreted the *Public Safety Officer Bill of Rights Law* to include the right to see statements taken of employees before answering internal affairs division questioning (Americans for Effective Law Enforcement, 2005).

Employees must also understand that they have no recourse against incompetent or incorrect legal counsel. In *Silverio v. Municipal Court of Boston* (1969), the discharge of a public employee was not barred because he relied upon the erroneous advice of counsel. The employee's attorney erroneously informed him that he had a legal right not to answer certain questions in the internal investigation (Americans for Effective Law Enforcement, 2005).

Truthfulness in Administrative Investigations

The *LaChance* decision extended the *Garrity* decision by precluding officers from being untruthful during statements given in departmental investigations. In the case of *LaChance v. Erickson* (1998), the United States Supreme Court emphasized that an officer has no constitutional right to be untruthful. Under this ruling, a police officer may be charged with misconduct and with making false statements regarding alleged misconduct. Neither the Fifth Amendment nor previous United States Supreme Court decisions afford an employee the right to resort to making a false statement in administrative proceedings. In the decision of *Huemiller v. Ogden Civil Service Commission* (2004), the court affirmed that honesty is critical to an officer's performance of duty (Americans for Effective Law Enforcement, 2005; Whalen, 1998).

The foundation of the untruthfulness allegation will also be considered in context to the issue that is the subject of the alleged lie. For example, in a National Labor Relations Board decision in *U.S.A.A. and Williams* (2004), an employer improperly questioned an employee about distributing fliers on a coworkers desk after-hours, protesting the layoff of some employees, and then unlawfully fired her for lying about her activities. Because the subject matter of the disciplinary interview was improper (concerted labor activities) the employer could not terminate her for untruthfulness. In the decision of *Lacombe v. Lafayette City Parish Consol. Government* (2003), the appellate court found the decision to terminate a fire captain was not made in good faith or with just cause because the answers given during an internal investigations interview were "evasive." In addition, the window of opportunity for an agency to allege untruthfulness is also limited in scope. For example, the decision of *King v. Erickson, et al.* (1996), holds that public employees cannot be disciplined for falsely denying any misconduct after formal disciplinary charges have been made (Americans for Effective Law Enforcement, 2005).

Care must be taken in the definition of what constitutes untruthfulness in an administrative investigation. For example, the courts have ruled that witness recollection of an event may not be perfect and subsequently allow such testimony. According to John C. Klotter and Jefferson L. Ingram (2004) the courts have affirmed in the cases of *United States v. Lima* (1980) and *Staton v. State* (1981) that:

> In order for a witness to be competent to testify, it is not necessary that he or she have perfect recall. Defects in witness recollection are proper subjects for cross-examination and impeachment, but do not render the testimony inadmissible. The witness may testify to facts within his or her knowledge, although his or her recollection thereof is vague or imperfect. (p. 291)

Departments must avoid holding personnel to an unrealistic standard of recall when such standards do not reach such levels in the criminal courts where the burden of proof is beyond a reasonable doubt. This is a far higher standard than required in an administrative hearing where the standard of proof is only at the level of a preponderance of the evidence.

Truthfulness in Federal Criminal Investigations

In *Brogan v. United States* (1998), the United States Supreme Court greatly expanded the ability to prosecute false statements made by state or local law enforcement officers to any federal agents under 18 U.S.C. 1001. The decision eliminated the long-standing legal principle and precedent that permitted an "exculpatory no" to criminal allegations to be exempt entirely from federal criminal prosecution for making false statements to federal agents. In layman's terminology, an "exculpatory no" is a general denial of any and all allegations of criminal misconduct under federal investigation. The defendant in this case, a union officer, was questioned concerning allegations of bribes and gratuities. The union officer provided a simple "no" answer to the question and, based upon this singular answer and general denial of criminal conduct or culpability, which was in fact untrue, the officer was subsequently convicted of making a false statement (Americans for Effective Law Enforcement, 2005; Scuro, 2000a).

Figure 6-2. Former L.A.P.D. detective Mark Fuhrman was convicted of felony perjury charges after testifying at the O. J. Simpson murder trial that he had not used a racial slur in the previous ten years (CNN).

Disclosure of Exculpatory Evidence

Cases such as *Brady v. Maryland* (1963) require the release of exculpatory information to the defense in a prosecution. Mark Newbold (2001) states with respect to the prosecutor's duties in the *Brady* case that the rule:

> Places on the prosecutor an affirmative constitutional duty to disclose exculpatory evidence to a defendant. This constitutional duty is triggered by the impact that the favorable evidence has on the outcome of the criminal proceeding. It requires the prosecutor to evaluate a case in its entirety and look at the cumulative effect that withholding the information has on the outcome of the trial. (p. 10)

This type of criminal case law also has implications in the internal investigation process. Under *Brady,* evidence affecting the credibility of the police officer as a witness may be exculpatory evidence and should be given to the defense during discovery, for example, evidence that the officer has had in his file a sustained finding of untruthfulness is clearly exculpatory to the defense (Noble, 2003). In addition, certain exculpatory evidence needs to be released to defense which may also include personnel information related to criminal activity (Ferrell, 1997; Noble, 2003).

The internal investigator must also review relevant state case law with respect to these types of evidentiary rules. For example, in the *People v. Rosario* (1961) decision handed down in New York State, requires the prosecutor to provide the defense with prior statements of a prosecution witness relating to the subject of that witness's testimony.

This rule also extends to law enforcement personnel involved in the cases as well. Officers can be liable in federal courts if they fail to disclose to a prosecutor any evidence that may be favorable to a defendant and if that disclosure does not take place, the officer may be found to have committed an "affirmative abuse of power" (Newbold, 2001).

In the case of *Giglio v. United States* (1972), the United States Supreme Court expanded the prosecutor's duty to disclose evidence relative to the credibility of a governmental witness. This decision was extended in the case of *United States v. Agurs* (1976) wherein the Court made it clear that the defendant need not request exculpatory information from the prosecutor. Rather the duty to disclose attached regardless of whether the defense requested the evidence (Newbold, 2001).

In *Kyles v. Whitney* (1995), the Court found three circumstances where the duty attaches: (1) where previously undisclosed evidence revealed that the prosecution introduced trial testimony that it knew or should have known was perjured, (2) where the Government failed to accede to a defense request for disclosure of some specific kind of exculpatory evidence, and (3) where the defense failed to request information or made a general request for exculpatory evidence. In addition, the favorable evidence must be material in nature and the failure to disclose the information undermines the confidence in the outcome of the trial. An officer withholding such information can be liable under Section 1983 (Newbold, 2001).

CASE LAW: USE-OF-FORCE

The next section discusses the various case laws that are related to the internal investigations process with respect to establishing justification for the use-of-force by law enforcement officers. An additional citation under this section deals with the courts opinions in police exercise of control in situations in efforts to maintain order.

Deadly Force

The United States Supreme Court decided the issue of the circumstances for the use of deadly physical force in the case of *Tennessee v. Garner* (1985). The ruling restricts police use of deadly force against a fleeing suspect, and permits such force only if the suspect poses an imminent threat to that officer or someone else, or that officer has probable cause to believe the suspect is fleeing from a violent crime, and only when the officer has precluded other options for preventing his escape, and when feasible gives a warning. This type of force falls under the Fourth Amendment to the United States Constitution (Grossi, 2002b; Gundy, 2003; Makholm, 2002a; J. J. Sullivan, 1999; G. T. Williams, 1999c).

In *Vaughan v. Cox* (2001) decided in the Eleventh Circuit, the Court reiterated the test for using deadly force to seize a fleeing felon by stating: (1) the officer has probable cause to believe the suspect poses a threat of serious harm to the officer or others, or that the felon has committed a crime involving infliction or threatened infliction of serious physical harm, (2) the officer reasonably believes that deadly force was "necessary" to prevent escape, and (3) that the officer has given some warning of the use of "deadly force" . . . if feasible (Makholm, 2002a).

The Reasonableness and Justification of Force

In the *Graham v. Connor* (1989) decision, the "objective reasonableness test" was introduced, under the Fourth Amendment, and is a balancing test that weighs the person's right to privacy and physical integrity against the government's legitimate interests in taking action against the person. Under the provisions of this test, the use-of-force needs to be reasonable in relation to the circumstances presented to the officer (Gundy, 2003; McKee, 2000; Meyer, 1999; Meyer, 2001; Milazzo, 1998; Scuro, 1998; G. T. Williams, 1999c).

Chief Justice Rehnquist, with respect to the standard of objective reasonableness wrote that this "calculus of reasonableness" must recognize that police must make split-second decisions in situations that are "tense, uncertain, and rapidly evolving" (Meyer, 1999; Meyer, 2001; Milazzo, 1998). Interestingly enough, the Court used terminology that referred to an officer's decision making process should not be held to an "unrealistic standard of perfection" in making these evolving decisions (Milazzo, 1998). The Court commented that in the reasonableness of an officer's decision to use deadly force "must be viewed from the perspective of the officer on the scene . . . [and] . . . not . . . from the calm vantage point of hindsight" (Hopper, 2001a; Weiss & Davis, 2002).

The *Graham* decision mandates that every police use-of-force, whether it be non-deadly or deadly, requires a case specific review of: (1) the severity of the crime at issue, (2) the apparent threat posed by the subject to officers and others, (3) whether the subject is resisting seizure, (4) whether the subject is attempting to flee, and (5) the use-of-force is to be judged from the perspective of a reasonable officer coping with a tense and fast evolving situation (Gundy, 2003; Newbold, 2002). In addition, the officer is not required to use the minimal amount of force necessary to effect an arrest or control a suspect. An officer needs only to select a level of force that is objectively reasonable.

One final point is the issue of more restrictive departmental policies affecting this decision. In *Smith v. Freeland* (1992), decided in the Sixth Circuit Court, the issue was whether the officer violated the Constitution, not whether he should be disciplined by the local police force (Gundy, 2003).

Police Control of Persons and Situations

In keeping with these thoughts, the Court has also recognized the need for officers to be proactive in maintaining control of situations so as they don't debilitate further. In the United States Supreme Court case of *Michigan v. Summers* (1981), the Court recognized that the risk of harm to both the police and others "is minimized if the officers routinely exercise unquestioned command of the situation." In *Maryland v. Wilson* (1997), the Court also ruled that this case offered guidance in a vehicle stop situation (Ward, Parsons, & Connor, 2000).

CASE LAW: CIVIL

The next section discusses the various civil case laws that are related to the internal investigations process. Specific attention is paid to training, policy, and tactical issues of liability.

Law Enforcement Training Issues

The lead case in law enforcement training issues is *Canton v. Harris* (1989), wherein a federal court ruled that a municipality is civilly liable for the failure to train its police force, where the plaintiff proves that the lack of training was so reckless or grossly negligent that it deprived a person of their constitutional rights. In general, the facts have to demonstrate that: (1) training does not currently meet acceptable standards within the law enforcement training community and omits important aspects, (2) is not satisfactorily documented, (3) is not properly taught, or (4) contains inadequate standards. This deliberate indifference is proven in cases where the need for additional training is "so obvious" and the failure to provide the additional training is "so likely" as to result in a constitutional violation. In addition, a person alleging inadequate training does not have to show a past practice or course of conduct. The courts in some jurisdictions have held that a single incident can be enough to raise a claim such as the case of *Board of County Commissioners of Bryan County v. Brown* (1997) decided in the United States Supreme Court (Dahlinger, 2001; Hill & Logan, 2001; Martinelli & Pollock, 2000; Rohr, 2001; Scuro, 1998). Municipalities cannot only be sued for failure to train and deliberate indifference, but also for custom and practice issues of outdated or inadequate training (Weissberg, 1999).

Proving deliberate indifference is difficult because the plaintiff must prove the need for different training is so obvious that policymakers deliberately turned a blind eye to the problem (Hopper, 2001b; Nielsen, 2003a). In addition, actions by personnel that are so egregiously or obviously outside of the realm of normal behavior are not subject to claims under *Canton*. For example, in *Sewell v. Town of Lake Hamilton* (1998), an officer was accused of sexually molesting a female after a traffic stop. As such, the civil suit alleged failure to adequately train and supervise the officer. The court determined that the municipality had no liability as the officer's proper response to the situation would have been obvious to all without training or supervision (Zeichner, 1998). A similar allegation of failure to train occurred in Rochester, New York. Former police officer, Clint Jackson, was convicted of 15 counts of third degree sexual abuse against eight separate women he had stopped. Jackson claimed the cause of his conduct was from the Rochester Police Department's failure to "train and adequately supervise" him in his duties (Armon, 2003).

Canton revealed the Court's attitude with respect to training in department policy as it stated the city's policy was inadequate "in light of the duties assigned to specific officers" (Rohr, 2001). The *Canton* case also noted that officers should receive training to use and apply acquired skills to reasonably foreseeable circumstances and conditions and the adequacy of the training must be determined in relation to the tasks the particular officers perform (Weissberg, 1999).

Figure 6-3. Former Rochester, New York police officer Clint Jackson was convicted of numerous counts of sexual abuse of women he had stopped for traffic violations (Courtesy of WHEC-TV Channel 10, Rochester, New York).

Similar cases decided in relation to *Canton* were *Leite v. City of Providence* (1978) wherein the police department was responsible for a plaintiff's injury that were the result of inadequate training and supervision of an employee; *Whitney v. Warden* where the training provided was not enough to avoid liability as well as training that was not properly documented did not exist; *Popow v. City of Margate* (1979) where the failure to properly train officers in safe and proper use of weapons in realistic force type situations as well as no policy for realistic use in heavily populated areas resulted in the Court ruling that the department was "grossly inadequate in training and supervision" (also see *Zuchel v. City and County of Denver,* 1993) (Hill, 2003; Hopper, 2001b; Martinelli & Pollock, 2000; Oberlander, 2004; Ryan, 2004; Spaulding, 2001).

In *Walker v. New York* (1993), the implications for the future of litigation against the police is a failure to train individual officers was applied through a three pronged test: (1) Do we know that officers perform a particular task? (2) Does this task present difficult choices? And (3) If the officer makes the wrong choice, will it harm someone's constitutional rights? (Law and Order, 2001c). Consistent with the decision in *Sewell v. Town of Lake Hamilton* (1998), the Court asserted that, "If the conduct on which the claim is based is such that a common person would know the right response without training, there is no duty to train" (Ryan, 2004).

Liability Through Policy, Practice, and Custom Issues

There are several cases that have been decided that relate to the liability of governmental agencies that exercise authority through custom and practice to violate the civil rights of others. In *Monroe v. Pape* (1961), the United States Supreme Court held that behavior prohibited by the letter of state law but carried out with state or local government authority violates Section 1983. This decision allowed Section 1983 to be used to file suit against state and local officials who were misusing their government power to violate federal constitutional rights (Means, 2004).

In the *Monell v. New York City Department of Social Services* (1978) case, the United States Supreme Court decided that federal jurisdiction could be exercised over a public entity for the acts of its employees where there was an allegation that the civil rights violation was the result of an official policy, custom, or practice of that public entity (Scuro, 1998; Sullivan, 1999).

In the *Monell* decision, the Court wrote that a "city is not liable under a Section 1983 claim unless a municipal 'policy' or 'custom' is the moving force behind the constitutional violation (Hill & Logan, 2001; Martinelli & Pollock, 2000; Means, 2004). Only where a failure to train reflects a 'deliberate' or 'conscious' choice by the municipality can the failure be properly thought of as an actionable city policy" (Hill & Logan, 2001).

In proving a claim, the plaintiff must demonstrate two elements: (1) a municipal employee committed a constitutional violation and (2) a municipal policy or custom was the moving force behind the constitutional deprivation. If both elements are met, there is still another series of barriers that need to be met to establish a claim for inadequate training. The plaintiff must show: (1) the officers exceeded constitutional limitations on the use-of-force, (2) the use-of-force arose under circumstances that constitute a usual and recurring situation with which police officers must deal, (3) the inadequate training demonstrates a deliberate indifference on the part of the city towards persons with the police come into contact, and (4) there is a direct causal link between the constitutional deprivation and the inadequate training (also see *Allen v. Muskogee,* 1997) (Hopper, 2001b; Ryan, 2004).

In other words, in order to establish a *Monell* claim, the plaintiff, must establish a nexus between the failure to train, supervise, or hire and the injury, whether it is a physical injury or a violation of civil rights. A plaintiff's attorney will invariably file discovery motions to view involved officer personnel records to obtain evidence of prior misconduct and the employer's failure to sufficiently discipline such unacceptable behavior. Plaintiff's need only demonstrate that the municipality's failure to discipline a repeat offender was a discernible act of indifference by policymakers or administrators (Martinelli & Pollock, 2000). The recurring problem in federal civil rights actions is the test for determining who and which public official is in fact a policymaker for the governmental entity involved (Scuro, 1998). However, according to recent United States Supreme Court rulings, "policy, practice, and custom" can exist de facto or in writing or be proven to exist "by a single act of a municipal official if that official was, as a matter of state law, the final policymaker for the act in question" (Martinelli & Pollock, 2000).

The *Monell* decision also created an opportunity for the plaintiff, if the "prevailing party," to have attorney's fees paid by the defendant. In addition, while the ruling extended the reach of Section 1983 to municipal entities, it declined to expose them to vicarious liability (Means, 2004).

In *Owen v. City of Independence* (1980), the United States Supreme Court eliminated any immunity or affirmative defense to a governmental entity based on its good faith or legitimate motivation behind such a custom, policy, or practice as determined in the *Monell* decision. However, in *Gomez v. Toledo* (1980), a public employee could avoid liability by claiming legitimate motivation in taking official action to claim and receive an immunity or affirmative defense of good faith (Scuro, 1998).

Liability Through Police Use of Tactics

Liability can also be realized through tactics used. In *Young v. City of Killeen* (1985), a District Court, based upon the expert testimony of a criminal justice specialist, ruled in the case of an officer that had fatally shot a suspect involved in an apparent drug deal that even though the shooting was found to be justified, the officer acted negligently because he: (1) failed to radio for back-up and wait for assistance, (2) positioned the patrol car to cut off any escape route of the suspect, (3) ordered both suspects out of the car instead leaving them there, hands exposed, (4) increased the risk of the incident by ordering both suspects from the car at once, (5) abandoned a position of cover to advance to the suspects, (6) used poor tactics that created more risk than was already at hand, and (7) even though the officer was properly trained, his actions imperiled the suspects by creating a situation where fatal error was likely to occur. Vicarious liability was not applicable in this case as only the officer was found liable (Hill, 2003).

Purported tactical errors were also cited in the case of *Billington v. Smith* (2002), decided in the Ninth Circuit Court of Appeals. Based upon the circumstances, the Appellate Court enunciated the test for "prior act" liability as follows: "When an officer intentionally or recklessly provokes a violent confrontation, if the provocation is an independent Fourth Amendment violation, he may be held liable for his otherwise defensive use of deadly force." Simply put, if an officer provokes the use of deadly force, he will not be held liable unless that provocation in and of itself amounts to a Fourth Amendment violation (Spector, 2002b).

However, divergent court rulings also address the issue by stating that qualified immunity was afforded to a police involved use-of-force that is not otherwise justified because it might have arguably been avoided because of police tactics as cited in the Eighth and Tenth Circuit Court opinions in *Mettler v. Whitledge* (1999) and *Romero v. Board of County Commissioner's* (1995) (MacLatchie, 2000). Although it is unlikely that officers will be held liable merely because of the tactics employed before the use of deadly force, they likely will have to defend against this theory (Spector, 2002b).

CASE LAW: LABOR LAW

The next section discusses the various labor case laws that are related to the internal investigations process. Specific attention is paid to the right of representation and the right of due process in the investigative and disciplinary processes.

The Right of Representation for Union Members

The right of employees to have representation in investigative proceedings has been an issue of controversy since the United States Supreme Court ruled in the *National Labor Relations Board v. Weingarten* (1975) case. In the *Weingarten* ruling, employees of a collective bargaining unit who have a reasonable expectation of what they say is being used against them in a disciplinary action have the right to union representation in an administrative interview. In essence, this right mirrors the constitutional protections of the *Miranda* decision. "A lone employee, confronted by the employer's investigation and the possibility of discipline, may be either too afraid to face accusations, too inarticulate to accurately explain, or simply too uniformed to raise extenuating factors. A knowledgeable union representative could assist this employee by drawing out favorable facts or applicable mitigating circumstances" (International Brotherhood of Teamsters, 2006).

In 2000, that decision was modified to include employees not represented by a union in the decision handed down on the *Epilepsy Foundation of Northeast Ohio* (2000) (Siegel, 2000). In 2004, this decision was reversed, returning the rule to the original requirements for representation of union members as decided in *IBM Corporation,* 341 NLRB No. 148. The National Labor Relations Board decision concluded that, "an employer's right to conduct prompt, efficient, thorough, and confidential workplace investigations" outweighs the right of non-union employees to have co-workers present during investigatory interviews (Boddy, 2005).

The *Weingarten* rule applies to any employee interview that may reasonably be believed to result in discipline. This would include interviews that are related to: (1) sexual harassment complaints or allegations of unlawful discrimination, (2) suspicion of violation of workplace policies, (3) investigation of insubordinate conduct, workplace violence, or other inappropriate behavior, (4) inquiries into theft or misappropriation of goods or funds, and (5) investigations of suspected violations of substance abuse policies, etc. In addition, there is no right to representation if there is no possibility of discipline resulting from the interview, nor if the interview does not constitute and investigatory interview (Siegel, 2000). Case law supports that employees must be affirmatively advised of these rights as in the decision of *Prince George's County and Prince George's County Police Civilian Employees Association* (2005), an arbitrator reduced a termination to a demotion, with loss of back pay, and salary reduction for a police civilian employee who was untruthful at an interview as management failed to provide her with the assistance of a union representative at the official interview (Americans for Effective Law Enforcement, 2005).

The representative has the right to consult privately with the interviewee, be present during the entire interview, ask questions of the investigator and interviewee, offer evidence in defense of the interviewee, and object to questions asked of the interviewee. The suggested practice is that since any law enforcement action or omission can ultimately result in some type of culpability, whether departmentally, civilly, or criminally, all interviewee's should be allowed representation in order to protect the integrity of the statement and due process rights of those involved. The presence of the representative cannot prevent the internal investigator from asking questions or allow the interviewee the opportunity to refuse to answer in the internal investigation interview. As such, the presence or offer of a representative can only enhance the integrity and fairness of the case under investigation. The International Brotherhood of Teamsters (2006) offers these points for the union representative to consider during the investigative interview process as a tangible knowledge of *Weingarten* is vital, since it allows the union representative to:

1. Serve as a (non-silent) witness to this interview
2. Contradict a supervisor's possibly false account of said interview
3. Prevent intimidating tactics or confusing questions by supervisor
4. Prevent the member from making self-incriminating statements or admissions
5. Advise the member, under certain circumstances, to deny everything
6. Warn the member about losing his or her temper
7. Discourage the member from informing on others, i.e., co-workers
8. Identify any extenuating or mitigating factors that could benefit the member

If an employee exercises this right, the employer has three options available under the *Weingarten* rule: (1) Grant the request, arrange for a union or legal representative to be present and then continue the interview, (2) Deny the request and stop the interview, or (3) Inform the employee that it is his or her choice either to continue the interview without a representative or to terminate the interview. If the interview continues without the representative present, the employee must be advised that he or she can elect to stop the interview (International Brotherhood of Teamsters, 2006).

This *Weingarten* decision, while having evolved over the last 30 years, amounts to allowing protections for employees who may be the subject of discipline. In the system of jurisprudence, certain rights and protections are afforded to those accused of transgressions. The *Weingarten* decision is likened to those rights afforded under the *Miranda* decision and as such, the spirit and letter of the law must be adhered to in these types of proceedings.

Privileged Communications for Union Members

Communications between union members and officials may not be considered privileged communications in the eyes of the law. For example, in a decision from New York State in *In re Grand Jury Subpoenas* (1998), the "Union Official-Member Privilege" does not bar a prosecutor or grand jury from inquiring into conversations between a union member and his union representative. A companion decision is also found in *Walker v. Huie* (1992), which was a civil rights damage suit in Utah that was filed against police officers for excessive use-of-force. The court ruled that a conversation between an officer and the union president was not privileged against disclosure (Americans for Effective Law Enforcement, 2005).

Due Process Rights of Public Employees

The right of due process in protecting property rights in employment is embodied in the United States Supreme Court decision in *Cleveland Board of Education v. Loudermill* (1985). In this case, the Court held that all public employees who hold a "property interest" in their employment are entitled to due process prior to dismissal from their positions. Based upon the protections of the Fifth and Fourteenth Amendments, employees are entitled to respond to proposed discipline prior to a dismissal proceeding.

Justice Marshall articulated his defense of the rights of public employees in his decision which stated in part:

> I continue to believe that before the decision is made to terminate an employee's wages, the employee is entitled to an opportunity to test the strength of the evidence by confronting and cross-examining adverse witnesses and by presenting witnesses on his own behalf, whenever there are substantial disputes in testimonial evidence. (Findlaw.com, 2006)

Opponents of the practice of *Loudermill* in law enforcement organizations see the use as more of a method of depriving rather than affording the rights intended in the spirit of the decision (Leibig, 2001).

Procedural problems cited in the *Loudermill* process as experienced in law enforcement organizations are: (1) lack of officer access to evidence and (2) curtailment of due process rights in the post-termination process (Leibig, 2001). Because the process is for the most part secretive, law enforcement officers are most often deprived of the right to review and examine all of the evidence against them. Consequently, the process then becomes unfairly weighted towards the organization and the rights of the employee become secondary, and in some cases non-existent, which was not the intent of the Court's decision.

In keeping with the Court's decision, several mandated elements of a due process proceeding must be adhered to when an employee has earned property interest in his or her job: (1) an unbiased tribunal must be offered, (2) a notice of proposed action and the reason for the action offered, (3) an opportunity to present reasons why the proposed action should not be taken, (4) an opportunity to present evidence and call witnesses, (5) an opportunity to show opposing evidence, (6) a right to counsel or representation, (7) a right to a recorded proceeding, (8) a right to a decision that is based only on evidence presented, (9) a right to written findings of fact and the reason for the decision, and (10) both pre and post-disciplinary procedures are required to assure a full evidentiary hearing. Following these steps will ensure the rights of the employee, the validity of the hearing or proceeding, and the final disposition of the case will withstand court scrutiny.

Abusive and Coercive Interviews

There are several cases that control the conduct of the internal investigator during the administrative interview process. These interviews should be treated no differently than those of a criminal suspect. As a point of fact, they should be treated with a much higher level of respect for the individual as well as the protection of their due process rights. Such issues of abuse were identified the cases of *Karmel v. City of New York* (2002), *Alvarez v. City of New York* (1998), *Miller v. WCAB* (1999), *Prettyman v. State of New Jersey* (1997), *Angara v. City of Chicago* (1995), and *Buege v. Lee* (1978) (Americans for Effective Law Enforcement, 2005).

Law enforcement organizations are also being held accountable for unduly coercing employees in interviews in direct violation of their individual due process rights. In *California Correctional POA v. the State of California* (2000), a California appeals court ruling

Figure 6-4. Psychological coercion, deceptive tactics, and undue pressure have created situations where false confessions have been given to the police such as in the Central Park jogger rape case. The internal investigator must take care in their use of coercion and tactics in interviews to prevent such cases of false admissions and statements from occurring in the internal investigation process (CNN).

upheld and tightened an injunction against management attempts to deny constitutional and statutory rights of correctional officers being interviewed as witnesses and targets in a criminal investigation. Another case involved the reinstatement and back pay for employees who were subjected to "intrusive, lengthy, and coercive-styled interrogation" as decided in *Oddsen v. Board of Fire and Police Commissioners of Milwaukee* (1982) (Americans for Effective Law Enforcement, 2005).

COLLECTIVE BARGAINING AGREEMENTS AND UNIONS

The National Labor Relations Board enforces the laws covered in the *National Labor Relations Act.* Labor laws provide protections for employees that cover such issues as allowing employees the right to file complaints against an employer who violates the law through discrimination or penalization. Labor laws in law enforcement can cover areas such as ticket issuing quotas and the like. States also have similar acts for state redress of violations of enacted labor laws. For example, the New York State Public Employee Relations Board (PERB) has control of labor law and the *Taylor Law* which regulates the powers of unions and employers in such matters.

The internal investigator and administrator should be versed in federal and state laws as well as any prevailing collective bargaining agreements when conducting an internal investigation. Collective bargaining agreements can limit the powers of agencies in the disciplinary process, the conduct of an investigation, and the ultimate penalties levied against an employee accused of misconduct.

Grievances result from adverse actions taken against union members. Successful grievances result from violations of labor agreements. Violating a contract for the good of the case is no different than violating the law. As such, the internal investigator and administrator should act and bargain in good faith when questions arise concerning the progression of an internal investigation and how it may be in violation of current law or contract. Two excellent examples of this are concerned with the application of the exclusionary rule in the violation of collective bargaining agreements. In *Conwell v. City of Albuquerque* (1981) the court ruled that the collective bargaining agreement concerning questioning of an employee must be complied with. The violation resulted in the officer being reinstated and back pay ordered. In *Cymbalsky v. Dilworth* (1983), the failure to record an interview as provided by collective bargaining agreement also resulted in having

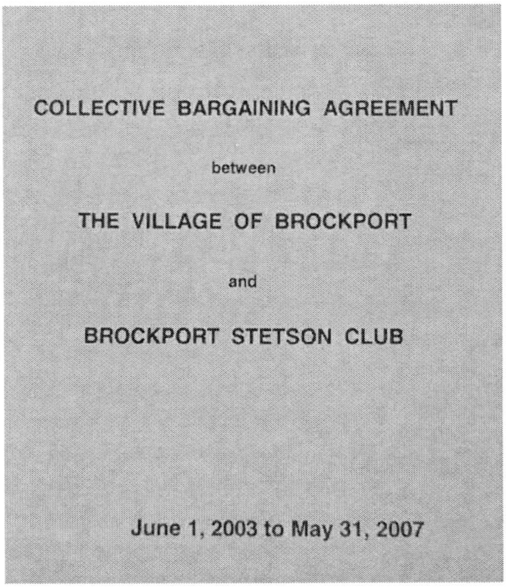

COLLECTIVE BARGAINING AGREEMENT

between

THE VILLAGE OF BROCKPORT

and

BROCKPORT STETSON CLUB

June 1, 2003 to May 31, 2007

Figure 6-5. Labor contracts should be followed closely by the membership, collective bargaining unit, and the law enforcement administration. Law enforcement administrators should consider that a violation of a contract provision is analogous to a violation of the law (Photo courtesy of the Brockport, New York Police Department).

the levied discipline set aside (Americans for Effective law Enforcement, 2005).

POLICE OFFICER BILL OF RIGHTS

The *State and Local Law Enforcement Discipline, Accountability, and Due Process Act of 2001* was introduced to establish minimum procedures governing internal investigations, interrogation of law enforcement officers, and administrative disciplinary hearings in which legislation would preempt any state law that fails to meet the standards (Horne, 2001). Currently, several states have enacted a *Police Officer Bill of Rights* in order to ensure protections of police personnel in the internal investigations process.

These types of legislation emerge from allegations of unjust treatment of police personnel in administrative investigations. What occurs is that the pendulum swings towards law enforcement organizations until such time that the process is abused and individual rights are violated necessitating the courts and legislature to intervene and bring balance back to the system. Law enforcement organizations have a set of rules that have been in place for a significant period of time. While not attempting to infringe on management's rights to manage the organization, management should practice following the rules rather than testing them. When the limits are pushed, many times the response is as extreme in order to bring balance. Internal investigators and administrators must concentrate on what can be done in the process as opposed to testing what shouldn't be done and then blaming the system for their own mistakes. A tried and true adage is that the only way to avoid the constrictions of regulation is through self-regulation.

RECORDS RETENTION LAW

The laws and rules surrounding records retention are ambiguous with respect to their applications in organizations. This section does not offer specific, but rather general guidance in the topic area. Records retention is mandated by statutes at the state level, for example the *New York State Education Law,* and de facto rules by case law such as in *Canton v. Harris* (1989) wherein all training records can be subpoenaed for production in a civil trial. Hence they must be maintained for the minimum time periods as mandated by law as well as the tenure of the employee. If state law allows though, a policy should provide a means to periodically remove adverse personnel actions from employee files when conduct is not repeated and the incidents are low-level, the action is corrected, or remedial training has been effective (Field & Meloni, 1999).

Other issues may impact records retention such as collective bargaining agreements that will allow for destruction or return of disciplinary or training records to the employee after a "probationary" period. These codicils in collective bargaining agreements may be not only illegal, but may bring undue civil liability upon the organization. The emergence of "paperless" packages should also be of concern as technology evolves and organizations adopt software programs that obviate the use of hard copies, policies must be in place to protect those records from destruction as well as unauthorized access.

An example of this is contained in the regulations for law enforcement personnel in New York State. Records retention for public safety and emergency services such as training and remedial training (e.g., memorandum of record/training memorandum) must remain in the personnel file for six years after the individual leaves service (University of the State of New York State Education Department, 1993, p. 90). Therefore, the individual state laws should be reviewed and advice of legal counsel sought prior to the destruction or return of any personnel records.

The following list is a general set of guidelines for purging records in a law enforcement organization. While this list is offered as a guide, the agency should consider keeping records as long as the employee is in the organization because of the requests for all personnel records when an employee is the subject of civil litigation:

1. *Sustained Cases:* Ten years after termination of employment.
2. *Exonerated, Unfounded, and Not Sustained:* Five years after the incident.
3. *Administrative/Incident Reviews/Office Cases:* Three years after the incident.
4. *Stenographic Notes:* Seven years after the incident.
5. *Civil Action:* Six years after the completion of litigation.
6. *Use-of-force/Subject Management Reports and Packages:* Six years after the incident.
7. *Police Fleet MVA's Without Litigation:* Ten years after the accident.
8. *Police Fleet MVA's With Litigation:* Ten years after the completion of the litigation.
9. *Counseling Memorandum/Memorandum of Record/Training Memorandum:* Six years after termination from employment.
10. *Administrative Report/Intradepartmental Correspondence/Special Report:* Six years after the incident.
11. *Missing Property Report:* Six years after the incident.
12. *Injured Officer Report:* No time limits (See Americans with Disabilities Act).
13. *Background Investigations:* Six years after termination from employment.

RECORDS RELEASE AND THE RIGHT TO PRIVACY

Another confusing area of law with respect to internal investigations is that of records release and rights to privacy. Records release and rights to privacy in this area include internal investigations reports and investigative packages as well as the personnel records of law enforcement employees. Some general guidelines and thoughts are provided in this chapter, however, the internal investigator, administrator, and person assigned to process *Freedom of Information Law* (FOIL) requests must first consult with legal counsel prior to the release of any such records.

FOIL requests are filed consistently with law enforcement agencies for legitimate and nefarious reasons. Those involved in an auto accident may request copies of the motor vehicle accident investigation report for insurance and litigation purposes. Career criminals may also request all records pertaining to them that a department maintains in order to learn if an active investigation is being conducted. The former would be released while the latter would be reviewed based upon the department's need to withhold certain types of information that may interfere with legitimate operations.

In general, all records are available, unless an exception permits an agency to deny access. Most exceptions are based upon common sense and the potential for harm that would arise by means of disclosure. If disclosure of records would be damaging to an individual or preclude a government agency from carrying out its duties, it is likely that some aspects of the records may be withheld (New York State Department of State, 2002). Commonly-used exemptions include various types of records whose release would impair law enforcement investigations or proceedings, many types of internal records, and records whose release would cause an unwarranted invasion of personal privacy.

Exemptions are also included in superseding laws. For example, in New York State, the *New York State Civil Rights Law,* Section 50-a, precludes the release of any personnel records to the public. This exception to the FOIL mandate extends to internal investigations packages wherein the law enforcement officer was the subject as they are also considered personnel records. Other exceptions in New York State are included in such statutes as the *New York State Public Officers Law* Section 87, *Access to Agency Records* and Section 89, *General Provisions Relating to Access to Records* that regulate records release. These laws as well as current case law must be reviewed before any release of records can take place.

While access to information must be controlled for legal and operational reasons, the right to the personal privacy of the law enforcement officer must also be considered in the equation. Certain types of information release of personal information by a law enforcement organization can be actionable by the employee. In *Kallstrom v. City of Columbus, Ohio* (1998) the United States Court of Appeals for the Sixth Circuit held that the plaintiffs, who were undercover police officers, had a constitutionally protected interest in not having certain personal information contained in their personnel files released to a criminal defense attorney. The court held that the constitutional right implicated was the officers' and their families' right to personal security and bodily integrity. Although the state has no affirmative duty to protect citizens from private acts of violence, it may not cause or greatly increase the risk of harm to its citizens through its own affirmative acts (Reak, 1998b). Therefore, when examining a request for records release, the legal, organizational, and personal issues involved must be weighed against the legality, validity, and extent of the request.

SUMMARY

This chapter discussed the issues of the legal and labor issues to be considered in the internal investigations process. The chapter reviews, in the broadest sense of legal and procedural issues, those matters that have an impact on investigative conduct and the disciplinary process. Covering all case law in this format would be impossible and impractical, however, this chapter is intended to guide the internal investigator and administrator in the proper legal and procedural edicts for the conduct of an internal investigation.

As law enforcement officers, the charge is to protect the rights and privileges guaranteed by the United States Constitution in a free society that is intended to be enjoyed by all. Law enforcement agencies are not exempt from these regulations and cannot cede from the requirements of the Constitution when dealing with its own employees. Simply stated, a law enforcement organization that is charged with enforcing the law cannot also break the law, even when dealing with its own employees. This principle is profoundly stated in the text *Local Government Police Management* as:

> Police chiefs should see that their employees are given all the personal safeguards afforded any civilian member of the community. Procedures must be fair and reasonable. Only arbitrary and capricious actions in administrative hearings should be subject to review by a court, and chiefs should never make efforts to protect officers from the consequences of their misconduct. (Garmire, 1982, p. 285)

In order to fulfill the legal and labor issue requirements, the internal investigator must consider the following issues when conducting the inquiry of any complaint against an employee of the law enforcement organization:

1. Departmental rules of conduct.
2. Labor laws and rules in investigative process.
3. Criminal implications of conduct.
4. Civil implications of conduct.
5. All due process rights of the involved officer.
6. Maintaining a strong liaison with the municipality's legal/corporation counsel and Civil Service Commission.
7. In cases where an investigation has revealed a sustained finding that will (or could) result in a disciplinary action, elicit legal review before preferring charges/disciplinary action.

Chapter 7

INVESTIGATIVE TECHNIQUES AND PROCEDURES

INTRODUCTION

This chapter discusses the conduct of the internal investigation in general and process terms. The chapter addresses investigative techniques in terms of policy and procedure as well as situations that the internal investigator may face in this assignment. Later chapters are devoted to the unique requirements of special and administrative investigations as well as evidence and scene processing requirements.

FUNDAMENTAL PERSPECTIVE

The role of a criminal investigator in most police organizations is considered an esteemed position. There exists a proliferation of writing in the area of criminal investigation that all have a common theme throughout; the discovery of facts. Charles E. O'Hara (1981) states that, "An investigation may be considered a success if all the available information relevant and material to the issues or allegations of the case is uncovered" (p. 6). However, the lines become blurred when the internal investigation is mentioned.

The internal investigation is the most complex and challenging investigation conducted by the investigator as well as in the organization. As such, it comes with its own rules and burdens. Whether justly or unjustly based, the internal investigator is the most scrutinized member of any police organization. There seems to be no margin for error in their actions and no right answer when working in an environment that has so many masters with divergent interests to satisfy. Consequently, these investigations must be thorough, fair, and well-planned to protect all of the rights of parties involved (Close, 2001).

AGENCY POLICY DEVELOPMENT

To portray an image of true responsiveness, a department should accept complaints in any form and by any reasonable means, including telephone, mail, or e-mail, as well as anonymous complaints (Thurnauer, 2002). Policy development for complaint intake is a necessary task for all law enforcement administrators. Agencies must have a complaint policy in place to set a standard for operations in the organization. Complaint intake, case investigation, and proper disposition criteria must be developed for all strata in the organization as well. Use of other agency policies as guides, especially accredited agencies, as well as model policies such as those from the International Association of Chiefs of Police can assist an organization in their development and implementation (International Association of Chiefs of Police, 2000b).

Complaint intake policy will very likely be agency specific dependent upon size, command structure, community needs, union agreements, and accessibility of complainants to the process. Many organizations have a multiple option system that allows several vehicles for a complainant to file a complaint. Organizations can set standards of filing a complaint as high as only taking signed formal complaints, to accepting telephone and mail complaints. This should be researched and designed to meet the intrinsic needs of the department, community, and collective bargaining unit involved in the process.

Complaint intake policy should be clear with respect to the authority and responsibility to take a personnel complaint by any identified rank in the organization. Complaint intake policy should also include a comprehensive list of the case progression and responsibilities of all department personnel who will be involved in the investigation, including investigators, reviewers, and union or legal representation. Unless aggravating circumstances exist, the target of the investigation should be notified that a complaint has been filed and an investigation is commencing.

The law enforcement organization should also identify what complaints can be mediated or conciliated (e.g., minor procedure v. an excessive force complaint), what level a complaint can be mediated or conciliated in the organization (e.g., sergeant v. captain), the types of complaints that will be accepted in the organization (e.g., all as opposed to a defined list), and formal complaints as opposed to informal or semi-formal reviews (e.g., formal personnel complaint v. command level review v. incident/administrative review). The policy should allow for discretion on behalf of the identified complaint intake officers to resolve complaints at the lowest level possible. An excellent example of this is provided through the Washington State Patrol which has a system in place that identifies lower level cases as Non-Investigative Matters (NIM). As such, they have the following policy:

1. The accused employee acted in accordance with a department regulation, order, procedure, or policy.
2. All available means to identify the employee have been exhausted with negative results.
3. A court must adjudicate the legality of a complainant's arrest, citation, notice of infraction, the legality of a warrant, or the legality of seized evidence.
4. The complainant requested that no formal administrative investigation be initiated.
5. The complainant supported supervisory intervention (counseling, discussion of complainant's concerns with the accused employee, remedial training, or a combination of those things) in lieu of formal investigation. (Serpas, Olson, & Jones, 2003)

Some agencies definitively state that a formal personnel complaint will be taken in all instances where a complaint is made. Policies of this nature are far too rigid and unworkable in the practical world of law enforcement. A policy that is also too vague or allows too much discretion also works to the detriment of the organization. Complaint intake policy should involve the input of department command, industry standards, collective bargaining unit, line level personnel, and community input in order to meet the needs of all stakeholders in the process.

If the complaint is of a criminal nature, or has the potential for leading to criminal conduct, the policy should also address who should conduct this investigation. Depending on the severity, a criminal investigation can be conducted by the immediate supervisor, specialized units in the organization such as a detective bureau or special investigations unit, designated command officer, county sheriff's department, state police, or a states attorney's office.

Figure 7-1. Complaint intake is a process that requires the supervisor to be inquisitive, vigilant, and tolerant of the concerns of those who believe that they have been the subject of police misconduct or abuse (Photo courtesy of the Brockport, New York Police Department).

COMPLAINT INTAKE

Complaint intake should be distinguished by the level of violation. In many cases, the complaint is for some low level of alleged procedural violation. The complaint may many times turn out to be a question about police policy, procedure, or the law. In all of these cases, the complaint may be resolved by merely allowing the person to convey their side of the event. Allowing the person to vent may be all that is needed to de-escalate the situation and resolve the issue or complaint. Good listening skills and allowing a complainant to talk can facilitate the determination of the base problem and assist the internal investigator in quickly finding a solution to the problem. The internal investigator should give complainants options rather than ultimatums (Nowicki, 2002c). The majority of complaints result in some type of field conciliation where the complainant is satisfied with the supervisor's or internal investigator's explanation.

Complainants will usually bring a broad array of issues to the table when voicing their concerns. The internal investigator should clarify the salient issues into specific allegations that may have the potential for violations of organizational policy. Broad or vague complaints of behavior are not sufficient to initiate a complaint investigation.

The next stage is to determine if the complaint is procedural and/or criminal. This will require the investigating supervisor to either decide if the complaint can be handled at his or her level and also if the complaint needs to be taken to a higher level. In addition, if the complaint is of a criminal allegation, two separate and distinct investigations should be conducted by separate and distinct investigators or investigating bodies.

The following is a checklist of considerations for the internal investigator when conducting a complaint intake:

1. Determine the complainant's desire to pursue a formal personnel complaint weighed against the seriousness of the allegation(s).
2. In cases where the complainant does not want to pursue a formal personnel complaint, endeavor to have them sign a sup-

porting deposition/affidavit attesting to this fact.

3. If the complainant desires a formal personnel complaint, or if the allegation is of a serious nature (e.g., excessive force, allegation of a crime, etc.) initiate a complaint form and conduct a thorough preliminary investigation. Thorough means statements, investigative reports, photographs, and physical evidence collection. The internal investigator should not take anything for granted.
4. In excessive force allegations where the complainant has, or will receive medical treatment, have the complainant sign a medical records release form.
5. Don't release personal information concerning the officer to the complainant or witnesses in the case. The complainant is only entitled to information that is already available to them. In cases where the complainant must identify the involved officer from a photo array, use the number of the photograph in the statement the complainant signs and not the name or identity of the officer.
6. Don't indicate to the complainant that the officer will be disciplined. The investigator will not know the final disposition of the case until the investigation is completed and reviewed.
7. If the complainant identifies a witness or witnesses that are not present for the initial complaint intake, send a certified letter with a return receipt to all involved requesting their cooperation.

ALTERNATIVE STRATEGIES

While conciliation and mediation are alternative strategies to complaint resolution, some departments have implemented innovative systems for complaint resolution. This is a progressive step as a policy for taking every complaint in an organization is neither practical nor recommended. Complaints have varying degrees of severity and the few resources that agencies have should be directed to the most serious of allegations. In contrast, lower level complaints of policy and procedure may be best handled by more informal means in order to provide a system that is more responsive and satisfactory to customer complaints than the formal internal investigations process.

For example, the Washington State Patrol complaint system was designed to resolve complaints at the outset by offering officers the opportunity to avoid the investigative process. The system is designed: (1) to allow accused employees to avoid lengthy investigation either by admitting a mistake, receiving a sanction, and moving on or by volunteering information to exonerate themselves, (2) to deal with minor misconduct at the lowest possible level of the department, and (3) to ensure predictability, reliability, and validity of punishment attached to certain behaviors. Under this system, accused employees are advised of the allegations through their representatives and allowed to come forward and respond to the allegations. Many disciplinary cases have been settled without any need for additional investigation (Serpas, Olson, & Jones, 2003).

To implement such a system, legal counsel should be consulted along with the collective bargaining unit, if applicable. The system should also be marketed to the line staff so that they will understand and consider using the system when a complaint is filed against them. A policy should be developed that includes a formalized system of interaction between the internal affairs staff who have the authority to authorize such resolutions in cases and the collective bargaining unit personnel who will liaison between the organization and the accused personnel. One additional recommendation is that the organization should use an independent third party (e.g., command officer not attached to the internal investigations unit) in the process as the primary contact to the union in order to prevent tainting of the case if it should go forward to formal investigation as opposed to the commanding personnel officer in the internal investigations unit. All communications between the third party and the union should also be confidential unless the officer does plead guilty.

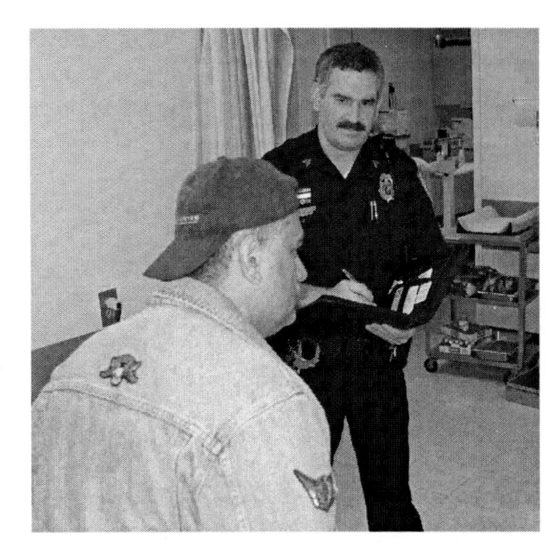

Figure 7-2. Any claims of excessive force should be immediately evaluated by appropriate medical staff and the results documented in the internal investigation (Photo courtesy of the Brockport, New York Police Department).

MEDICAL ATTENTION

Because of court rulings such as *Canton v. Harris* (1989), departments are responsible to offer and provide medical attention to those subjected to force by law enforcement personnel. At times, allegations of excessive force are made by those arrested or subjected to the force. In order to reduce liability, law enforcement organizations should develop policies requiring that these subjects be given medical attention upon request or if there are obvious injuries or the potential for injury based upon the level of force used. If the person refuses treatment, a written record of the refusal should be obtained (Stine, 2001). Under some federal case law, if the plaintiff was injured while being taken into custody and later sentenced to prison, he does not have to file a federal lawsuit against the officer or department until he had completed his time in prison (Smith, 1998).

In excessive force allegations, the investigator must determine if the complainant was subjected to force, the type or complaint of injuries, and was medical attention requested by the complainant? In addition, was medical attention offered by the arresting officer or required by policy? If not, the internal investigator should offer and accompany the complainant to the hospital for the evaluation and any impending treatment. Medical records release forms can be signed at this time and the records can be obtained as part and parcel to the investigation and case file.

In developing a medical records release form, each medical provider may have different requirements for records release. In addition, the requirements for the *Health Insurance Portability and Accountability Act of 1996* (HIPAA) should also be consulted when a form is developed for the internal investigation unit's use in medical records release.

CASE PLANNING AND STRATEGY

Case planning and strategy should begin when the formal personnel complaint is filed. Later discussion in the text reviews the interview hierarchy, evidence collection, and case assembly; however, all of these components need to be considered in the context of planning and strategy. While most internal investigations should be treated with the same tenacity as a homicide investigation and the best tools for investigation are in-depth investigation and research, the need for planning and strategy should not be disregarded. Even the simplest of cases requires an investigative strategy as that can lead to serious consequences dependent upon the information uncovered during the investigation as well as the history of the target officer. If the investigation takes a serious turn or if the officer is found guilty because of a poor or biased investigation, no justice is served. The internal investigator must always be cognizant of the ramifications of this process and the investigation should never be the vehicle for the needless "professional death" of an employee.

MULTIFACETED CASE INVESTIGATION

A multifaceted case investigation model is a recommended strategy for an internal investigation. While a criminal investigation primarily serves one singular purpose, to identify and arrest a criminal offender, the internal investigation will often have multiple implications and thus, multiple purposes. Therefore, cases should be investigated from three perspectives: (1) adherence or disobedience to departmental policy and procedure, (2) the civil implications of the actions, and (3) the potential for any criminal conduct of the involved personnel.

Departmental Policy and Procedure: The internal investigation primarily determines whether or not organizational policy was adhered to in the incident being investigated. In addition, the internal investigation should also review the efficacy of policy and procedure, the training issues that may be involved in this investigation, and the training that may be needed throughout the organization.

Civil Implications: The majority of internal investigations have the potential for civil litigation. Albeit, most do not incur a civil suit, the implications should not be ignored as the initial investigation is the time to address all of the potential issues rather than awaiting a lawsuit and the attempting to backtrack the case.

Potential for Criminal Conduct: In rare cases, there is a potential for criminal conduct, both at the state and federal levels. Any allegation of excessive force, if proven, can lead to departmental sanction, civil litigation, and criminal prosecution in state and federal courts.

An example of this is an officer who uses unauthorized equipment, such as non-issued pepper spray. While the officer may have violated policy, their actions may be reasonable under the state and federal constitutions and thus be justified at those levels (Nowicki, 2001i). Hence, the investigation would reveal that a departmental sanction was in order for the violation of policy, but no criminal or civil liability would attach to the officer's actions. All three of these issues should be addressed in the internal investigation for the investigation to be a complete and multifaceted approach to the process.

HIERARCHY OF THE PROCESS

Every law enforcement organization should have a policy in place not only for complaint intake and investigation, but also the hierarchy of the review and disposition process. The following is a general guideline to the process:

Complaint Intake: Complaint intake should be done by a supervisor in the organization. Complaints should always be answered by the next higher rank to the target of the investigation (e.g., lieutenant for sergeant, captain for lieutenant, etc.). If the complaint is conciliated or resolved at this contact, some type of documentation should be placed in the file in order to track the number of complaints and dispositions for later early intervention system reviews.

Conciliation or Supervisory Investigation: If the incident results in a conciliation, the organization can leave this review at the first-line supervisor or receiver of the complaint or a next level review in order to ensure integrity in the process. If a formal personnel complaint is taken and preliminary investigation conducted by the intake supervisor, approval should be obtained from a higher supervisory authority for the intake supervisor to complete the investigation.

The investigation may require review by experts such as defensive tactics, accident investigators, corporation counsel, or district attorneys. This review is included in the investigation and included for the justification of recommended findings for the command review.

Command Review: Complaint intake and completed investigation should also have some type of intermediary review prior to review by the chief of the organization. In larger agencies, this would simply encompass the chain of command and the internal investigations unit. In smaller agencies, this can be accomplished by the use of another supervisor such as one on afternoons and one on days to check the completeness, accuracy, and justification for the findings as recommended by the investigating supervisor. A command board or civilian review process would be appropriate at this stage of the hierarchy for their recommendations as well.

Chief's Review: The final review stage in the process is conducted by the chief. The chief must review the entire case in-depth as well as considering the opinions of all of the previous reviewers before making a final recommendation and disposition in the investigation.

Notifications to Complainant and Involved Officer: The final disposition stages include notifications to the complainant and officer and copies of the memos to the personnel file of the subject or target of the investigation in order to properly complete the case.

INTERVIEW PROCEDURES AND TECHNIQUES: GENERAL

This next section discusses general interview procedures and techniques. This section covers the different types of techniques, the mediums for documenting different types of statements, and protocols for varied interview processes. Later sections discuss specific interview settings.

At the outset, the internal investigation interview is more a matter of attitude than technique. Experts in the field of interview and interrogation advocate for the respectful treatment of all parties involved in the process, regardless of the allegation or nature of the offense. As law enforcement personnel, the requirement is for fair, respectful, and impartial treatment of accused offenders. There exists no exclusion of law enforcement personnel accused of transgressions from this rule. Therefore, when interviewing a complainant, a witness, or an accused officer, respect to all should be tantamount.

In general, interview questions have a foundation in both types of interviews whether law enforcement or civilian. Direct questions help to clarify an issue, while confrontational questions are used if there is evidence or facts to the contrary, and challenging questions are used if the responses

Figure 7-3. Interview practices should be thorough and respectful in the interviews of complainants, witnesses, and involved personnel alike (Photo courtesy of the Brockport, New York Police Department).

are not believable (Arnold, 1999). While conducting the interview, care must be taken in how questions are framed, presented, and perceived by the interviewee and any reviewers of the case.

Because of the involved nature of these investigations, the internal investigator should schedule as many interviews as possible in advance to save time unless the investigator needs the element of surprise. The internal investigator should develop a list of prospective witnesses and first send certified letters to each with return receipts for inclusion in the investigative file. These contacts should be accompanied by telephone contacts and personal visits with a business card left at locations where the prospective witness was not located. These efforts should be documented in the case file in order to demonstrate that reasonable attempts were made to solicit the cooperation of parties who could offer insight into the facts of the investigation.

In as far as humanly possible, the internal investigator must be briefed with all of the known facts of the investigation prior to the interview. The investigator must have a working knowledge of the facts before an effective interview can take place. Therefore, preparation is the key to conducting the interview right the first time. While the investigator is not precluded from follow-up interviews, these should be limited as much as possible. The following is a list of suggested interview preparation strategies for the internal investigator to consider:

1. Review all available reports, documents, statements, etc. before the conduction of the interview.
2. Prepare references ahead of time to use for review (e.g., photographs, evidence, policy/procedure references, witness statements used for confirmation or rebuttal, etc.).
3. Prepare a separate copy of all documents the officer will need to refer to during the interview. Provide the officer a copy of the documents they prepared and are entitled to and allow them the opportunity to review them with their representative or in private prior to beginning the interview.
4. Prepare and mark (number) exhibits/photographs ahead of time. Use numeric coding for photographs and exhibits so they can be referred to and tracked in the documentation of the interview. Photographs can be numbered and loose for referencing during the interview or placed on card stock or in page protectors as described in chapter 13: "Case Investigative Summary and Package–Case Preparation and Presentation." The internal investigator should take care in what photographs should and should not

be shown to the interviewee. Therefore, the photographs should be separated prior to the interview to prevent this from occurring.

5. Prepare as many questions as possible ahead of time. The internal investigator should not rely on memory as the interview should only have to be conducted once if the investigator is properly prepared.
6. The internal investigator should not engage in the use of sarcasm or trickery during the interview that are sometimes standard tactics for a criminal suspect. Most police officers are well aware of these techniques and can actually use the same techniques against the investigator. Direct, specific, and respectful interview procedures should be observed in the interviews of all involved parties. Always allow the interviewee to maintain their dignity in the interview process.
7. When identifying specific techniques or procedures, the internal investigator must use the specific techniques or terminology as well as laymen's descriptions for the official record.
8. The internal investigator should also take great care in not trying to sound like a lawyer. The investigator should not be suggestive or plant seeds of thought in the mind of the reviewer as well as not appear to be something they are not, an attorney. The proceeding, while formal, is also of an investigative nature, not a legal proceeding.
9. Remember the basic questions of who, what, when, where, why, and how?

There should also be an interview protocol with respect to when an interview is conducted with the involved parties. This speaks more to planning and strategy of the investigative process. If at all possible, the interviews should be conducted in the following order:

1. The complainant (after evidentiary document review).
2. Independent or uninvolved witnesses.
3. Witnesses known to and identified by the complainant.
4. Employees who witnessed or were involved in the incident.
5. Possible re-interview of the complainant based upon any new information developed in the follow-up interviews.
6. The subject or target officer(s).

The internal investigator occupies an extremely powerful position with respect to the conduct of the investigation and the interviews of all of the involved parties. This all but omnipotent role carries with it an immense responsibility. The responsibility is to objectivity and fairness to all of the parties involved including the complainant, organization, community, and the involved personnel. The internal investigator must ascribe to the principle that the rights of the complainant should be balanced with the rights of the officer, not overshadow them.

Providing for the Physical Needs of the Interviewee

This simple component is sometimes lost in the process. No matter who the interviewee is or represents, the internal investigator should attempt to provide for their physical needs in the interview. An ulterior motive is to develop rapport and confidence in the investigator while a more altruistic motive is to empathize with the interviewee and attempt to provide some physical comforts. Issues such as temperature of the room, lighting, background noise, proximity, and interruptions all may have a negative impact in the interview. The simplest method that can be employed is ensuring some type of refreshment is available for the interviewee such as water, coffee, and soda. These may be considered tactics, but more importantly, a humanistic mindset in providing for the needs of any interviewee, whether a witness or the officer who is the target of the investigation.

Figure 7-4. A police sergeant takes the statement of an independent witness to a personnel complaint who was located during a neighborhood canvass (Photo courtesy of the Brockport, New York Police Department).

Supporting Depositions and Affidavits

In documenting the statements of involved parties, the internal investigator can use several different vehicles for documenting the result of the interview and personal statements of the involved parties. In taking statements from complainant's, civilian witnesses, witnesses who are classified as lay and expert when offering qualified opinions as to some specific aspect of the investigation, and personnel from other law enforcement organizations, the internal investigator may consider the use of a supporting deposition or affidavit. These evidentiary statements usually include some type of warning that untruthful statements can be punished by criminal statute and are in effect, a sworn statement of the party. The affiant or deponent swears under penalty of signing a false instrument, or presenting the false instrument for testimony can be also charged with perjury. These types of warnings and sanctions are important for the witness to be held to so as the integrity of the statement can be maintained to the highest possible standards.

Stenographic, Video, and Audiotaped Statements

When the organization has the capabilities for conducting recorded interviews, they should be used as often and as practicably possible. The actual words of the complainant, witnesses, and involved personnel are documented verbatim which limits the opportunity for misinterpretation. When taking written statements, most often they are paraphrased and great care must be taken in their accuracy as well as comprehensiveness. This problem is obviated when a verbatim recorded statement is taken. This is not always within the means of an organization and not practical in every case for every interview. When possible, these types of recording procedures should be used in the higher priority cases such as allegations of excessive force and crimes. When conducting a recorded interview, the following is a recommended protocol for the order of the interview process:

1. Identify everyone in the room by name and title for the record.
2. Investigating supervisor(s) should conduct the first round of interviews.
3. Any union or legal representative of the employee is allowed to ask questions of the interviewee.
4. Follow-up questions may then be asked by the investigating supervisor(s).
5. The interviewee should be allowed to make closing comments or a closing statement.

In addition, the following is a list of recommendations that the investigator should consider when conducting interviews of all involved parties:

1. Obtain a signed advisement form from involved personnel, complainants, and witnesses. These forms should include the *Garrity* warnings and *Weingarten* protections for law enforcement personnel as well as truthfulness requirements for all other interviewees.
2. Have ready a prepared script for each statement and build interview questions around the foundational questions.
3. Ask open-ended questions that lead to more focused and probing questions.
4. Don't be suggestive. The investigator must remember that everything said is being recorded.
5. Focus should be maintained on the specific issues in the complaint.
6. The internal investigator must use factually-based questions, not conjecture or innuendo. The internal investigator should not plant seeds of conjecture in the mind of the interviewee, or more importantly, the reviewers of the case. Questions framed such as the following should be avoided: Is it possible that. . .? Could the other officer have been thinking. . .? Do you expect me to believe. . . ?
7. Information elicited should be limited to the interviewee's observations and perspectives alone, not what the interviewee may believe what another person observed, felt, or believed. The interviewee can only recount what they observed or heard. Limiting the scope of the interview allows for as objective an account as possible given the fact that there will always be some subjectivity in a person's ability to accurately recall information.
8. The interviewee should describe their observations in their own terms and these terms should be clarified on the record when the definitions are ambiguous.
9. The internal investigator should also clarify specific defensive tactics techniques when they are described by the complainant, witnesses, and personnel involved.

The internal investigator will also be involved in the interview of expert witnesses during the course of many case investigations. For example, when interviewing an accident reconstructionist, the terms drag factor and yaw mark, to name a few, should be clarified in laymen's terms for the reviewers to understand. There are many experts that can be utilized during the search for the truth in an investigation that will require the same level of clarifying information such as evidence technicians, laboratory personnel, fingerprint experts, and handwriting analysts to name a few. Another example is the interview of medical personnel. When interviewing medical personnel, the doctor, physician's assistant, or nurse should describe the injury in technical and laymen's terms. The following issues should be considered for medical personnel who have evaluated, diagnosed, or treated the complainant in an internal investigation:

1. The lack of injuries, or
2. The extent of, and permanence of any injuries incurred.
3. An expert opinion if the injuries indicate the use of excessive force.
4. Any and all medical procedures rendered or not rendered.

One final note deals with the videotaping the interviews of law enforcement personnel. An employee may voluntarily consent to such videotaping of the interview. This can also be an issue that is addressed in a collective bargaining agreement. The Federal Labor Relations Authority in *Customs Service and NTEU* (2000) addressed this as an issue within federal agencies in that this must be bargained for and consider the "impact and implementation" of the procedure prior to use (Americans for Effective Law Enforcement, 2005).

Telephone Interviews

The use of telephone interviews can be problematic. There are times when a telephone interview is the only option available for the interview of an involved party. The ability of the internal investigator to interact with the interviewee, read body language, offer visual aids in the interview such as photographs of the officer or scene are all obviated in the telephone interview. In addition, the investigator has no constructive means of interviewee identification other than the word of the person at the other end of the telephone. The telephone interview is not recommended, however, it should be considered if an in-person interview cannot be conducted.

In consideration of all of these factors, two points must be measured when a telephone interview is used as direct evidence in an internal investigation: (1) the weight and merits of a non-sworn statement and (2) the tenuous nature of the identification of the interviewee. As such, an adverse finding in an internal investigation should never be solely based upon a telephone interview. In addition, the internal investigator should take the following steps in verifying and documenting the identity of the interviewee: (1) the interview should be tape-recorded and the interviewee advised that the interview will be taped, (2) the interviewee should provide the internal investigator with some type of identification unique to the interviewee (e.g., date of birth, Social Security number, etc.), and (3) at the end of the tape, the internal investigator should include a statement verifying the date, time, internal investigator's name, the case number, the number dialed, and the person who was interviewed. The tapes should be preserved until the case is finally resolved (including any civil or criminal litigation) and a separate tape should be used for each individual interview.

Oral Synopsis

An oral synopsis is used in investigative reports when the information elicited from the interviewee is of importance, however, a formal statement is impractical or the interviewee is uncooperative or unable to offer a written or recorded statement. An example of the use of the oral synopsis is also demonstrated in the results of a neighborhood canvass. A complaint is filed for discourtesy. A person is located who states that they observed the officer and complainant together and that they heard a loud interchange between the subjects, but cannot recall the exact words used. An oral synopsis of the information can be included in the investigative report as the information is probative, but does not offer direct evidence to confirm or refute the allegations in the complaint.

In the use of an oral synopsis, the sum and substance of the interview can be documented in the Investigative Action Report as later described in this text. The internal investigator should clearly document exact statements and quotes as well as the reason for the oral synopsis as opposed to the written or recorded statement.

Administrative/Special/ Intra-Departmental Reports

The administrative or intra-departmental report is completed by personnel in the organization and is used quite often. They are completed by personnel within the agency who are involved or have information relevant to the incident being investigated, but have not given a stenographic or taped statement. These reports are very useful in the investigation of all procedural complaints, requests for information in a complaint, and for cases where multiple personnel were involved and the extent of the personal knowledge of the potential witness may be in question or limited in nature. The internal investigator is also not limited to one report or one interview. During the investigative stage, the internal investigator can conduct personal interviews and request multiple reports as needed to clarify emerging issues, however, this is not a recommended strategy in the interest of case quality, planning, strategy, and time management.

The internal investigator must also understand that the restrictions of *Garrity* and *Weingarten* also apply to requests for these types of written reports from employees. If the action could be construed as having criminal implications or lead to a disciplinary action, then the employee must be afforded all due process rights and protections under the law. One example is found in an arbitrator's decision in *City of Lansing and Capitol City Post* (1996), wherein the *Weingarten* rights were extended to written reports requested by a supervisor. The arbitrator ruled that management must inform subordinates of their right to representation if the inquiry can lead to discipline (Americans for Effective Law Enforcement, 2005).

The request for the administrative report/intra-departmental correspondence should be a standardized form designed for this purpose. The form should include the following information:

1. The case number.
2. The date of the request.
3. The name and assignment of the employee involved who will be required to submit the report.
4. The name and assignment of the investigating supervisor.
5. A statement advising the involved employee that an administrative investigation is being conducted by the organization and that they are being ordered to submit the report based upon department policy and regulations.
6. An advisement to the employee whether or not he or she is the target, subject, or witness of the investigation.
7. That the employee may be represented by an attorney or collective bargaining unit representative and have this individual review the statement prior to submission. A reasonable time period should also be included for the return date which should be three to five days, but not less than two days from issuance, unless exigent circumstances exist.
8. An advisement to the employee to review all relevant documentation of the incident prior to completing the statement.
9. That the employee is required to be truthful in their statement and untruthfulness can result in disciplinary action which may include dismissal. In addition, the employee must be advised in writing that the responses given, because they are being compelled as a term and condition of employment, cannot be used in a criminal proceeding involving the officer, but can be used in any departmental proceeding.
10. A brief synopsis of the complaint, including the date, time, location, complainant's name, and the allegations involved.
11. A series of questions that are specific and narrowly connected to the job function as they relate to the corresponding allegation.
12. A statement affording the officer the opportunity to waive these rights voluntarily and knowingly with a place to sign

and date the waiver (Note: The officer does not need to sign for receipt, only if they exercise their option to waive their rights).

13. The time, date, and location of the issuance of the request.
14. The identity and signature of the issuing supervisor.

Jail (Inmate) Interviews

At times, the need may arise to interview a complainant or witness who is incarcerated. The internal investigator will have to identify the particular protocol required for conducting these types of interviews. There are a few issues for the internal investigator to consider when arranging these interviews.

The internal investigator should research beforehand any protocol that is required of the jail or correctional facility administration in order to adhere to the required rules. There may be specific time periods that the internal investigator may be limited to in conducting such interviews. The jail personnel will most likely assist the law enforcement officer in their investigation, however, the internal investigator should understand the rules ahead of time in order to practice professional courtesy.

The internal investigator must also consider that if the complainant is represented by legal counsel in the matter being complained of, they may need permission from their counsel prior to giving the statement. The internal investigator should explore this issue at the first opportunity presented. If the complainant states that they would like their attorney present arrangements should be made prior to the interview. If the complainant states that they do not desire to have their attorney present during the interview, or the attorney has granted permission for the interview without being physically present, this should be placed clearly in the record at the outset of the written statement or the taped/stenographic statement.

Figure 7-5. In-custody interviews should be conducted with the complainant as needed for the investigation (Photo courtesy of the Brockport, New York Police Department).

A witness in a case does not need legal representation, however, these are voluntary interviews. The witness can refuse to give a statement or state that they would like a legal representative present prior to the interview. The internal investigator will have to abide by the request of the witness in these types of scenarios.

Law Enforcement Interviews

Due to the use of multiple agencies in large operations, multi-jurisdictional investigations such as police pursuits that cross political boundaries, and task forces, the need may present itself on occasion to solicit the statements of other law enforcement agency personnel in the progression of the investigation.

These interviews are also strictly voluntary unless they are compelled through a separate internal investigation of the affected agency. The internal investigations unit command and police chief should endeavor to develop a liaison and collaborative policy in multi-jurisdictional case investigation. In these scenarios, the affected agency would develop its own investigative case file and the interview would take place with both agency investigators present. The affected agency employee would most likely be allowed union representation at such an interview. When a policy is developed, these requests may go directly through the commanding officers of the respective internal investigations units or designated supervisors in each agency that would arrange for the interviews.

Where a policy doesn't exist, the internal investigator must, out of professional courtesy, obtain permission to conduct the interview at the very least through the employee's immediate supervisor. These circumstances are also voluntary in nature and the employee of the affected agency cannot be compelled to give the statement. The employee may request a union representative or legal counsel be present for the interview and should not be precluded from exercising this option.

The witness statement can be documented by affidavit/supporting deposition, audio/video recording (if permission is obtained), or stenographic statement. The internal investigator should also make arrangements to provide a copy of the employee's statement to the employee and affected agency if requested. A confidentiality warning should be attached to the statement if provided to the affected officer or agency.

INTERVIEW PROCEDURES AND TECHNIQUES: COMPLAINANTS/WITNESSES

The interview of complainants and witnesses in complaint investigations is similar to the basic tenets of crime or offense investigation. The goal of any interview is to obtain information that is relevant to the matter in question. Chief Bob Harrison (2001) very adeptly asks, "What is the goal in a complaint interview?" (p. 151). Understanding what the goals and objectives are will direct the course of the interview. The goal or objective of an internal investigation interview is to determine what information or observations the interviewee may have that relates to employee conduct. Additional objectives of the complainant or witness statement are to: (1) allow the complainant or witness an opportunity to tell their side of the story in their own words, (2) demonstrate the complainants or witnesses independent recollection of dates, times, distances, descriptions, other relevant information, and (3) lock complainants and witnesses into their versions of the incident (Arnold, 1999).

The internal investigator must be both sensitive to the needs of the complainant as well as the need to establish the best evidence that will determine the truth of the matter. Therefore, the internal investigator must not be afraid to challenge inconsistencies offered or discovered during the interview. Consistent statements can indicate credibility while inconsistent statements can indicate a lack of credibility. The internal investigator should be prepared for the interview ahead of time and have as much information about the case available at the time of the interview in order to correlate facts and use evidence such as other statements, photographs, medical reports, and any other documentation to corroborate or challenge the interviewee's version of the incident.

The complainant may also be a suspect/defendant in the original actions that led to the complaint. As previously mentioned, their Fifth and Sixth Amendments rights must be considered. If the complainant decides to waive their right to have their legal counsel present, this should be clear in the written or recorded documentation of the interview.

INTERVIEW PROCEDURES AND TECHNIQUES: LAW ENFORCEMENT PERSONNEL

This area of discussion no doubt causes much consternation with law enforcement officers, unions, police administrators, and the community. While the legal requirements are fairly simple, each separate population seems to have its own interpretation of the boundaries which span the entire spectrum from no right to interview and full legal representation to every right to a compelled interview with no right to representation. The problem lies in internal investigators and police administrators who attempt to push the limits in compelling statements. While that right already exists in the law, the problem is the administration of due process. Chief Ronald S. Neubauer, (1999) former president of the International Association of Chief's of Police, recognized this issue as he states that, "The head of the agency also has an obligation to ensure that a police officer is afforded the same rights as any other citizen or suspect who is accused of wrongdoing" (p. 6). These rights have been afforded based upon the letter and spirit of the law and are inalienable.

By law, a public employer can develop a policy to compel an employee of a police department to give a statement, but also hold that employee to the highest standards of truthfulness in the offering of the statement. The *Garrity v. New Jersey* (1967) decision is the basis for this procedure in compelling statements that are used in internal investigations without violating an employee's Fifth Amendment rights against compulsory self incrimination that may lead to criminal charges. The *Garrity* warnings are similar to *Miranda* warnings, but warn the employee that failure to fully disclose information that is related to the office held may result in discipline up to and including dismissal (Thurnauer, 2002). Several cases have laid the legal foundation for these warnings beyond *Garrity* such as *Gardner v. Broderick* (1968), *Uniformed Sanitation Men Association v. Commissioner of Sanitation* (1968), *Lefkowitz v. Turley* (1973), and *Kelley v. Johnson* (1976). Such warnings include that the employee be informed that although they have the right to remain silent and not incriminate themselves, their silence can be deemed as insubordination and will result in administrative discipline. The employee is further advised that any statements made under compulsion of the threat of such discipline cannot be used against the employee in a later criminal proceeding. In the issue of refusing to answer,

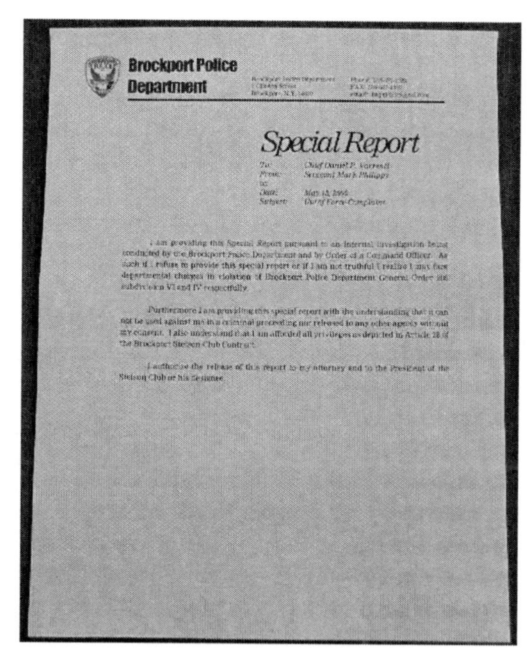
Brockport Police Department

Special Report

To: [illegible]
From: [illegible]
cc:
Date: [illegible]
Subject: [illegible]

I am providing this Special Report pursuant to an internal investigation being conducted by the Brockport Police Department and by Order of a Command Officer. As such if I refuse to provide this special report or if I am not truthful I realize I may face departmental charges in violation of Brockport Police Department General Order [illegible] subdivision VI and IV respectfully.

Furthermore I am providing this special report with the understanding that it can not be used against me in a criminal proceeding nor released to any other agency without my consent. I also understand that I am afforded all privileges as depicted in Article [illegible] of the Brockport Stetson Club Contract.

I authorize the release of this report to my attorney and to the President of the Stetson Club or his designee.

Figure 7-6. The Garrity Warnings should be in written format when issued to the employee (Photo courtesy of the Brockport, New York Police Department).

several cases have been decided in favor of the organization's right to discipline and terminate on this basis alone, such as *Blunier v. Board of Fire and Police Commissioners* (1989), *Thomas v. Brevard County Sheriff's Office* (1984), and *Lemoine v. Department of Police* (1977) (Americans for Effective Law Enforcement, 2005).

Understanding the officer's rights to due process and adhering to them is key to the admissibility of a statement. These emanate from the *Garrity* decision. Therefore, employees should be given the following series of admonitions prior to an administrative interview:

1. You are advised that this is an internal administrative investigation only.
2. You will be asked and are required to answer all questions specifically related to the performance of your duties and your fitness for office.
3. If you refuse to answer these questions, you can be subject to discipline that can be as much as discharge or removal from office. You may also be subject to discipline for knowingly giving false statements.
4. I want to reassure you that any answers given are to be used solely for internal administrative purposes and may not be used in any subsequent criminal prosecution should such occur. (International Association of Chiefs of Police, 2000b, p. 47)

A second example of a set of *Garrity* warnings includes the right of representation as included under the *Weingarten* decision as follows:

1. You are under orders to answer all of the questions being asked.
2. Your answers must be truthful.
3. Your statements made during this interview cannot be used against you in a criminal proceeding.
4. Your refusal to answer questions and/or answering untruthfully may result in disciplinary action.
5. You have the right to be represented by an attorney or union representative of your choosing during this interview.

The interviewee should be served with reasonable notice of the interview unless exigent circumstances exist. The notice should include: (1) the date, time, and location of the complaint, (2) the complainant's name (3) the specific allegation(s), (4) the date, time, and location of the interview, (5) the advisement of the right to representation, and (6) the investigator's name under the auspices of the chief executive officer of the agency. The interviewee should be allowed to review the complaint itself. The interviewee's right to representation is afforded though the *Weingarten* decision, however the interviewee can't unreasonably delay interviews in most jurisdictions (Arnold, 1999).

No information obtained during the internal investigation can be shared with the criminal investigator. If criminal activity is admitted, the internal investigator should cease conducting the interview and turn the case over to a criminal investigator (Thurnauer, 2002). All other aspects of the internal investigation can proceed except for the interview of the target or subject officer until after the criminal interrogation has been completed. This is done so as any allegations of tainted evidence by the target or subject officer can be adequately defended by the internal investigator.

Once the internal investigator has ensured that all due process rights of the subject or target of the investigation have been provided for, the interview can proceed. In conducting the interview the use of standard interview techniques is acceptable with the understanding that the need for sensitivity and empathy to all involved is necessary. This level of sensitivity and empathy must also extend to the consideration of the trauma level of the incident being investigated and the law enforcement officer's well-being in the timing of the interview. Because of the stress factors that transcend most all encounters, physiological changes in the body can adversely affect memory, and as such failed memory does not automatically equate to untruthfulness (Colaprete, 2003).

The interview should begin with a protocol of identifying the specific details leading to the incident and then open-ended questions that lead to more focused interview questions. Questions can be developed ahead of time by the review of the available evidence and statements as well as evolve during the course of the interview. Open-ended questions can include: Do you recall. . .? Do you remember. . .? Have you ever. . .? The internal investigator must also be careful in asking questions like, "Is it possible. . .? Asked improperly, and given that anything may be possible, this may lead to undue influence and supposition when no evidence exists to support such a conclusion.

Specific interview questions can include a line of inquiry as: (1) The complainant states that you were discourteous by characterizing him or referring to him as an "[Expletive]." Did you make this statement? (2) Did you refer to the complainant in any other manner? (3) Did any other officer at the scene refer to the complainant in this manner? (4) Did anyone else at the scene refer to the complainant in this manner? These are direct questions that establish if the interviewee either committed the act or has knowledge of the act occurring.

The internal investigator should also be prepared for evasive or uncooperative responses. In these scenarios, the investigator must first consider that the interviewee will most likely not have the ability to recall every detail of an event, especially one that is traumatic or chaotic. When the interviewee makes the affirmation, "I don't recall" this may not be out of the realm of possibility.

If the internal investigator believes that the interviewee is not being entirely candid, he or she should not become upset or resort to threatening tactics. The internal investigator should also avoid the use of "high-risk high-gain" tactics such as threats of false evidence or non-existent witnesses. These tactics are practiced by the interviewee and will most often do more harm than good to the case and the search for the truth. The cadence of the interview should be calm, collected, and tenacious in tone and delivery. The internal investigator should continue to ask pointed questions related specifically to the facts of the investigation. The internal investigator should also use evidentiary documents and photographs to refresh memory and impeach testimony as needed.

The manner in which a question is framed can also lead to the impression that the interviewee is not being cooperative. Clear, concise, and direct questions are required for these types of interviews. Questions that are designed to confuse, that can have multiple implications from an answer, or are sarcastic are all unacceptable. Questions that also include unrealistic expectations are also unacceptable. For example, an interviewee is asked to recall intricate details of an event that occurred removed in time from the event will most likely be telling the truth as they know it when giving their statement. When the internal investigator adds in a statement an affirmation to the effect that the interviewee is a "trained observer and is responsible to testify in court settings to their observations," and then implies that because of this training they are being untruthful is blatantly unacceptable. This statement implies to the case reviewer that the interviewee is being untruthful based upon conjecture and innuendo, not on evidence. The addition of questions that have unrealistic expectations is also an unacceptable tactic. For example, when an officer applies handcuffs in an arrest and during a later interview of the circumstances, the officer is asked, "Did you count the clicks from the handcuffs when placing them on the suspect?" This would imply to the case reviewer that there is some level of training and testing for this and that there is an acceptable limit of "clicks" when neither is true.

The final consideration is the avoidance of patently illegal questions that violate an interviewee's civil or human rights. Such issues as protected classes of information should be avoided in the interview. Even when the allegations of a complainant are of this nature, if they are protected and are not a part of the job function, they must not be explored in the interview or investigation. The exclusionary rule or "Fruits of the Poisonous Tree" doctrine are an excellent guide for these types of situations. That, and the fact that no matter how diligent the investigator may be, there will most likely never be a time when all of the facts will be gained in an investigation. The internal investigator's responsibility is to make every effort to gain the facts and objectively present the available evidence for review by higher authority.

Additional considerations must be given to the linkage between the types of questions asked and their relationship to the official job function. Questions must be directly and narrowly related to how the alleged conduct is aligned with or in conflict with the official job function as delineated in organizational policies, procedures, rules, or relevant civil and criminal laws. Questions should also be framed so as to not violate an employee's right to privacy. Some allegations made by complainant's may prove to not be an issue for the interview and pursuing such a line of questioning may invite an investigation through a state level human rights division or organization. Such questions can also lead to a civil suit brought against the internal investigator and the chief executive of the organization.

Several cases have been decided with respect to this issue wherein the courts have ordered reinstatement with back pay. For example, in the decision of *Ronayne v. Lombard* (1977), a New York court limited the scope of questioning in a disciplinary matter to the official duties of the officer. In the decision of *Cox v. City of Chattanooga* (1974), the high court of Tennessee reinstated a captain who was terminated for failure to answer questions unrelated to official duties. These types of restrictions extend to such issues as allegations of inappropriate sexual relations as well. Decisions have limited the opportunities for internal investigators to interview in some of the most serious of allegations. In the decision of *J. R. Lopez v. Idaho Department of Law Enforcement and Idaho Personnel Commission* (1984), a district court ruled that a state trooper was improperly terminated for refusing polygraph questions pertaining to his sex life. The relief ordered by the court was a $50,000 judgment against the agency and reinstatement to the department. In *Shuman v. City of Philadelphia* (1983), the court affirmed that a department's inquiry into an officer's off-duty relationship with a female violated his "zone of privacy" and his subsequent refusal to answer questions was justified. In the decision of *Young v. Winkle* (1986), a fire chief could not require a firefighter to answer questions about a complaint of sexual contact with a 12-year-old child. However, in *Blunier v. Board of Fire and Police Commissioners of Peoria* (1989), firefighters accused of oral, anal, and vaginal sex with a citizen while on duty, refused to answer questions during an internal investigation. The appellate court concluded that there was insufficient evidence to affirm their termination for sexual misconduct, but their dismissal was warranted for their refusal to answer questions pertaining to the incident (Americans for Effective Law Enforcement, 2005).

The internal investigator and administrator must understand that the rights of the complainant should be tantamount to and not overshadow the rights of the accused officer (Colaprete, 2003).

INVESTIGATIVE CONDUCT IN EMPLOYEE INTERVIEWS

Other rules that are in place that emanate from federal and state protections, case law, and Civil Service rules are those directed towards personnel who are entitled to representation and fair notice if they are the subject or target of an investigation. Reasonable notice of an interview of the target or subject must be in writing to provide fair notice. The employee must also be afforded a reasonable amount of time to respond to questions or prepare for the interview. As a general rule, this time frame can be equated to a period of 48 hours unless other local or state rules prevail or exigent circumstances exist. Exigent circumstances such as a police-involved shooting or criminal activity can justify an earlier interview. The internal investigator and administrator should also consider the psychological issues involved in interviews that are too close in time to the incident as well as the physiological responses to stress that affect memory capacity.

The internal investigator must allow the interviewee a reasonable time to obtain counsel or representation. The questioning can commence if a representative isn't present in a reasonable amount of time. The internal investigator should document all efforts to contact legal counsel or representative so that the interview can be justified in any later hearing. An administrative law judge or hearing officer may have the power under statute to exclude the statement if they determine that a reasonable amount of time was not afforded. Depending on the severity of the incident, the need to ensure the admissibility of the statement, and the psychological condition of the interviewee, it may be a better tactic to wait for a more appropriate time to conduct the interview.

In relation to the relevant case law, several cases have been decided on this issue. For example, in *Upland POA v. City of Upland* (2003), a California appeals court decided that a compelled disciplinary interview where the officer's attorney was unable to appear for a rescheduled interview was legal. A companion case was decided in *Brougham v. City of Normandy* (1992), wherein an appellate court upheld the right to discipline an officer who refused to answer a superior's job-related questions without first consulting with legal counsel. However, a similar case decided in the New Jersey appeals court affirmed reinstatement of an officer who was terminated because he declined to answer questions without the assistance of an attorney. In the *Matter of William Carroll* (2001), the New Jersey officer was supported by state criminal justice guidelines that specifically afforded him that right. In the *City of Manchester and Manchester Police Patrolmen's Association* (1995), an arbitrator delivered a similar ruling requiring management to delay an employee interview until a labor representative was present whenever the employee "reasonably believes" that disciplinary action might be taken. The fact that management chooses to characterize an interview as "non-disciplinary" is not the controlling factor for failure to provide representation. In New York, the courts have split decisions in this area. For example, in *May v. Shaw* (1977), a trial judge found that an officer was deprived of due process rights when an interview proceeded without the assistance of counsel that was not available. In contrast, under the ruling of *Donofrio v. Hastings* (1976), an appellate panel in a 3 to 2 decision ruled that there was no right to an attorney during the interrogation process even though a collectively bargained agreement granted that right. These rights extend beyond internal investigations and attach even when external bodies are conducting an investigation. This was apparent in the decision of *NASA v.*

National Labor Relations Authority (1979), wherein the Supreme Court held that a federal employee who is a member of a bargaining unit is entitled to the presence of his union representative at an interview conducted by the Office of Inspector General, even though the OIG is not a part of the management hierarchy, discipline could result from the interview (Americans for Effective Law Enforcement, 2005).

An additional note with respect to right to counsel in compelled interviews is that they are afforded in many states. In the decision of *Nichols v. Baltimore Police Department* (1983), the lawyer is entitled to object and consult with the client (Americans for Effective Law Enforcement, 2005). This would be consistent with the rules that apply in states that allow such representation. The internal investigator should respect this right while also controlling the interview. The attorney may object and clarify issues, but may not unduly interrupt the proceedings or prevent the interview from continuing to completion.

Preliminary interviews can be conducted when few facts are known to the internal investigator and no information exists at the time for the internal investigator to believe that any wrongdoing has occurred. These types of interviews are generally referred to as fact-finding interviews. Fact-finding interviews can be conducted if at the time of the interview, the officer was not believed to be the subject or target of an investigation. In addition, the information known prior to the interview could not potentially lead to discipline. One example of such informal interviews is found in the Illinois Supreme Court decision in *Ehlers v. Jackson County* (1998), wherein the Court upheld the termination of a sergeant who refused to speak with the sheriff without her union representative present. The Court concluded that the protections of *Weingarten* were not applicable because the interview was "informal" and non-disciplinary (Americans for Effective Law Enforcement, 2005). The interview should end if the status changes such as through an admission of some violation of policy or law. The interviewee should then be offered the opportunity for legal or union representation. The interviewee can knowingly and voluntarily waive his or her legal rights to representation. This should be gained in writing from the interviewee. In addition, these types of hearings are civil in nature and compliance with strict technical rules may not be as strict as exercised in criminal proceedings. The internal investigator and administrator must consider the exclusionary rule or the "Fruits of the Poisonous Tree" doctrine when developing the investigative strategy for any specific case. Following the stricter rules should ensure the admissibility of evidence in these types of proceedings.

Figure 7-7. The fact-finding interview can be conducted by the internal investigator when the information known cannot potentially lead to a disciplinary situation involving the employee being interviewed (Photo courtesy of the Brockport, New York Police Department).

As an example of this, the general rule is afforded through the example of a police-involved shooting. An officer radios that he has been involved in a shooting. The first responding supervisor arrives and walks directly to the officer, and through a fact-finding interview asks, "What happened?" The officer admits at the outset that he didn't see a weapon when he fired at the suspect. At this point, there is a potential for culpability on the officer's behalf in violating policy. The interview must then end and the officer's rights afforded. Any further interviewing would most likely result in the statement being excluded at a criminal trial and subsequent departmental hearing.

In alternate circumstances to the same scenario, the supervisor arrives at the scene, and while walking towards to subject officer, the supervisor is approached by an independent witness who states that the suspect did not have a gun. Since the officer may now become the target or subject of discipline, the officer's rights must be afforded at the outset and prior to any interview taking place.

The tipping point in these scenarios is the knowledge the supervisor had prior to contact with the involved officer. The supervisor must be able to justify their knowledge and actions at a legal and/or administrative proceeding if any admissions or statements of the involved officer are to be introduced.

REFERENCE MATERIALS

The value of a reference library in the internal investigations process cannot be understated. In criminal investigations, crime reports, intelligence files, criminal records, and the like are the primary sources for investigation. The internal investigator must have an extensive and interdisciplinary library that addresses the legal, procedural, civil, training standards, and psychological issues of investigation just to name a few of the sources that may be pertinent to a case.

The internal investigations unit commander or law enforcement administrator should authorize the development and maintenance of such a library. The use of contemporary computer programs in cataloging resources should also be available to the investigator for ease of access to reference materials. Departmental policy should not be the sole source for determining the outcome of a case. Several flaws exist in this methodology including outdated policy, contemporary thought in the field, and the advanced knowledge or practices of the employee are but a few of the issues to be considered in a case investigation and review.

Access to the Internet and electronic libraries for peer-reviewed and professional journals should also be provided to the internal investigations unit. These are excellent tools in the research process and are timely in developing the needed research information. The electronic libraries should be augmented by textbooks and hard copy articles categorized by topic such as use-of-force, deadly physical force deployment, legal issues, etc.

There are other references that will prove to be invaluable in the internal investigation process. For department-based materials there are rules, regulations, policy, and general orders as well as in-house training programs, specialized unit manuals, and the like. Discipline-based materials are those of the law enforcement discipline such as national and local standards for policy, procedure, force training and continuums, also just to name a few.

Empirical records are numbers based such as crime statistics, use-of-force records, early intervention systems records, and others. These records will assist in demonstrating the department's records for such incidents as well as the target officer's comparison to accepted threshold-type standards.

The last resource is to historical records. Historical records are those of department policy or legal changes that were in effect at the time of the incident, not allegation. Copious records of policy, procedural, and legal changes should be kept in chronological order so that the internal investigator can apply the appropriate and not retroactive standard to the findings of the investigation. This would also apply to such reference materials as criminal records or intelligence information that is germane to the case. For example, an officer is accused of unjustly harassing the complainant due to a field stop in a high crime area such as burglaries. The officer may have knowledge that the individual is a career burglar or the criminal/intelligence record of the complainant may prove this. These materials should be attached to the case file as evidence that the officer was justified in the basis for the stop.

Figure 7-8. A police supervisor interviewing an independent witness located during a neighborhood canvass (Photo courtesy of the Brockport, New York Police Department).

NEIGHBORHOOD CANVASS

The neighborhood canvass is as much a part of the internal investigation as it is a part of the criminal investigation. This will prove to be one of the more important tasks performed and is far more extensive than the investigation of a crime in many cases. This task should be mandated in every internal investigation where there exists a potential for locating witnesses. If the area is remote or the incident occurred out of the view of the public, then this fact should be clearly documented in the investigative report.

The internal investigator should consider a neighborhood check during the times the incident occurred and similar days of the week in order to attempt to identify those who had business in the area, and those who were at home or present during the time of the incident. An effort should also be made to identify other occupants of a residence who may have been present during the time of the incident and a potential witness. This should also be documented in the investigative report and a follow-up should be done in an effort to locate any subjects who may have been present, but not yet interviewed. If the internal investigator receives no response at a location, a business card with the case number written on it should be left for the occupants and this effort also documented in the investigative report.

The internal investigator will also find subjects who purport to know nothing or are uncooperative with the investigator. The names and statements of uncooperative witnesses who say they saw nothing or refuse to cooperate should be documented to refute any later unanticipated testimony. Documenting these statements will help to insulate the department and officer from manufactured statements brought out after the incident has occurred (Mayer & Coble, 1998).

CASE NOTES/INVESTIGATIVE ACTION

The internal investigator will be involved in ongoing development of information in the case and must use a method of documenting the information developed. There are two recommended methods that the investigator can use beyond that of making notebook entries that later lead to the final report. The follow-up and information developed during the evolution of the case should be a separate report or reports from the final summary report that is discussed later in the text. Those methods are Case Notes and an Investigative Action Report.

Case Notes: Case notes are individually written reports of all investigative activities as the case progresses. They are completed and submitted as part of the case file contemporaneously to the actions taken. This methodology of investigative documentation has an advantage of being submitted in a timely manner, however, can become extremely cumbersome in the process. Each individual report will need to be referred to in the final case summary and each should be a separate attachment or appendix to the final case package.

Investigative Action Report: The internal investigator may also choose to document all investigative follow-up activities in one administrative report/intra-departmental correspondence directed to the case file. This type of report is an account of all case follow-up activities and the results, including the neighborhood canvass, evidence recovery and processing, activities such as attempts to contact witnesses, the documentation of relevant dates and activities that may be relevant to the case but not to the final summary analysis. This type of report is easy to produce as a computer or Microsoft Word document template. The report can then be saved under new case file numbers and completed as the investigation progresses. This allows for consistent and contemporaneous documentation as well as one final report that is an appendix or attachment to refer to in the final case summary. An example of this is provided in Appendix A.

These reports should be completed on an administrative form and not a public document such as a department general report or incident report in order to protect the confidentiality of the findings of the investigation.

CASE INVESTIGATIVE FINDINGS

The next section discusses the issue of case investigative findings, not from the identified definitions such as exonerated and unfounded, but from the level of evidence, the discretionary powers of police officers, and the inclusion of exculpatory evidence in the internal investigation case file.

The Preponderance of the Evidence Standard

The preponderance of the evidence is the standard in civil cases that is applied to the level of proof required in internal investigations. Understanding that there is a difference between local, state, and federal standards is an issue. While departments can hold employees to a higher standard than those of local, state, or federal laws, even the United States Supreme Court understands the inexact science of policing and allows for latitude in its decision-making processes in police events. The Court often applies the "totality of the circumstances test" to its decisions in order to develop a fair and just decision that follows both the spirit and letter of the law

(Holcomb, 2002; Hopper, 2004; Makholm, 2000b).

While policy may have an impact on liability, the standards are set in state and federal courts for ultimate liability. For example, in an incident of deadly physical force, if the shooting falls outside of a department's use-of-force policy, this doesn't mean that the shooting was unconstitutional, especially where the policy is more restrictive than the governing legal standards. In response, the federal circuit courts addressing the issue have widely rejected efforts to establish constitutional liability through violations of department policy as decided in the cases of *Drewitt v. Platt* (1993), *Ramirez v. Ahn* (1988), *Gravely v. Madden* (1998), *Soller v. Moore* (1996), *Edwards v. Baer* (1988), *Wilson v. Meeks* (1995), and *Ensley v. Soper* (1998) (MacLatchie, 2000). As such, departments should consider using the Constitutional standards in applying rules and orders keeping in mind that state standards and department policies fall second and not primary to this concept.

Police Discretion

In keeping with the previous thoughts, policy and procedure should be considered as guides and not ultimate edicts to operational decisions. An important turning point in the discussion so far is to fully understand the concept of police discretion. Case findings need to be based upon a multitude of factors, including the officer's discretionary powers. The highest court in the land has agreed with this concept as expressed by Chief Justice Warren Burger who stated, "The officer working the beat makes more decisions and exercises broader discretion affecting the daily lives of people everyday and to a greater extent than a judge will exercise in a week" (Strong, 2004). Police administrators champion the position of accountability and responsibility on behalf of line personnel, however, this level of answerability most often brings with it an unrealistic expectation of perfection in all law enforcement actions.

There is an immense difference between fact and supposition and between policy and humanity (Colaprete, 2003). Absent computerized robots answering calls for service, the standards set may at times be far too high to reach. Standards that are unachievable will always bring disappointment to all involved. There are also times when, because law enforcement officers are only human, they will make mistakes, wherein organizations must not cover up, but may have to admit the mistake and apologize to the aggrieved party and the public (Daily, 1998).

The internal investigator and administrator must think in terms of the profound wisdom in the following statements. Dr. Ellen Kirschman (1998) notes that, "It is almost impossible to perform work with such high consequences and avoid doing something that someone thinks is wrong. It is impossible to work as a cop and avoid getting disciplined" (p. 134). Martin J. Mayer and Paul R. Coble (1998) also note with respect to the most controversial and volatile police actions, the use-of-force that, "The truth of the matter is that most actions taken by officers are done for the right reasons and in the right way. Most police shootings are legally and morally justified. Most uses of force are proper" (p. 8). These notions seem to somehow get lost when comparing law enforcement actions to strict and frequently unachievable standards. In the issue of police discretion, humanity must not be lost in a sea of policy.

Thorough Investigations and Exculpatory Information

An internal investigation is not complete unless all investigative tasks have been accomplished. This also means that all discovered information should be included, including all information that is exculpatory in nature for the officer. Information that clears the officer should also be included if found.

The internal investigator is responsible to all parties of the investigation, including the subject or target of the investigation. The redacting of exculpatory witness statements, collection of evidence that is not introduced, or other aspects such as germane factors of a complainant's criminal record or history that are excluded from the investigation all tear away at the very foundation of a thorough and unbiased investigative process.

An example of this would be a complainant who alleges they were "pistol-whipped" during their arrest. The officer's service weapon is collected as evidence at the scene and sent to an evidence laboratory for processing. As a result, the lab report returns revealing no obvious or trace evidence, or, trace evidence has been found, but not analyzed. This may or may not indicate that the complainant was struck, but is relevant to the case and must be presented and fully explained for the final review. Nothing damages the credibility of the internal investigations process more than only including facts that indict the subject employee while ignoring those pieces of information that would prove his or her innocence (Thurnauer, 2002).

ANONYMOUS COMPLAINTS

The issue of the validity and investigative responsibilities of law enforcement organizations is one of considerable debate. Should or shouldn't a law enforcement organization be responsible to investigate anonymous complaints? The answer rests in four considerations: (1) the level of responsiveness to the community that the organization has made or is otherwise mandated through such issues as federal oversight, (2) the level and severity of complaint as well as the complaint history of the identified officer, if applicable, (3) guidance from the courts in criminal case law, and (4) case-by-case evaluation. Each is addressed separately below:

Responsiveness: A law enforcement organization may enact a strict policy of investigating all complaints, no matter the source or validity. This may also be part and parcel to a commitment to responsiveness or a mandate of community or federal oversight in extreme cases. This policy leaves no discretion to the police administrator and dependent upon the number of anonymous complaints received on an annual basis, may be an unworkable or unrealistic expectation of the organization. An even deeper issue needs to be considered with the level of credibility when a complainant refuses to identify themselves or come forward to swear to the validity of the complaint.

Severity and History: Severity of the complaint is a better barometer for the decision-making process in anonymous complaint investigation. Complaints of excessive force and allegations of crimes deserve far more attention than that of an anonymous complaint of discourtesy. Another consideration is if a specific law enforcement officer is identified and the officer has a history of aberrant or questionable behavior. This type of anonymous complaint may also warrant further investigation.

Criminal Case Law: The criminal case law is another resource for determining whether or not a complaint investigation should be initiated in an anonymous complaint. The organization can look to the courts for some guidance in the levels of evidence required in such cases. For example, in *Florida v. J.L.* (2000), the United States Supreme Court held that an anonymous tip that a person is carrying a gun is not, without more, sufficient to justify a stop and frisk of that person. In a contrasting decision, in *Terry v. Ohio* (1968), an officer must have a reasonable suspicion that a suspect is engaged in criminal activity and may be armed and dangerous. Whether a suspicion is reasonable depends upon both the content of the information possessed by the officer and its reliability. In *U.S. v. Valentine* (2000) and *U.S. v. Thomas* (2000), which both involved face-to-face anonymous tips, the courts found sufficient indicia of reliability where the informants approached the police and where the suspects acted suspiciously when approached. Valentine indicates that when an informant places his anonymity at risk, it tends to increase his reliability, even if the police make no efforts to obtain enough identifying information to hold the informant accountable (Reak, 2001).

These decisions provide some guidance as to the opinions of the courts in these matters and companion guidance in the issue of anonymous complaints to law enforcement organizations with respect to the actions of their personnel.

Case-by-Case Evaluation: Case-by-case evaluations are also an option for the organization to exercise in anonymous complaint investigation. This option at the outset provides an immense amount of latitude to the agency. This also brings with it some problems as the organization must identify which investigations will be conducted, which will not, and have to justify the difference. An additional issue is that when any action is taken it may be precedent setting and thus every subsequent similar case may need to be addressed in the same manner.

Regardless of which system of selection that is chosen, a system should be in place for handling these types of complaints. The organization should also make a part of policy that the complaints can be received in many ways such as by mail, telephone, and the Internet. The most workable rule absent a departmental policy is to consider the level of severity of the complaint and to conduct an incident review/administrative/precautionary investigation into at least the most serious anonymous complaints.

DEALING WITH FALSE COMPLAINTS

Another issue that causes immense controversy in the ranks and with the community is the issue of dealing with false complaints filed against law enforcement personnel. Even when a law enforcement officer is vindicated in the internal investigation, there still exists a level of desire to have the complainant prosecuted for filing the false complaint. The courts, police administrators, unions, and line personnel are all divided on this issue and the resolution lies with the opinion of the local courts in the jurisdiction where the criminal prosecution would take place. If the local courts are unwilling or case law precedents preclude criminal action, then the point is academic when brought for further discussion. The agency, aggrieved officer, and collective bargaining unit may explore options of civil sanctions against false complaints of citizens.

With respect to resolving the internal investigation, one avenue of investigation of potentially false complaints is offering the complainant the opportunity to voluntarily take a polygraph examination (Thurnauer, 2002). While the polygraph cannot be introduced in criminal court proceedings, if the complainant admits to the lie, the admission or confession can be introduced as evidence to support the criminal case. The internal investigator can also introduce evidence of a refusal to take the polygraph or failure to meet a scheduled polygraph appointment in the internal investigation package.

Figure 7-9. False complaints of stolen property, excessive force, and discourtesy are the bane of many police departments throughout the world (Photo courtesy of the Brockport, New York Police Department).

There also must be some type of warning and criminal redress for making such a false statement. For example, in Section 210.45 of the *New York State Penal Law,* a provision is included for filing false statements which are usually in the form of the original complaint and statements such as supporting depositions and affidavits. The warning and sanction must be clearly written on the statement and the person signing the statement must be made aware of the sanctions for making a false statement.

The next requirement is that the finding of the case must clearly reach a level of evidence that equates to probable cause for arrest that demonstrates the complainant knowingly lied in their statement. In a case where the complaint is unfounded, such as an allegation that a complainant was subjected to excessive force and the officer and independent witnesses say otherwise, a case for the untruthful statement can be made. On the other hand, if the allegation is for excessive force and the officer is exonerated, or if the evidence in the complaint does not provide clarity in the actions and is disposed of as not sustained, then a criminal action could not be supported.

The final requirement is that the statutes, contemporary case law, judges, and prosecutors should all be consulted prior to making an arrest for this type of offense. These cases should have the approval of at least a district attorney and law enforcement administrator prior to making an arrest.

The internal investigator must immediately bring this information forward to the law enforcement administrator when discovered in an investigation. The law enforcement administrator must also demonstrate the fortitude to prosecute those cases that are appropriate and can be legally prosecuted when false allegations are made against the personnel of their agency. A paradox exists wherein a police administrator is willing and able to sanction a law enforcement officer for being untruthful, to include suspension, termination, and leaving a career in ruins, however, not sanction the same behavior on behalf of those who commit crimes against the organization's personnel.

SATELLITE/ANCILLARY ISSUES

Satellite and ancillary issues are those that are developed during the course of the internal investigation and not alleged as part of the original personnel complaint. An example may be an allegation of excessive force wherein the original complaint is exonerated, however, the law enforcement officer is found guilty of some minor and unrelated infraction. Satellite and ancillary issues should be severely limited to those of significance and have a relationship to the original complaint itself. Issues that are minor in nature and unrelated should be handled separate from the complaint and informally if they are a first-time offense or offender. The problem arises when satellite and ancillary issues are used as a means of disciplining an officer for an incident when no other evidence supports a sustained finding for misconduct. These are inappropriate tactics and weaken the integrity of the investigative process as well as the integrity of the internal investigator and law enforcement administrator.

This method of investigation should be used judiciously and not abused by the internal investigator and administrator. The internal investigator and law enforcement administrator should not mask or hide politics, opinions, grudges, and the lack of credible evidence in a sustained satellite or ancillary issue in an internal investigation. These tactics are transparent to not only the recipient, but the entire organization as a whole. The internal investigation must always be beyond reproach.

Figure 7-10. A police sergeant conducting a remedial training session (Photo courtesy of the Brockport, New York Police Department).

REMEDIAL TRAINING

During the investigative process, there will be occasions where the violation of organizational policy or procedure is clear and a sustained finding is imminent. In these cases, the supervisor conducting the investigation may find a prudent course of action in conducting a training or remedial training session in order to rectify the problem, minimize the damage to the involved personnel, and mitigate any future liability issues. This documentation should be included in the final case summary and package.

Training and remedial training are not considered discipline under such states statutes as the *New York State Civil Service Law.* Discipline defined, is some type of adverse action that affects a property right in a position such as pay (e.g., suspension or demotion) or officially designated discipline (e.g., Letter of Reprimand as opposed to a counseling or training memorandum). Therefore, if the actions of the employee were not in accordance with policy, procedure, or the law, then training or retraining will be necessary, regardless of any final discipline levied in the case. This proactive approach may however, minimize the need for disciplinary action.

When the completed investigation clearly determines that training/remedial training is needed, the supervisor or internal investigator should arrange to conduct the training or have a subject matter expert conduct the training such as a need for defensive driving, defensive tactics, or firearms training. An example is that an employee, during a use-of-force, improperly applies a leg restraint device such as the Hobble in an inappropriate manner, such as a "hog-tie." While the original force may be justified and the subject who received the force suffered no injuries, the employee would need to be retrained in the use of the Hobble because of the liability in the issue of positional asphyxia. This should be arranged by the investigating supervisor and included in the investigative package. This can also be documented on a separate departmental training or remedial training report rather than a formal memorandum of record or counseling memorandum.

IDENTIFYING DEPARTMENTAL POLICY AND TRAINING ISSUES

Case review may lead to not only the individual officer training needs, but larger issues of inadequate policy, procedure, and training on an organizational level. The case review should be an excellent opportunity to explore these issues if they surface and should become a catalyst for change in the organization. Identifying officer safety issues that may be cause for policy change or remedial training are: (1) verbal de-escalation, (2) ground fighting, (3) arrest control tactics, (4) firearms safety and proficiency, (5) defensive and pursuit driving, (6) use-of-force statutes and policies, (7) building search practices, (8) weapon retention, (9) less lethal force options, and (10) response to in-progress calls (Garner, 2002).

A comprehensive review process should also be in place to review all use-of-force/subject resistance reports regardless of the lodging of a complaint. A subject matter expert such as a defensive tactics instructor should review all submitted force packages in order to determine justification, tactics, and the quality of the documentation. This procedure should result in higher quality documentation along with a component of an early intervention system that identifies problems and patterns in force practices.

The review process can also work to protect the internal investigator and trainer in documenting problems that are revealed and management's actions or inaction. The internal investigator and department trainer must be willing to bring these issues forward in the organization in order to recommend positive change, or in the worst cases, protect themselves from individual liability when the organization fails to take appropriate or timely action to correct the discovered deficiencies. These protests can have a bearing in court as they tend to protect officers from individual liability, but inflict further liability on the agency and management for refusal to address weaknesses (Soto, 1998).

A collaborative and not competitive relationship should be developed between the organization's internal investigations unit, research unit, training unit, and legal counsel. For example, internal investigations units and firearms training units need to analyze shooting performance data in order to identify training needs and translate that to continued training program development (Morrison & Shave, 2002). These actions should also involve the training unit personnel, defensive tactics, and legal counsel in order to draft policy and lesson plans that withstand court scrutiny.

DOCUMENTING THE INVESTIGATION

Every internal investigation will require the strictest and highest standards of documentation in order for the case to be acceptable and credible. The form and format of the final summary are included later in the text as well as examples of the proper methodology for final case assembly. The documentation of the case should leave no question unanswered, no witness uninterviewed, and no evidence unrevealed. Every relevant piece of evidence and documentation should be included in the final package for presentation through the chain of command. The measure of case quality is in the agreement of the internal investigator's recommended findings by those of the organization, legal community, and the industry standards of measuring evidence and determining the appropriate disposition of the case.

SUMMARY

Charles E. O'Hara (1981) states that, "Investigation is an art and not a science; hence it must be discussed in terms of precepts and advice rather than laws and rigid theories. The element of intuition or felicity of inspiration in the choice of methods has its effect on the outcome despite the most methodical and exhausting treatment of a case. Then, too, there is the matter of chance which cannot be omitted from consideration" (p. 5). Internal investigation is an art, science, and attitude. While it is an art based upon the development of tacit skills and technique, a science based upon the evaluation and interpretation of evidence based upon legal and scientific standards, it is also a measure or proper attitude. The internal investigator must conduct the investigation without bias, grudge, animus, political, peer, or command influence. An internal investigation should be based solely upon the discovered information as measured against the standards of evidence that apply.

The key aspects of the internal investigation amount to some fundamental precepts: (1) investigator integrity, (2) case findings based upon facts and evidence, not conjecture, innuendo, or unqualified opinion as opinion-based evidence should be strictly limited to those of experts such as district attorneys, technical advisors, medical professionals, and the like, and (3) case quality should be measured by thoroughness, accuracy, and objectivity of findings. The level of work that is demonstrated in the case determines the amount of care and attention that has been paid to it by the internal investigator. When conducting any investigation, the internal investigator must proceed from the perspective of how they would want to be personally treated if they were the subject or target of the allegations. The internal investigator would most likely expect a standard of investigation that is thorough, fair, and with the utmost respect.

Chapter 8

INCIDENT INVESTIGATIONS: CRIMES AND USE-OF-FORCE

INTRODUCTION

This chapter discusses the investigative requirements surrounding the allegations of crimes in both the local/superior court levels as well as federal investigations. The chapter then leads to force investigations and pays particular attention to the varying degrees of force available and the investigative needs of each type when deployed by law enforcement personnel.

COLOR OF LAW INVESTIGATIONS

Because of the state level problems encountered in the administration of justice, the federal government was forced into a position of enacting federal laws that would supersede the states rights when injustices were reported or discovered in the state level criminal justice systems. As this issued applied to law enforcement, the United States Supreme Court in *U.S. v. Classic* (1941) defined action taken under the color of law as misuse of power, possessed by virtue of state or federal law, and made possible only because the wrongdoer is clothed with the authority of state or federal law (Gundy, 2003).

The most contemporary application is through 42 *United States Code* (U.S.C.) Section 1983 as the legal vehicle to investigate and prosecute those who act under "color of law" in depriving United States citizens of their civil rights. The most common types of police misconduct include excessive force, sexual assault, intentional false arrest, falsifying evidence, extortion, and other related offenses (Schafer, 2000).

These investigations are conducted and prosecuted by the Department of Justice (DOJ). The ratio of complaints to prosecutions is small. Approximately 74 percent of all civil rights investigations reported each year allege police misconduct. Of the 10,000 color of law complaints received by DOJ each year, approximately 30 officers are prosecuted (Schafer, 2000). The majority of complaints are handled by a preliminary review of the documentation on file with the agency that is related to the event complained about.

As previously stated, the authority is derived from 42 U.S.C. Section 1983, which is a federal statute that creates a right to sue any person who, acting under color of state law, deprives an individual of their constitutional rights (Means, 2004). Also included in Title 18 of the U.S.C. are Sections 241, 242,

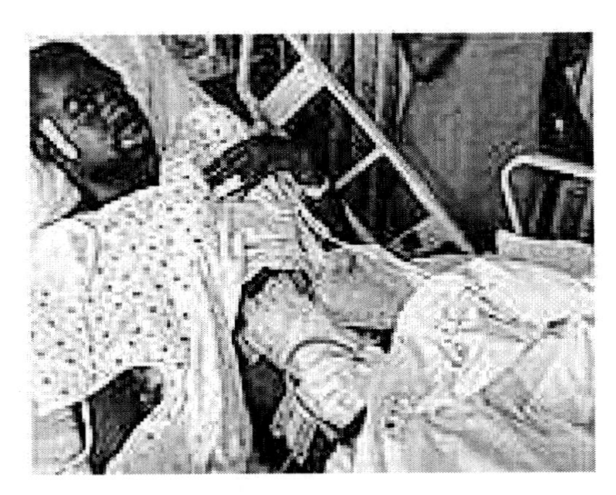

Figure 8-1. The Abner Louima case is an egregious example of a color of law violation by an on-duty police officer (CNN).

and 1001. Within those statutes are prohibitions against Deprivation of Rights Under Color of Law, Conspiracy Against Rights, Obstruction of Justice, and False Statements (Schafer, 2000). Several high profile cases have also demonstrated that law enforcement personnel can be prosecuted at both the state and federal levels for the same incident or offense. This is possible through the decisions in *United States v. Price* (1966) and *Screws v. United States* (1945), as a favorable decision in a state court does not bar federal prosecution based upon the legal principle of "double jeopardy" (Scuro, 2000a).

Most color of law investigations are initiated by a preliminary investigation that includes a paper review of the incident. If further investigation is warranted, then a substantial investigation takes place much like standard investigative protocol would require. One of the recommended strategies for avoiding color of law substantial investigations is to maintain high quality documentation of all events that fall under the categories of federal purview (Schafer, 2000).

Color of law investigations also are comprised of two categories: (1) criminal wrongdoing and (2) pattern-and-practice misconduct. In criminal cases the level of evidence must be beyond a reasonable doubt, while in civil cases, it is a preponderance of the evidence that prevails. In civil proceedings, a judge orders the police department to correct any deficiencies in their administrative, training, or policy procedures (Schafer, 2000).

As part of any federal criminal investigation, it is also highly probable that the agent assigned will contact the subjects for a verbal, taped, or written statement. It is at this point that *Brogan v. United States* (1998), as discussed in chapter 6 "Legal and Labor Issues," creates a critical if not radical change in the approach that an officer under investigation, as well as the attorney, must take when making any statement as to the circumstances of the incident with particular emphasis and concern for 18 U.S.C. 1001 consequences (Scuro, 2000a).

The law enforcement organization should cooperate with such investigations while also using the assistance of their own municipal counsel in order to liaison and guide the investigation in as much as possible.

CRIMINAL INVESTIGATIONS

Criminal investigations place the law enforcement organization in a precarious position with the method and process of investigation. The allegations of a police officer committing a crime are extremely serious in nature and deserve immediate and adequate attention. When these charges are founded, they all but obliterate the work of those ethically sound officers who serve the public in a manner that reflects the highest standards of law enforcement. One tragic case involved a New York State Trooper who falsified evidence in numerous criminal cases. New York State Trooper David L. Harding was convicted for falsifying fingerprint evidence in four criminal cases. The judge in the case, Betty D. Friedlander of Tompkins County Court, accused the investigator, of "willfully destroying or attempting to destroy public confidence in the criminal justice system" (Copyright 1992 by the *New York Times* Company. Reprinted with permission). Cases such as these exemplify the need to act swiftly and judiciously in the investigation and proper disposition of these matters in order to restore confidence in the police service. In addition, because of the *Garrity* ruling, the investigations must be completely separate and distinct so that any allegations of the violation of rights or impropriety can be defended by the internal investigator and organization.

When an allegation of a crime is to be investigated, two separate investigations must commence. The criminal investigation can proceed and information developed by the criminal investigators can be immediately and completely shared with the internal investigators contemporaneously to its discovery. Therefore, the criminal investigation should proceed without interference and information gained should be communicated to the separate internal investigator also assigned to conduct the administrative investigation. During the criminal investigation, the law enforcement officer must be afforded all of the same rights that an accused suspect or criminal would enjoy. A violation of these rights will most likely result in the exclusion of the evidence obtained at that stage of the investigation. The law enforcement officer can also exercise their Fifth and Sixth Amendments rights against self-incrimination (*Miranda* rights) and the assistance of counsel. In the criminal realm, these rights are inalienable and the law enforcement officer as well, cannot be forced to waive them. This may also be an area of civil liability for the criminal investigator if they violate these rights.

Once the law enforcement officer is interviewed, or refuses to give a statement, at this point the internal investigator can enter the investigation and proceed with the administrative investigative steps. The internal investigator should then conduct the administrative interview under the *Garrity* warnings and the provisions of *Weingarten* and take a separate statement. This is to ensure that if the criminal case is lost due to a technicality or favorable verdict from the judge or jury, the internal disciplinary action can proceed based upon the weight of the statement taken during the administrative interview. The reason for the second and compelled statement is that a hearing administrator, superior court, or appellate court judge may rule that if the statement was excluded in the criminal trial, it may be excluded from the internal disciplinary proceeding. In taking these precautions, the information developed and the statement taken for any criminal investigation is less likely to be challenged if it can be definitively shown that it was developed prior to the compelled internal interview.

Figure 8-2. Former NYPD officer Justin Volpe was investigated both criminally and internally for the torture of Abner Louima (CNN).

USE-OF-FORCE

The use of physical force is one of the most studied areas in law enforcement. Researchers, experts, and practitioners alike have examined the topic from a multitude of viewpoints from tactics, to effectiveness, to the medical and trauma issues. This section discusses the investigative perspective of a use-of-force along with the training and policy implications. The section further discusses the various methods of force deployment and investigative considerations for the internal investigator.

The United States Supreme Court has held that the proper response to potential and actual violence is for the government to ensure adequate police presence and to arrest those who actually engage in such conduct (Rohr, 2001). In addition, the Court has also held that "the right to make an arrest or investigatory stop necessarily carries with it the right to use some degree of physical coercion or threat thereof to effect it" (Milazzo, 1998). The use-of-force must also be justified from the individual officer's perspective and not the perspective of other officers involved (Chudwin, 1999). In using force, officers are often observed by citizens as they take defensive actions which are perceived as aggressive actions (Mueck, 1999). In addition, the largest lawsuit settlements are related to high-speed police pursuits, police involved shootings, and incidents that relate to use-of-force (Hill, 2003). In order to clarify the legal issues involved in use-of-force deployment Judge Emery Plitt, Jr. has developed the concept of ten legal truths concerning justified use-of-force:

1. There is no legal duty to retreat before using force.
2. The use-of-force is not inherently suspect or unlawful.
3. The use of deadly force is not limited to any particular list of tactics and /or weapons to the exclusion of others.
4. Roadblocks and ramming are the use-of-force, possibly even deadly force.
5. No court has ever banned outright any specific technique, tactic, or weapon.
6. What an officer learns about a suspect or situation after force is used may never be used to justify the force.
7. An officer need not see a weapon first before using force.
8. An officer need not be attacked first before force is used.
9. The force used does not have to be the best alternative for resolving the situation, only a reasonable one.
10. Prior uses of force by an officer do not necessarily make his or her later uses of force improper. (Massine, 2002, p. 45)

Generally, an officer's use-of-force is judged according to the circumstances existing at the moment the force was used (Spector, 2002b). However, most officers struggle with the legal justification as well as the available force options in making an arrest (Baratta, 1998). Officers will also be inhibited by concerns of civil litigation and hesitate in taking the proper action in an arrest (Stevens, 2001). When force is used, most often the question will be concerning the justification for the force. All lawful force is reactive in nature (Nowicki, 2001f). Unfortunately, there will always exist a perception of excessive force in police actions to overcome resistance. *Black's Law Dictionary* defines excessive force as, "Force which is not justified based upon the totality of the circumstances known to the officer at the time" (G. T. Williams, 2003b). The International Association of Chiefs of Police (IACP) defines the term excessive force as, "the application of an amount and/or frequency of force greater than what is required to compel compliance from a willing or unwilling subject." In addition, a national study by the IACP revealed that police do not use force in 99.966% of all incidents (Henriquez, 1999).

The study involved an extensive analysis of the types, variables, and demographics of force deployment in the United States. The study revealed that: (1) force was used only 4.9 times for every 10,000 responses to police calls for service, (2) major injuries as a result of use-of-force on subjects was very low, with female subjects at 2.1 percent and male subjects at 1.5 percent, and (3) 35 percent of reported confrontations were intra-racial (officers and subjects of different races), while 52 percent were inter-racial (officers and subjects of the same race) (International Association of Chiefs of Police, 1998b).

With the force standard being judged according to the circumstances existing at the moment the force was used, several high profile incidents in the country have, on the surface, appeared to be excessive, but later determined to be justified given the totality of the circumstances. For example, one interpretation of the Philadelphia case involved the belief that officers were responding to a dangerous situation and performing a duty mandated by the public. As such, through the officer's eyes, the "extra kicks" were a reasonable response to danger and were not intended as punishment (Westrick, 2000).

Many police use-of-force situations are sudden close contact situations that require immediate, instinctive response (Meyer, 2001). Another stark consideration is found in the belief that the only control officers have over anyone is what they are allowed to have (Papenfuhs, 2003). Use-of-force situations that may appear excessive or for an extended period of time may be attributed to numerous legitimate factors and not the use of excessive force. Offender skill, physical condition, and officer capacity are just a few of the variables that may affect the level and intensity of force needed to effect an offender's custody. Other considerations in force delivery deal with threat assessment such as ranges when considering a suspect attack. Based upon the Tueller Drill a suspect represents an imminent threat from up to 21 feet. Also of serious concern is that a suspect who sustains a wound can continue to be a lethal threat to an officer from much further distances (Borelli, 2001; Demetriou, 2002). There are myriad issues that determine the level, intensity, and justification for force deployment and each situation is not only unique, but must be judged from the specific circumstances involved. The internal investigator must be aware of the multitude of variables that can impact the level and intensity of force in order to properly evaluate the incident in question. Therefore, experts posit that the use-of-force should not be evaluated based upon properly delivered tactics, but rather, the tactics used and the type and duration of the force, based upon the totality of the circumstances known to the officer at the time the force was used as the law requires reasonableness in the officer's attempt to problem-solve, not the best answer to the problem (G. T. Williams, 2001a).

Use-of-force training models often operate in a vacuum. They are delivered in classroom environments that do not take into consideration the dynamic situations faced in practical force deployment situations in the field. Most use-of-force training is developed in and taught in ideal circumstances and needs to take into account that street level situations are not textbook or well-defined scenarios (Demetriou, 2002; Nowicki, 2000b). There is also inadequate attention paid to the aftermath of police force situations when training programs are developed and delivered to law enforcement officers (Chudwin, 1999).

One method of case review that is recommended for the internal investigator and administrator is outcome-based evaluation criteria of a use-of-force incident which recognizes that there is more than one way to solve a defense problem (G. T. Williams, 2001a). In essence, this is the concept of equifinality, which means that there is more than one acceptable way to reach a justified end. The internal investigator and administrator must maintain an open mind in investigating and evaluating the use-of-force as there exists numerous resources to consult such as departmental policy, defensive tactics standards, the legal justification based upon state and federal standards, the skill levels and condition of the suspect and officer, and the immense variation in defensive tactic deployment and effectiveness in and endless possibility of situations.

Policy and Training Considerations

This next section discusses both the policy and training issues involved in use-of-force deployment. The development of policy should emerge from a sound research base that is augmented by the expert opinions of defensive tactics and firearms staff, training unit, police administration, municipal counsel, and internal investigations. All of these entities should be involved as they all share responsibility in training, investigating, and defending the policy and practices of the law enforcement organization.

With respect to policy development in the issue of police use-of-force, the courts have not established specific guidelines for officers in regards to what level of force is appropriate for a specific situation which affords the law enforcement organization a great deal of discretion in the writing of policies and force continuum design models (Gundy, 2003). Sound policies use the language of the courts to guide officers in the use-of-force. By using the language of the courts, the officers' use-of-force is clearly definable and defensible (G. T. Williams, 1999c). However, policymaking should also be approached scientifically and should be grounded in empirically-based research rather than unqualified opinion or individual experiences (Meyer, 1999). To be effective, force policies should be brief, concise, be general enough to provide for limitless variations of attack and defense that

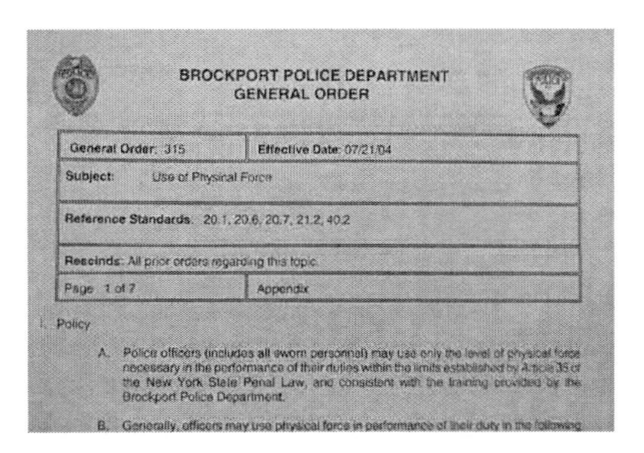

BROCKPORT POLICE DEPARTMENT
GENERAL ORDER

General Order: 315	Effective Date: 07/21/04
Subject: Use of Physical Force	
Reference Standards: 20.1, 20.6, 20.7, 21.2, 40.2	
Rescinds: All prior orders regarding this topic.	
Page 1 of 7	Appendix

I. Policy

A. Police officers (includes all sworn personnel) may use only the level of physical force necessary in the performance of their duties within the limits established by Article 35 of the New York State Penal Law, and consistent with the training provided by the Brockport Police Department.

B. Generally, officers may use physical force in performance of their duty in the following

Figure 8-3. Every department should have a policy in place that regulates the use of force as well as specific reporting procedures (Photo courtesy of the Brockport, New York Police Department).

officers face, yet be restrictive enough to meet court requirements for properly supervising officer behavior (G. T. Williams, 1999c).

Use-of-force policies should include two salient components: (1) they must be tactically sound and (2) they must be administratively sound (Grossi, 2002a). These components of a policy work together to protect the officer in their deployment of force in street encounters as well as protect the officer in administrative and legal proceedings when the officer was acting in good faith and in accordance with the letter and spirit of the policy. Policies should also not prescribe specific conditions and responses as they should be based upon the facts the officer knew at the time of the incident, the options available to the officer in responding to the threat, imminent danger to themselves or a third party, and the reasonableness of their actions (Weiss & Davis, 2002). The problem with policies and training usually emerges from advising and directing law enforcement officers of the proscribed conduct rather than the acceptable conduct in a use-of-force incident. Law enforcement officers need policy that identifies what tactics and instruments can be used so that they can be clear in their actions (Rosenbaum, 2001).

Great care should be exercised in policy development as they are often used against the law enforcement officer and organization in impending litigation. Policies are often written in such a restrictive manner that the law enforcement officer may be placed in a situation where every situation encountered results in some violation of policy. This becomes fodder for the plaintiff's attorney in a civil suit. Force policies should not micromanage or mandate certain techniques, tactics or defensive tactics systems as they offer officers two poor choices: (1) violate policy and hopefully survive unhurt through needed improvisation, or (2) risk injury using obligatory methods of control and defense in a situation the officer's policy and directed "techniques" failed to adequately address (G. T. Williams, 1999c).

Correct policy language should afford the law enforcement officer the options of force to resolve the situation faced while protecting themselves and their organization from unjustified or frivolous litigation and media scrutiny. For example, a force policy should include language in the following manner: "An officer may employ deadly force when he or she has a reasonable belief that his or her life, or that of another's, is in imminent danger of death or serious bodily injury based on the totality of circumstances known to the officer at the time" (G. T. Williams, 1999c).

From a policy perspective, use-of-force applications must be broad enough to allow officers to have reasonable options to use in the field, yet these options must be specific enough to provide parameters for officers to work within (Nowicki, 2001b).

A force policy should also include definitions of conditions, terms, and techniques in order to provide consistency and clarity of actions. For example, the term compliance is defined as a complete lack of physical resistance, a condition in which the suspect willingly moves in agreement with conditions and lawful orders, and is a function of obeying lawful orders and moving in a manner required by the officer, as reasonably perceived by the officer (G. T. Williams, 2003b). Another example of a term which should be included in a force policy is a contact weapon, which is defined as any object fabricated out of metal, wood, plastic, glass, wire or any other material capable of holding an edge, a point or rigidity that can be used to lacerate, puncture or otherwise inflict damage to the human body by physical contact (M. Williams, 2002). Providing for terms and definitions in policy development ensures a consistent language in deployment of tactics, documentation, and defense of justification in the legal and administrative arenas.

With respect to training issues in use-of-force, several barriers exist that are not limited in nature or scope. Barriers include resources, expertise, cognitive ability of the student, and sparse budgets are just to name a few. A noted problem is that defensive tactics skills are among the hardest skills to retain (Sanow, 2001a). In addition, because of such barriers as limited training opportunities, state mandates, and the highest liability considerations in deadly physical force deployment, force training is consistently being overshadowed by firearms training (Massine, 2002). Law enforcement organizations should make force training a significant priority in agencies because the probability of a lawsuit based upon the average arrest has a much higher propensity than that of a litigation based upon the use of deadly physical force, which for some agencies has been non-existent. As Rick Baratta (1999) profoundly states, "Not enough training time is spent on instant motor response" (p. 67).

Most training rules are also presumptuous as they are based on the officer taking the first action when in reality, it is the subject who most often takes the first action for which the officer has to respond. In addition, the opponent controls the confrontation as the officer is forced to react to the attack (Weiss & Dresser, 2000a). A paradox is faced when the officer is an aggressor and defender at the same time, protecting the subject from harm while trying to establish control (Sanow, 2001a). Defensive tactics trainers must also convey to trainees that most techniques learned in the classroom will most likely not work on highly motivated and skilled assailants as control holds have a very remote chance of success on dangerous individuals (Papenfuhs, 2000).

When developing training, the two factors that should determine the focus of training are: (1) the criticality of the task (Is it deadly?) and (2) the frequency of the task (Is this done often?) (Nowicki, 2004). The force triangle (ability/opportunity/jeopardy) should be a conceptual lesson plan to a force training model (Weiss & Davis, 2002). Use-of-force training should also focus on a few effective techniques that are easily retained and easily performed and training should be taught in a conceptual manner rather than in exact specifics (Nowicki, 2000b). Use-of-force training should be consistently delivered in small, workable units in training environments such as roll calls in order to keep the skills fresh and ingrain the techniques for use as second nature (Nowicki, 2004). All such training should be documented whether formal or informal and placed as a part of the law enforcement officer's personnel and training files for use in any later proceedings to defend the officer and the organization.

Greg Meyer (1999) states that, "Progressive law enforcement officials provide policy, training, equipment, tactics, and review processes designed to support legitimate use-of-force while reducing the number and severity of injuries to officers and suspects" (p. 29). In extending these concepts and issues to the internal investigation, the internal investigator must be familiar with force requirements and training in the agency to effectively investigate and provide an informed judgment in all use-of-force incidents.

Force Continuums and Matrices

Force continuums and matrices are guides for the internal investigator to work from when determining the justification for force deployment in an internal investigation. The force continuum or matrix can be developed in-house, or adopted from another agency or entity. The force continuum or matrix may also be included in the final internal investigation summary and package for reference by the reviewers in aiding in the recommended findings and final disposition of a case.

Thomas Aveni (2003b) presents the purpose of force continuums as a conceptualization tool used as a sort of:

> Graphical interface for unraveling the complex and inflammatory realm in which police are tasked with using force with requisite objective reasonableness. They almost universally reflect a logical and reasonable progression of force response to what are usually illogical manifestations of non-compliant and/or aggressive behavior. (p. 74)

Force continuums come in many variants such as: (1) linear designs, (2) modified linear designs, (3) non-linear designs, (4) wheel variants of non-linear designs, and (5) perception continuums (Aveni, 2003b). An example of a force continuum can be found in the Federal Law Enforcement Training Center (FLETC) force continuum or model that advocates placing resistive subjects into five categories: (1) Compliant Level, (2) Resistive (Passive) Level, (3) Resistive (Active) Level, (4) Assaultive (Bodily Harm) Level, and (5) Assaultive (Serious Bodily Harm or Death) Level (Nowicki, 2001b). The force continuum or matrix should be considered as a guide to actions and afford the user the latitude to make response decisions based upon the conduct of the aggressor rather than a strict steppingstone or gradient process of decision making in force deployment. The key consideration in continuum and matrix development is the delineation of options the officer is authorized by departmental policy and law to use (Rosenbaum, 2001).

Force continuums also bring with them many problems. Force continuums in a use-of-force policy carry a high potential for increased civil liability at a trial as many use-of-force incidents do not unfold in an ascending process. This provides the plaintiff's attorney with an opportunity to second-guess the defendant's use-of-force policy. Force continuums should be included in training, not policy. Workable models preclude escalation and de-escalation clauses as they should be written in accordance with the requirements of *Graham v. Connor* (1989) where an officer needs to respond reasonably to a suspect's resistance (G. T. Williams, 1999c). In addition, escalation and de-escalation are not recognized terms in a legal sense and should not be introduced into any subsequent testimony to a force incident (G. T. Williams, 2000).

The internal investigator must understand the difference between action and reaction, where officers are most often in reactionary modes in a use-of-force. Force continuums and matrices focus on interpreting subject action or intent and then "responding" appropriately. Officers interpret suspect actions in order to counter (respond) to the violence they are faced with (Westrick, 2000). From an investigative perspective, the perceptual continuum is recommended as it attempts to unravel what the officer perceived during an event, and at what stage of the event. Using this continuum, the suspect's actions that precipitated the officer's reactions can be evaluated factoring in the timeline of the officer's knowledge of the incident such as past history and emerging events (Aveni, 2003b).

Subject Considerations

One missed opportunity in most force investigations is the investigation of the subject's history. An important factor in the deployment of force is the law enforcement officer's previous knowledge of suspect background such as violent offender, or special skill level such as martial arts expertise. Special factors may exist that were not available to the officer at the time, but may provide guidance in the final case investigation and mitigating factors for the case disposition and any litigation.

The internal investigator should research such issues as suspect special skills, background, military, martial arts, street-fighting experience, criminal record, psychological history, alcohol and/or substance abuse, and domestic violence history. The fact that an officer did not have prior knowledge of the suspect's violent or aberrant behavior is not a preclusion for the suspect to demonstrate these behaviors in the arrest or control situation. In contrast, it is equally important to understand if the officer did have knowledge of the subject's special skills. This would be relevant when the officer knew that the subject was a champion boxer or martial artist and may reasonably believe that a higher level of initial force may be required because of the officer's lack of personal skills that may not match the subject's ability to resist or become violent.

Such an investigation should be limited to the factors that are germane to the case when considering offering the evidence as a mitigating factor. For example, an officer may have an encounter with a violently resisting suspect during a domestic violence arrest. A subsequent records check reveals that the suspect has a previous petit larceny conviction and no violent history. The inclusion of the petit larceny conviction in the investigative package would be inappropriate. If the record check revealed a history of violence and resisting

Figure 8-4. Subjects may have a special fighting skill or expertise that should be determined and not be overlooked when completing the internal investigation.

with the police or previous mental hygiene arrests for violent behavior, then these would be appropriate for inclusion in the case file.

Force Sustained by an Unintended Third Party

There are infrequent occasions when force is sustained by an unintended third party in an incident. These types of situations are usually low level such as in the use of chemical agents when arresting an individual in a public place or crowd situation, or active countermeasures with an impact instrument such as a PR24 in like situations. The most serious of these incidents and most often garnering the greatest media attention are the unintended victims of a police involved shooting.

The first consideration in the investigation is the reliance on the wording in the organization's force policy and training requirements. The internal investigator must be aware of the policy requirements for the use-of-force and how exactly a law enforcement officer was trained. The defensive tactics and firearms records should be researched with respect to judgment training. The computer training and simulation records should also be researched with respect to the scenarios provided and the officer's responses to the scenarios presented. This documentation should all be collected attached or included in the case file.

Prior to any final recommendation and disposition to the investigation, the legal and civil issues should also be reviewed. From the criminal perspective, cases such as the use of deadly force will most likely require review by a district attorney and possible presentation for grand jury decision. In civil proceedings, several case law precedents have been set that are favorable to law enforcement in these situations.

For unintended victims or third parties struck by a police bullet where the plaintiff is the unintended victim of police gunfire directed at a criminal suspect, there is no seizure within the meaning of the Fourth Amendment, and the victim's right to recover damages under Section 1983 requires liability be established, if at all, under the Fourteenth Amendment's substantive due process clause (MacLatchie, 2000).

In the context of force being used outside of a seizure such as when an officer unintentionally or accidentally strikes someone who is not being detained or arrested, the Court has relied upon the Fourteenth Amendment's substantive due process standard. The concept protects people from wanton and arbitrary governmental actions, therefore, the officer's actions must be malicious with the intent to harm an individual and must "shock the conscience" of the Court in order to be actionable (Newbold, 2002).

The final point in this issue is evidenced in the court's decision in *Elliot v. Leavitt* (1996), wherein the Fourth Circuit Court ruled that the number of shots by itself cannot be determinative as to whether the force used was reasonable, since the fact that multiple shots were fired does not suggest the officers shot mindlessly as much as it indicates that they sought to ensure elimination of a deadly threat (MacLatchie, 2000).

While these incidents are tragic, they are in essence, accidental in nature and must be treated as such despite the emotions they may draw from all involved, both in and outside of the organization. The internal investigator and administrator must proceed from the position of law and policy in the context of the incident rather than the emotional or political rhetoric that is not permitted in the legal review of the outcome of the law enforcement officer's actions. Furthermore, in the development of policy and training, both should not be formed to present insurmountable restrictions on officer actions. They should be aligned with the legal standards that will prevail in criminal and civil proceedings.

USE-OF-FORCE REPORTING PROCEDURES

The use-of-force reporting procedures are the foundation for any use-of-force justification as well as investigation. While great latitude may exist in reporting procedures, the fact remains that some reporting system must be in place for the monitoring of the actions of the officers in all force deployment situations, no matter how minor the force may be. As previously mentioned, force litigation is among the major threats facing law enforcement organizations in modern society. Law enforcement trainers, administrators, and internal investigators must work in concert to minimize these threats through proper policy development, training, and reporting procedures. This next section discusses report writing procedures, proper terminology and report contents, and the report review process.

Report Writing Procedures

The axiom of, "If it's not written down, it didn't occur" is on the lips of most police instructors when they deliver classes in report writing requirements. Somehow, this statement is lost when pen meets paper. The loss is due to many legitimate reasons such as a lack of training, loss of cognitive skills due to infrequent use, and limited resources such as an officer being limited in time to complete the report. Even in the most serious of incidents, one of the most neglected areas of lethal force training is the report-writing process (Nowicki, 2002a). These skills should be taught, refreshed, practiced, and when a use-of-force occurs, there should be ample time and support for the officer to properly complete the required reports.

With respect to training, more emphasis should be placed on teaching officers how to properly write comprehensive evidential statements to truthfully and properly justify their use-of-force (McBride, 2001; Nowicki, 2001a). This can be accomplished by formal in-service training and roll call training where examples can be provided on a consistent basis to refresh the skills taught and provide new skills as they emerge in the department's training portfolio.

With respect to reporting systems, several schools of thought exist from one report to multiple reports that document one incident. In developing a new system or reviewing a current system, comprehensiveness and simplicity should not be diametrically opposed concepts. Experts in the field suggest that the process include only a limited number of reports and forced responses to standardize the reporting procedure. For example, force should be reported on one form and not multiple forms. Multiple forms, short forms, and the like may create confusion and civil liability where there is none (G. T. Williams, 2000). In addition, use-of-force report forms should

Figure 8-5. A police supervisor reviewing a submitted police use of force report (Photo courtesy of the Brockport, New York Police Department).

be mostly check boxes and fill in the blanks and minimal room should exist for any narrative since the extensive narrative properly belongs in the incident report (Nowicki, 2001f).

Several additional factors will also impact how and what an officer documents in the documentation of the use-of-force. Jeff Chudwin (1999) speaks of officer survival in the aftermath of a use-of-force incident and recommends the following:

1. Limiting report and statements to the involved officer's actions and observations only. Recount information known to the officer at the time of the incident. The law does not require the officer to be factually correct, only reasonable in his or her belief. The involved officer should not engage in speculation or conjecture. Unless absolutely necessary, do not write or speak for another officer. The officer should write and speak about what they did and their perceptions based upon their five senses.
2. Officer should not estimate distance and time if they are uncertain or do not know. Experts and evidence technicians complete their own investigation and their informed findings should be used. The human mind does not capture events in life-threatening circumstances in ordered, real time sequence.
3. Officers should not attempt to write or verbally report detailed information until they have attained a normal heart rate and blood pressure. Officers who are forced to produce reports without sleep or the opportunity to reflect on the circumstances of their involvement will likely produce inadequate reports.
4. Officers should always have the assistance of knowledgeable and competent legal counsel. (p. 16)

The courts have also agreed and supported the concept that the officer involved in a use-of-force should have representation in the completion of such critical documents. For example, in the decision of *Long Beach Police Officer Association v. City of Long Beach* (1984), the trial judge held that officers may consult with union representatives or their attorney before completing a shooting report. A companion decision involved a federal court injunction in *Watson v. County of Riverside* (1997), wherein management was prevented from introducing a use-of-force incident report in the disciplinary hearing. Department superiors required the involved officer to complete the report without the presence of a union attorney and the Court placed these compelled reports in the same category as formalized internal investigations interviews. Contrasting case law also exists in the decision of *Ward v. City of Portland* (1988), wherein the court ruled that the chief may lawfully require police officers involved in fatal shootings to write incident reports before they have consulted with an association attorney as the City has a strong, compelling interest in obtaining prompt, accurate, and "unvarnished" reports of fatal shootings for training purposes (Americans for Effective Law Enforcement, 2005).

The internal investigator should be aware of the unworkable nature of some use-of-force policies and procedures that inhibit proper use-of-force reporting. Factoring in all of the physiological and psychological barriers to effective recall, compounded by administrative pressures to complete reports on duty rather than overtime, and an onerous reporting system may all factor into inconsistencies in the officer's account of the incident. The internal investigator should be prepared to objectively review the circumstances of the incident and the mitigating factors that accompany the reporting of a use-of-force.

Proper Terminology and Contents

Terminology is also a conundrum in force reporting. The French essayist Joseph Joubert stated, "Words, like glass, obscure when they do not aid vision" (Nowicki, 2001f). Use-of-force terminology can be confusing to defensive tactics experts, let alone officers who infrequently use techniques, and civilians who only understand inaccurate street or slang terms. This maligned parlance causes irreparable problems at all levels in the reporting and investigative processes. Terminology in report title such as use-of-force, subject resistance report, subject management report, force management report, level of resistance report are all important distinctions. Another unique title is Use of Control Report (Nowicki, 2001a).

The first concern in use-of-force reporting is documenting the officer's knowledge and fear levels contemporaneously to the application of force. The officer must justify their actions as well as the reasonableness of their actions. For example, using a baton strike as an active countermeasure requires that the officer articulate why the level of force was needed as well as the reasonableness of using the baton as opposed to other options available at the time of the incident such as chemical agents, hands-on techniques, proximity, threat level, and the like. The fear an officer felt based upon imminent threat cues must be clearly articulated in the use-of-force report for the internal investigation and subsequent courtroom testimony (Aveni, 2003a; Nowicki, 2001f).

The second concern is that the aggressor is the suspect and the officer engages in a defensive or control-type orientation. Terminology such as use-of-force should be changed to more accurately reflect this mindset. Use-of-force implies that the officer was the initiator rather than subject resistance report or subject management report that accurately depicts the nature of the contact. Officers respond rather than initiate force-related actions which necessitates a different orientation in how force-related incidents are reported. Therefore, the language of force must constantly change to more accurately describe an officer's behavior while using force. The words "use-of-force" convey a meaning that puts the burden upon the officer as the user of force and force is most often a reaction to a subject's behavior of resistance to the officer (Nowicki, 2002h).

The third concern is that the terminology must accurately reflect the intent of the technique. For example, many control techniques have no pain associated with them when used in a specific way. A pain compliance technique should be replaced with a control technique as the goal is not to cause pain but gain control (Nowicki, 2002h). Furthermore, most use-of-force techniques have some type of formal name for example: (1) a nerve pressure point penetration is not a gouge, (2) a heel strike is not a stomp, and (3) a baton can be used as a control tool rather than an impact instrument (Nowicki, 2002h). The internal investigator should have a visual reference guide for each technique that is taught and used in the organization. The examples can then be used in the interview of complainants, witnesses, and involved officers in accurately describing the incident and included in the investigative package.

Another problem in reporting is when a chemical agent is used in attempting to gain control of an aggressive subject. A person who is pepper sprayed is not contaminated; they have been sprayed with or exposed to pepper spray. The person will go through the process of post-exposure cleansing or post-exposure recovery (Nowicki, 2002h). All of the previous terms are not a matter of semantics, but more accurate descriptions of the nature of the cause and nature of force application.

Documenting the facts of the force application is incumbent upon the officer. Several factors of the force must be clearly documented for the internal investigator to make the proper assessment of the reasonableness and justification. The following is a list of components of the report that should be included for the officer to use and the internal investigator to use as a guide in investigating the application of force:

1. The basis for the response and all relevant actions that led to the use-of-force.
2. The reason force was used.
3. The progression and level of force applied. This should also include the effectiveness and ineffectiveness of techniques and the reason for any escalation of force.
4. The suspect's resistive actions, conduct, and verbal statements.
5. The specific warnings given by the officer and any verbal or physical responses to the warnings.

Figure 8-6. All contact and actions with the subject should be fully documented including transportation to a medical facility by police vehicle or ambulance dependent upon the subject's injury level (Photo courtesy of the Brockport, New York Police Department).

6. The specific identification of all active countermeasures and effectiveness/lack of effectiveness. The report should document a progression of action and reaction in chronological order of use.
7. The equipment used and whether the equipment was issued and/or approved for use by the officer.
8. The consistency/inconsistency with statutory and case law, department policy, and training. If an officer hasn't been trained in a specific technique they can't be held liable for its use.
9. Collect and include all involved officer and witness officer reports (e.g., Crime, Incident, Use-of-force, etc.).
10. The scene and subject should be photographed and relevant evidence collected. A scene diagram should also be included whenever possible.
11. Determine what medical attention was offered/rendered, the extent or lack of any injuries, and any previous injuries.

12. Uninvolved and involved witness statements should be completed and included in the investigative case package or file.
13. Any and all post-incident actions such as medical treatment, transportation for interview, transportation to a booking facility, etc.
14. Expert witness review should be considered such as a defensive tactics and firearms instructors as well as civil and criminal counsel for justification.

A law enforcement organization should also provide to its employees a list of trained and acceptable defensive tactics terms for use in the completion of the use-of-force report. A manual that provides photographic depictions of trained defensive tactics techniques would be an invaluable reference tool in completing use-of-force reports as well as an investigative reference for the internal investigator. Defensive tactics techniques can vary from agency to agency and instructor to instructor, so it is extremely important to have a standardized example of the acceptable and trained tactics in an agency.

A final note in the documentation of a use-of-force is the inclusion of any injuries sustained by the officer during the incident. Injuries to officers need to be specifically documented so that any later disabilities claims can be substantiated and protect the officer. This can also support the officer's need for escalation in applied responsive force, optional force tactics, and the level of fear experienced dependent upon the type and extensiveness of the injury.

The internal investigator is responsible to investigate, not make unqualified judgments. Investigation requires that the incident be clarified, not scrutinized. The internal investigator must explore the nature and justification for the force as well as the techniques and terminology. For instance, an officer may describe a technique in the documentation as the application of a clavical notch. The subject resistance report documents this technique. The internal investigator during the interview determines through physical reenactment that the technique was a mandibular angle. The officer was found to be mistaken in the terminology used, however, the application of the mandibular angle was the correct and reasonable technique for the situation. The internal investigator must clarify and justify the use-of-force in the investigation as despite the inaccurate description, the officer's actions were justified. The internal investigator must consider every aspect of the incident and the consideration must be the reasonableness of the force applied in the unique circumstances of the incident. This orientation is necessary to fairly and impartially evaluate a use-of-force scenario as only a fraction of the incidents will be definitive, or black and white as it were. Most often, the scenario will be a judgment call based upon the circumstances faced by the officer at the time and as such, must be considered in the light of the limited knowledge at the time of the incident, not the subsequent brilliant light of hindsight.

The Review Process

The review process for force incidents is primarily tasked to the first level of supervision in a law enforcement organization. This review must come from a trained and qualified reviewer as the process is the critical entry point for the incident into the system. Use-of-force should be treated as a significant incident and some level of investigation and review should take place when it occurs. The depth of the review should be based upon the nature of the force used. In addition, a nondisciplinary method of conveying the message to officers of the kinds of force that are appropriate to use in all situations should be a part of a continuous improvement process in the organization (Rosenbaum, 2001). This review should extend to the effectiveness or the lack of effectiveness of techniques used and correlate the training to this reality-based view of the actual incidents faced on the street (Nowicki, 2002e).

Reviewing supervisors should also ensure that use-of-force reports must be complete, accurate, and fully descriptive of the incident at hand, and written in a thorough and straightforward manner. Reviewing supervisors should also be able to quickly discern appropriate from questionable conduct to quickly investigate the discrepancy and avoid civil and criminal litigation (Harrison, 2001; Meyer, 1999; Meyer, 2001; Nowicki, 2001f).

Figure 8-7. The taser is an alternative to the use of deadly physical force only in limited situations (Photo courtesy of the Brockport, New York Police Department).

LESS LETHAL/NON-LETHAL DEPLOYMENT

The entire arena of less lethal and non lethal weapons deployment is one of great debate in law enforcement. The battle for law enforcement lies in the good faith effort to minimize the need for lethal force deployment that is fought with internal and external politics that vie against all police use-of-force. One truth is that law enforcement is tasked with the responsibility to protect society from those who are intent on imposing harm. In building that wall of protection, there will be a need to use force in some situations in order to maintain a level of safety for the remainder of society.

Another truth is that in this dichotomy of needs, less lethal and non-lethal force options may not be perfect, but they are viable alternatives to lethal force deployment. The internal investigator, administrator, legal entities, and the community need to be edified in the intent of these instruments and their unpredictability in the most dangerous and dynamic scenarios. Dr. Cynthia Bir (2002) brings a sensible understanding of the use of non-lethal instruments as she states that: "Both the law enforcement and military communities know that non-lethal is a goal, not a promise. A trade off exists between the risk of injury to the combatant and the risk to the community due to the behavior being controlled" (p. 94).

Sid Heal (2001) also sincerely speaks to this intent as he states that, "Less-lethal munitions are testaments to law enforcement's desire to keep peace and safety within its communities" (p. 88).

The use of less-lethal devices is a matter of consideration for every contemporary law enforcement organization. There are several issues of concern that the law enforcement administrator should consider. Some of these issues are the intent of the particular device selected and the mechanics of the device, such as operation and accuracy. Dr. Cynthia Bir (2002) speaks to the intent of kinetic energy devices as she states that: "Kinetic energy rounds are designed to cause a blunt impact to the subject at such a level as to inflict enough pain to deter the individual from the deviant behavior or delay an event to allow for more controlled intervention" (p. 96).

While kinetic energy devices have had successes, their accuracy and ineffectiveness are also an issue. Accurate ranges for a kinetic energy device are up to 75 feet, however, distances objects can be thrown by hostiles hard enough to cause injury is up to 180 feet based upon testing (American Society of Law Enforcement Training, 2003). So the deployer of the less-lethal device may have to enter a danger zone and compromise their personal safety in order to increase the effectiveness and accuracy of the device being used. This is important information for the internal investigation as effectiveness is contrasted by the increased risk factor of the officer which may wholly mitigate an allegation of arbitrary use.

Another area of consideration is the use of terminology in less-lethal force deployment. Impact weapons are generally considered intermediate weapons and are commonly referred to as less-than-lethal (Borrello, 1999). Terminology such as Scalable Effects Capabilities (SEC) are also used by the military to describe less-lethal devices (Bir, 2002). When a law enforcement organization decides to select and use terminology, it should be appropriate for use in the description of the methodology in the law enforcement, media, political, and legal realms. A significant part of the process is the defense of the tactic in all of these arenas.

Less-lethal devices have not evolved to a state of perfection. Several factors will impact the effect of the devices including environmental, human, and deployment issues. While the technology is still evolving, and some risks have been identified, options of less-than-lethal force must be demonstrated by a law enforcement organization (Hill, 2003). A National Institute of Justice study revealed that fatal impacts occurred in less than one percent of the deployments (Bir, 2002). Less-lethal, while an alternative to lethal force in many incidents, may still have unintentional and tragic outcomes as a result of deployment (Heal, 2001; Ijames, 1999). As such, severe or fatal outcomes as a result of a kinetic energy round deployment are critical to investigate (Bir, 2002). In consideration of the small percentage of fatal outcomes of less-lethal force deployment a poignant point is made by Jaime Cuadros (2002) concerning kinetic energy device deployment as he states that: "As tragic and regrettable as it is whenever an individual is injured or killed in a less-lethal encounter, it must be remembered that before the less-lethal alternative was available, these individuals would most almost certainly have been handled with lethal force" (p. 101).

There are also concerns voiced on behalf of officers who are placed in the position of having to make a choice in these tense and fast-evolving scenarios. For example, Chief Donald Dorsch (2001) argues that:

> Many situations that require the decision of whether to use less lethal or lethal force to be made can get an officer killed. . . . If a good officer uses all the training and other tools he has and must rely on his handgun, the burden squarely lies on the subject, not the officer. . . . It is getting to the point where all actions of the violator, no matter how irresponsible, reckless and disorderly, are the officer's problem and his responsibility. Officers are scapegoats; they are picked apart by the media and the public no matter what they do. (p. 102)

This is compounded by the issue of prospective civil liability when a substantial injury or death occurs and less-than-lethal options were available and not used nor considered (Newbold, 2002; Nowicki, 2001h).

Police trainers, administrators, and internal investigators should accept the fact that less lethal force options are one small piece of the problem-solving puzzle and should not be considered an end unto themselves (Ijames, 2002). While not always effective, less-lethal options continue to demonstrate merit in police encounters with violent offenders. Greg Meyer (1999) offers the reality of not considering or using less-lethal options as he states that:

> The aggressive use of available non-lethal weapons or relatively low levels of force to control resisting suspects early in deteriorating confrontations predictably results in fewer and less severe injuries to suspects and officers. The tactical alternative of prolonging confrontations often leads to more injurious–even deadly–degrees of force. (p. 27)

Research Methodology and Liability

Less lethal and non-lethal deployment options must be researched prior to use. There are numerous options available to departments that choose the available technology. Departments should research the available technology as compared to department needs and resources. Manufacturers will often have a research base, however, care must be exercised when using only the manufacturer's sales information to make a decision on product reliability and effectiveness. Each department is different and the individual needs such as budget, product utility, civil liability, and community acceptance are all issues to be considered when making the final decision. The internal investigator should have this research available for use in the internal investigation when these devices are used in order to adequately assess their justification for use and defense of the organization's decision to employ such tactics and equipment. The internal investigator should be aware of the legal and civil issues, research and selection issues, and the documentation of the use of less-lethal instruments and tactics.

The legal and civil issues are concerned with the justification for the use of less-lethal or non-lethal devices. The courts have thus far concluded that officers may use justifiable lethal force; however, at their discretion, officers may use less-lethal alternatives. The case law has been very clear that officers and their employer (local or state) shall not be liable where an officer-involved shooting is reasonable and justified. There is no court ruling requiring the use of less-lethal weapons. The ultimate goal is to protect the community and subdue the suspect with the least injury to police, bystanders, and the threatening person (Sifling-Aardema, 2000).

In the civil litigation side of this issue, Professor Darrell Ross of East Carolina University conducted a study of 4,000 published decisions on litigation involving use-of-force cases. He found that there are nine specific categories that most frequently arise in police training lawsuits. The highest litigated use-of-force issue was non-lethal force (including hands-on defensive tactics, handcuffing, use of baton, and aerosols). Lethal force was at number six on the list (Massine, 2002).

The irony of the above is that less-lethal alternatives are viewed as an opportunity rather than an obligation in some courts. For example, in *Plakas v. Drinski* (1994) decided in the Seventh Circuit Court, and *Roy v. Inhabitants of City of Lewiston* (1994) decided in the First Circuit Court, the plaintiffs alleged that officers were obligated to, "Use all feasible alternatives before ultimate resort to deadly force," and "the city had not adequately trained the officers in non-deadly alternatives for subduing dangerous but intoxicated persons." Summary judgment was granted on behalf of both agencies and upheld on appeal, with the courts summarizing, "there is no constitutional duty to use non-deadly alternatives first" (Ijames, 1999; MacLatchie, 2000; Sifling-Aardema, 2000). The Second and Ninth Circuit Courts also provided similar rulings in *Salim v. Proux* (1996) and *Scott v. Henrich* (1994) as well as *Martinez v. County of Los Angeles* (MacLatchie, 2000; Sifling-Aardema, 2000).

One case that provides some guidance in the decision to use less-lethal options is *Deorle v. Rutherford* (2001), which was decided in the Ninth Circuit Court of Appeals, wherein an emotionally disturbed person confronted officers, arming himself with several weapons and a bottle of lighter fluid. In addition, Deorle moved towards the officer at a steady and unhurried gait. The officer did not order Deorle to stop and he did not warn him that he would fire. As a result, the beanbag inadvertently veered off course and struck Deorle in the face causing multiple injuries. The Court's opinion directly addressed four critical points that were never thoroughly explored in previous decisions involving beanbag rounds as follows: (1) firing beanbag rounds at an unarmed suspect without first issuing a verbal warning constitutes excessive force, (2) Deorle was deemed as "unarmed" despite the fact that he was still holding a bottle of lighter fluid at the time, and despite his arming himself with numerous weapons during the standoff, (3) the practice of announcing "less-lethal" or a similar statement prior to firing is not considered sufficient warning to the suspect, and (4) the beanbag round "constitutes force that carries a significant risk of injury" (Hopper, 2001a). In essence, the Court ruled that the deployment of less-than-deadly force that may lead to injury should be preceded by a warning when feasible and a failure to provide that warning may result in significant civil liability. The Courts also require that a specific command with consequence be given such as "Drop the weapon or I'll shoot," or "Drop the weapon and get on the ground or I'll release the dog" (Lesh, 2003).

Concerns of civil litigation also emerge from administrators who believe that the use of less-than-lethal devices is precedent-setting and thus may create an undue burden on smaller agencies to acquire these technologies in spite of limited resources. For example, Chief Donald Dorsch (2001) argues that, "Another grave concern is the impending potential litigation for departments who do not have the resources to deploy less-lethal weapons while neighboring departments do" (p. 102).

With respect to research and selection, many departments have adopted less-lethal munitions without any realistic testing or any true understanding of their effectiveness (Sanow, 2001b). Therefore, the need to carefully select new technologies and equipment exists so that the agency can ensure there is a real benefit from deployment, or if the tool just consists of the latest new trend (Nowicki, 2001b). With this in mind, there are three main considerations when choosing a less-lethal weapon or projectile: (1) accuracy, (2) effectiveness, and (3) potential for causing death or serious physical injury. In choosing a specific less-lethal implement, the department should test products at the anticipated ranges of deployment, set acceptable standards, and accept only those instruments that meet those standards (Kester, 2002). The department should write requests for proposals (RFP's) based upon the recommendations of a committee of defensive tactics instructors, fire-arms instructors, subject matter experts, mu-nicipal counsel, internal investigations, and medical physicians in order to select the proper device and training regimen that will withstand internal investigation and court scrutiny.

This process must be recorded to later use in the internal investigation process and court defense of the selection and deployment philosophy. Chief Robert E. Cansler (1998) recommends a series of steps to follow in documenting research and limiting liability in the use of less lethal technology improvements as follows:

1. *Document Your Research:* Maintain a file containing references to all research performed prior to adopting the technology.
2. *Review Your Insurance Needs:* Obtain written opinions from your insurance carrier that the use of the technology you are implementing is covered by existing insurance.

3. *Adopt and Enforce Written Guidelines on Use:* Guidelines should be practically oriented. Submit any guidelines you write to your manufacturer or distributor and make sure they approve them in writing.
4. *Involve and Educate the Community:* Utilize the community policing concept to create buy-in to technology use and provide a forum for community input into the decisions of the organization.
5. *Use Manufacturer-Distributor Approved Training:* Use trainers who are certified by the manufacturer or distributor to conduct department train-the-trainer sessions. If an in-house training program will be developed, include in the contract a requirement for the manufacturer or distributor to work with the department to approve the training and provide real-time updates of emerging training developments and liability issues.
6. *Document Your Training:* Consider having at least one training session videotaped for the training file. Good attendance records and some form of competency testing can be very valuable in establishing the existence and scope of your training.
7. *Verify Results of Field Use:* Developing a track record of successful use without excessive injury can be vital to your defense when the unexpected does occur. (p. 53)

The research into a product's effective range and selection should be documented in the internal investigation summary report along with practical testing by subject matter experts. When deployed, the report should be included in the internal investigations package in order to defend the less-lethal choice and organization in a lawsuit.

Less-lethal and non-lethal will continue to be researched and tested because of the controversy and litigation that surrounds the use of deadly force. Because of this, Sid Heal (2001) states that: "In spite of the tragedies . . . less lethal options will continue to grow in popularity because the standard is not perfection. The standard is the alternative. The use of less-lethal options declares the dignity and reverence for human life and provides moral options in inherently amoral environments" (p. 93).

Terminology

Terminology is a matter of concern for all involved in a force deployment situation, from the defensive tactics instructors who teach techniques, to the officers who deploy the force, to the administrators who are vicariously liable for the use-of-force, and to the attorneys who defend the officers and agencies. Terminology is also an important aspect of communication to the community as terms should be understandable to the general population with minimal need for explanation. The force vernacular is a topic of intense discussion between force experts, police administrators, and the courts and a necessary part of the vocabulary of the internal investigator.

Terminology should be designed to be accurate and not politically correct. Legal settings do not recognize attempts at political prowess, only how the instrument is defined in the law. An example of this is demonstrated in the Court's decision in *Deorle v. Rutherford* (2001) mentioned earlier. In this decision, the Court described the beanbag as, "A euphemism that grossly underrates the dangerousness of the projectile that is not some sort of hackey-sack; it is a projectile capable of inflicting serious injury or death, rather than a child's toy" (Ijames, 2002).

The use of ambiguous terms only creates problems with the use of these devices; problems that relate to both political and civil liability. Therefore, the devices should not be characterized as "non-lethal" or "less-lethal" if they have the potential of inflicting serious or lethal injuries. The lethality of an impact weapon, pepper spray, or a stun device is determined by how it is used, not by the name given. Andrew Borello (2002a) proclaims, "Just because a baton is a weapon does not make it a liability-generating instrument of brutality. It is the malicious, unreasonable, or negligent use of the baton that causes problems" (p. 34). The application of indefinite names actually causes confusion and criticism should something occur that is inconsistent with what the name implies. For example, with kinetic energy devices, the label should suggest the injury potential inherent in the round as opposed to in how the round is used (Borrello, 2000; Ijames, 2002). A profound understanding of the injury potential of these types of devices is communicated through the statement, "Less-lethal does not mean non-lethal" (*Law and Order,* 2001b). In addition, Steve Ijames (2002) states that, "Calling a particular tool less than or non-lethal doesn't make it so. Labels are innocently attached, but they can generate unrealistic expectations concerning the potential injury outcomes. Impact projectiles are just that and they should be referred to accordingly" (p. 88).

In identifying such instruments, defensive tactics instructors and police administrators should work from the perspective of practicality and potential for end result. For example, policymakers and trainers should consider naming such instruments as "defensive weapons" or "intermediate weapons" to avoid politics and liability when the use of a less-lethal instrument inadvertently results in a death or serious injury (Borrello, 2000). Instruments should also be identified by their real name and purpose whenever possible in order to avoid confusion and additional liability. The law enforcement officer can describe a service weapon as a weapon, firearm, duty-weapon, or handgun without having to worry about the perception.

Some appropriate and unique alternatives in labeling such tools as the beanbag a "lethal-force option" as opposed to "less-lethal" may provide a clearer definition for use since the officer could use the option only when lethal force was justified (Nowicki, 2001b). This type of terminology provides a definitive understanding of the use of the device as opposed to a vague and politically correct term. Another option is renaming the use-of-force report as "levels of resistance report" (Nowicki, 2001f). A use-of-force report places the onus of aggression on the officer wherein most force is in response to a subject's aggressive actions. A subject resistance report or subject management report does not clearly identify what actions the subject engaged in to precipitate the force or the level of resistance. Departments may consider identifying varying levels of resistance as done in force matrices and apply these definitions to the level of resistance report in order to more clearly compile statistics and categorize the application of force in the agency.

The internal investigator should have a reference list of acceptable and trained terminology to use in the investigative process. These terms, even if confused by the officer who demonstrates the technique, as long as the technique was justified and properly deployed, should be used in the investigative summary in order to clarify the issues from an investigative perspective.

Impact Instruments

The police impact instrument, while standard issue with most agencies and having been a part of the uniform for over a century, is one of the most controversial of defensive weapons. The contemporary example of this was revealed through a study conducted by the International Association of Chiefs of Police that revealed the baton was used in only one percent of the force deployments during the evaluation period, however, it accounted for 11% of the total force complaints (Nowicki, 2001k; Sanow, 2001b).

Traditional use of the baton has been to control a suspect via pain compliance or by causing a structural injury. However, the baton may not be effective with those who have high resistance to pain due to intoxication, drug influence, or rage wherein many such individuals continue to fight despite broken bones or other severe injuries (Borello, 1999; Papenfuhs, 1999). This should be explored in the internal investigation through officer and witness statements of the reactions of the subject to the techniques used.

With respect to the legal issues in the use of batons against resistive suspects, the *Deorle v. Rutherford* (2001) ruling revealed that a warning prior to use may not be required for ordinary baton use (Lesh, 2003). Because of the legal, procedural, and political issues surrounding the use of the baton, a renewed emphasis on baton training should be undertaken by police departments (Sanow, 2001b).

Figure 8-8. The police baton is one of the most useful and controversial pieces of issued equipment because of the number of complaints generated by its proper and improper use (Photo courtesy of the Brockport, New York Police Department).

The evaluation of baton deployment in an internal investigation should be based upon training, recertifications, proficiency, availability, and appropriateness in the given situation. The baton as an issued piece of equipment should be available at all times to the officer. Many reasons exist for not having the baton available such as the need for an immediate foot chase from the vehicle, a situation encountered while on break, as well as many others. Liability may occur when an officer must resort to a higher level of force when the baton, due to controllable or uncontrollable reasons was not available and may have been a more appropriate and reasonable force option in the situation (Borello, 1999). Because an officer didn't have the option available may not be a determining factor in its use, for example, the baton may have not been available, however, due to a close quarters force application, the baton may not have been of practical use. The final evaluation of the use of an impact instrument should be based upon: (1) the level of resistance offered by the subject that necessitated the use of an impact instrument, (2) the reasonableness of the use of the impact instrument in the situation, and (3) if a reasonable officer would use the same level of force if placed in a similar situation (Borello, 1999).

Kinetic Energy Devices

Impact weapons testing was pioneered by the Army in the 1960s. Less-lethal devices are intended to incapacitate dangerous persons, and stop or reduce the behavior that justified their use. Impact weapons are designed to deliver non-penetrating contact energy from a safer distance than a police baton (Ijames, 2002). While controlling countless situations, they have also caused critical injuries and deaths as well. A handful of deaths have been documented in North America since their use in 1970. The most successful uses in policing have been related to their use in controlling or subduing deranged or suicidal persons (Ijames, 1999; Ijames, 2002). The purpose of impact munitions is to de-escalate potentially violent confrontations. Typically, these scenarios involve armed and non-compliant individuals and suicidal subjects. With current technology, the impact munitions are an excellent force option against a violator armed with a knife or other impact/contact weapon, or against the person intending to commit suicide by cop (*Law and Order,* 2001b).

The National Tactical Officers Association (NTOA) has conducted studies that have revealed that 61 percent of suspects engaged with less-lethal munitions are done so inside 21 feet, while 19 percent are engaged between 21 and 42 feet. Most beanbags have a safe distance of 21 feet (*Law and Order,* 2003c). Continued research in the law enforcement realm has revealed limited data concerning the effectiveness and appropriateness of use in specific situations. Imparted momentum defines a projectile's impact that can vary widely by cartridge and manufacturer (American Society for Law Enforcement Training, 2003). Reliable human effect data are all but non-existent for determining the amount of force required for impact munitions to be effective. In addition, accuracy also figures into deployment as practical experience shows, for a variety of reasons, just one out of six flat bags impacts the target properly. This results in the need for more than one kinetic energy device being deployed in situations requiring this level of force. Research has revealed that more than one beanbag has been fired in 65 percent of these scenarios (*Law and Order,* 2001b). The current research has revealed that no standards can be developed that would apply to the wide diversity of applied kinetic energy munitions (Heal, 2001).

With respect to the legal and civil issues involved in kinetic energy device deployment, the courts have offered some guidance to the legal designation of the level of force that the kinetic energy device is at in the force continuum. The United States Court of Appeals for the Ninth Circuit ruled that beanbags fall short of the standards for lethal force (Nowicki, 2001h). In addition, from a criminal and civil perspective, most manufacturers support the proper, reasonable, and justified use of their products in court actions (Borrello, 1999). In order to minimize the risk of liability, departments should implement policies that delineate: (1) the designation or dedication of weapons for the less-lethal munitions, (2) officers who are responsible for less-lethal deployment should load their own ammunition, (3) a back-up system with a lethal option in instances where the less-lethal option fails, and (4) the need for a verbal warning, when possible, to the suspect prior to firing (Hopper, 2001a). Additional measures to minimize the risk of liability are to dedicate weapons for such purposes through the use of brightly colored stocks as this will relieve confusion on behalf of other officers at a crisis site who may perceive a regular shotgun, loaded with kinetic energy munitions, as real and may present a situation of sympathetic fire (Ijames, 2002).

The justification for deployment will rest on a few considerations. Kinetic energy devices are considered as an "extended range baton" or "extended-range, impact munitions" (Heal, 2001; *Law and Order,* 2001b). As such they have both an effective maximum range and minimum safe usage range. There is also no device that can address every climate, range, or circumstance (Heal, 2001). The decision to use the kinetic energy device may also not be well-defined such as in a deadly threat situation. Impact projectile scenarios never involved such clear-cut imminent danger, and the impact projectile decision is not based on self-preservation, but on a variety of factors placed on a scale that balances the need to stop the suspect's behavior v. the acceptability of the potential injury (Ijames, 2002).

Several psychological, physiological, and environmental issues will also influence the effectiveness of the kinetic energy device. For example, the type (or lack) of clothing worn by the target individual will affect the damage to the skin. Other factors that affect the outcome are distance, point of aim, age, and the mental attitude of the target individual (e.g., drug-induced pain insensibility) (Cuadros, 2002). Steve Ijames (2002) states with respect to the justification for deployment that: "Impact rounds should generally be used when a baton strike is appropriate, but the situation is too dangerous to move into police baton range. . . . The rounds should not be limited to deadly force situations, as some agencies have done out of concern for past deaths" (p. 92).

The deployment should also be supervised if at all possible.

The internal investigator will need to investigate these incidents when the level of injury is severe or lethal or when a complaint is filed. The International Association of Chiefs of Police recommends those incidents that do not result in a hospital stay be investigated as a baton strike and not a shooting incident (*Law and Order,* 2001b). For investigative purposes, the internal investigator will need to know: (1) accuracy of the munitions, (2) acceptable and safe ranges of the munitions, (3) any results of testing, including accuracy in the department tests including comparisons to other munitions and the reason for selection, and (4) the training, if any, the deploying officer received as well as training given at the department level.

Chemical Agents

Chemical agents are a non-lethal force choice, used for individual and crowd situations (Nowicki, 2002f). Handheld aerosol subject restraints (ASR's or OC) have been in use in law enforcement for approximately 37 years (Cataldo, 2003). Some 97 percent of today's law enforcement personnel carry some form of ASR (Dallett, 2004; Nielsen, 2003a). Even as a non-lethal force option, the internal investigator needs an awareness of the legal, research, and procedural issues surrounding the use of chemical agents in subduing subjects.

Courts in different circuits have issued varying rulings on when the use of aerosol pepper spray is justified. Because of this, it is critical for department heads to ensure their policies comply with court rulings in their circuit (Orrick, 2004b). Policies must be consistent with the law and not overly restrictive of police actions. Cases have been decided in the Courts that have used policy as a factor in ruling against the department's otherwise appropriate actions. For example, in the United States Court of Appeals for the Ninth Circuit in California, a case was decided concerning the use of pepper spray against non-violent protestors. In *Headwaters Forest Defense, et al. v. Humboldt County, et al.* (2001), The Humboldt County Sheriff's Department had dealt with non-violent protestors on several occasions. An alternative to gaining compliance from the protestors was to place pepper spray on a Q-tip and place it on the eyes of the protestors. In reviewing the facts, the Court considered that: (1) no other jurisdiction had been found to use pepper spray on non-violent protestors, (2) the district attorney refused to affirmatively sanction the use of pepper spray in this situation, and (3) as a part of the Department's general orders, pepper spray was defined as a "defensive weapon for the protection of department members" and that it was meant to be used in cases where an officer was "attempting to subdue an attacker or a violently resisting suspect, or under other circumstances which under the law permit the lawful and necessary use-of-force, which is best accomplished by the use of a chemical agent" (Devanney, 2003). The divergent opinion of the Court's ruling has been realized in the use of pepper spray since this technique would constructively be acceptable given the circumstances that law enforcement was facing at the time of this incident (Makholm, 2002b). This is an excellent example of an internal investigation that would have its findings, in this case, exonerated, based upon the totality of the circumstances involved as well as no precedent-setting case in place prior to the incident.

Continued research has revealed that according to an International Association of Chiefs of Police study on use-of-force, the use of chemical force, primarily OC products, was greater than the combined totals for electronic, impact, and firearm force (Henriquez, 1999). Some specific agency research has also revealed that agencies like the City of Baltimore Police Department experienced a 53 percent decrease in use-of-force-related complaints during its pepper spray test period (Meyer, 1999). In addition, the use of OC has resulted in reduced injuries to officers and subjects, as well as a reduction in workmen's compensation claims (Nowicki, 2001e). Studies have also concluded that the use of pepper spray has no serious long-term medical effects on a suspect (Bragg, 2000; Reilly, 2003).

Research has also revealed the effectiveness and ineffectiveness of this non-lethal force option. For example, pepper spray is effective in 80–85 percent of the scenarios it is used in. In addition, the failure of pepper spray is usually attributable to improper application of the spray (Nowicki, 2001e; Orrick, 2004b). Pepper spray may also have a rate of failure that is as high as 50 percent (Reilly, 2003). Officers need to be cautioned that even the best pepper spray may not work against an emotionally disturbed person, highly goal-oriented individuals, or individuals under the influence of drugs or alcohol (Nielsen, 2003a; Orrick, 2004b).

For deployment purposes, pepper spray was designed for application to the facial area and works in the eyes, nose, and mouth to cause an extreme burning sensation to the mucous membranes (Cataldo, 2003). There are many factors that can influence the performance and safety of pepper spray devices including: (1) the strength and characteristics of the solution, (2) the efficiency and accuracy of delivery, (3) individual differences in sensitivity to the solution, tolerance, case-specific differences (drug use, goal orientation and altered mental status), and (4) environmental conditions (space, ventilation, and wind) can also influence the performance and safety of these products (Reilly, 2003). One of the more common mistakes in pepper spray deployment is to not spray enough chemical agent, or to spray a short burst and then stop (Orrick, 2004b). One of the strongest attributes of pepper spray is that it works as a distractionary technique. Pepper spray can also pose a problem as it may not have the desired effect and actually enrage the attacker and cause him or her to be even more of a threat (Cataldo, 2003).

An emerging tool in the use of chemical agents is the pepperball. The pepperball has multiple uses including a certain intimidation factor when it is displayed in crowd situations. Pepperball munitions also produce a three-pronged effect: (1) the psychological shock of being shot and hit, (2) the pain from the actual impact, and (3) the release of the irritant agent. The pepperball was designed to produce blunt trauma causing pain and contusions (*Law and Order,* 2003c; Nowicki, 2002f). The use of the pepperball has resulted in positive results in most patrol situations (Heal, 2000; Kester, 2002). However, in October of 2004, the use of the pepperball proved to have a tragic outcome when a police officer attempting to clear crowds inadvertently struck a female victim in the eye causing her death (*Cable News Network,* October 22, 2004). In this case, the pepperball was being used for the proper purpose and produced an unintended, but tragic outcome.

To investigate complaints of the use of chemical agents, the internal investigator should consider that chemical agents are low on the force continuum. By virtue of use, intent can be presumed in the officer's attempt to subdue the subject by means of the chemical agent prior to escalating to higher levels of force. This factor should not be absent from the investigation as in many cases, the officer could have justifiably opted for a higher level, but instead opted for the lowest level and a reasonable progression of force. The internal investigator must consider myriad factors in determining the justification and reasonableness of the use of an ASR such as: (1) effectiveness, (2) the history, statistics, and strength of the product used, (3) deployment problems, (3) tolerance, (4) drug involvement, (5) previous encounters with the subject where an ASR was used and any reactions to the chemical agent, and (6) department statistics on effectiveness. These all affect the outcome of the investigation. An example of an investigative consideration may be an officer who executed a "short burst" and did not apply enough chemical agent to cause the intended physical reaction from the subject. This may significantly impact an allegation of excessive force when the force applied was not enough to subdue the subject.

Taser

The taser, also termed as a conducted energy weapon (CEW), discharges an electrical current into the subject, immediately and temporarily immobilizing him or her (Newbold, 2002). The taser is a non-lethal use-of-force option when properly used. The taser has been in use since 1974 and is immediately effective in approximately 95 percent of the deployments. Suicide by cop incidents, dangerous mental subjects, violently hallucinating individuals that are under the influence of drugs are typical incidents where the taser can be used (Nowicki, 2001j). The taser is considered the most effective less-lethal weapon currently on the market (Kester, 2002).

The legal and civil issues concerning taser use would center on an evaluation based upon the *Graham v. Connor* (1989) ruling and reasonable force. In addition, the Fourteenth Amendment protects persons from being subjected, under color of law, to the intentional and wanton infliction of physical harm. As such, it must be demonstrated that the conducted energy weapon or taser was used for the purpose of only controlling the subject (Newbold, 2002). Even with these considerations, a constitutional challenge is less likely where a police officer is confronted with a legitimate need to use deadly force and is able to deploy a conducted energy weapon instead (Newbold, 2002).

The research in the use of the taser has revealed many positive outcomes. For example, the Phoenix Arizona Police Department conducted a study that revealed a significant reduction in the number of injuries during violent confrontations with subjects. In studying 475 incidents of police force, the taser was used 128 times. Injuries to suspects dropped from 33 percent to nine percent when the taser was deployed. Officer injuries were also reduced from nine percent to two percent in the same study. Officer-involved shootings were decreased from 15 to eight over the first six months of 2003. In addition, the Orange County Florida Sheriff's Office reported that it has reduced officer injuries by over 80 percent since adapting the taser for patrol use (*Law and Order,* 2003a; *Law and Order,* 2003b).

The mechanics of the taser involve the interruption of the body's nervous system through an electrical pulse. The taser transmits high voltage and low wattage to deliver a pulsating electrical output that causes involuntary muscle contractions, which result in the incapacitation of the subject and a loss of balance that compels the person to drop to the ground (Nowicki, 2001j; Weiss & Davis, 2003). The taser is safe because it interferes with the communication between the brain and the nervous system and doesn't rely on impact or penetration, nor does it destroy nerves or muscles. Mental focus, training, alcohol, body size, or drug-induced dementia cannot override the taser's effect and its use will not cause long-term injuries. Studies have also shown that the electricity produced will not interfere with a pacemaker or cause a heart attack (Weiss & Davis, 2003).

For deployment purposes, the taser should be placed on the high end of use-of-force non-lethal options of the force continuum where the officer would be justified in using closed hand strikes or baton strikes against a subject, the taser should be justified (Nowicki, 2001j). The taser can also be used where an impact weapon or higher level of force is justified. It is most likely to be used in situations such as: (1) detaining and arresting a subject, (2) controlling a pretrial detainee, and (3) controlling a convicted person who is incarcerated (Newbold, 2002). Optimum ranges vary from as wide as 3–21 feet (Nowicki, 2001j) to as narrow as 12–18 feet (Kester, 2002). There also exists a limited failure rate, however, taser failures can most often be attributed to failure in deployment rather than the taser itself (Nowicki, 2001j). Deployment consideration should also extend to prohibiting the combined use with pepper spray that is flammable to prevent an unintended ignition and set the subject afire (Nowicki, 2001e). Post-deployment activities should include medical treatment after penetration (Nowicki, 2001j).

While the taser has proven successful, its use is not without controversy as it has been banned from use by some federal agencies. Despite this, surveys have indicated that there is general acceptance of its use as a viable option for police use-of-force incidents.

To investigate a taser deployment, the internal investigator must consider all of the factors that led to the use, including the level of justified force for the situation encountered. Other reasonable options that were available as well as the imminence of the threat should be included in the investigation. The taser itself also includes a computerized tracking device for use as well as safety measures to prevent overuse. These records should be included in the investigative package as well as manufacturer documentation and statistics. The ineffectiveness should also be documented when situations are encountered where the taser had no effect due to a failure to penetrate clothing and the like, which necessitated the escalation to a higher level of force being employed to control the subject.

Carotid/Lateral Vascular Neck Restraint

One of the final less-lethal or non-lethal force options is the use of the Carotid or Lateral Vascular Neck Restraint (LVNR). The LVNR may be the most effective method of controlling subjects who have a high resistance to pain such as drug influence, alcohol, or rage (Papenfuhs, 1999). Almost 30 years of research in the Kansas City, Missouri Police Department on the use of the Lateral Vascular Neck Restraint has revealed that no single death, serious injury, or litigation has resulted (Uhrig, 1999).

Also termed the Bi-lateral Neck Restraint, the technique involves pressure applied to either side of the throat to slow the blood supply returning from the brain, causing the subject to struggle less. Pressure on the venous system is likely to cause unconsciousness in four to seven seconds. Slowing the blood flow away from the brain backs-up the carbon dioxide in the brain and causes loss of consciousness. The technique has risks when applied to subjects suffering from cardiac disorders or hypertension. It should not be applied to the very young or very old. Additional risk occurs when the technique is held too long after the subject has fallen unconscious or when post-care procedures are inadequate or non-existent (Sanow, 2001b).

Most agencies refuse to consider this technique because of the controversy surrounding the use of chokeholds. The LVNR is not a chokehold, but rather an alternative strategy in the force continuum. Agencies that do use this technique should be credited for providing as many options for their personnel as possible in order to control violent and resisting subjects in the most dynamic and violent situations. Investigative protocol should emerge from the training and acumen of the application of the technique of the subject officer. The organization should have a strong trail of documentation that justifies the technique from the legal and medical fields in order to defend against any litigation when the technique is properly and appropriately applied. The subject officer's training record, record of application, and the department's overall statistics should also be included in the package for justification in criminal, civil, and personnel complaints.

SUMMARY

This chapter discussed investigations that involve crimes and use-of-force. From the criminal perspective, color of law investigations and criminal investigations were examined in their relationship to the internal investigator's role and responsibilities when these allegations are brought to the attention of the organization. The chapter then progressed through the varying issues surrounding the use-of-force and specific policy, operational, legal, and investigative considerations in force deployment. Among the topics covered were the uses of impact instruments, chemical agents, and the taser as well as several others. The emphasis was placed on the options available to the officer in controlling a subject, the reasonable use of options, and the investigative consideration of the totality of the circumstances involved in every force deployment scenario.

Chapter 9

CRITICAL INCIDENT INVESTIGATIONS: DEADLY PHYSICAL FORCE AND IN-CUSTODY DEATH

INTRODUCTION

This chapter discusses the investigative requirements surrounding critical incidents such as the use of deadly physical force and in-custody deaths. The chapter discusses the investigative requirements for critical incident scene management, police-involved shootings, the phenomenon of victim-assisted suicide, and in-custody death investigations.

CRITICAL INCIDENT SCENE MANAGEMENT

Critical incident scene management should be a process that is in place long before an incident occurs. Policy, procedure, notifications, the designation of an incident commander, and many other considerations should be at the forefront of any discussion in a law enforcement organization if a process does not exist since these incidents are difficult and unpredictable. This section discusses issues beyond those of basic crime scene investigation and explores the use of legal advisors, reporting procedures at these scenes, the family of the deceased, and critical incident investigation teams.

Fundamentally, the crime scene should be immediately secured and no person, including any police officer or commanding officer, should be allowed within the cordoned-off area until the scene is processed. In addition, nothing including dead bodies should be removed from the crime scene until it is processed. One person should be designated as the person-in-charge of the crime scene, and that authority should be respected by all command officers at the scene, including the chief. No actions should be taken outside the plan developed by the person-in-charge. All involved officers should be separated so that there can be no allegation of collusion (Close, 2001). In addition, any questioning of personnel should be done in private and not in open or unsecured crime scenes as they may be recorded or overheard and surface in later legal proceedings (Chudwin, 1999).

The command and supervisory personnel should also not lose sight of the needs of the personnel involved. Few situations in an officer's life will be more stressful and occur in a shorter period of time than a critical incident (Oberlander, 2004). Special consideration should be given for their psychological and

Figure 9-1. The most critical investigations conducted by internal affairs involve the use of deadly physical force and in-custody deaths (Photo courtesy of the Brockport, New York Police Department).

emotional needs both after the incident and during post-incident follow-up. The officer will also be hypersensitive to every action taken, observed, or comment overheard so great care is necessary in appropriately dealing with these needs and avoiding short and long-term issues because of intentional or inadvertent comments or actions of those involved in the investigation.

The Criticality of Legal Advisors

These types of incidents are fraught with liability and a wise administrator and internal investigator should welcome the advice of competent legal counsel. The agency's first and most important role is in support of the prosecutorial process (Mayer & Coble, 1998). The internal investigation is tantamount to the criminal but the criminal must proceed first. With this in mind, legal counsel should come from such parties as prosecutors, municipal attorneys, risk managers, subject matter experts, and the like. An agency's attorney can provide insights and expertise to the chief or other designee with a detachment and objectivity that may not be possible for agency members who are directly and personally involved in events and decisions (Mayer & Coble, 1998).

Agencies that have the resources should employ the services of a specialized police legal advisor. Smaller agencies can combine resources to hire one attorney to work full-time providing assistance to several agencies. The police legal advisor can counsel police administrators and investigators in the criminal, civil, and protection of officer rights at critical incident scenes. A police legal advisor is an attorney who has an understanding of police operations and the legal knowledge required to be helpful in advising the police at these types of scenes. The duties that a police legal advisor may perform are as diverse and wide-ranging as the law-related needs of police agencies and officers. A police legal advisor can provide support in such areas as: (1) reviewing and drafting policies, (2) training, (3) discipline, grievances, and labor support, (3) litigation support, (4) legislation and public relations, (5) operations, and (6) community policing (International Association of Chiefs of Police, 1998d).

The law enforcement administrator as well as internal and criminal investigators should document the advice of the police legal advisor and the follow-up actions that are consistent with the advice given. The documentation should be included in the investigative package and readily available to the police legal advisor for use in any future defense or litigation.

Report Review and Consistency

Critical incident scenes will most likely involve numerous involved and investigative personnel and subsequent reports. These reports will be both criminal and administrative in nature. Because of this, one supervisor should be assigned to review all reports that are generated and none of the reports should be forwarded for additional processing until all reports from the incident have been reviewed by the assigned supervisor (Cope, 2002). A review of the reports should ensure that agreement takes place in all written documentation (Nowicki, 2001f). The organization should also consider the use of two supervisors or command officers assigned to the review, one responsible for any criminal investigation, and the second supervisor or command officer conducting an additional review for department procedure and civil litigation issues.

The Family of the Deceased

Where a critical incident involves the death of the subject, the department should have a plan in place to deal with their needs and offer counseling services to the family of the decedent (Close, 2001). While the family can refuse, the organization should make an effort to assist in any means possible.

In contrast, the decision to meet with the family to discuss the incident is ill-advised. The results of the criminal investigation can be discussed, however, the results of the internal in most states cannot. Families and relatives will be quick to file lawsuits in these cases, many times before the investigation is truly completed. These types of meetings, while well-intended, may cause more harm than good from a community service perspective as well as a civil litigation perspective. The administrator will most certainly be placed in a position to answer difficult questions where the resulting information release would be inappropriate for dissemination prior to the matter being reviewed in the court setting. If the administrator decides to arrange such a meeting, they should be scripted and under the strict guidance of legal counsel in order to ensure that the investigation is not compromised and the organization and officer are not exposed to any undue litigation or scrutiny.

Critical Incident Investigation Teams

Some agencies have decided to have a specialized group of personnel that investigate critical incidents such as police-involved shootings and in-custody deaths. The efficacy of their use may be in question as in theory they work, however, in application, problems may exist. These issues should be resolved prior to any specialized team being involved in the investigation of these types of incidents.

From a positive perspective, the Washington, DC police conducted an immense amount of research in this area in developing a high performance, police-involved shooting team. One of the considerations in concept development was the identification of their "customer" population. The Washington concept identified five primary customers in the process design: (1) citizens, (2) officers involved in the shooting with consideration for the civil, criminal, and departmental ramifications of the use of deadly force, (3) critics and public interest groups, (4) the police industry, and (5) the media. A key consideration was given to the fact that officers were entitled to high quality investigations and objective reviews of their conduct, whether they were found to be justified or not in their actions. The system was divided into two major components with two subcomponents each: (1) deadly force deployment that involved intentional firearms discharge at any person and those involving animal shootings, accidental discharges, and police officer suicides and (2) non-deadly force occurrences such as in-custody deaths, arrestee hospital admittance, non-lethal weapon strikes to the head, and excessive force criminal violations (Ederheimer, 2000).

From a negative perspective, these terms can pose significant problems in the investigative process if not researched and administered properly. For example, these types of teams should consider that they are at the forefront of the case and their actions impact three separate and distinct areas of the case: (1) criminal, (2) internal, and (3) civil. Planning the strategy and progress provides for protections for all involved. The team mission must also be clear and communicated to all involved in the process as are they criminal or internal investigators? This question will prevail in every subsequent proceeding where legal testimony and review are required. This is critical in the interview of involved personnel due to their varied protections under the labor, civil, and criminal laws. The approach to these types of interviews should be well-planned in order to satisfy the needs of all three previously mentioned impact areas.

The issue of interview and interrogation of involved personnel should not be taken lightly. These incidents involve scene fact-finding interviews, criminal interviews, and internal interviews. These should be extremely limited and every interview session well-documented. From an interview and interrogation perspective, officers who are interviewed should be interviewed once if at all possible as multiple statements present a logistical nightmare for civil litigation. In addition, if an officer is to be required to give a formal sworn statement in an interview, then no written report should be needed (G. T. Williams, 1999a). This planning should begin before an incident occurs with a protocol in place that starts at the first line of supervision that will be responding to scenes and extend through the ranks to the highest level administrators who will be responsible for the outcome of the investigation in the criminal, internal, and civil realms.

POLICE INVOLVED SHOOTINGS

Approximately 400 people are killed in police-involved shootings in the United States each year (Paynter, 2000). Police-involved shootings are some of the most traumatic and dangerous events in a law enforcement officer's career (Makholm, 2003b). This section discusses the research, legal issues, as well as officer and offender considerations in a police-involved shooting.

According to a study on use-of-force conducted by the International Association of Chiefs of Police, of the 5,395 police uses of firearm force reported in 1997–1998, the largest concentration (1,256 incidents) took place in jurisdictions of 170,000 to 499,000 persons (Henriquez, 1999). In addition, statistics compiled by the Los Angeles Police Department revealed that over 37 percent of such shootings occur within one minute of the officer's arrival on the scene, and over 35 percent occur within 30 seconds. Combining these statistics with the FBI statistics concerning officers killed and assaulted in the line of duty, which states that the majority of these incidents occur between the hours of 6:00 p.m. and 6:00 a.m., and considering that it takes the average person at least 40 minutes for their eyes to adjust to the darkness, it is obvious that most officers are not prepared for a lethal confrontation (Rayburn, 2000).

An independent research study in police-involved shootings also revealed five key factors were apparent that include: (1) commission of a serious criminal offense by the offender, (2) alcohol and drug involvement on behalf of the offender, (3) mental disorder/irrational behavior on behalf of the offender, (4) mistaken facts on behalf of the police, and (5) victim-precipitated suicide (Parent, 2000).

With respect to officers injured or killed in the line of duty, several stark factors must be considered in the investigation of police-involved shootings. About 10 percent of the officers who are shot and killed each year are shot with their own handgun or another officer's handgun (Nowicki, 2002d; Parent, 2000). Eighty-five percent of officers who were killed in the line of duty were unable to fire their handgun before being killed (Aveni, 2003a). In addition, there is an 85 percent probability that the officer being disarmed will be shot or another officer will be shot with the officer's handgun (Nowicki, 2002d). A study in the New York Police Department revealed that 82 percent of officers who were killed in the line of duty were slain within six feet of their attacker (Aveni, 2003a). Still another study of statistical information associated with deaths and assaults on police and peace officers has revealed several common factors:

1. The incident is usually spontaneous.
2. The incident is life-threatening.
3. The incident occurs at very close range, 75% under 10 feet.
4. Most incidents occur under poor visibility.
5. Offender has the initiative and the officer reacts to a lethal threat.
6. There is no time to think of response.
7. The officer experiences extreme life-threatening stress.
8. There may be more than one suspect.
9. The assailant may not be the original target of the officer's attention.
10. There may be a physical altercation involved.
11. The suspect will be 10 years younger than the officer and in better shape.
12. The suspect will anticipate the officer's actions and responses.
13. The officers will not anticipate the suspects responses.
14. The officer may hesitate to evaluate the situation: What degree of force should be used?
15. The suspect decides to use force and acts: Officer must react, but cannot respond in time. (Baratta, 1998, p. 191)

Proximity to the suspect and hit ratios are also a significant factor to consider in the investigation of police-involved shootings. For example, in a police-involved shooting, the probability for hits ranges around 20 percent even with half of these shootings occurring within less than 5 feet (Black, 2001). In addition, only about half of all officer-involved shooting incidents where a suspect is struck, at least one police bullet strikes one opponent (Morrison & Shave, 2002).

An understanding of the legal and civil issues is also necessary for the review of a police-involved shooting investigation. In civil cases, departments should seek summary judgment whenever the genuine issues of material fact are not in dispute. Just because there may be some conflict in the evidence over what led up to the shooting doesn't mean summary judgment isn't viable. Examples of cases where summary judgment was given to police departments in spite of facts in dispute are, *Krueger v. Fuhr* (1993) where a fleeing felony suspect armed with a knife was shot in the back, *Valance v. Wisel* (1997) where a plaintiff testified that he did not believe he was engaging in wrongful conduct, *Wood v. City of Lakeland, Florida* (2000) where a suicidal person with a knife was fatally shot and the autopsy report disputed the officers' claim the decedent was holding the knife in a threatening manner when shot, and *Drewitt v. Pratt* (1993) where an officer shot a motorist despite an alleged factual dispute over whether the officer could have jumped out of the car's path and therefore avoided the need to shoot (MacLatchie, 2000).

Several additional factors must be considered in the investigation of a police-involved shooting including the officer, offender, threat proximity, and training issues. From the perspective of the officer, data suggests that the perception of a firearm attack is enough to degrade and adversely affect human performance (Aveni, 2003a). In evaluating the officer's actions and performance at a police-involved shooting, performance and decision-making skills may be significantly diminished in the progression of the event. As such, the outcome should be evaluated based upon a set of minimum standards or expectations as opposed to a set of maximum or ideal expectations.

Another consideration from the officer's perspective is that of the occurrence of the associative firing impulse. Thomas Aveni (2003a) states with respect to the associative firing impulse that:

> Officers experience an associative threat assumption phenomenon, as one or more officers conclude that the officer that initiated fire correctly identified an imminent lethal threat; or one or more officers experiences a mistaken origin of fire phenomenon, whereby an officer believes shots being fired by another officer are in fact shots fired by the suspect. (p. 85)

This is a critical concept for the internal investigator to understand as many high profile police shooting incidents have led to such incidents as sympathetic fire that have brought undue media, legal, and departmental scrutiny for a legitimate and recognized conditional response to such highly stressful and emotionally-charged situations. The internal investigator must understand that an officer is often confused about the suspect's intentions, and most often only identifies the threat at the last possible moment. Consequently, the suspect controls the violence, not the officer (G. T. Williams, 1999b).

The offender issues are also a concern for the internal investigation. Offenders most often are the precipitator of these incidents, leaving the officer in the position of a victim having to respond rather than as the aggressor initiating the action. Internal investigators must understand the concept of action is faster than reaction. An officer's defensive response to a suspect's action is going to be slower than the suspect's initial action of pulling a weapon. It takes more time for the officer to realize he is under attack than it takes for the suspect to decide to launch an attack (Rayburn, 2001). Studies have revealed that the majority of suspects, as high as 87 percent, are "instinctive" shooters (Baratta, 1999). This compounds the problem of action v. reaction.

Threat proximity has been previously discussed with statistics demonstrating that most police-involved shootings occur in close quarters environments in a matter of seconds. Only five percent of all police-involved shootings occur beyond twelve yards (Aveni, 2002b). Threat cessation is also another concern for police-involved shootings. Threat cessation may not occur with the placement of one shot. Bullets have unpredictable and sometimes minimal short-term effects on an adversary, thus continuing, and sometimes increasing the threat. Even with the advent of large caliber and high capacity issued weapons, this may not cease the threat and over-dependence on this may be a dangerous psychological disadvantage to the officer (McKenna, 2001). Suspects who are also aware that police personnel wear protective body armor purposely shoot at the head of the officer to inflict the stopping wound or fatal hit. One study indicated over a period examined that close to half of the officers involved received fatal hits to the head (Baratta, 1999). The examination and evaluation of the incident should encompass the suspect's side as well as the officer's in order to be fair and impartial.

The internal investigation should also include and address any training issues involved in the investigation and evaluation of the incident. For example, current firearms training philosophy is being questioned with respect to the extensive amount of time spent with techniques and principles that officers cannot be expected to use in a police-involved shooting. An officer under the stress of a shooting will not be able to perform multiple techniques in order to ensure accurate shot placement (Nowicki, 2002a). To address this problem, organizations need to consider viable options to firearms training that are directly related to street experiences based upon analysis of officer-involved shootings. For example, studies have shown that laser sights greatly enhance firearms training and accuracy. A laser sight will help an officer shoot more accurately and with greater speed (Nielsen, 2003b).

In the event of the death of an individual subjected to police actions, the stress levels exceed those encountered in most other police actions. When the death is due to an auto accident that resulted from a pursuit or an in-custody death because the subject had overdosed on an illicit drug, the officer will most likely suffer from psychological and emotional trauma. In the event of a use of deadly force wherein the officer was forced to be the instrument of a subject's death, the problem is only magnified. With this in mind, Dr. Alexis Artwohl and Loren W. Christensen (1997) state that, "The officer deserves and needs the most professional, thorough, and accurate investigation you can do, and he needs the respect and compassion you would show any person who has experienced a traumatic event" (p. 249).

Deadly Physical Force

To understand the use of deadly force, the internal investigator must understand the definition of deadly force as well as the practical considerations or reasons in which deadly force can be used. George J. Franscell and Ann M. Maurer (2000) present the *Model Penal Code* definition of "deadly force" used by some jurisdictions as:

> Force by which the actor uses with the purpose of causing or which he knows to create a substantial risk of causing death or serious bodily harm. Purposely firing a firearm in the direction of another person or at a vehicle in which another person is believed to be constitutes deadly force. A threat to cause death or serious bodily harm, by the production of a weapon or otherwise, so long as the actor's purpose is limited to creating an apprehension that he will use deadly force if necessary does not constitute deadly force. (p. 145)

While deadly physical force is authorized under the law it is often perceived as a deviation or act of aggression on behalf of an officer, no matter the circumstances involved. Quite the contrary is the case in the majority of incidents of deadly force. George T. Williams (1999a) states that, "Killing or injuring a person by employing deadly force is a matter of duty for police, not an act of passion." While a person chooses to be a police officer and protect the public, they are often forced to protect themselves and the lives of others due to the acts of those in society who demonstrate the propensity for instilling violence against others.

There are a series of reasons in which an officer can use deadly force. Frank Borelli (2001) cites four reasons to justify deadly force deployment as: (1) the assailant's proximity to bring a lethal threat to the officer, (2) the assailant's ability to bring a lethal threat to the officer, (3) imminent jeopardy is presented as a result of the first two components, and (4) preclusion based upon a duty to protect others wherein the officer has no duty to retreat from the threat (p. 15). Included in the investigative summary should be the delineation of these requirements and the conduct of the involved officer with respect to each.

The internal investigator must also consider that if an officer has to resort to deadly physical force, then they may employ some unconventional, albeit, reasonable methods of force to defend themselves and cease the threat to themselves or a third party. For example, subjects attempting to disarm an officer present a lethal threat that justifies higher levels of lethal force by the officer. The officer must do virtually anything to prevent a disarming, including the use of unorthodox deadly force tactics (Nowicki, 2003). The internal investigator must recognize that officer safety is paramount in these situations for if the officer is incapacitated or mortally wounded, they will not be able to fulfill their duties in protecting the general public. In addition, with respect to officer safety, the potential of a lawsuit should not be considered when facing a lethal encounter (Nowicki, 2001h).

Considerations for the Officer Interview

There are several factors that need to be considered for the interview. Many are addressed in the following sections; however, tactics and officer welfare are tantamount as being critical to the process. The internal investigation interview can be stressful to both the involved officer and investigator (Artwohl & Christensen, 1997). While the search for the truth is paramount, it should not be at the behest of other factors in the case, including the involved officer. Such considerations include: (1) understanding what the involved officer is experiencing mentally, (2) the goal of the interview, including information required by the prosecutor, agency, and civil defense attorney, and (3) the tone of the interview itself (G. T. Williams, 1999a).

From a legal perspective, a foundational case was decided in Colorado in *People v. Probasco* (1990). This case involved an on-duty shooting that resulted in the deputy's indictment for criminally negligent homicide. Probasco was questioned at the scene by responding deputies and disclosed information that led to his arrest. The issue for the court to decide upon was if the interview of Probasco was "custodial" and subsequently entitled him to the protections against compulsory self-incrimination under *Miranda v. Arizona* (1967). The court decided that even though the interview was technically an interrogation, Probasco was not in "custody" within the meaning of *Miranda* at the time of the questioning. This ruling thus negated the need to advise Probasco of his *Miranda* warnings. The court noted that at the time of the questioning that Probasco was subjected to only a fact-finding interview as no information existed at the time to lead the responding officers to believe that any criminal wrongdoing had occurred. The interview included only questions that were merely framed to determine what had transpired. Since Probasco was not deprived of his freedom in any significant way, the Court did not consider him to be in custody as it is interpreted in the legal sense. The requirement to stay at the scene and report to his superiors resulted from normal employment obligations. In a related decision entitled *Faniel v. Chesapeake and Pot. Tel. Co. of MD* (1979) an employee who claimed false imprisonment due to being directed to submit to an on-the-job interview concerning a misconduct complaint was not entitled to a jury award (Americans for Effective Law Enforcement, 2005).

Operational and policy issues should be based upon the legal and tactical aspects of interviews as well as the psychological issues. For example, the human memory is subject to distortions and omissions even under nonstressful circumstances and the stress of a traumatic incident only compounds the problem. Participants and witnesses may be unable to recall events, or their minds may invent complex sequences as to their behavior and what they perceive others have done. Honest officers have been accused of untruthfulness when in fact they have offered the truth in internal investigation statements, subsequently being disciplined and even terminated for being untruthful, when in fact they were telling the truth as they knew it (Artwohl & Christensen, 1997).

Because of the officer's mental and/or physical condition after a police-involved shooting, the interview may need to be postponed from 48 to 72 hours as an interview conducted under adverse conditions can be inefficient and perhaps harmful if conducted too quickly. During this period, the officer should be allowed to sleep, rest, and if desired, consult with a psychologist. Allowing the officer this opportunity will often lead to the officer's increased ability to offer a more comprehensive and chronologically complete statement which results in a better, more accurate account of the officer's actions and state of mind (G. T. Williams, 1999a). Therefore, it is common not to require the officer to give a statement or write their report immediately after the incident as the officer may not be able to relate a coherent version of the incident (Artwohl & Christensen, 1997). The officer should also be admonished on refraining contact with other principles and witnesses in the case so as the subsequent statement will be solely a product of the officer's recollection and not from those pieces provided by others who were involved.

For the interview protocol, first and foremost is the tone of the interview which should be formal and respectful (G. T. Williams, 1999a). In addition, Dr. Alexis Artwohl and Loren W. Christensen (1997) offer the following list of recommendations for officer-involved shooting interviews:

1. Upon first contact with the officer, advise him of the procedures that will be followed in order to allay as many fears as possible.
2. Offer to make arrangements for family contacts and other immediate personal needs. Also offer peer support, employee assistance, and other supportive programs available to the agency.
3. Provide the opportunity for the officer to do a scene walk-through with his personal attorney.
4. When confiscating the weapon, ensure an exact replacement is offered.
5. Provide the officer with an escort or personal bodyguard from the time the incident to the time he or she is safely brought home. The officer should be provided a driver for personal transportation during this time period as well as transportation for the immediate family.
6. Evaluate and offer trauma counseling to all involved personnel including supervisory staff.
7. The post-shooting interview should occur at the discretion of the officer after he has consulted with his attorney. The officer should be allowed to go home, and de-stress in an appropriate manner. If the officer chooses to be interviewed contemporaneously to the incident, then he should be given the opportunity to shower and change clothes first.
8. Interviews should take place in a large and comfortable room such as a conference room. The officer should not be isolated and should have access to friends, family, and support personnel.
9. Provide access to food, beverages, and a quiet room where the officer (and his family) can retreat to get temporary relief from the commotion.
10. Do not expose the officer or his family to conversations that are transpiring by administrative and investigative staff concerning the progression of the investigation.
11. An officer can only report what they have perceived, not necessarily on what actually occurred. If perceptions differ from the physical evidence, either from the officer or witness accounts, doesn't mean that the officer is being untruthful. Differing or fragmented memories of the event are the result of cognitive, sensory, and perceptual distortions that are the inevitable result of physical changes in

the body due to high arousal states during the event.

12. Do not pressure the officer into providing events of the detail he or she does not legitimately remember. Don't imply that the officer is being deceptive, incompetent, evasive, or dishonest when he or she report memory gaps or confusion. Stress leads to several physiological responses that will cause tunnel vision and second-guessing of the progression of the event. This second-guessing is an inevitable consequence of any trauma (not just shootings) and should not be seen as evidence that they, or anyone else, has necessarily acted improperly.
13. Cognitive memory may be distorted close in time to the event, but may return over the time following the event. Therefore, officers may remember salient details later and should be allowed to amend their recollection at the time of the recall. (p. 245)

Visual Impairment

In police action, visual acuity can have a significant impact on an officer's ability to make decisions in dangerous or life-threatening situations. Thomas Aveni (2002a) states with respect to diminished visual acuity that, "Little if any thought has been given to addressing the cognitive impairment officers are routinely expected to render critical decisions with" (p. 71). Visual acuity can be diminished by medical reasons as well as environmental conditions. The internal investigator may need to explore these issues when conducting the internal investigation of a police-involved shooting. This section discusses the statistics surrounding environmental conditions and visual impairment, the physiological responses, environmental conditions, equipment, training, and investigative considerations involved in determining the impact of visual acuity in the deployment of deadly force.

There are different definitions of visual ability. For example, focal vision is primarily involved with objects in the center of vision. This visual system is strongly linked to consciousness. Among its main functions is identification through distinguishing fine points, i.e., what is it? It is sometimes called "cognitive vision," because it is tightly tied to cognitive tasks. Focal vision is used most effectively in endeavors that demand fine eye-hand control. Indeed, focal vision tends to be inhibited in high-stress situations that demand gross motor control and rapid body movement (Armstrong & Nibler, 1999).

Ambient vision is unlike focal vision and is used for the entire visual field. Also unlike focal vision, decreasing illumination does not have important effects on its acuity, and information from ambient vision can be used without conscious awareness. One of its main functions is to answer the question "Where is it?" It is sometimes called "motor vision," because it is involved in movement behavior and control. In high-stress situations that include body movement and demand balance coordination, focal vision comes naturally into play (Armstrong & Nibler, 1999). Ambient vision may have an impact in police-involved shootings with respect to the response of the officer to a perceived threat.

The statistical propensity for being involved in a shooting is during the evening hours. As such, most police shootings occur in diminished lighting conditions. As a matter of fact, six of every ten police involved shootings have occurred in diminished lighting conditions (Aveni, 2002b). The Uniform Crime Report statistics have also revealed that the majority of officers killed or injured in the line of duty occurred between the hours of 6:00 p.m. and 6:00 a.m. (Aveni, 2002a; Baratta, 1999). Based upon these statistics, the internal investigator must understand the affect of diminished lighting and include those affects if they are applicable and relevant to the investigation.

A person's vision is severely impaired in the first three to four minutes of entering darkness. The eyes need approximately 20 to 30 minutes to adjust to the darkness. In addition, colors are affected by our lack of visual acuity as our minds fill in the missing colors, as well as the use of prescription glasses. It takes approximately 40 minutes in a consistently dark environment for our eyes to completely adjust to a point as well as they will be in a darkened environment. Many factors influence adaptations including, genetic programming, age, general health, diseases of the eye, environmental influences, medications, and stress due to biological changes in the body related to stress (Myers, 1998). Other factors such as the use of caffeine can produce a negative physiological response to a person's visual acuity as well.

There are also certain physiological reactions of the body that affect sight when working in diminished lighting conditions as well as stress-induced responses. Night vision is sensitive to contrast and to movement, but insensitive to details (Myers, 1998). As a threat emerges, the human eye does not see rapid movement, but rather a composite of that movement. In reality, the officer may only see the culmination of the suspect's actions (Aveni, 2002a). As stress rises in a critical incident, the phenomenon of backing away from a suspect is related to visual impairment due to physiological changes in the body. Visual systems begin to deteriorate with respect to peripheral vision, therefore, the body reacts by backing away in order to widen the peripheral field of vision. With these physiological and psychological changes in the body, visual tracking also becomes difficult (Laur, 2002). With respect to peripheral vision, the affects of darkened conditions and the brain integrates complex processes including memory, selective suppression, and enhancement of images to compensate for the limitations in both our direct and peripheral vision. The perceptions that result (i.e., what we think we see) are heavily influenced by our prior experiences, knowledge, expectations, training and survival instincts, and we are often unaware of the true limitations of our vision (Myers, 1998). Michael T. Rayburn (2000) poignantly states that: "It is hard enough to tell the difference between a handgun, a pager, a cell phone, or even a wallet under low-light conditions–even without the stress of thinking that you might be shot by the person you are confronting" (p. 104).

Compounding the issue of physiological responses is environmental conditions that also have a negative effect on the officer's ability to properly perceive the circumstances that are being presented. According to Dr. Paul Michel, an expert in the forensic evaluation of visual ability, "The acuity of human vision is completely predicated upon the availability of ambient light" (Aveni, 2002a, p. 73). Diminished lighting may reduce an officer's vision to a point of legal blindness. This impairment then becomes a significant issue in evaluating an officer's observations in a critical incident such as a police-involved shooting (Aveni, 2002a; Hopper, 2001b; Myers, 1998). In very dark conditions, vision is reduced from 20/20 to 20/800 which is four times the impairment that constitutes legal blindness (Myers, 1998).

Inconsistent light may also be a contributing factor in officer deaths as lighting, shadows, and the like may skew the perception of the suspect as not being armed when in fact, the suspect is (Spaulding, 2001). In contrast, substantive cognitive impairment occurs at light thresholds consistent with dawn or dusk light conditions. This problem is increased by distance, movement, and physiological reactions to stress wherein innocuous objects cannot be properly discerned and interpreted as a threat (Aveni, 2002b). In addition, officers seldom work in a consistently dark environment. As a matter of fact, it is likely that the light will fluctuate, meaning that an officer's eyes will never fully adjust to a single light or dark environment (Spaulding, 2001).

Rick Baratta (1999) discussed the merits and results of surveying deadly force characteristics and deployments. In the surveys, the majority of assaults and deaths of police officers occur between 6:00 P.M. and 6:00 A.M., which he believes may be indicative of visibility. Diminished ambient lighting results in:

1. Perception in identifying the threat and determining the threat level.
2. Ability to use concealment.
3. Ability to control the situation.
4. Accuracy of shooting.
5. Tactics.
6. Use of artificial light (flashlight/spotlight). (p. 66)

Equipment considerations revolve around a few issues related to lighting conditions. The first is the use of a flashlight as well as type, intensity, and operability. In deadly force situations, a flashlight may have been available, but not used because of such reasons as immediacy of the contact. A flashlight may not have the proper intensity or low battery volume which may impact proper illumination of a subject or area. Flashlight use may also impede night vision because of light reflected back into the officer's eyes (Myers, 1998). A flashlight may have been available to the officer, but lost during a foot chase or struggle. All of these possibilities should be explored in the internal investigation where lighting may have been an issue.

There has also been the advent of laser sights in departments. Some issued by agencies, while officers may purchase them on their own. In either case, the agency should have a policy and possibly a series of what sights are approved for duty use. Because of the successes, agencies should strongly consider the issuance of laser sights as a part of the duty weapon. Traditional hit ratios are in the 18 percent to 20 percent range and studies have shown that laser sights may not only improve accuracy, but may also prevent some deadly force encounters from becoming fatal confrontations. Laser sights also allow the officer to concentrate on the threat in confrontations as opposed to the sights of their duty weapon (Grossi, 2002b). However, lasers only provide an aiming mechanism; illumination may still be a factor to consider in threat level identification.

Because of the serious nature of shooting in diminished lighting conditions supported by statistics that demonstrate need, and case law that mandates realistic training, departments should make low light shooting training a priority. Training should include the perceptual, cognitive, and judgmental aspects of when deadly force is most appropriately applied (Aveni, 2002b). Any training that is received by the involved officer should also be included in the investigative package.

To investigate a police-involved shooting, the internal investigator should have knowledge of how the eyes adjust which can also help to evaluate the reports of witnesses, and the documentation of the lighting conditions at crime scenes. Accurate measures of the existing conditions, including the length of time that an individual spent in those conditions should be copiously documented by crime scene and internal investigators. In police-involved shootings, this is critical in order to determine the actual perceptive ability of the officer under these conditions. The location, type and amount of ambient light should be documented. The height of the sources of light should be included in the diagram to help vision experts later to determine and testify to visual perceptions and complex cognitive processes of the officers involved (Myers, 1998). Other considerations are for day officers who may enter dark environments in homes and building searches quicker than their eyes can properly adjust and thus be visually impaired during the confrontation.

The final consideration in this aspect of the internal investigation is the medical condition of the involved officer and any witnesses with respect to visual ability. The internal investigator may need to explore the vision level and range of the involved officer and witnesses, whether the need for and use of corrective lenses was in place, if any specific eye diseases may have impacted the visual perception of the incident, and the like. The internal investigator may even request documentation of the visual capacity of the officer through the officer's optometrist or through a departmentally authorized eye exam by a professional.

Fatigue

Fatigue in these types of incidents may be in two forms: (1) fatigue and exhaustion related to a defensive tactics encounter and (2) general fatigue due to lack of sleep, shift assignment, and overwork during the shift. Fatigue related to exhaustion while perhaps experienced during a violent struggle with a resisting subject may have a significant impact on the decision-making process to escalate force levels in order to gain control of a subject or to simply survive the incident. An officer may have no viable alternative but to use deadly physical force dependent upon their condition and rapidly deteriorating ability to stay in the fight until control of the subject is gained.

Also, as identified in officer stress factors and fleet motor vehicle accidents, general fatigue may have a significant impact on officer performance. Officers may realize they're tired, but may not realize how much fatigue impacts their personal performance. Fatigue may also have a significant impact on judgment and motivation. The result of being tired may place the officer in a position where they will give up quality and safety just to complete the assignment (Pedersen, 2001).

In either case, the internal investigator must explore the reasons for force and if those reasons were legitimate. The level of fatigue may be a salient factor in why the officer resorted to the use of deadly force and thus a mitigating factor for consideration in the final case disposition.

Threat Indicators from the Suspect

Many interviews of police officers involved shootings center, quite inappropriately, on only the officer's actions. This mindset has evolved from a thought process that places an undue burden on the officer to wholly justify his or her actions. Much, if not of all of the justification constructively emerges from the suspect's aggressive actions and the officer's response. An important factor for the internal investigator to uncover is all of the suspect's actions that led to the officer having to resort to deadly physical force. A suspect's motivation to shoot may be dramatically different from an officer's because of the way he grew up, or he may be under the influence of alcohol or drugs (Weiss & Davis, 2002). Hence, this becomes a critical area to explore in the interview process of officers and witnesses. A study that revealed that threat indicators or warning signs were displayed in 74 percent of the officers murdered and many of these warning signs were displayed by the suspect's stance and body language (Baratta, 1999).

The body language displayed by others may be an important component of a report when force is used. The preferred tactic for reporting officers would be to specifically quantify a subject's aggressive behavior, rather than reporting in non-specific terms that a "subject was aggressive" (Nowicki, 2001g). During the investigation, the interviewer should ascertain if the suspect demonstrated any threat indicators to the officer. For example: (1) bladed stance, (2) folded arm stance, (3) hands on hips, (4) invasion of personal space, (5) finger pointing, (6) wandering attention, (7) ignoring verbal commands, (8) other indicators such as pacing, clenched fists, clenched teeth, (9) spitting, (10) grabbing the groin area, and (11) emotional mood swings (Hurley, 2000). Other examples are nervousness, feigned passivity, inappropriate silence or calmness, and verbal distraction (Baratta, 1999).

The internal investigator should also ascertain if the subject was a skilled fighter and has demonstrated such skill through his or her use of tactics or indicators. For example, skilled fighters possess certain attributes that need to be understood by the officer involved in a use-of-force such as: (1) balance, (2) mobility, (3) protected stance, (4) protects his head, (5) takes a position of advantage, (6) tests his opponent, and (7) presses the attack and continues the assault after the officer has initiated his offensive (Papenfuhs, 2000). The officer may not have documented these demonstrated skills or attributes, but used them in his or her decision-making process to escalate the level of force. Along these lines, an individual may not have a specialized skill, but may demonstrate a characteristic (e.g., bladed or defensive stance) and then proclaim they are a martial arts or fighting expert. If the officer's base of knowledge is from this contact, they will have to assume that the subject has a specialized skill and would be justified in raising their level of force to meet the purported threat.

A final indicator in threat perception from the subject deals with the misidentification of objects that the subject may have in their possession or threaten the use of. Objects are normally misidentified due to three factors: (1) the suspect's actions and/or body language just prior to the object being seen, (2) the angle from which the object is seen, plus the absence of other angles for verification, and (3) lighting or reflection (Messina, 2000). What is most important to the investigation is the perceptions of the officer at the time of the incident, not the clarity of hindsight.

Tactical Disarmament of Suspects

The use of tactical disarmament of armed subjects is one of significant debate with regard to the legal, operational, and ethical issues involved. Some dramatic examples have been profiled in the media and have demonstrated some successes, however, much care needs to be taken in developing policy and making the ultimate decision to use this tactic. The purpose of this section is not to condemn the decision to use this tactic, but to offer some understanding of the investigative concerns.

The ethical issues can be summed up by Derrick D. Bartlett (2000) who states that, "The idea of keeping an individual from killing himself by shooting at him is frightening, dangerous, and, in most states, illegal" (p. 84). An examination of state and federal law, as well as agencies that have opted to practice this type of technique should be undertaken far before employing the practice. A review by the criminal and civil attorneys will also be in order before this can be placed into policy and practice. A civil review would be based upon *Graham v. Connor* (1989) and the question would be in light of the totality of the circumstances of the incident, "Was tactical disarmament a reasonable force option?"

Research has also revealed that the practice is imprecise. A study conducted with controlled firearms tests found that several issues surfaced that would make this practice impractical. Such problems as shot placement, secondary targets being struck by fragmentation, and rounds detonating as a sympathetic response to the weapon being struck by a high-powered round were all considerations for limiting or restricting such a concept or tactic to the most egregious of situations (Bartlett, 2000). Departments should consequently conduct their own testing in firearms and specialized teams to develop an empirical database to justify use.

The internal investigator must have available all records of such testing as well as the firearms training records of those involved in the decision to employ the practice. These types of incidents would then need to be reviewed by specialists such as department firearms staff involved in the testing and policy development, criminal, and civil attorneys before a finding could be rendered as to the justification for the use of this tactic.

The Debate Over Warning Shots

Warning shots carry an even higher level of controversy than do incidents of tactical disarmament. For example, a tactical disarmament incident will most likely only occur after much discussion and numerous agency and specialized unit command approvals. On the other hand, warning shots are spontaneous and solely the decision of the involved officer in tense and evolving situations.

From a legal perspective, in *Minnesota v. McKissic,* the court suggested or endorsed a warning shot would or could have stopped the activity and prevented the individual's injury or death in the event. A major part of this case was questioning whether the shooting was justified and if the defendant had an alternative to the use of lethal force. The state courts have ruled that warning shots are viewed as an option to lethal force where none may exist otherwise in an ultimate effort to avoid injury or death. The court viewed these as a lifesaving option and no legal support for a ban on warning shots was found as long as there was no danger to other, uninvolved parties (Mulroy & Santiago, 1998).

Most agencies however, forbid the use of warning shots (Grossi, 2002b). In spite of court support, agencies are most often holding their personnel to a more restrictive and higher standard for firearms use. For example, there was a case of an officer who, while off-duty and walking his own dog, was confronted by two other dogs who began to bark. The officer fired his service revolver into the ground to scare the other dogs away and was subsequently terminated for this action (*Law and Order,* 2000e). In this case, there was no threat to human life as a result of the warning shot; however, the department chose to exercise the higher standard of firearms use.

This type of investigation will also be primarily based in published and trained departmental policy. While the legal and civil issues will fall to case law, such as the example provided in *Minnesota v. McKissic,* the justification and/or discipline will be based upon the acceptable standards of firearm use by the agency.

Questionable Shootings

As previously discussed, for the most part, the overwhelming majority of police-involved shootings are determined to be justified. There exists however, a category that deserves discussion concerning shootings that may appear to not be justified upon initial review, but may later prove to be justified based upon the review of the totality of the circumstances involved. These are shootings that occur where the officer may not appear overtly justified in his or her actions to employ deadly force. They are referred to as questionable shootings and can be defined as those that occur when the suspect who was shot by the police was unarmed and not assaultive at the time of the shooting (Aveni, 2002a).

Thomas Aveni (2003a) states that, "Questionable shootings are largely attributable to misidentification of threat level due to impaired visual contrast sensitivity in low levels of ambient light, precipitating suspect behavior, and context-based expectations relative to the nature of the assignment or call" (p. 85). Anecdotal evidence places the number of questionable shootings in the range of 10–15 percent (Aveni, 2002a). A contemporary example of this was the case of Amadou Diallo, which involved a street stop of a subject who was unarmed. The officers involved fired at Diallo which resulted in his death. The officers were indicted and later acquitted of all charges based upon the officer's belief that they were being threatened and the interpretation that they were at some point under fire. While a case of extreme media and public controversy, the officers were found justified in their actions despite the later investigation revealing that Diallo was not armed at the time of the encounter.

To understand the differentiation between incidents that appear completely justified and those that appear questionable, the criminal and internal investigator should understand some basic rules of engagement. The first distinction is between the concepts of an immediate threat, when one is faced with a an edged weapon or deadly instrument within contact distance, as opposed to an immediate threat, wherein one is faced with a suspect with an edged weapon or deadly instrument charging from a distance (Aveni, 2002a). The outcome of both scenarios can be equally fatal.

Likewise, consider the hypothetical scenario of a suicidal suspect who confronts the officer holding a weapon to his own head. The subject states that he will enter the house to kill his wife and then commit suicide. The only options are to allow the subject to enter the house or end the proclaimed threat by shooting the subject. The investigation later reveals that the weapon was a realistic looking toy gun and no one was in the house. While this may be branded a suicide-by-cop scenario, it can also be branded as a questionable shooting as the subject really posed no threat to anyone. The facts leading up to scenarios of this nature are critical to bring out during the investigation in order to ensure that a just finding is applied to the incident.

These cases are the true test of the objectivity of the criminal and internal investigators involved in the case. While the public, media, and police administrators may all be calling for the officer's "head on a spear," the reality is the criminal and internal investigators must be influenced by one thing only, the evidence in the case and the finding that the evidence supports. The criminal and internal investigators must be tenacious and resilient in their search for and communication of the truth.

Recommended Question Format

The internal investigator should have a prepared list of questions for when such critical incidents as police-involved shootings occur. While no list can be all encompassing, they present a checklist to cover the foundational issues that can lead to more probing and incident specific questions. The following list is an example of a series of questions that can be used in the interview of the involved officer:

1. What is the officer's current assignment?
2. What was the officer's attire (e.g., uniform or plainclothes)? Was a badge or identification clearly visible on the offi-

cer's plainclothes attire if worn at the time of the incident?

3. Was the officer operating a marked or unmarked vehicle?
4. What type of issued and authorized equipment was being carried by the officer and was it immediately available at the time of the incident (e.g., pepper spray, PR-24, bulletproof vest, other, etc.)?
5. Does the officer need corrective lenses? Was the officer wearing them at time of shooting? If not, was it voluntary, or involuntary, such as glasses lost during a foot chase or struggle?
6. Did the officer have any prior information that the suspect was armed?
7. Did the officer have any prior information that the suspect has been violent prior to the arrival at this incident or any past history of violence? Does the officer know if the suspect had a history of previous weapons possession or use?
8. The officer should describe the escalation of verbal and physical force (if any) before the shooting occurred. Could the officer have reasonably and safely utilized another means of force (e.g., pepper spray, PR-24, etc.)?
9. When was the officer's weapon drawn?
10. Why did the officer discharge his or her weapon? Important: The internal investigator should allow the officer the opportunity to describe the threat without leading him/her.
11. When was the safety on the officer's weapon removed?
12. What type of weapon was used by the officer and the suspect?
13. What type of ammunition was used and available to the officer (e.g., issued or authorized) and suspect?
14. Number of rounds fired by officer and suspect?
15. The succession and sound of the rounds.
16. Was any reload performed including why and when? What was done with spent magazine/rounds?
17. Was there any weapon malfunction including the nature of the malfunction?
18. What stance was used by officer and suspect?
19. Was there any stance change as shots were being fired?
20. What was the distance between officer and suspect during the incident?
21. Which hand(s) were used to fire weapon for both the officer and suspect?
22. The officer should describe the suspect's actions before, during, and after the shooting. The internal investigator should also have the officer describe the suspect's body movements while being shot.
23. Was there any muzzle flash observed by the officer from the suspect's weapon?
24. The officer should be asked about the position of any witnesses to the shooting.
25. The officer should describe the background behind the suspect at the point of the shooting. The officer should also describe the line of fire between the officer and suspect.
26. Was the officer or suspect injured as a result of the shooting?
27. The officer should describe any attempt to seek cover before or during the incident.
28. Could the officer determine what the suspect was aiming at?
29. Does the officer know where the suspect's rounds struck? Where his rounds struck?
30. Where was the suspect's weapon recovered? Did anyone touch or move the suspect's weapon? The officer should describe the weapon as best as possible.
31. Did anyone examine/secure the officer's weapon? If so, who and why?
32. Did anyone examine/secure the suspect's weapon? If so, who and why?

Scene Management and Responsibilities

There are a series of tasks that should be completed at the scene of a police involved shooting. These tasks are divided into three categories: (1) investigative, (2) administrative, and (3) medical records. The following is a list of these tasks by category.

Investigative Tasks: The investigative tasks are those directly related to the search for evidence, interviews, and related tasks of documenting the scene from the perspective of the criminal and internal investigator. These tasks include:

1. Scene diagram prepared by an evidence technician, internal investigations investigator, and the involved officer(s).
2. Photographs of the scene, suspect, and involved officer(s) by an evidence technician, internal investigator, and officers at the scene.
3. Photographs of the weapon, gun belt, and all issued equipment worn at the time of the incident.
4. Video of the scene.
5. Dispatch or emergency communications copies of 911 tapes, radio channel traffic of the event, and the need to secure master tapes as evidence.
6. Rundown for all working the geographical area of employment for that shift.
7. All involved investigative reports (e.g., crime, investigative action, grand jury package, etc.).
8. Reports that document crucial statements (e.g., gun did not fire because safety was on; is there a report documenting that someone found the safety on?).
9. Suspect/victim criminal history.
10. All witness statements to include affidavits and depositions.
11. Results of the neighborhood canvass.
12. Ballistics report(s).

Administrative Tasks: The administrative tasks are those directly related to the collection of all administrative reports and documents that relate to the internal investigation and potential civil liability. These tasks include:

1. All involved administrative reports (e.g., use-of-force/subject management package, supplemental reports, officer injured, post-pursuit, etc.).
2. Any separate administrative or special reports completed by involved and investigating personnel.
3. Involved officer complaint and use-of-force history.

Medical Records Tasks: The medical records tasks are those directly related to the collection of all medical reports and documents that relate to the internal investigation and potential civil liability. These tasks include:

1. Medical Records Release Forms collection.
2. Preliminary and final hospital reports.
3. Ambulance personnel notes and reports.
4. Medical Examiner/Coroner report(s) and evidentiary photographs.

Post-Incident Debriefings and Comprehensive Reports

This section discusses the concept and practice of post-incident debriefing for the purpose of examining the critical incident from a policy, procedure, and tactical perspective in order to improve future operations. These are specifically used for the purpose of identifying concerns, lessons learned, resolving problems, and formulating better plans of action for future deployments in a method of continuous improvement. In the post-incident debriefing session, personnel should describe their duties, activities, and perceptions. Supervisors should review the thinking process, how the incident met departmental policy, and if policies are contemporary and workable (Bar, 2003; Meyer, 2001). There are two types of debriefings that are relevant to this discussion: (1) group and (2) individual.

General Concepts: Post-incident debriefings are not a new idea and if used as a training concept, can be of immense value. For both types, the purpose of the debriefing should be clear to all involved. Rules should also be in place mandating that all discoveries will be treated solely as training issues. The administrator should not engage in these types of interchanges unless they are fully prepared to follow through with these types of promises. In addition, prior to any debriefing occurring in an agency, the administrator must understand the legal and civil ramifications of any disclosures that are made. These interchanges are not protected by any privilege and as such, all of those involved can be summoned to testify in any subsequent departmental or court proceedings. If the organization chooses to conduct debriefings of this nature, then notes/minutes, or a final report should be generated in order to document the outcome and defend against claims of a cover-up should they arise in the future. The administrator, facilitator, and involved personnel must understand at the outset that any document relating to a specific case is subject to the discovery process (Nowicki, 2001f).

Group Debriefings: Group debriefings are effective for gaining the perspectives of all individuals involved. While conveying the aspects of the incident, the facilitator should start at the initial responder and work upwards through the rank structure to gain not only a chronological picture of the progression of the event, but more importantly, to identify real time information that was the impetus for decisions that were made along the way. This prevents the ominous influence of hindsight in the review and keeps the process on track to its original intent of being a training concept.

Individual Debriefings: Individual debriefings also have an immense value in working an officer through the details of the incident in order for them to document every aspect of their memory of the incident. Individual and small group debriefings, such as in the case of two or three officers involved in a police shooting, as opposed to everyone on the scene or involved in the investigation carry value in that they are conducted by a facilitator who is a subject matter expert in the organization's firearms and defensive tactics training as well as departmental policy. These debriefings are critical because of the consequences of a police-involved shooting that can be realized by the officer, agency, and community. Thomas Aveni (2003a) speaks to the critical nature of clearly and accurately recalling and documenting these types of incidents as he states, "All too frequently, the delineation between an in-policy shooting and one that isn't will fall within a fraction of a second" (p. 87). An independent facilitator can walk the involved officer through the event so that the facts can be recounted in the chronology they occurred.

Because of numerous reasons that affect the officer's ability to convey the details of the event, including the stress of being involved in these types of incidents, the officer should be afforded this opportunity to accurately recount and document their version of the event. For example, due to stress, officers can be disoriented and often cannot recall the minor details of an incident accurately in the immediate aftermath. A structured debriefing process can help this recollection. To facilitate this, a pocket guide or software program can be provided to help the officer gather their thoughts and accurately document the incident. Officers never seem to have enough time to give their own statement the time they deserve (McBride, 2001). In addition, when conducting a debriefing, even in incidents of minor uses of force, the agency also needs to review the incident from several different perspectives. Techniques that an officer uses may be reasonable from a legal perspective, but there may be another option that could be used from a safety or injury reduction perspective (Nowicki, 2001b).

Officers should be debriefed and assisted in preparation of their written evidence by an expert. Such an expert would: (1) guide officers through their statements, (2) helping them with the structure, (3) providing guidance to describe the techniques used, and (4) reminding officers to include those technical and anatomical terms which were covered in their officer safety training course. A comprehensive statement will not only state what technique was used, but also describe it in layman's terms. A comprehensive report will also protect officers from malicious complaints or civil litigation (McBride, 2001).

A few additional concerns arise when the issue of post-incident debriefings is discussed. The first is the need for a facilitator who is a subject matter expert. This will keep the debriefing and comprehensive report on track and in line with the intent of this process. The second issue is that great care must be taken in the distribution of such a report, whether it consists of the officer's comprehensive statement through the use-of-force/subject management report, or the records of the group debriefing of the incident. Not only are they discoverable, but can also be used in a maligned way in the organization. For example, an incident debriefing is conducted and a summary presentation is provided to the command staff of the organization prior to the completion of any internal investigation. If this case results in the contemplation of discipline, the claim could be made that the command staff who reviewed the disciplinary package or who were members of any subsequent command review board were not impartial, but rather, tainted by the original review and presentation. While the practices of post-incident debriefings and comprehensive reports are a recommended strategy, they must be done correctly to have the desired outcome.

ACCIDENTAL DISCHARGES

Accidental discharges are a concern of police administrators and police trainers alike. The safety and liability issues are replete in incidents where an innocent party is struck by a police bullet by accident. There are several reasons that may be attributed to an accidental discharge to include unsafe handling of the weapon, mechanical failures, and failure to adhere to training standards. They are also attributable to physiological responses of the body in stressful situations. Phil Messina (2000) states that research in this area:

> Strongly indicates that officers who are trained to disengage into a fisted position when under stress are likely to have an involuntary weapon discharge when they disengage with their gun in their hand. . . . Unfortunately, when these discharges occur, agencies are slow to take responsibility and instead leave their officers 'swinging in the wind.' The fact is that most involuntary discharges are caused by unavoidable physiological reactions or reactions that were conditioned into officers during training. (p. 32)

The internal investigation into an accidental discharge should include the basic investigative responsibilities of scene examination and evidence recovery as well as identifying witnesses. This type of investigation should also include confiscating the officer's weapon and having the firearm tested for operability and functional safety mechanisms by lab and firearms instructor staff. In the interview process, the internal investigator should explore the firearms training history of the officer involved as well as the tactics or techniques used prior to the accidental discharge. The internal investigator should ascertain if the discharge occurred as a result of a weapons malfunction, a violation of safety protocol, or during an uncontrollable confrontation with a suspect as in the case of an officer wrestling for custody of a weapon with a violent or resisting suspect.

Figure 9-2. Victim precipitated suicide can be extremely traumatic to the involved officer who is forced into this situation and has no alternative but to use deadly physical force to protect themselves and others (Photo courtesy of the Brockport, New York Police Department).

VICTIM-PRECIPITATED SUICIDE

Victim-precipitated suicide (also termed victim-assisted suicide and suicide-by-cop) is a complex issue for the internal and criminal investigator to grasp. More importantly, it is a difficult issue to investigate as the incidences may be grossly underreported because an investigation did not reveal enough evidence to support such a finding. This section discusses the definition of victim-precipitated suicide, the legal considerations, offender considerations, officer considerations, investigative considerations, and death by indifference.

Several issues affect the entire schema of the victim-precipitated suicide phenomenon. For example, because of deinstitutionalization, the propensity of officer contacts with emotionally disturbed persons has grown immensely over the years. In the Tampa, Florida area, the rate of incarcerated persons that are estimated to have some type of mental illness is in the range of 16 percent (Weiss & Dresser, 2000b). Research conducted in this area has revealed that there is a lack of awareness with criminal justice professionals who do not fully understand the issues and complexities concerning incidents of victim-precipitated suicide. Law enforcement needs to educate both the private and public sectors, especially groups such as medical examiners, coroners, and the media, regarding this phenomenon of victim-precipitated suicide. In the vast majority of cases reviewed in the research, the medical examiner/coroner ruled the manner of death a homicide rather than a suicide (Pinizzotto & Davis, 1999).

Several empirical studies have supported the existence of this phenomenon. For example, a study of 58 cases in British Columbia found that roughly 48 percent had characteristics associated with victim-precipitated homicide. In the majority of the cases, the victim's statements, actions, and bizarre behavior clearly reflected suicidal intent (Parent, 1998). Another study in the Los Angeles County Sheriff's Department consisted of the review of 437 officer-involved shootings which revealed that victim-precipitated suicide accounted for 46 or 11 percent of the shootings. The study also revealed that these types of incidents are on the rise (Paynter, 2000). Still another study completed in Philadelphia found that of 588 homicides studied, 26 percent were victim-precipitated (Parent, 1998). It is estimated that 10 percent to 50 percent police shootings involve victim-precipitated suicide (Burke & Rigsby, 1999).

Victim Precipitated Suicide Defined

In order for the issue of victim-precipitated suicide to be understood by law enforcement, a clear definition must be developed at the very least, within the agency that recognizes this phenomenon. This also should be extended to development and adoption by agencies and medical examiners/coroners throughout the country (Pinizzotto & Davis, 1999). The development and use of this theory in policy as a method of fostering an understanding in both the officer's, administrator's, and jury's minds that the officer was not at fault, but merely the vehicle for a person's ultimate desire to die at someone's hands other than their own.

The psychological foundation of victim-precipitated suicide encounters are based upon the interactional theory of violence that is the act of the participant precipitates the act of the police which may lead to the use of deadly physical force (Burke & Rigsby, 1999; Parent, 1998). In theory, police may be chosen as executors because of the stigma attached to suicide, convenience, those who are unwilling or unable to take their own life, or insurance recovery for surviving family members (Burke & Rigsby, 1999).

In the definition of victim-precipitated suicide, several experts have explored those similar characteristics in the act that are prevalent in such incidents. For example, victim-precipitated suicide is an incident in which an individual bent on self-destruction, engages in life-threatening and criminal behavior in order to force law enforcement officers to kill him/her (Burke & Rigsby, 1999). Dr. Audrey L. Honig (2001) also defines a victim-precipitated suicide incident as, "An event in which an individual engages in behavior that poses an apparent risk of serious injury or death to others, with the intent of precipitating the use of deadly force by law enforcement personnel" (p. 89). Victim-precipitated suicide is also termed as victim-assisted suicide and victim-precipitated homicide (Parent, 1998; Paynter, 2000).

Legal Considerations

Beyond the psychological issues that are faced by the involved officer as well as the subject, there is also a concern for the legal and liability issues involved in these types of incidents. These issues are compounded by the notion that lawsuits can result when an officer fails to recognize that a person suffers from a mental illness (Hill & Logan, 2001). Officers are faced with uncooperative and sometimes violent subjects on a consistent basis. A realistic expectation of the officer's capacity to recognize these types of individuals is necessary for the officer, agency, and community as a whole.

An example of liability in suicide cases can be found in *Quezada v. County of Bernalillo* (1991) decided in the Tenth Circuit Court, where the district court found an officer was negligent when he placed himself in jeopardy by leaving cover and "forcing the confrontation" which resulted in the shooting and killing of a suicidal woman, who pointed a gun in an officer's direction (Ijames, 1999). However, conflicting cases exist such as in *Adams v. Fremont* (1998), wherein the California Appellate Court ruled:

> We will not impose a duty that requires police officers to choose between refusing to offer assistance at the scene of a threatened suicide or assuming full responsibility for the

> suicidal individual's welfare. This choice discourages police officers from rendering assistance in these inherently unpredictable situations in which even highly trained mental health professionals cannot guarantee success. Any reduction in the availability of police assistance at the scene of a threatened suicide would severely compromise public safety and likely result in more deaths or injuries. (Milazzo & McNaught, 2002)

Another interesting note is that litigation has commenced on the grounds that emotionally disturbed persons are protected under the *Americans with Disabilities Act* (ADA) in that the act prohibits discrimination against qualified individuals with disabilities in the delivery of government services, programs, or activities. With respect to use-of-force, the federal district courts have decided in *Hainze v. Richards* (2000) and *Gohier v. Enright* (1999) that an officer has no duty to reasonably accommodate a subject demonstrating violent behavior or the officer's actions that are a result of the subject's conduct. A general guideline is that the courts have held that the ADA does not prohibit officers from taking enforcement action, including the use-of-force, necessary to protect the officer or provide for public safety (Litchford, 2000).

While the courts have been supportive of police actions in these types of incidents, the mentally ill are a special-needs population. Law enforcement organizations can mitigate liability through the development of a training program, targeting this special needs population by crisis intervention training (Hill & Logan, 2001; Honig, 2001). An officer cannot be held liable in a victim-assisted suicide unless the officer's actions were unjustifiable (Burke & Rigsby, 1999).

Figure 9-3. Because of deinstitutionalization law enforcement is forced into a position to handle an increasing number of emotionally disturbed persons in their daily contacts (Photo courtesy of the Brockport, New York Police Department).

Offender Considerations

To conduct the investigation, the internal investigator should have an understanding of the offender characteristics involved in victim-precipitated suicide incidents. The underlying characteristic is one of mental illness in these subjects. Mental illness can be psychotic, which is a progressive disintegration of an individual's personality and due to overwhelming stress coupled with an individual's inability to adequately cope. Lesser conditions known as personality disorders result in an inability to behave in a socially acceptable manner. Known as sociopathic or psychopathic personalities, this group makes up a large part of the career criminal population in our jails and prisons (Fuller, 2000). These characteristics can be manifested through drug and alcohol abuse, history of domestic violence, documented mental problems history, the murder of a significant other, terminal illness, traumatic experience, criminal record indicating a history of violence, planning one's own death, and suicide notes (Burke & Rigsby, 1999; Honig, 2001; Paynter, 2000). Precipitators are often able to withstand severe pain and discomfort while persisting in their efforts to force the victim officers to use deadly force (Honig, 2001). Steve Ijames (2002) also identifies these types of individuals as an unconventional adversary by describing them as, "One who is potentially very dangerous, but clearly outside the realm of the armed and assaultive hardened criminal" (p. 93).

Research conducted into other cases revealed similarities in these types of incidents such as: (1) the subjects initiated the contact, (2) the subjects refused to comply with repeated commands to drop their guns, and (3) the subjects displayed replica guns (Pinizzotto & Davis, 1999). Further research involved a study in the Los Angeles County Sheriff's Department which revealed that verbal dissuasion consisting of commands to drop the weapon were used in 95.7 percent of the cases reviewed and had minimal success in defusing the situations. The study also found that in 23 percent of the cases officers tried to subdue the individual through less-lethal tactics that included beanbags, pepper spray, Taser systems, tear gas and hand-to-hand combat, but, in every case, these tactics failed (Paynter, 2000).

The psychological illness coupled with such aggravating factors as alcohol or drug abuse, make the subject intent on victim-precipitated suicide one of the most difficult, if not impossible situations faced by modern day law enforcement officers. The motivation of these subjects is a significant mitigating factor in investigating and reviewing an officer's actions who is involved in attempting to gain control of emotionally disturbed individual's intent on committing suicide in this manner.

Officer Considerations

Sadly, the officers are the true victims in these incidents. Officers are most often placed in impossible situations wherein a motivated subject is not amenable to any resolution strategy other than the completion of their intended act. Officers will often feel guilt, anger, a sense of failure, a sense of being used, may believe that more could have been done to prevent the incident, may experience diminished self-confidence, and a sense of responsibility to the victim's family (Burke & Rigsby, 1999; Honig, 2001). The organization must provide crisis intervention counseling for those officers who need the psychological support to survive these encounters. Organizations should also develop training and policy that will provide department and legally sanctioned options for when these situations arise. The concept of management of officer jeopardy is an operational philosophy committed to preventing an unnecessary officer/suspect confrontation (Ijames, 1999). Through training and policy, these incidents can be minimized and safer resolution strategies provided for the officer and subject.

Investigative Considerations

From the investigative perspective, in order to determine the true nature of the incident, the investigator must examine areas not traditionally explored in a criminal or internal investigation. Criminal and internal investigations conducted after shootings have rarely examined the mental state of the precipitator–the person forcing the shooting (Honig, 2001). Criminal and internal investigators have, at times, added to problems created by this situation by failing to examine the root causes of the victim's behavior (Parent, 1998). This is the cause of the confrontation and must be a significant part of the investigation if it can be determined.

There are several mental illnesses that subjects may suffer from that need to be understood so that they can be recognized and included in the investigation when learned. Mental conditions include psychosis, schizophrenia, depression and manic-depression, Post-Traumatic Stress Disorder (PTSD), and substance abuse. In addition, the risk of violence is high when substance abuse is involved, especially with alcohol (Clede, 1998). While psychological diseases may be well-hidden to the responding officer, another problem is created when no immediate or overt signs exist of suicidal intent that can be detected by the responding officer. Dr. Audrey L. Honig (2001) states that there may be no specific indicators of suicidal intent discovered until after the incident, but persons at risk for suicide by cop may display a variety of indicators, including the following: (1) prior thoughts of suicide, (2) feelings of helplessness and/or hopelessness, and (3) drastic mood swings. In addition, observable behaviors may include the following:

1. Failing to comply with orders and directions.
2. Advancing toward the officer.
3. Forcing a confrontation and/or engaging in acts which escalate the situation.
4. Not attempting to escape, surrender, or retreat.
5. Demanding that the law enforcement officer kill the suspect.
6. Expressing a desire to go out in a blaze of glory.
7. Making a last will and testament verbally.
8. Telling family members or friends of a desire to die.
9. Declaring that prison is not an option. (p. 91)

The true nature may be difficult to discover as there is usually minimal to no documentation of the victim's intent (Parent, 1998). The internal and criminal investigator should endeavor to determine if the subject was (or is) under medical supervision and contact the physician to conduct an interview (Pinizzotto & Davis, 1999). Several recommended interview questions of witnesses in these incidents include:

1. Has/was the subject drinking prior to the incident? Is there a history of alcohol abuse?
2. Has/was the subject abused/abusing drugs prior to the incident? Is there a history of drug abuse?
3. Does/did the subject have a history of violence?
4. Does/did the subject suffer from mental illness?
5. Does/did the subject ever attempt suicide?
6. Was there a weapon involved?
7. Does/did the subject ever confront others with a weapon in the past?
8. Does/did the subject ever threaten to kill a police officer or express a desire to be killed by a police officer in the past?
9. Does/did the subject experience domestic problems?
10. Did the subject appear to be out of control? Yelling? Rage?
11. Was the subject ever arrested in the past? If so, what for? (Burke & Rigsby, 1999)

Beyond the traditional evidence recovery methods, another recommended strategy is to collect and place into evidence all recordings and 911 tapes (Pinizzotto & Davis, 1999). These records may also indicate the subject's intent, or at least give an additional dimension to the investigation after review and transcription. The internal and criminal investigator should also ascertain if less lethal options were available and viable at the time of the incident (Burke & Rigsby, 1999). If so, they should not be used as a stand-alone tactic, but with lethal force back-up in the event that the less-lethal option fails (Honig, 2001). The internal investigator should also include any previously developed or disseminated information of this nature on the subject to patrol and the officer involved in the shooting. The information needs to be captured and made part of the investigative package.

Death by Indifference

An interesting legal concept being discussed in the realm of victim-precipitated suicide is that of "Death by Indifference" (Praet, 2002; G. T. Williams, 2003a). Subjects who are intoxicated by drugs, alcohol, or some forms of mental illness may not demonstrate their willingness to commit suicide by actions, but rather act in a manner that provokes a deadly physical force situation.

Absent any substantive information concerning the subject's intent to commit suicide, in the defense of the police in the resulting civil suit, it may be difficult to convince a jury that the decedent truly intended to commit suicide. Experience also dictates that some juries will be unwilling to render a verdict that tells the grieving relatives that their now departed loved one committed suicide-by-cop.

While not a victim precipitated suicide in the textbook definition, in the case of death by indifference, the person is probably not a victim. He or she really doesn't assist in bringing about his or her own death. It is simply that the subject was willing to take action without regard for the possibility that they may die. Unlike suicide by cop, the concept of death by indifference is much more palatable to a jury. Therefore, it is highly recommended that situations that do not fit the classic suicide-by-cop, but which instead fit within the death by indifference profile, be classified as such from the outset and throughout all related legal proceedings (Praet, 2002; G. T. Williams, 2003a).

IN-CUSTODY DEATHS

The issue of in-custody deaths is a perplexing and serious concern for law enforcement officers, administrators, the community, medical researchers, and legal counsel alike. These incidents occur infrequently, but evoke great controversy and liability. The most obvious of cases deal with trauma sustained by a subject during the efforts of law enforcement to gain control or custody. Additional considerations are those cases that involve other aggravating factors brought on by the subject. For example, in the case of Nathaniel Jones, who was arrested in Cincinnati in 2003, his death was a direct result of factors beyond the control of the arresting officers. While the officers were involved in using force to take him into custody, an autopsy by Hamilton County Coroner Dr. Carl Parrott revealed that Jones suffered from obesity, had an enlarged heart, and "intoxicating levels" of PCP, embalming fluid, and cocaine in his blood (Cable News Network, December 1, 2003; Cable News Network, May 6, 2004). An insignificant number of these cases results in any culpability on behalf of the involved personnel. Those that do are usually clear concerning the actions and culpability of the involved personnel.

The majority of these incidents aren't as clear cut. This will leave questions in the minds of all involved if unresolved. The investigation will center on two issues: (1) the cause of death and (2) the justification for taking custody or control of the subject and the reasonableness of the force exerted to achieve this objective. The cause of death is as critical to determine as the methods and level of force used. The cause of death may have no relationship to the use-of-force and subsequently will relieve the involved officer and agency of significant culpability as well as liability. These investigations should proceed as do others discussed in this text; however, a significant effort should be made at determining medical history and the medical state of the subject at the time of the incident.

Positional Asphyxia

The controversy surrounding the issue of positional asphyxia is even greater than that of the issue of in-custody deaths. Part of the controversy emerges from a lack of expertise and research compounded by the unreasonable need of society to blame the police for the death of person who is in their custody.

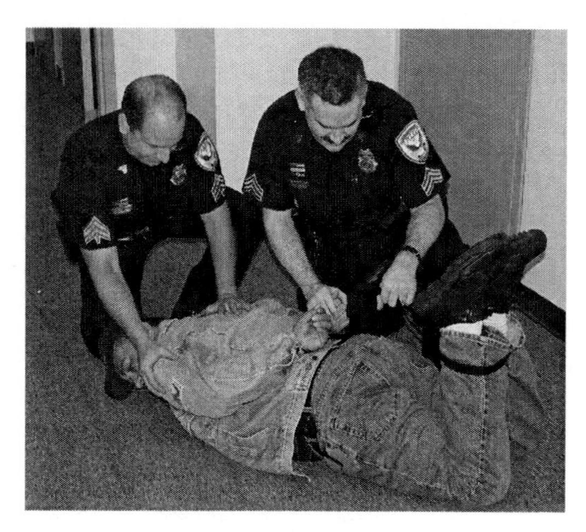

Figure 9-4. Positional asphyxia is a phenomenon that is based in confusing research, however, it is also an area of serious concern for police administrators (Photo courtesy of the Brockport, New York Police Department).

Time has made the issue more confusing and more lucid.

At the outset, to define the medical reason, asphyxia is a decrease in blood oxygen levels or an increase in blood carbon dioxide levels (Byrd, 2000). The theory is that sudden in-custody death syndrome occurs as a result of "excited delirium" (also known as "acute exhaustive mania") brought on by schizophrenia or acute drug intoxication, particularly cocaine, phencyclidine (PCP), or methamphetamine. To the extent that the effects of schizophrenia and drug abuse are uncontrollable, it may be that many of these deaths cannot be prevented (Meyer, 1999). The theory of positional asphyxia is appealing to forensic pathologists because it assists them in determining a cause of death when there is no anatomic evidence. It is appealing to the families of people who die in custody because it allows them to blame someone other than the deceased (Reak, 1998a). These types of incidents are sometimes confused with, or accompanied by, some type issues which suggest positional asphyxia and, therefore, sometimes the cause of death is attributed to positional asphyxia. Dependant upon the expertise of the medical examiner, the cause of death is undetermined or misdetermined and therefore leaves open the suggestion that the police are responsible for the death of the individual (Makholm, 2002d).

The problem with the theory of positional asphyxia is that no one has proven it to be true (Reak, 1998a). Early studies attributing cause of death in cases categorized as positional asphyxia have been disproven by Dr. Chan and Dr. Neuman of the University of California at San Diego, and further studies by Paul Schmidt of San Diego County (Bragg, 2000). A review of autopsy reports involving restraint deaths reveals that people, particularly mental patients and persons under the influence of drugs, die while being restrained in all sorts of positions, including face-up in bed and sitting upright in chairs. These cases suggest that it is the struggle against restraint, not impaired breathing, which triggers the arrhythmia that causes death (Reak, 1998a).

In addition, maximal restraints such as "hog-tying" have been attributed to the phenomenon of positional asphyxia. The courts have been presented with conflicting research studies examining the physiological effect, if any, of these restraints. More recent research has suggested that such restraints may be "physiologically neutral" (Byrd, 2000; Meyer, 1999; Reak, 1998a). Contemporary medical research accompanied by legal opinion strongly suggests that this condition may not be the panacea for medical examiners, litigation specialists, and the vocal community.

Legal Issues of Positional Asphyxia

Since the inception of the phenomenon of positional asphyxia has entered the law enforcement realm, several cases have been decided against the efficacy of the concept. For example, the case of *Fernandez v. City of Cooper City* (2002) decided in the Eleventh Circuit Court involved a resistive male suspect who stopped breathing after being restrained. Witness testimony in the case revealed that the officers did not use any excessive force on the plaintiff. Despite the plaintiff's medical expert's testimony that the officer's actions contributed to the plaintiff's death, the Court ruled in favor of the officers and department rendering summary judgment. The Court acknowledged that it was of course an unfortunate occurrence, but sympathy for a plaintiff does not transform law enforcement officials' objectively reasonable responses to a volatile situation into a constitutional violation (Makholm, 2002d).

In *Price v. County of San Diego, et al.* (1998), the Court:

> Finally concluded that the evidence for positional asphyxia has fallen completely. . . . The hog-tie restraint in and of itself does not constitute excessive force–when a violent individual has resisted less severe restraint techniques, applying a physiologically neutral restraint that will immobilize him is not excessive force. (Byrd, 2000)

Several additional cases that have been decided against the concept of positional asphyxia are *Phillips v. Milwaukee* (1996) and *Cottrell v. Caldwell* (1996), while a case decided in support of the concept was *Animashaun v. O'Donnell* (1995) (Reak, 1998a). While all medical precautions should remain in effect for the treatment of injured prisoners, this should not affect the lack of culpability on officers for unforeseen tragedies involved in the normal course of the officer's duties.

Also for consideration in the investigation is an interesting case involving expert testimony in an in-custody death decided in the Eleventh Circuit Court in *Cottrell v. Caldwell* (1996) where the Court stated that in order to hold the police liable under section 1983 for an in-custody death the plaintiff must produce a great deal more evidence than expert testimony that the police violated "generally accepted police procedures" (MacLatchie, 2000).

Investigative Considerations

An investigator protocol should be developed in the investigation of all in-custody death situations. Chris Lawrence and Wanda K. Mohr (2004) have developed an excellent and thorough protocol for in-custody death investigation where consideration should be given to all of the following:

1. Subject's personal history.
2. Residential history to include all past residences.
3. Educational history to include school records of maladaptation, propensity for violence or outbursts, maltreatment, physical and sexual abuse or neglect, special education needs, major traumatic events such a deaths in the family, out-of-home placement, major illnesses or surgeries, history of truancy, medically suspicious events such as fainting, frequent accidents, or incidents suggestive of substance or alcohol abuse.
4. Family history to include genetic and environmental influences, domestic violence or domestic disturbances that may indicate drug or alcohol abuse, family history of mental illness, illnesses sometimes associated with sudden death such as cardiovascular problems, history of drug or alcohol abuse, or major stressors encountered in life.
5. Employment history to include the determination of occupational functioning as it is an important indicator of psychological adaptation, indicators of psychiatric difficulties or patterns of interpersonal

conflict or violence, history of behavioral problems at work or during military service, long gaps in employment indicating hospitalization or incarceration, health insurance records, doctors, and prescription medications.

6. Financial history to include as it is an indicator of stability or conversely, high stress and the presence of mental illness, unusual patterns of bank activity, civil suits, bankruptcies, large unserviced debts, active collections, can all serve as intense stressors that might exacerbate pre-existing psychiatric conditions.
7. Police contact history to include psychiatric illness, substance abuse, or violent behavior, arrest records, domestic violence or disturbance calls, drunk driving records, probation, parole, presentencing reports, and court-ordered psychiatric assessments.
8. Medical history to include acute or chronic illnesses, past medical treatment, a family history of risk factors, a list of current prescription medications and over-the-counter drug purchases, a search of the residence for all medications and any illicit drugs, medication information such as date of prescription, amount dispensed, and amount remaining, or if the subject has stopped using any medication, recent medically related purchases, health plan records, local pharmacy records and physician records specifically the months before the incident to indicate any change in from the usual state of functioning, search for double doctoring, conditions such as diabetes, asthma, psychotic hallucinations, epilepsy, and acute mania, consult a clinical toxicologist or pharmacist when multiple drugs may have or have been taken to determine possible side effects.
9. Nutritional history to include as to what the subject had to eat that day and any marked changes in eating habits as different foods and medications/drugs can exacerbate such conditions as polydipsia and other potentially fatal medical conditions.
10. Behavioral history to include friends, relatives, neighbors, and coworkers who can speak of unusual behavior, whether the subject's physical or mental condition has worsened in recent history, and anything that could lead to significant stress.
11. Substance abuse to include history, duration, frequency, to what level, and types such as cocaine, amphetamine, alcohol, or over-the-counter stimulants, or alcohol.
12. Determining the common link between psychosocial stressors as precipitants of violent behavior in predisposed individuals, and their role in the exacerbation of mental illnesses.
13. The incident to include the duration of objectionable behavior prior to police contact, details of the person's behavior leading up to police intervention documenting everything that was said and done by the subject, aroused states such as hyperventilating, hallucinating, shouting, running, pacing furiously, or the presence of an exaggerated startle response, the nature and duration of the resistance, documenting such descriptors of emotional state such as anger, fear, rage, subject's aggression towards the police whether or not if it was a defensive or offensive posture, efforts needed to bring the subject under control, fitness level, age, size, and experience of the officers necessary to gain control of the situation, how was the subject transported, how the subject was restrained, how vigorously the subject struggled against the restraints, duration of the subject's agitated state including agitation prior to police response, which may exacerbate such

medical conditions as rhabdomyolysis, calmness may also mimic a state of compliance, need to document that the person is breathing and that they have a pulse when they cease to struggle, when transported to the emergency department, it is important that the subject's body temperature be recorded, core body temperature should be obtained before, at the time of, and after the subject's death, also include any observation indicating the subject's body temperature, thyroid or cricoid conditions can actually impede airflow and cause injury during intubation.

14. Environmental factors to include climatic conditions, including noting temperature trends during the week prior to the incident, if the subject was overdressed, if there was a prolonged struggle on a hot day, temperature and relative humidity readings at the time of the incident, inside temperatures as well including lack of climate control systems, and the climate data of the room where the deceased has been stored in, if medical personnel made attempts to restrain the subject, if the subject was able to expel body heat or not through sweating, which may be a side effect of medications or narcotics taken, dimensions of the room in question and the number of people present, data collected from all locations from which the subject was placed, if restrained on the ground, consideration must be given to the surface temperature, may need the services of a forensic climatologist.

SUMMARY

This chapter discussed investigations that involve deadly physical force and in-custody deaths. The chapter began by discussing the importance and major components of critical incident scene management. The chapter then progressed through the internal investigator's responsibilities at a police-involved shooting, stressing such mitigating factors as the affects of physiological and environmental impacts on officer capacity and perception. The chapter also provided a recommended list of questions that can be used during the officer interview as well as a list of tasks to be performed in the event of a police-involved shooting. The chapter also discussed in-depth the issues surrounding the phenomenon of victim-precipitated suicide along with the psychological and investigative needs of these types of investigations. The chapter concluded with a discussion and protocol for the investigation of in-custody deaths.

Chapter 10

SPECIAL INVESTIGATIONS

INTRODUCTION

This chapter discusses the investigative requirements surrounding special types of investigations that the internal investigator will also be responsible for in the law enforcement organization. The chapter discusses the investigative requirements for fleet vehicle accidents, pursuits, specialized units, substance abuse, hostile work environments, domestic violence, and racial profiling.

FLEET VEHICLE ACCIDENTS

Fleet vehicle accidents, while distressing to most police administrators, are a fact of life in law enforcement. Operating in an emergency mode in some of the worst traffic and weather conditions will at times, result in a fleet motor vehicle accident. Many organizations function from the perspective that by virtue of an accident occurring, it is automatically attributable to the operating officer. Because of politics, budgets, and liability, organizations take a zero-tolerance type policy that ultimately has not been empirically proven to reduce fleet vehicle accidents. Therefore, police administrators should temper reasonable policy with strictly objective investigation techniques and resolution strategies. There is an unrealistic expectation in this investigative realm that there should never be a personnel complaint or fleet vehicle accident, in spite of the nature of the daily work of a law enforcement officer.

Legal Considerations

The legal considerations encompass criminal and civil liability on behalf of officers and departments in police vehicle operation. This is an area of significant liability for the officers and agencies involved. Cases have also been brought to trial for officers who have been criminally charged for negligent police vehicle operation. The internal investigator may be forced to examine two areas in these types of investigations: (1) officer culpability in vehicle operation from the criminal, civil, and departmental policy perspectives and (2) the department's liability in vehicle acquisition, maintenance, training practices, and policy.

With respect to officer culpability in vehicle operation from the criminal, civil, and departmental policy perspectives, the internal investigator will rely on the prevailing laws and departmental policies to determine the final disposition in the fleet vehicle accident. Caution should be taken in trying to set a

Officer Alan Neel
January 30th, 2000 - Taylor, Texas

Figure 10-1. Taylor, TX, January 30, 2000 – Police Cpl. Alan Neel is trapped inside his Crown Victoria when it is rear-ended at 84 miles per hour by a drunk driver. The crash jams both front doors shut. Neel manages to kick his way free and runs from the car as it explodes in fire. "If anything had delayed me at all, I wouldn't be here today," Neel says later (Photo courtesy of the Safety Forum, Washington, D.C.).

Figure 10-2. Jason Schechterle, a Phoenix officer who was severely burned when his Crown Victoria police car was hit, says Ford must make the car safer (Photo courtesy of The Salt Lake Tribune).

tone or "make an example" of an officer as this may set the foundation for the pending litigation when none in fact may exist.

With respect to the department's liability in vehicle acquisition, maintenance, training practices, and policy perspectives; this area is much more difficult for the internal investigator, but a part of the overall investigation. For example, the history of the Ford Crown Victoria's catching fire after an impact has been brought to the attention of law enforcement administrators across the country. The controversy surrounding the Crown Victoria surfaced in 2002 when reports implicated the car in the death of approximately 12 police officers. All of these police officers died after being involved in rear-end crashes that caused their vehicles to burst into flames. In response to these fires, Ford installed rubber and plastic shields to cover sharp parts around the fuel tank of the Crown Victoria police car to help minimize punctures and fires (Parker & Waichman, 2006). The departments that fail to respond can incur significant civil liability. Another issue is poorly researched equipment placement such as airbag deployment that leads to officers suffering more injuries than would have normally been sustained in a similar type of accident. Another example is demonstrated through a Ford Motor Company published study in which they identified that police vehicles, because of the nature of operation of police vehicles during night hours where the propensity for drunk driving was highest, that police vehicles experience four times more accidents than civilian vehicles (Wells, 2004).

This also creates a civil liability issue when the study proves the need and departments fail to respond with training and equipment.

In addition, lawsuits can be brought against agencies and officers personally for failing to conduct a proper and complete motor vehicle accident investigation. There is also an issue if negligence arises with agencies that fail to have a policy for accident investigation in place. While laws are in place such as qualified immunity, aggrieved parties still have a right to be heard in the courts (Badger, 2003e).

Policy Considerations

Agencies should have a fleet vehicle accident policy in place that is beyond that of a basic accident investigation policy. These types of accidents are fraught with liability and as such a strict protocol for investigation, evidence collection, and command/legal notifies should be in place when they occur. Dale H. Close (2001) also states with respect to fleet accident policy and tracking that:

> Crashes should be tracked according to the age and experience of the officer, the shift, the day of the week, the nature of the action of the officer at the time of the crash, the type of crash, and the weather conditions at the time. The purpose of this tracking is to determine when and under what circumstances most crashes take place so that training and supervision can be geared to resolving the crash problem. (p. 22)

Investigative Considerations

The investigative considerations in fleet vehicle accidents mirror those of a serious or fatal accident investigation as the internal investigator must go beyond the basic accident investigation techniques in order to discover the true cause of the accident and defend the officer and agency when appropriate.

To start with, it is the driver's action, inaction, or inattention that causes the majority of accidents (Badger, 2002b; Close, 2001). There are several additional factors that need to be considered in fleet vehicle accident investigation as well. For example, fatigue is strongly associated with traffic accidents. A study in one police department found that of all preventable traffic accidents involving police vehicles, 50 percent occurred between midnight and 6:00 a.m. Twenty percent occurred between 1:30 p.m. and 3:00 p.m. Further analysis revealed that these accidents involved officers who normally worked the graveyard shift, but were headed to court at the time of the accident (Pedersen, 2001). Another factor is perception response or perception reaction time (PRT), which in normal conditions is 1.5 to 1.75 seconds. However, in varying human and environmental factors such as diminished lighting, fatigue, physical limitations, glance behavior, eye fixations, and others, this time can be significantly delayed (Badger, 2002b).

Physiological considerations must be contrasted with environmental conditions at the scene, such as sun glare and shadows that are also a part of accident investigation in determining all contributing factors. When analyzing a fleet vehicle accident, the investigator should consider sun and shadow as to how they may have affected driver vision and obtain a survey or forensic map of the scene in order to complete the investigation properly (Gravesen, 2003). Human factors training is also essential to accurate accident investigation (Badger, 2002b). Still another consideration is from traffic control and roadway engineering systems that may have contributed to the accident. The internal investigator may need the assistance of an accident reconstructionist, municipal attorney, and civil engineer in these investigations.

These incidents will also be heavily dependent upon physical evidence as witness statements can often be in question. Joe Badger (2002a) states that, "Physical evidence analysis can assist the investigator in pursuing a productive path by providing clues from the characteristics of the physical evidence. . . . Physical evidence may link a suspect with a vehicle, disprove or support witness testimony, or provide leads" (p. 26). The collection of physical evidence should be trained, a part of policy, and be the responsibility of all personnel involved from the initial responder to the chief.

Officers often draw premature conclusions regarding fault or causation (Badger, 2003c). The following is a series of steps necessary for the completion of a thorough and proper accident investigation (Badger, 2002a; Badger, 2002b; Badger, 2003a; Badger, 2003b; Badger, 2003c; Badger, 2003d):

Photographs, Evidence, and Measurements: Photographs, evidence, and measurements are essential at most fleet vehicle accident scenes. Photographs, evidence, and measurements will be the most significant probative evidence available to determine the dynamics of the accident:

1. Ensure photographs of vehicles even if no damages are noted.
2. Photograph the entire scene before paint-marking evidence.
3. A minimum of 18 camera angles should be used in the evidence photography of a vehicle involved in an accident.
4. Include all landmarks in photos as well as vehicles, tires, bodies, skidmarks, gouges, scrapes.
5. Take photographs of everything that cannot be absolutely eliminated as not being a part of the accident.
6. Take interior panoramic and exterior panoramic photos looking out and looking in, photos from correct eye height for both (all) drivers.
7. The internal investigator should return to the scene during daylights hours for further evidence search, photographs, and measurements.
8. In a nighttime collision with a pedestrian, document exactly what the person was wearing. The issue is the driver's ability to perceive the pedestrian's presence. Also take photographs to compare clothing pattern imprints.
9. Ensure consistency in all measurements taken.
10. Secure all physical evidence such as shoes and driver's pedals.
11. Fingerprint dust the rearview mirror and steering wheel for latents.
12. Use evidence collected to confirm or refute witness statements.
13. Analyze the airbag sensor module information.

Witnesses: Accidents will most often involve witnesses that consist of the drivers, passengers, and bystanders. Securing and interviewing these individuals is a necessary step to the completion of the accident investigation, however, statements should be weighed against all other statements as well as the analysis of the physical evidence at the scene:

1. Collect witness statements even from vehicle drivers and occupants.
2. Accurately document witness statement attribution (officer personally heard statement, or was told something was said).
3. Witness accounts offer some probative value, but vary and are highly subject to individual perception and interpretation. They should be evaluated in the context of the incident.
4. Witnesses and passengers not named in reports should also be located and interviewed.

General Duties: There are also a series of general or additional duties the internal investigator should complete that will add to the final investigation:

1. Documentation of all aspects of the investigation as well as collection of all reports to be added to the investigative package.
2. Maintain all notes taken and keep them as a part of the investigative package.
3. Discuss the case with the prosecutor or district attorney to establish if any criminal culpability is present and the contemplation of any criminal charges.
4. Take note of the roadside conditions as they may be possible explanations for the actions of the drivers.
5. Note the vehicle identification numbers of all vehicles involved.
6. Ensure that officers are trained in taking proper measurements.

During the follow-up investigation, the officer involved may need to be interviewed. The internal investigator must also follow the rules of protection of statements in these cases where the involved officer may be the target of the investigation and possibly subjected to a disciplinary process. Questioning of officers needs to include vehicle inspection, vehicle condition, driver training (basic and specialized), driver experience, relationship to similar pursuits and outcomes, and their interpretation of how safe they believed they were in the vehicle operation, whether if it was during normal or emergency operation.

PURSUITS

In investigating a police pursuit, the internal investigator may have to examine two distinct aspects: (1) justification for the pursuit and (2) and resulting motor vehicle accident. The propensity for an accident or injury that results from a police pursuit is of concern to all involved including the police and the community. In general, statistics show that once a pursuit has been commenced, accident probability is at approximately 40 percent, while injuries occur in approximately 20 percent of those accidents, and death occurs in approximately one percent of all pursuits (Eisenberg, 1999). More specifically, according to the NHTSA Fatality Analysis Reporting System (FARS), a five year analysis revealed that 1,641 deaths resulted from vehicular pursuits. Of these, 18 (one percent) were the pursuing officer, 1,058 (65%) were the driver or occupants in the violator vehicle, and 565 (34%) were innocent third parties generally struck by the fleeing vehicle (T. Miller, 2002).

Figure 10-3. The investigation of police pursuits impacts a department's policy, procedure, liability, and the safety of law enforcement personnel and the public alike (Photo courtesy of the Brockport, New York Police Department).

While suspects are primarily responsible for attempts at escape, the onus seems to consistently be placed on law enforcement for the consequences of the suspect's actions. Quasi-experimental research indicates that an average of 50 percent of suspects continue to drive dangerously after ground units terminate their pursuits, therefore suspects may drive dangerously independent of the presence or absence of police units, or the decisions made to continue or discontinue pursuits (Martin, 2001a). Suspects will also flee for myriad reasons, from minor traffic violations to major crimes. Some states have responded by enacting legislation that makes flight in a vehicle a felony.

In consideration of the involved officer, several factors impact the ability to properly initiate, manage, and terminate a pursuit when conditions become too dangerous. Officer training, experience, and the unknown all weigh heavily on an officer's ability and decision to initiate and continue a pursuit. During any stressful driving situation, a physiological occurrence called "siren syndrome" also takes place when adrenaline is released into the bloodstream which can cause the driver to focus on a single aspect of the emergency response or pursuit (Schembra, 2002). Another aggravating factor concerns the reality that some officers are not suited, either physically or psychologically to handle a pursuit (Daniels & Spratley, 2003b). Wayne Daniels and Lynnette Spratley (2003a) also state that:

> The officer has to justify his actions if he decides that continuing the pursuit poses a greater danger to the public than breaking it off. Civil suits stemming from what is perceived as law enforcement's failure to protect the public by chasing and apprehending a violator are becoming more common. (p. 58)

These investigations can be extremely complex to conduct for the internal investigator given the fact that the law is supportive of managed police chases, while departments have developed restrictive policies concerning the circumstances when a chase can commence, along with the political backlash of a chase resulting in a serious injury or fatal accident.

Legal Considerations

In 1995, the courts indicated that the standard of care to be applied to the operation of an emergency vehicle is the "reckless disregard standard." Therefore, the courts may find liability in police pursuits where the emergency vehicle was operated in a reckless disregard for the safety of others. "This standard demands more than a showing of a lack of 'due care under the circumstances. . . .' It requires evidence that the 'actor has intentionally done an act of an unreasonable character in disregard of a known or obvious risk that was so great as to make it highly probable that harm would follow and has done so with conscious disregard to the outcome" (J. J. Sullivan, 1999).

In a subsequent ruling, the Supreme Court decided in the case of *County of Sacramento v. Lewis* (1998) to reduce the potential civil liability for departments involved in police pursuits. In this case, the Court held that a pursuit is not a seizure and that high-speed chases with no intent to harm suspects physically or worsen their legal plight do not support police liability for deprivation of process (Close, 2001).

While this case law has indicated that there exists a higher burden of proof in order to establish liability on behalf of an officer involved in a chase, the use of roadblocks and extreme measures to stop a pursued vehicle has been met with less enthusiasm by the courts. For example, *Graham v. Connor* (1989) and *Tennessee v. Garner* (1985) are the ruling cases in reasonable force and should be applied to the use of vehicle stop tactics such as shooting out tires, coolant systems, or roadblocks (Warren & Olsen, 2002). The United States Supreme Court has also considered roadblocks a seizure, and as such, because of the high risk of injury, they should only be used as a last resort (J. J. Sullivan, 1999). Empirical evidence suggests that a high number of color of law investigations stem from pursuits (Schafer, 2000).

Wayne Daniels and Lynnette Spratley (2003a) state with respect to lawsuits filed in pursuits that, "Lawsuits are not about being right or wrong, but about jurors who feel sympathy for the person who was killed, and sympathy for the bereaved family" (p. 54).

Policy Considerations

Traffic enforcement stops and pursuits are some of the most hazardous duties that officers participate in daily (Papenfuhs, 2003). An agency must have a policy in place to manage the pursuit process. Absent a policy, the internal investigator will not have the guide for examining the incident beyond the federal and state standards that are in place at the time of the incident. Many police organizations have no policy or procedure in place for pursuits as well as high-risk traffic stops, instead leaving this to the discretion of the officers and supervisors in the field in which tactics vary greatly (Borello, 2001).

A well-written policy forms the foundation for any defense of a vehicle pursuit (Daniels & Spratley, 2003a). A recommended strategy for reducing liability is: (1) establish written policies for the initiation and termination of pursuits, (2) educate and train all officers in the published pursuit policy, (3) require supervisors and command officers to monitor and terminate pursuits when necessary, (4) take appropriate remedial or disciplinary action when pursuit policy is violated (Close, 2001). The policy should also be clear so officers have a solid basis on which to base their decisions. The circumstances under which they are authorized to drive with their emergency equipment activated should be listed (Schembra, 2002).

Jeff Martin (2001b) recommends utilizing a risk v. benefit standard in a decision-making model entitled 3QFC or Three Question, Forced Choice. The model takes a gross-motor skills approach to the problem. In answering yes or no to the following questions, a determination can be made as to the continuance or termination of a pursuit: (1) Was the suspect an immediate or future threat to the public before the police pursuit? (2) Is the non-compliant driving by the violator hazardous? And (3) If pursuing, what is the plan to end the pursuit as soon as possible? (p. 16). Clyde B. Eisenberg (1999) also recommends a Total Pursuit Management model that is comprised of five essential elements that allow law enforcement agencies to apprehend criminals, train their personnel, and minimize civil liability:

1. A clear and concise written policy.
2. Extensive training.
3. Pursuit prevention techniques.
4. Pursuit termination devices.
5. Pursuit termination techniques (police vehicle involvement). (p. 73)

To investigate these types of incidents, the internal investigator must have a keen awareness of the vehicle and traffic laws of the affected state, the federal and state standards as they relate to the pursuit of fleeing vehicles, civil case law, and the department's policy on initiating, managing, and terminating pursuits.

Investigative Considerations

Crashes that result from pursuits should be considered crime scenes (Close, 2001). The assistance of civil and criminal counsel as well as crash management and civil engineering experts should be used whenever possible. There are numerous considerations for the investigation including environmental conditions, vehicle condition, training or lack of training, and the reason for the pursuit.

The investigation should include copies of communications tapes, event printouts, all involved reports, and any expert opinions as to the cause of the accident. A review of all available videotapes and proof of any training the officer has received in pursuit training should be reviewed by the internal investigator and added to the investigative package (Daniels, 2002).

The stress involved in pursuits can play havoc on an officer's ability to remember details, especially the fine points that can emerge into major issues when recounting the incident in court or an internal investigation. In high-speed pursuits, it is recommended that any interview and reports be delayed for a day or two while the officer calms down and has an opportunity to accurately and thoroughly collect their thoughts (Daniels & Spratley, 2003a).

SWAT ISSUES

Specialized units must operate under the same sanctioned rules as the department (Makholm, 2000a). Specialized teams such as SWAT have unique training and responsibilities. The internal investigator should be allowed access to their specific training regimen, unit policy, and training/research records into the particular tactics that are sanctioned by the organization. To properly and effectively investigate these incidents, the internal investigator must have an understanding of what is acceptable conduct for specialized unit personnel from the organizational as well as national levels. This section addresses primarily the legal issues involved in SWAT team use.

A case decided in the United States Court of Appeals Tenth Circuit involved the plaintiff, Samuel Allen Heflin and his family filing against the La Plata County Sheriff's Department in Colorado concerning a SWAT entry in 1996. While several allegations were made concerning tactics, in the case made to the United States Court of Appeals, the Court found that qualified immunity did not apply with respect to three specific issues: (1) the reasonableness to use the SWAT team, (2) the SWAT team's use of weapons against minor children, and (3) the officer's alleged failure to knock and announce their entry into the residence. In addition, the Court also refused to grant qualified immunity to the SWAT team leader in the case (Devanney, 2002). With this in mind, legal training needs to keep pace with the emerging technology used in confronting dangerous tactical situations (Milazzo & McNaught, 2002).

SWAT teams may also be used in the rescue of hostages. Hostage situations are tenuous at best and compounded by concerns of liability. Generally, there is no federal civil rights liability for accidentally killing a hostage, but there may be state liability for negligence and wrongful death (Milazzo & McNaught, 2002). The primary task of most SWAT teams is high-risk building entries. In conducting high-risk building entries, the general rule is that police need one of three things to enter a private premises: (1) consent, (2) a warrant, either for arrest or search, or (3) exigent circumstances (Milazzo & McNaught, 2002). While a warrantless entry would most likely be justified in a hostage situation, the consideration for a search warrant may be necessary when only the suspects are present at the location.

An emerging issue is the use of diversionary devices or "flash bangs." Flash bangs and diversionary devices are designed to create disorienting physiological and psychological effects and as such, medical screening is an important post-deployment concern. In *Langford v. Gates* (1987), the California Supreme Court ruled in favor of LAPD's use of a flash bang because of several factors including: (1) proper documentation, (2) teams professionalism, (3) training, and (4) operational experience (R. K. Miller, 2002). Courts generally support the use of flash bangs or other diversionary devices as long as two conditions are present: (1) there must be some factual justification supporting why the use was necessary in a particular case and (2) deployment is not routine, or indiscriminately without regard to the known threat. Any injury that occurs will inevitably lead to an analysis of whether the initial entry was lawful (Milazzo & McNaught, 2002). An example of this is the use of flash bangs in dynamic entries. In January of 2005 in Niagara Falls, New York, an 18-year-old woman who was not the intended arrest target suffered second and third degree burns as a result of the use of a flash bang during the service of a high-risk warrant (Democrat and Chronicle, January 22, 2005). Because of the potential for incidents like this, the investigative and liability concerns require that technicians retrieve as much of the spent device as possible (R. K. Miller, 2002).

In addition, specialized units such as SWAT have different training and techniques than those in patrol services, thus the need for an internal expert/advisor, preferably someone who has expertise on team tactics, or who is a former member is necessary for qualified review of deployment of tactics in the internal investigations process. The department may also consider the use of an expert consultant in reviewing these incidents so that an outside or independent reviewer can guide and support case findings.

CANINE ISSUES

The use of canine units in law enforcement has set unparalleled precedents for efficiency and enforcement techniques. As such, many police and sheriff's departments have adopted canine units or request their use from larger agencies that have these resources. Canine searches happen on a consistent basis in organizations and the potential for liability grows each time a dog is released. This section examines legal issues, policy issues, and investigative issues of canine use in law enforcement.

Legal Considerations

Several legal considerations are related to the use of canine teams insofar as operational tactics and liability. The Ninth Circuit Court of Appeals in *Cruz v. City of Escondido* (1997) decided that the officer's use of a trained police dog to stop fleeing suspects was not deadly force under the Fourth Amendment as pursuant to *Tennessee v. Garner* (1985), the force used must have been reasonably likely to kill for a jury instruction on use of deadly force to be given. In addition, the case of *Mendoza v. Block* (1994), also decided in the Ninth Circuit Court of Appeals holds that for at least those circumstances where the crime is serious and the suspect is potentially dangerous, it is not unreasonable to allow the dog to continue to bite the suspect until the suspect has stopped struggling and is handcuffed (Franscell & Maurer, 2000).

Several additional cases have been decided in the federal courts, including the Sixth and Ninth Circuit Courts of Appeal, for example *Robinette v. Barnes* (1988), have held that the use of properly trained police dogs does not constitute deadly physical force. In 2003, federal district courts have held that under certain circumstances, officers and/or their employers can be held liable when a police dog is used in apprehending suspects. As a recommended practice, a warning about the presence of police dogs should be given to pursued suspects. In addition, the department should keep statistics in all canine tracks and the ratios of apprehensions to bites (Devanney & Summers-Devanney, 2003b; Franscell & Maurer, 2000). With respect to warning suspects of a canine use, this falls also under the *Deorle v. Rutherford* (2001) ruling

(Lesh, 2003). *Graham v. Connor* (1989) sets the standard in that before a dog can be deployed, the handler must consider the "totality of the circumstances." This includes: (1) the severity of the crime, (2) whether the suspect poses an immediate threat to the safety of law enforcement officers or others, and (3) whether the suspect is actively resisting arrest or attempting to evade arrest by flight (Smith, 1998).

Canine usage also has the potential for significant liability in a police agency. While some states provide for exemptions of liability for police dog bites during apprehension or detention of criminal suspects, such as the State of California, they may not protect against claims based on common law theories, such as negligence and intentional torts, or claims, premised upon federal civil rights law for violations of constitutional rights (Franscell & Maurer, 2000). Such was the case in *Priester v. the City of Riviera Beach, Florida* (2000) decided in the Eleventh Circuit Court. In this case, a canine officer was found to have used unreasonable force in deployment of the canine. In addition, the Court also found, with respect to an assisting officer, if a police officer, whether supervisory or not, fails or refused to intervene when a constitutional violation such as an unprovoked beating takes place in his presence, the officer is directly liable under Section 1983 and can be held personally liable for his nonfeasance (Makholm, 2000a; Makholm, 2002c; Martinelli & Pollock, 2000).

Policy Considerations

For policy to be effective in canine use, there are relevant components that must be present. First is that a warning policy should be in place for the handlers to use in every case possible. Next, a comprehensive policy for medical treatment and documentation should be in place and followed by the handlers. The organization should also require handlers to keep all documentation of training records, both departmental copies and personal. The policy should include a fluid resume for the canine and its handler listing all training and activities of the dog as well as a chronological listing of the handlers training and experience (Smith, 1998). This documentation should be included in the internal investigations package.

Investigative Considerations

The investigative considerations will be based upon the department's specialized unit policy on canine deployment, contemporary case law, and severity of the crime. The case should also be determined upon such case law as those used in determining the justification for the use-of-force. In citing *Graham v. Connor* (1989), which states that in the standard of objective reasonableness, all determinations of the reasonableness of force must be evaluated in light of the particular circumstances from the perspective of a reasonable officer on the scene. As such, when conducting the investigation, the investigator should focus on three issues: (1) the severity of the crime at issue, (2) whether the suspect poses an immediate threat to the safety of officers or others, and (3) whether the suspect is actively resisting arrest or attempting to evade arrest by flight (Franscell & Maurer, 2000; MacLatchie, 2000).

SUBSTANCE ABUSE

Law enforcement personnel experience some of the highest stress levels of any profession. Many personnel are unable to develop a healthy release system for such pressures and resort to purported stress relievers as alcohol and illicit drugs. The *Americans with Disabili-*

ties Act of 1990 was enacted to prevent certain types of discrimination. The ADA does not prohibit drug testing or an employer's right to prohibit alcohol or illegal drug use in the workplace. There have been numerous states that have also enacted such laws. Drug testing should be based upon clearly defined policy and existing labor agreement. Testing can be done both randomly and through reasonable suspicion. Department policies should be followed in such areas as the establishment of the basis of the test, notification procedures, testing, and evidence recovery/ analysis. A department should also provide the employee with an opportunity to have a second test conducted in a lab of their choosing provided proper evidence handling is adhered to in the process. The organization should also consider a referral to an employee assistance program if such results are positive and the employee is willing to participate in a rehabilitation program.

HOSTILE WORK ENVIRONMENTS AND SEXUAL HARASSMENT

A hostile work environment takes an extreme toll on the individual employee as well as the organization and community served. Costs include immense potential for civil liability and decreased production by all who are touched by such incidents. These incidents are often covered-up and tolerated in many organizations to the point where a civil rights investigation may be the only recourse for an aggrieved employee. The internal investigator has an obligation to take these claims seriously and conduct a thorough and fair investigation when allegations are made, no matter who in the organization is involved. Sustained allegations can be adjudicated through federal and state laws as well as carrying severe civil penalties.

Hostile Work Environment

Robert Boertien (2002) offers a policy definition of hostile workplace as, "Conduct that has the effect of unreasonably interfering with an individual's work performance or creating an intimidating, hostile or offensive working environment" (p. 70). Professor Philip E. Carlan (2000) also states that, "A hostile work environment arises when a co-worker or supervisor, engaging in unwelcome and inappropriate sexually-based behavior, renders the workplace atmosphere intimidating, hostile, or offensive–as occurs most frequently in male-dominated professions such as law enforcement" (p. 126). The results can be devastating to even the largest of organizations in lawsuits, lost productivity, stress claims and sick time usage, and the loss of valued employees.

The Supreme Court has identified that conduct to support a claim of hostile work environment must be "severe or pervasive." In the same vein, the conduct must be beyond low-level comments, teasing, sporadic use of abusive language, jokes, etc., unless the conduct was extremely serious, and also linked to a tangible employment action (Byrd, 1998). In *Harris v. Forklift Systems, Inc.* (1993), the United States Supreme Court extended its ruling in *Meritor* to include conduct that does not actually cause psychological injury. Title VII is violated when a workplace is permeated with unwelcome discriminatory intimidation, ridicule, and insult that is sufficiently severe or pervasive to alter the conditions of the victim's employment and create an abusive working environment. Title VII also applies before the harassing conduct leads to a nervous breakdown. There is no need for the conduct to be psychologically injurious (Carlan, 2000).

Sexual Harassment

Sexual harassment is an overt form of discrimination premised on gender and nearly 95 percent of all such incidents go unreported. Harm caused by sexual harassment is often extreme. It can include humiliation, loss of dignity, psychological–and sometimes physical injury, and damage to professional reputations and careers (Carlan, 2000). Sexual harassment is an attempt to establish power over the other person (Mueck, 2000). Quid pro quo is a request for sexual favors in exchange for some benefit (Carlan, 2000).

Compelling evidence suggests that sexual harassment is prevalent in even the most professional of police agencies. Despite this evidence, many police administrators are reluctant to acknowledge this fact in their own agencies. In addition, a recent survey indicated that 34 percent of law enforcement agencies in the United States have no written sexual harassment policy and fewer than 25 percent would promptly investigate a filed compliant. In 1997, federal and state monetary losses from sexual harassment were almost a half billion dollars. These losses resulted from absenteeism, lower productivity, increased health care costs, poor morale, and employee turnover, and do not even include the large costs related to litigation and court-awarded damages (Carlan, 2000).

Timothy L. Fuss and Dr. Lynn L. Snowden (2000), through literary research and an empirical study involving 44 randomly selected women in law enforcement state that based upon their research, "It is evident that sexual harassment still occurs" (p. 71). Police administrators must recognize that this problem exists and work to combat the problem at all levels in their agencies.

Legal Issues of Sexual Harassment

Based in Title VII of the *Civil Rights Act of 1964,* the Equal Employment Opportunity Commission defines sexual harassment as unwelcome sexual advances. Congress amended the *Civil Rights Act* in 1991 to include compensatory damages beyond back pay and made jury trials an option. The legislation further provided for damages in the form of future monetary loss, emotional pain and suffering, inconvenience, mental anguish, loss of life enjoyment, and other non-monetary losses. Plaintiffs also were entitled to collect punitive damages from employers shown to have acted with malice or reckless indifference (Carlan, 2000).

Another consideration is that some type of tangible employment action must take place. Included under the definitions of sexual harassment and hostile work environment, a tangible employment action has been defined by the Supreme Court as a significant change in employment status, such as hiring, failing to promote, re-assigning with significantly different responsibilities or a significant change in benefits resulting from the employment decision, and inflicts direct economic harm (Byrd, 1998).

Professor Philip E. Carlan (2000) states that, "Today, the courts will likely find a hostile environment present when the workplace includes sexual propositions, pornography, extremely vulgar language, sexual touching, degrading comments, or embarrassing questions or jokes" (p. 126). According to the United States Supreme Court's decision in *Meritor Savings Bank v. Vinson* (1986), the challenged conduct must be unwelcome in the sense that the employee did not solicit or incite it and regarded the conduct as undesirable or offensive. In addition, the sexual misconduct does not have to be linked to the granting or denying of an employee benefit for it to be illegal.

In developing a prima facie case, the courts have held that incidents involving employees other than the victim are also relevant in establishing a generally hostile work environment (Carlan, 2000). In addition, plaintiff's have attempted to expand the quid pro quo category to include "unfinished threats," such as when a supervisor requests sexual favors in exchange for some benefit or threatens to take some adverse action against the employee, but the threat is never fulfilled (Byrd, 1998).

Torts involving vicarious liability with respect to sexual harassment claims also involve supervisors who engage in such acts. In *Faragher v. City of Boca Raton* (1998), a supervisor (lieutenant) and command officer (chief) sexually harassed a female subordinate on a consistent and egregious basis. The chief also had the authority to hire new employees and issue discipline. No complaint was made to management by the plaintiff. After court review, the Eleventh Circuit Court of Appeals found in favor of the City of Boca Raton in that neither of the supervisors were acting as the city's agents and beyond the scope of their employment. In addition, the supervisors were not aided in their actions by the agency relationship, and that the city did not know nor should it have known of the harassment (Byrd, 1998).

A second case, *Burlington Industries, Inc. v. Ellerth* (1998) a female employee also alleged repeated and egregious sexual harassment from a supervisor who was a mid-level manager. This supervisor also had authority to make hiring and promotional decisions. No complaint was made to management by the plaintiff, despite a policy in place that prohibited sexual harassment. In this case, the Seventh Circuit Court of Appeals found the employer was liable for the harassment by the supervisor (Byrd, 1998; Carlan, 2000).

The Supreme Court, in reviewing both cases utilized two cases in which sexual misconduct was committed by police officers. In *Primeaux v. U.S.* (1996) and *Mary M. v. Los Angeles* (1991), officers used their official positions to obtain an advantage in order to commit the rapes of both plaintiffs. This agency relationship was the deciding factor for holding the agencies liable. The Court found this analogous to *Faragher* and *Ellerth's* claims as the supervisors were assisted in accomplishing the tort by the existence of the agency relationship (Byrd, 1998). This is also the doctrine of respondeat superior, where the employer is liable even if the employer had no knowledge of the misconduct as in *Henson v. City of Dundee* (1982) wherein the United States Court of Appeals reasoned that because the supervisor is acting within at least the apparent scope of his authority entrusted to him by the employer when he makes employment decisions, his conduct can fairly be imputed to the source of the authority. This made an agency responsible for a supervisory employee's action if that employee wielded authority delegated by the agency. Furthermore, the perpetrator does not have to be an employee, but only an agent attached to the department (Carlan, 2000).

In response to these cases, the Supreme Court has developed a two-prong test to determine employer liability in hostile environment claims: (1) the employer exercised reasonable care to prevent and promptly correct any sexual harassing behavior, and (2) the plaintiff employee unreasonably failed to take advantage of any preventive or corrective opportunities provided by the employer or to avoid harm otherwise (Byrd, 1998; Carlan, 2000).

Supervisory Issues

Supervisory issues are two-fold: (1) direct involvement as the harasser and (2) failure to take action when conduct is reported. Sadly, supervisors are often implicated as the harasser. In a recent study of sexual harassment of female law enforcement officers, surveys indicated that some 72 percent of the female victims were sexually harassed by their supervisor (Fuss & Snowden, 2000).

Under Equal Employment Opportunity Commission guidelines, employers are liable when their supervisors or agents create a hostile environment or if the employer knew or should have known of the sexual harassment and failed to take immediate and appropriate corrective action. According to Equal Employment Opportunity Commission, employers are usually deemed to know of sexual harassment if it is: (1) openly practiced, (2) well-known among employees, and (3) brought to the employer's notice when a victim files a charge (Carlan, 2000).

The supervisory aspect of these investigations presents a very precarious situation for the aggrieved party as well as the organization. Very strict policies must be developed and enforced by the administration in order to take measures to protect employee rights and protect the administration from sexually deviate or rogue supervisors.

Policy Issues

The Supreme Court through case law such as *Faragher* and *Ellerth* have mandated that employers must have adequate sexual harassment policies in place, disseminate those policies, train in the policies, and then continue to adequately apply those policies (Byrd, 1998; Fuss & Snowden, 2000). Professor Philip E. Carlan (2000) also states that:

> A basic sexual harassment policy should set forth: (1) an express commitment to eradicate and prevent sexual harassment, (2) a definition of sexual harassment including both quid pro quo and hostile work environment, (3) an explanation of penalties the agency will impose for substantiated sexual harassment conduct, (4) a detailed outline of the grievance procedure employees should use, (5) additional resource or contact persons available for consultation, and (6) an express commitment to keep all sexual harassment complaints and personnel actions confidential. (p. 126)

The organization needs a clear policy in place before an agency can proscribe conduct and then enforce sustained violations. The policy should preclude derogatory language, display of offensive materials, unwanted touching, offensive behaviors. The policy should also include specific links to protected classes such as race, national origin, religion, age, gender, sexual orientation, union affiliation, or disability. Supervisors and managers must recognize conduct, enforce rules, and offer a support mechanism to aggrieved parties. The policy should mandate supervisor and managerial responsibilities and hold them strictly accountable for malfeasance and non-feasance. The organization should also commit to training for all strata and periodic in-service follow-up refreshers. Policy, supervision, training, and enforcement through discipline should be a systematic approach to dealing with this problem (Close, 2001; Fuss & Snowden, 2000). The organization should implement counseling programs for victims of sexual harassment as well as monitor behaviors for retaliation attempts.

The organization should have some basic guidelines in place in the reporting and follow-up of these incidents to include:

1. Have the complaining employee document the incident as well as their actions/responses that the conduct was offensive.
2. Immediately initiate an investigation to include interviewing witnesses, collecting evidence, and documenting the findings with recommendations.
3. Resolution for sustained charges can range from conciliation between employ-

ees, to Departmental discipline, to criminal/civil charges.

Investigative Considerations

Few hostile work environment complaints are based upon a single incident and as such should be given serious attention, mediated or investigated to the satisfaction of the aggrieved party or proper investigative outcome, and be a part of a viable workplace intervention program (Boertien, 2002). In addition, employees sometimes delay or wait to report sexual harassment or hostile work environment complaints. This should never be interpreted as evidence that the complaint is void of merit (Carlan, 2000).

For the investigation of these type of incidents, the United States Supreme Court has set four criteria in place to determine if an environment is hostile or abusive by examining all of the circumstances of the case: (1) the frequency of the discriminatory conduct, (2) the severity of that conduct, (3) whether it is physically threatening or humiliating, or a mere offensive utterance, and (4) whether it unreasonably interferes with an employee's work performance (Carlan, 2000).

During the course of the investigation reassignment should take place while the investigation, mediation progresses. Consider administrative or paid leave for the suspected party pending a resolution if the previous options are not viable. Robert Boertien (2002) suggests the RITE method of, Reassign, Investigate, Take Steps to prevent a recurrence, and Evaluate as a policy based investigative process in an organization (p. 72). The department should also consider the use of outside mediators and professional counselors depending on the nature, size of the agency, relationship such as supervisor–subordinate, or the chief administrator or high level manager involved in the allegation.

In the event of a sustained complaint, the organization must act swiftly and decisively. The organization should consider past appropriate practice for handling these types of incidents as well as the severity and frequency of the sustained allegation. Robert Boertien (2002) recommends that, "Any sustained complaint against a member must result in a sanction sufficient to correct the unwanted behavior" (p. 72).

DOMESTIC VIOLENCE

Domestic violence in society is both pervasive and sinister. Intimate partner and family violence has only been recognized as a serious problem since states have moved to reduce the occurrence of domestic violence by enacting prohibitive legislation. Statistically, only 50% of domestic violence directed against women is reported to police (Prabhu & Turner, 2000). In addition, only one out of every three American women has reported physical abuse by an intimate partner. It is also estimated that some 74 percent of domestic abuse will happen in the workplace (Paziotopoulos, 2003).

In the law enforcement realm, research indicates that at least 40 percent of law enforcement families experience domestic violence each year, in comparison with about 11 percent to 12 percent of families in the general United States population. In addition, conviction rates of officers charged with domestic violence are miniscule (Graves, 2004; Lonsway & Conis, 2003). Other research estimates domestic violence committed by police officers against their intimate partners occurs at least as frequently as in the general population (Prabhu & Turner, 2000).

Alex Graves (2004) states that, "The very characteristics, techniques, and experiences instilled in police officers when used in intimate relationships, make police officers the most dangerous of domestic abusers" (p. 108). Dr. Kim Lonsway and Dr. Pete Conis (2003) state that: "The officer also knows how to manipulate the system to avoid detection and accountability, and abusive officers are often masters at shifting blame to the victim and creating the impression that the victim is the one who is crazy or perpetrating the abuse" (p. 133).

Sandy Prabhu and Nancy Turner (2000) also state that:

> Abusive officers, unlike civilian batterers: (1) have knowledge of the criminal justice system and those who work within it, (2) can use their authority to further silence and intimidate their victims, (3) are armed and trained in matters such as use-of-force, defensive tactics, and "police holds"; and (4) may use their position to access systems of information (p. 50).

Allegations and the investigation of law enforcement domestic violence must receive priority in order to prevent proven allegations from escalating into incidents of serious injury or fatality.

Legal Issues

Legal issues encompass two areas: (1) criminal liability and (2) federal law with respect to firearms possession. The area of criminal liability is set in the affected state's laws on physical abuse, assault, and domestic violence-related statutes. Law enforcement personnel are held to the same standard as the general population. As such, they should have at least the same level of investigative attention as any report of domestic violence as well as an increased level attention due to the egregious nature of a law enforcement officer engaging in such activity. Agencies should also hold the investigative standards to existing departmental policy as well as developing an internal policy for specifically investigating allegations of law enforcement related domestic violence.

Federal law was also enacted to address domestic violence ad the preclusion of weapons possession by those convicted of certain types of offenses. ATF's interpretation of the federal law concerning an officer possessing a firearm while subject to certain qualifying restraining orders has revealed that the federal law would be violated if an officer possesses a firearm in a personal capacity. Departments are also encouraged to develop policies that are stricter than federal law. In addition, based upon the *Lautenberg Act,* an officer previously convicted of a misdemeanor crime of domestic violence is prohibited from possessing any pistol, rifle or shotgun, even a firearm that is issued by the police department (International Association of Chiefs of Police, 2000a; Lonsway & Conis, 2003; Lonsway & Harrington, 2003; Prabhu & Turner, 2000). The offense does not need to be designated as domestic violence within state law, but is covered under the *Lautenberg Act* if it involves the use or attempted use of physical force or threat with a deadly weapon, and is committed against a current or former spouse, a past or present cohabitating partner, a person with whom the perpetrator has a child in common, or a person with whom the officer has or has had a dating relationship (Lonsway & Harrington, 2003).

The courts can also issue restraining orders or orders of protection for victims of these types of incidents. A "protection order" is defined as any injunction or other order issued by a court, including criminal or civil orders of protection, regardless of form, content, length, layout, or name (such as stay away, restraining, criminal, and emergency or temporary protection orders or injunctions), issued for the purpose of preventing the following. . . . Violent or threatening acts against another person, stalking or harassment of another person, contact or communication with another person and physical proximity to another person (Lonsway & Harrington, 2003).

Officer Considerations

While the law enforcement officer may be involved as the aggressor in a domestic violence incident, there are also times when the aggressor is the spouse or intimate partner. For example, a female officer may be the victim of domestic violence from an intimate partner who is not in law enforcement. Then too, the investigator must also consider that males, while infrequent, can be the victims of domestic violence. A male police lieutenant, Gregory Schmidt, was acquitted of domestic violence charges in Seattle and subsequently filed a 10 million dollar lawsuit against the agency for discrimination and harassment alleging that as a result of the incident he had been passed over for promotion, transferred capriciously, and forced to take sick leave and vacation (*Law and Order,* 2000c). Cases like these are a testament for the need for complete, thorough, and impartial investigations.

Family Considerations

Departments should have in place counseling and support services for the intimate partners and children of law enforcement personnel involved in domestic violence incidents. Approximately 3.3 million children witness their parents' interpersonal violence each year. Children exposed to domestic abuse often have behavior problems, difficulty concentrating, and often engage in rebellious behavior (Paziotopoulos, 2003). Based upon this, a department should contract for counseling and support services that help the entire family through these most difficult of situations.

Policy Considerations

Many police chiefs mistakenly believe that their standard domestic policies are sufficient to handle police involved domestic offense incidents (Prabhu & Turner, 2000). As such, most departments currently have no policy at all specifically addressing domestic violence perpetrated by one of their own employees, and the absence of a comprehensive policy as well as adequate training will leave a department at risk for charges of liability (Lonsway & Conis, 2003; Lonsway & Harrington, 2003). The International Association of Chiefs of Police has developed several model policies that may be of assistance to agencies contemplating the development of this necessary procedure.

When developing a policy, the first consideration is that a zero tolerance policy be implemented because of the serious nature of these incidents (Graves, 2004; Lonsway & Harrington, 2003; Prabhu & Turner, 2000). An Officer Involved Domestic Abuse Police policy should include several components: (1) victim safety and protection, (2) prevention and training, (3) early warning and prevention, (4) incident response protocol, (5) agency follow-up, (6) post-incident administrative and criminal decisions, (7) policies in employee handbooks, brochures, company produced video (Graves, 2004; Lonsway & Harrington, 2003; Paziotopoulos, 2003), (8) orders of protection should be on the victim at all times, along with copies given to the employer, school officials, and local police, building security, receptionists, as well as a photograph of the abuser (Paziotopoulos, 2003), and (9) a policy must include well thought-out practices for weapons seizure and storage, lethality assessment, victim safety, and cross-jurisdictional communication (Prabhu & Turner, 2000).

Margaret H. Culp (2000) recommends the following management protocol for responding to officer-related domestic violence incidents:

1. Include in a department policy for the officer to immediately notify internal affairs and their command of any order of protection, restraining order, served on them along with all particulars included in the allegations and scheduled court appearances.
2. Internal affairs in consultation with legal counsel (corporation counsel and the assigned prosecutor) reviews the order and determines the potential for the order to trigger the statute, attends the hearing, and reports the court's findings.
3. If an order triggers the statute, the department makes an immediate informed decision to assign an officer to non-law enforcement duties during the pendency of the order.
4. The department makes helpful resource information available to the officer.
5. Because it is critical to an officer that counsel be aware of the implications of the Statute for the officer's career, the union has been encouraged to consult with family law counsel to ensure that an officer receives thorough, knowledgeable representation at the court hearing of the order.

By policy, officers must be responsible to inform their supervisor and department when they are being investigated for domestic violence or are the subject of a restraining or protection order of any kind. Supervisors must also be responsible to monitor behavior for warning signs, and the department must be responsible to provide non-punitive avenues of assistance, confidential referrals to counseling, and fitness for duty evaluations (Lonsway & Harrington, 2003). Agencies should also consider developing agency contacts and written agreements for notification in all jurisdictions that department personnel reside in (Lonsway & Harrington, 2003; Prabhu & Turner, 2000).

Investigative Considerations

Domestic violence cases are complicated and the questioning cannot be confined to the incident at hand (Paziotopoulos, 2003). Domestic violence cases may be the result of years of systematic abuse or violent incidents as opposed to a single or isolated event. The internal investigator should determine the duration and extent of the physical and emotional abuse suffered by the victims of these cases in order to properly determine the appropriate disposition strategy.

The internal investigator should be aware of the warning signs that include: (1) unexplained bruises or explanations incongruent with injuries, (2) signs of distraction or difficulty concentrating; high absenteeism rate, (3) repeated upsetting phone calls, (4) signs of anxiety or depression, (5) fluctuations in quality of work for no apparent reason, (6) noticeable changes in the use of makeup and cosmetics, (7) inappropriate clothing, (8) disruptive visits from current/former partners, (9) frequent unexplained use of leave time, (10) discomfort when communicating with others, (11) sudden unexplained requests to be moved from public locations, (12) frequent financial problems, (13) requests for time off to attend court, (14) reluctance to field calls from former partners, (15) sudden changes of address or reluctance to divulge home address, and (16) reluctance to participate in informal activities outside of work (Paziotopoulos, 2003).

Additional considerations for the internal investigator are based on the psychological aspects of domestic violence. For example, domestic violence is about using power and control. Questions need to be addressed such as: (1) Does your partner try to isolate you from your friends and family? (2) Does your partner prefer to spend all your time together or at home? (3) Does your partner say things to criticize you? (4) Does your partner say things to make you feel bad? (5) Does your partner humiliate you in public? (6) Does your partner play mind games with you to make you think you are losing your mind? and (7) Does your partner use your children as blackmail or threaten to take your children away? (Paziotopoulos, 2003).

WORKPLACE VIOLENCE

Workplace violence rose to the limelight based upon several high-profile incidents. Organizations began to scramble to develop workplace violence policies that were intended to address the problem. Law enforcement is not immune to these types of incidents as the potential for workplace violence in this arena is high. Violence is not the only byproduct of stress and conflict in the workplace as employee conflict also causes enormous loss of effectiveness and productivity (Parks, 2000).

Workplace violence includes not only physical confrontations between co-workers, threats of violence, or deliberate destruction of company property, it also involves latent acts such as intimidation of co-workers, harassment of new employees by tenured employees when supervision is absent, and secret sabotage of departmental equipment, data, or records by a disgruntled employee. With respect to the policing culture, these issues may be much more pervasive and extremely difficult to identify and eradicate (Grimes, 2003).

Workplace violence often extends beyond employee-on-employee violence and reaches through the ranks as well. Dick Grimes (2003) also speaks of issues related to problems in creating a professional organization as he states:

> Much of this nonviolent violence begins when employees become frustrated as they try to do a good job in the midst of vague or conflicting goals, face unreasonable or nonexistent performance expectations from management, or work under the thumb of a tyrant who treats them like non-thinking children and then is surprised when they lash out. (p. 33)

The organization should be watchful of incidents of this nature as they may be overt and covert. While employees must be monitored and behavior of this type corrected, more importantly is the effect of poor supervision and management who become involved in these acts and negatively impact employee morale and performance.

Legal Issues

Courts and lawmakers have begun to hold employers increasingly accountable for workplace violence (Paziotopoulos, 2003). In defense of the organization, as well as the protection of its employees, likened to domestic violence incidents, these incidents should also be investigated and dealt with immediately.

Policy Issues

Progressive agencies that have recognized the potential for negative consequences and have responded by developing policy, investigative practices, and responses to reported incidents of workplace violence. For example, LAPD utilizes an Ombudsman process to resolve employee-on-employee conflicts. The Ombudsman Association (TOA), and international organization of practicing ombuds, defines an organizational ombudsman as, "a designated neutral or impartial dispute resolution whose major function is to provide confidential and informal assistance to managers and employees." The LAPD ombudsman resources include psychological services, employee assistance programs, a model peer counseling program, a women's coordinator who provides support for female employees, a wellness coordinator who assists employees who are sick or on injured-on-duty status, and the LAPD Memorial Foundation which provides financial support for employees and their families in times of crisis. The ombudsman office operates by two principles: (1) neutrality and (2) confidentiality (Parks, 2000).

Other policies include reporting procedures, the investigation, case resolution strategies, and follow-up procedures such as monitoring and counseling services. These incidents may also rise to the criminal level and the organization must be prepared to provide the appropriate criminal investigation and support through the court system for the aggrieved employee.

Figure 10-4. CNN reported on September 9, 1999 that a Grand jury indicted New Jersey State troopers John Hogan and James Kenna on attempted murder and assault charges in an incident that was believed to be motivated through racial profiling (CNN).

RACIAL PROFILING

An extremely divisive problem facing law enforcement today is the issue, whether perceived or real, of racial profiling. Agencies across the country have been burdened with a broad brush approach to an isolated problem in the discipline. Contrary to popular belief, the prevalence of racial profiling is not as widespread as many people believe (*Law and Order,* 2001a). In response, agencies have been mandated either by local, federal, or political standard to track and address any identified problems in the inequitable delivery of police services. The International Association of Chiefs of Police in 1999 opposed such measures as traffic stops legislation that led to officers asking certain questions in order to collect data. For example, "forcing an officer to inquire about the race or ethnic background of a motorist would likely serve only to trigger feelings of outrage and foster a perception of bias on the part of law enforcement" (Voegtlin, 1999). The negative affects of the problem are being experienced by all who are involved in this issue.

Officers most often fall victim to false perceptions, politics, and the media in these cases and may opt to not perform their sworn duties. From the perspective of false perceptions and politics, the reality is that officers make most traffic stop decisions before they're even close enough to a vehicle to determine the race of the driver (Meek, 2001). With respect to the media coverage and racial profiling, Jeremy Margolis (2000) profoundly states that, "The mass media has generated more heat than light with its extensive but often misguided coverage of racial profiling" (p. 18).

Professor David Harris states that, "The most observable impact of the racial profiling problem's fallout is in the courtroom, where the policemen need the benefit of the doubt" (Meek, 2001, p. 96). The constructive outcome of these issues is also stated by Johnny Hughes (2000) in that, "Officers will be afraid to stop anyone for fear of being labeled a racist and facing retaliation" (p. 24). Given all of these factors, Jeremy Margolis (2000) states that, "Giving credit to false allegations because of political pressure (something that is becoming increasingly difficult to resist) does a disservice to hardworking, fair-minded officers" (p. 23).

This section addresses the issues of racial profiling with respect to the operational issues, research and statistics, legal considerations, policy considerations, and investigative considerations.

Operational Issues

Jeremy Margolis (2000) states that, "Criminal elements exist in virtually every racial, national, tribal, religious, linguistic and cultural group" (p. 22). Therefore, race can be used as the basis for a stop if race is a legitimate intelligence factor (Nowicki, 2002g). The problem is that as a society, we have lost sight of the larger issues. Frank J. Gallo (2003) states that:

> The purpose of profiling is to provide a scientific method for focusing resources. . . . Profiling is not racial profiling and may include race as one factor among many. . . . Profiling includes assessing the current state of affairs and seeking relationships among variables for assessing criminal suspicion. It provides a snapshot of behaviors at a given time and place. (p. 19)

For example, profiling is used in drug trafficking cases. Johnny Hughes (2000) states that:

> Drugs are trafficked and used by people indigenous to an area. . . . Those who protest that members of specific ethnic groups are arrested for drug smuggling more than they are represented in the general population are not grasping reality. . . . It is 'Reason not Race' that directs the attention of officers to smugglers. Criminal Drug Interdiction Profiling is rooted in statistical reality, not racism. (p. 24)

With these issues in mind, the term bias-based policing should replace racial profiling, since this goes beyond the scope of just race. Bias-based policing is the unequal treatment of any person, which includes stopping, questioning, detaining or arresting on the basis of racial or ethnic characteristic, religion, gender, sexual orientation or socioeconomic status (Nowicki, 2002g).

Research and Statistics

Research studies have been conducted across the country with divergent results. Some agencies have been found to have demonstrated impropriety in their traffic stop practices. Albeit, the majority have been found to engage in legitimate practices, the specter of impropriety still exists. Care must be taken in the design and interpretation of any study of this nature due to the element of bias being built into the original research process that may skew the statistics both positively and negatively.

Some of the more noted studies have revealed that police engage in legal, proper, and justified traffic and field stops. For example, the State of Connecticut engaged in several studies in the effects of developing race data in traffic stops and found several positive results from the research (Cox, 2001). Another study conducted on 6,520 stops in the Richmond, Virginia Police Department revealed that stopped vehicle driver race proportions were 64 percent African American and 32 percent white. Additional review of the data suggested that there was no difference between African American and white officers in the rate of traffic stops of African American drivers (Oliver, 2001). Another positive result of officers conducting traffic stops is directly related to the war on drugs. According to the Drug Enforcement Administration some 40 percent of all drug arrests in this country are the outgrowth of traffic stops (Moody, 1998). To combine this information, the argument can be made that much good comes from legitimate and unbiased traffic and field stops.

Professor James Lasley and Professor Michael Hooper also conducted definitive research into the correlation between aggressive policing and institutionalized racism in police organizations. Their research revealed that aggressive policing does not automatically lead to the creation of a racist organization (Law and Order, 1998). Despite these factors, there will always be those who will not accept the fact that traffic and field stops are necessary, legitimate, and positive practices of police agencies.

Legal Considerations

Racial profiling is based in bias acts that are prohibited by law. The *United States Constitution* as well as individual state constitutions provide for such protective laws. Some attacks at the legality of street level and vehicular stops have been levied against police actions in pretextual stops. While the United States Supreme Court in *Whren v. U.S.* (1996) ruled that pretextual stops were constitutional, it left open the possibility of attacking racially based law enforcement activity under the Equal Protection Clause with civil suits (*Law and Order,* 2001a). In addition, these actions can also be filed under Title VI of the Civil Rights Act that provides that no person shall be denied the benefits of any program based upon race, color, or national origin from any agency that receives federal financial assistance (Close, 2001). The laws are clear in that when an act is found to be racially motivated, criminal and civil protections are in place to allow victims to seek redress. Several court cases indicate that police may act on a suspect's description that consists primarily of the suspect's race and gender. Absent evidence of discriminatory racial animus, such actions will not violate the Equal Protection Clause. Nevertheless, these cases also show that officers should not ignore non-racial/ethnic descriptors (Spector, 2002a).

Policy Considerations

Because of the issues involved in racial profiling and the potential for liability and loss of public trust, law enforcement organizations should develop a specific policy that addresses the phenomenon of racial profiling. While the investigative and disciplinary process will most likely remain the same, specific attention can be given to the topic in a separate and distinct policy based forum. With this in mind, a law enforcement agency should take the following steps in order to prevent such acts in the agency: (1) develop, implement, and train in agency policy prohibiting inappropriate police tactics that use racial profiling practices, (2) implement appropriate mechanisms to insure supervisory oversight and employee compliance, (3) develop a simple brochure that provides guidelines for citizens who are stopped by the police, and (4) develop a complaint process to investigate bias-based policing and report the findings to the complainant (Carrick, 2001).

Investigative Considerations

In the investigation of allegations of racial profiling, the internal investigator may be faced with individual as well as organizational allegations. From an individual case, the specific circumstances of the case will be the guiding factor. If an allegation is sustained, the history of the individual officer will then need to be reviewed to determine if any previous problems of a similar or exact nature are present. This may open the need to search deeply in the agency's records for arrests, field and traffic stop information, and patterns of conduct that must be balanced against officer effectiveness, productivity, and the demographics of the assigned patrol area. This will by no means be an easy task to fairly and impartially investigate.

The second consideration in allegations of racial profiling may rise to the team, group, or organizational levels. This is often referred to as "institutionalized racism." These can be vague and generalized allegations or based upon a series of lower level incidents that a discernible pattern of misconduct can be drawn from. These investigations must be based upon objective criterion applied to both quantitative and qualitative informational sources. For example, statistics alone do not prove or establish racial profiling, as racial profiling requires intent on the part of the officer that may not be established by statistical data alone since not everyone agrees to its reliability or usefulness (Close, 2001; *Law and Order,* 2001a; Meek, 2001). However, agencies can develop and analyze statistics that provide empirical evidence that counters exaggerated perceptions and problems before they occur (*Law and Order,* 2001a; *Law and Order,* 2001c). When statistics are used they should include officer race, department demographics, crime rates, driver's or subject of the field stop race, community demographics, economics, drug use enforcement, justification for searches and comparison to the rates of contraband located and seized. Steven J. Hill (1999) reported that:

> The International Association of Chiefs of Police (IACP), among others, has stated that the collection of such data could not only be easily impeded by truly biased officers, but would also lead to potentially volatile difficulties when police interview minorities concerning issues of race while engaged in the traffic stop situation. In such a stressful situation, the potential for offense to be taken by minority motorists is substantial. (p. 94)

Statistics are only one component of the analysis process. The internal investigator must also use the courts for guidance in these types of investigations. Research is emerging that strongly indicates that racial profiling is more a myth than it is a reality. The courts have examined the issue in some landmark cases and have provided some limited guidance in the criteria for evaluating whether or not an incident is racially motivated. The courts have examined such claims in light of factors such as ruling that there has been a failure to support these types of claims through statistical evidence alone (e.g., *Chavez v. Illinois State Police,* 1998) as well as equal protection claims wherein field stops were conducted with individuals who were of the same race and gender as a felony suspect (*Brown v. City of Oneonta,* 1999) (A. B. Anderson, 2000; Spector, 2002a).

The *Brown v. City of Oneonta* (1999) case involved two analyses: An analysis of the rights of officers to conduct a seizure under the Fourth Amendment. In this analysis, the Supreme Court ruled that using race in making street stops was permissible as long as race created the requisite probable cause or reasonable suspicion. The second analysis involved that of a claim for equal protection under the Fourteenth Amendment. The Supreme Court also ruled in favor of the police in this aspect as the police decision to conduct stops of black males was based upon a witness description and not through the discretion of the officers (Brooks, 2000; Spector, 2002a). The Court wrote:

> Officers rely on their ability to act on nonarticulable hunches, collected experience, intuition, and sense impressions–all of

> which are crucial in carrying out a criminal investigation. . . . Officers would be forced to justify these intuitive considerations in order to meet an accusation that race was the sole factor motivating the encounter. The unworkability of such a regime is self-evident. (Spector, 2002a)

SUMMARY

This chapter discussed the numerous special investigations that the internal investigator may be involved in. Some of the most common are fleet vehicle accidents and pursuits. The chapter then progressed through other limited opportunity but critical investigations such as specialized unit deployment as SWAT and K-9 and their unique duties and requirements. The chapter then reviewed such issues as substance abuse, hostile work environment, and domestic and workplace violence as they have been on the rise in the work world. The chapter closed with an in-depth discussion on the phenomenon of racial profiling with the need for proper statistical analysis and court precedent to guide a law enforcement agency's investigation and proper response to such allegations.

Chapter 11

ISSUES IN ADMINISTRATIVE AND CIVIL CLAIMS INVESTIGATIONS

INTRODUCTION

This chapter discusses the investigative requirements surrounding issues in administrative and civil claims investigations that the internal investigator will also be responsible for in the law enforcement organization. The chapter discusses the investigative requirements for insubordination investigations, untruthfulness, discourtesy, as well as several other general employment type claims. The chapter also discusses the issues involved in the investigation of training and policy development, line of duty deaths, and civil claims investigations.

INSUBORDINATION

Insubordination as well as many of the following issues, such as conduct unbecoming, discourtesy, and the like are not violations of criminal law, but can result in sanctions if misconduct is found on the part of the officer. As such, officers can also be disciplined and dismissed for unethical behavior. A general definition of insubordination is the failure to obey a departmental rule, regulation or procedure, or lawful order of a higher ranking officer without just or proper cause. Insubordination also involves more than expressing strong disagreement with a superior's decision. If the order is reasonable, the general rule traditionally upheld by the courts requires subordinate officers to carry out the orders under protest, and question them later (Collins, 1999). As such, the violation can carry serious penalties to include termination.

While insubordination is a serious violation of organizational edicts, situations may arise where the insubordination can be justified. The internal investigator and administrator must also be cognizant of these exceptions when bringing charges in an investigation of this nature. Just cause to disobey an order can be stated as: (1) the order was unlawful, (2) the order was outside the authority of the issuer, (3) obeying the order would require the officer to unduly jeopardize his safety, (4) the order was given to prevent the employee from exercising his rights under a state's collective bargaining law, or (5) the order infringes upon the officer's free speech or other constitutional right. An officer has no duty to obey an unlawful order (Collins, 1999).

An interesting case involving an Indiana State Trooper that was fired for insubordination concerning his refusal to work on a riverboat casino due to his religious beliefs was decided in favor of the trooper. After being fired for insubordination, both the Equal Employment Opportunity Commission and the Indiana Workforce Development Commission ruled in favor of the trooper in separate hearings (*Law and Order,* 2000b). As previously stated, while the penalty for insubordination can be termination, cases that support this severe action are: (1) an employee who failed to provide a list of friends at alleged drug parties, (2) employees who refused to submit to drug tests, (3) making untruthful reports of sexual harassment and discriminatory treatment, and (4) an officer who violated a "no arrest" policy (Collins, 1999).

The internal investigator should review organizational policy, organizational past practice with similar cases, and prevailing case law when making a decision in the penalty recommendation for a law enforcement officer who has committed an act of insubordination. Law enforcement administrators should also consider these factors strongly when levying a penalty as these factors will be important to the hearing administrator and the reviewing court if an appeal is filed.

UNTRUTHFULNESS

The issue of untruthfulness in police organizations is extremely problematic. While all who have an opinion will posit that there really is no issue in that law enforcement personnel should be ever vigilant in their search for and presentation of the truth, the fact of the matter is that like most issues facing law enforcement, this, too, carries many subjective areas of interpretation. This section discusses the practical implications of the truthfulness issue and its impact in law enforcement operations. This section discusses the clear as well as ambiguous nature of untruthfulness issues, practical implications of truthfulness in law enforcement, and strategies to abate untruthfulness.

The Clarity and Ambiguity of Untruthfulness

While police are allowed to make a mistake, the thought of telling an intentional lie is unacceptable (Sanow, 2001b). This holds true in such environments as with command personnel, internal affairs statements, and when testifying in any judicial or quasi-judicial setting. The Supreme Court however, does allow measures of untruthfulness in such areas as the interrogation process as long as the lie does not coerce or unduly place the subject in a position where a false confession could be had. In the former example, malicious lies are those told with bad intent and exceed the limits of legitimacy such as false testimony. Malice is the motive by which any sense of limits or constraint or fidelity to law and policy is destroyed (Noble, 2003). Untruthfulness must be scaled in the law enforcement environment dependent upon audience and severity of the issues at hand. Progressive analysts in this area recognize the unworkability of a zero tolerance policy and provide for distinct examples of the levels of deception that are and are not acceptable in the law enforcement realm. In the deception continuum concept, at one end of the continuum is intentional, malicious, and deceptive conduct which can take one of three forms:

1. Deceptive action in a formal setting, such as testifying in court or during an internal affairs investigation.
2. Failure to bring forward information involving criminal action by other officers, also known as observing the so-called code of silence.
3. Creation of false evidence that tends to implicate another in a criminal act. (Noble, 2003)

To determine the level of truthfulness in this environment is entirely dependent upon the circumstances rather than the explicit edicts. The issue of strict truthfulness then rests on the situation rather than the statement or the action of the involved officer. Several cases have been decided that may provide specific guidance in this arena and are sources for the internal investigator and administrator. These cases are: *Haney v. City of Los Angeles* (2003), *Ziegler v. City of South Pasadena* (1999), *Brogan v. United States* (1998), *LaChance v. Erickson* (1998), *Ackerman v. State Personnel Board* (1983), *Gee v. California State Personnel Board* (1970), and *Brady v. Maryland* (1963). Another case for consideration is *U.S. v. Whitted* (1993) wherein expert testimony with regard to the lack of candor or untruthfulness of an officer was highly inappropriate and constitutes legal error (MacLatchie, 2000).

One final issue in the issue of clarity and ambiguity in the area of untruthfulness manifests itself in the high stress levels that face officers on a daily basis. A proven fact is that stress impacts an officer's ability to accurately recall incidents. This is compounded by the fact that immense additional stress is created by an investigative process that will place an officer in a position where organizational pressure and survival may overcome the predilections of some of the most honest officers in the ranks. In addition, attempting to determine deceptive behavior in an officer is difficult at best and many times a matter of judgment involving many factors. Premature conclusions concerning an officer's truthfulness may lead to the conviction of an innocent person (Artwohl & Christensen, 1997, p. 245).

Zero Tolerance for Untruthfulness

One of the classic responses to internal corruption and complaints is to invoke a "Zero Tolerance Rule" for alleged acts of untruthfulness. Law enforcement administrators will employ this hardball measure as a tactic to finally put an end to all acts of deception in the organization. This is a problematic approach that most often causes far more harm than good, especially when the motivation is strictly for political reasons. Research in the field has indicated that ethical issues exist at all strata in law enforcement organizations and those at the lowest levels resent being held to higher standards than those who are in charge.

Research also suggests that the quantum of a "lie" is not as absolute as one might like to believe and that truthfulness should be measured more on the basis of a continuum that spans social lies or little white lies to egregious misconduct (Noble, 2003). Jeff Noble (2003) also states that:

> No lies, however, does not express the true concern of police administrators. Rather, the concern is with improper, intentional, deceptive conduct that affects an officer's credibility, whether that deceptive conduct consists of lying, making material omissions, or engaging in other unacceptable deliberate actions. (p. 92)

While accurate perceptual memory seems to always come into question, the issue of zero tolerance has both an absolute side and a practical side that need to be in balance in order for the organization to function properly.

Fact v. Fiction in Truthfulness

The slippery slope effect is one of the most popular explanations for the infancy stages of police corruption. In this ideology, if one subscribes to this theory, telling one lie will lead to a career of untruthfulness. Jeff Noble (2003) states that, "It may be true that some persons who engage in serious misconduct began with minor acts of deception, but it does not follow that all deception is a gateway to serious misconduct" (p. 97). The fact remains that there are those who will never lie no matter the circumstances, those who will lie through sanctioned means such as in the interview and interrogation process under limits set by the courts, those who will engage in lower level or inconsequential lies, those who will lie as a means of survival in organizations that have created insurmountable barriers to efficient and effective work practices, and those who are corrupt and lack any measure of integrity. The reality is that a distinction must be made between these groups and individuals instead of painting the entire spectrum of behaviors with a broad and imposingly restrictive brush.

Research into the motivations for dishonesty revealed that they fell into five separate categories: (1) anger, for which 41 percent of the responses dealt with excessive force situations, (2) peer pressure accounted for 20 percent of the incidents, (3) greed accounted for 16 percent of the incidents, (4) lust accounted for eight percent, and (5) other situations at 15 percent (Trautman, 2001). These facts reveal that the motivation for dishonesty is born from individual and external factors.

Much of the issue of untruthfulness emanates from an individual officer's perspective as well as a demonstration of the desire to protect other officers who are exposed to the same circumstances. Dr. Neal Trautman's (2001) research has revealed that, "One of the most powerful 'root causes' of officers throughout the nation participating in the code of silence is that they deeply believe they have been victimized by their own workplace." Understanding this perspective of the involved personnel is a priority for internal investigators as well as police administrators in evaluating if in fact a statement is untruthful, and whether the intent of the statement was a matter of a mistake in judgment or a fundamental and nefarious character flaw. This will be the test of determining the fact and fiction of the issue of truthfulness.

Practical Implications of Truthfulness in Law Enforcement

The practical implications of truthfulness connotes that there is an impractical side to the problem. The practical side is that law enforcement personnel must be able to function in an environment that demands the highest level of integrity in enforcing the laws of the land and the immense responsibility in being charged with the right to deprive others of their freedom, with cause, in a free society. The impractical side is that there are psychological, sociological, and environmental factors that have subtle and severe implications in the efficient and fair application of these types of rules. When examining this issue, the internal investigator must consider the contemporary issues in the relationship between general societal mores and law enforcement operations and organizational barriers, the allegiance to peers, and the impact of the courts.

David Nyberg (1994) asserts that acts of deception are such common practice in human communication that deceptive conduct would be impossible to prevent entirely by any rule, law, policy, or manner of enforcement (Noble, 2003, p. 97). Nowhere does this issue evoke more emotions and controversy than with law enforcement personnel who are the subject of allegations of marginalized integrity than from the American public. The rank and file recognizes that there are often occasions when citizen complaints are bolstered or fall to the level of vicious and blatant untruths perpetrated by those who capriciously decide that they are not pleased with the level of law enforcement services provided during a police contact. In an effort to exact revenge, they may file false complaints in hopes that the matter will not be investigated in depth, or that the mere filing of a complaint will bring problems or discredit upon the officer. Faced with this dilemma, an officer may see that since society lives to a lower standard and a complainant can allege the gamut of egregious acts, the need to lie may be more a matter of survival than one of intentional deception.

As briefly discussed in the previous section, loyalty and allegiance to peers is a powerful factor to contend with in the truthfulness construct. In uninvolved officers, it emerges as a sense of loyalty to protect a partner or coworker and feeling a sense of having to protect each other as all others work against the street officer often prevails (Gilmartin & Harris, 1998). The practical implications of this are that the feelings cannot be displaced or abated. Law enforcement officers will empathize with their immediate peers, as well as others known and unknown in the field.

The judicial, quasi-judicial, and departmental inquiries are the most important factors in balancing the practical side of this problem. For example, juries in criminal and civil cases evaluate officer credibility. The resulting verdicts reflect not only the jury's assessment of whether the officer did the right thing, but also whether the jury believed the officer's version of the events (Meyer, 1999). When issues of deception are brought to the table they must be measured in the context of the situation. The courts must weigh such deception in a probative rather than prejudicial manner, such as an officer that engages in a secretive extramarital affair. These types of deceptions would be considered administrative lies and would most likely not be allowed to be presented to a jury as true deceptive misconduct on behalf of the officer (Noble, 2003). These situations are likened to internal inquiries where the truth should be determined and measured in the context of the incident under investigation or being reviewed.

Jeff Noble (2003) places much of this issue into perspective as he states that:

> The difficulty for managers is balancing the need of the department and community to have officers that are beyond reproach against the recognition that all officers are human beings and that they have human failings. The officer's response may best be described as a spontaneous, unintelligent statement, and there are other factors that should be considered in making a final determination. Is the officer remorseful? Does the officer recognize the error? Does the officer have an otherwise acceptable record with the department? Was the underlying issue one of very little consequence? (p. 99)

Practical policy is then a critical issue in a law enforcement organization where the rhetoric of zero tolerance has no place. In developing policy and rules concerning the issue of untruthfulness, police administrators need to understand that there is a difference between deceptive conduct and deceptive misconduct. Acknowledging that some deceptive conduct is acceptable helps to define deceptive misconduct (Noble, 2003). Most, if not all officers know the definitive line of deception. The internal investigator and administrator may seek some guidance from the Constitutional test that allows for some deception in the interview and interrogation process to the point that an innocent person would falsely confess to a crime, again, a matter of interpretation for the courts with latitude that leads to an absolute. There are many gray or indistinct levels in the issue of truthfulness that need clarification and understanding from the internal investigator and administrator. Of paramount understanding is that statistics analyzed from some of the largest police agencies reveals that the "Blue Wall of Silence" seems to be based mostly in false perception than reality (Ferrell, 2003).

Figure 11-1. Officer Stephen Roach of the Evendale Police Department (Photo courtesy of the Cincinnati Enquirer).

Figure 11-2. Cincinnati Police Chief Thomas Streicher Jr. in light of this internal investigation issued a memo to all Cincinnati police officers stating, "Dishonesty cannot and will not be tolerated in our organization" (Photo courtesy of the Cincinnati Enquirer).

A case in point deals with a Cincinnati police officer who was involved in a police shooting. Officer Stephen Roach was subsequently investigated by the Cincinnati Police Department and found to have violated departmental policy and been untruthful during his statement. Officer Roach however, was acquitted in court of the criminal charges placed against him (Korte, 2002). Officer Roach was subsequently hired by the Evendale Police Department. The police chief, background investigator, and village officials, upon examination of the facts of the Cincinnati investigation, concurred with the findings of Hamilton County Judge Winkler that Officer Roach did not violate any laws and that his statement did not impede the Cincinnati investigation (Edwards, 2002). What this example very adeptly underscores is three critical areas: (1) the issue of organizational standards of truthfulness, (2) the vague and ambiguous nature of the interpretation of untruthfulness, and (3) the conflict between the levels of evidence required in internal investigations and a criminal court of law.

In dissecting these issues, to develop organizational standards of truthfulness, an administrator must consider the affect of strict hold-the-line standards. That is not to say that administrators should vacillate on consequential decisions involving integrity. However, they must consider the implications of edicts that hold unachievable standards as well. In examining the vague and ambiguous nature of the interpretation of untruthfulness, this case clearly shows that many involved in the investigation, who share equal credibility can view the same set of facts and come to starkly different conclusions. These conclusions will affect the lives of everyone involved, and not always for the better. The final issue is the conflict between the levels of evidence required in internal investigations and a criminal court of law. For example, Officer Roach was held to a standard of evidence in the Cincinnati internal investigation that was found to have violated policy where the evidence only has to reach a level of preponderance of facts; indicted based upon a level of evidence that must be marginally higher, that of probable cause; acquitted in a bench trial based upon the showing of reasonable doubt; and hired by another police agency that used the same preponderance of evidence standard to vindicate him as was done in a criminal court. For all intents and purposes, the issue of untruthfulness will never be as crystal clear as we would like it to be. Therefore, that fine line must be viewed from the side of the officer making these tough, critical, and life-altering decisions as a matter of convention and not aberration.

Strategies to Abate Untruthfulness

The internal investigator and administrator have two responsibilities; to uncover untruthfulness and to prevent it whenever possible. While the former responsibility will depend on the skill of the investigator as well as the available evidence, the latter requires a progressive thought process and organizational commitment. Policies, practices, and informal organizational culture may be the bane of this admirable goal. Therefore, the commitment has to begin at the highest levels of the organization and transcend to the lowest levels by the delineation of practical policies, expectations, and leadership by example.

While a salvo of information and research has been developed in this particular area, it seems we may be no further ahead than when these issues began to be substantively studied by researchers since Sir Robert Peel postured for a uniformed police force committed to service and integrity. Much of the onus for this falls to management's responsibility. Supervisors, managers, and chiefs bear much responsibility for ethical lapses as well as the perception of ethical lapses in police organizations. The extension to law enforcement officers rests with embracing a culture of an allegiance to principles and integrity rather than loyalty to people (Trautman, 2001; Trautman, 2002).

To offer some guidance in this area, Craig E. Ferrell (2003) recommends the following strategy to debunk the myth of pervasive untruthfulness in police organizations, "The key to influencing and changing public perception is the same as that for reducing municipal liability–proper training, proactive supervision, and open communication with the public" (p. 9). In addition, training must address the issue of the police code of silence, as when a trainer fails to do so, constructively, the code of silence is condoned (Martinelli & Pollock, 2000).

DISCOURTESY COMPLAINTS

The highest percentage of citizen complaints against officers is for discourtesy (Sanow, 2003). Many citizen complaints of discourtesy come from traffic stops which are a significant portion of the responsibility of many officers (Onder, 2001). Discourtesy complaints represent a proverbial oxymoron in that they are constructively an insignificant issue in the entire context of law enforcement services and problems, yet they consume an inordinately enormous amount of the organization's resources. This type of complaint is probably the most profound and disconcerting of all complaints received by a supervisor. John J. Fuller (2001) states that, "Cops saying the wrong thing at the wrong time account for the great majority of citizen complaints, whether justified or not" (p. 6). This is supported by research presented by Dr. Sandra Bass that shows the biggest indicator of officers receiving complaints is one of disrespect (Mueck, 2000). Further research conducted by Mervin F. White, Terry C. Cox, and Jack Basehart revealed four situational reasons why police use obscenity in interactions with citizens: (1) to gain the attention of the citizen, (2) to establish social distance, (3) to label and degrade citizens, and (4) to dominate and control citizens (Barker & Carter, 1994). These represent the community expectation of respect from their law enforcement officers as well as many of the negative reasons for those who are discourteous.

Two additional issues need discussion in the issue of discourtesy: (1) the definition of discourtesy and (2) situational examinations of discourtesy complaints. Most organizations have a blanket statement that proscribes discourteous acts in the furtherance of law enforcement duties. Most also do not have specific prohibited acts and exercise much latitude at both ends of the scale. This is in part because of politics, the vague nature of courtesy, and the limitations that would be placed on personnel and administrations. Having a blanket policy represents a double-edged sword though when investigating and determining if an interaction is either courteous or discourteous. Interestingly stated, investigations of this type can also be analogous to such types of behavior as conduct unbecoming, as these cases can also be as difficult to define as the age old argument of the difference between pornography and art (Martinelli & Pollock, 2000). Policies should include some definitive language defining discourtesy and interpretation should be in the most liberal sense to the benefit of the officer when making a determination in the investigation. Another consideration in this vane is to adopt the principle of Procedural Justice, which is defined as when the officer does his or her job, shows respect, and acts impartially with an absence of bias (Mueck, 2000). This connotes that the entire contact and not the individual comment or statement should be considered prior to rendering a finding.

Figure 11-3. Many personnel complaints are generated based upon routine traffic stops (Photo courtesy of the Brockport, New York Police Department).

The second component of assessment is to measure the complaint and actions in the context of the incident. One example is that while a patently discourteous term in normal circumstances can be construed as inappropriate, the use of a discourteous term that de-escalates a potentially violent situation should be considered in context and balanced with the final outcome. A second example is that some complaints arise from an officer raising their voice or yelling wherein the complainant alleges the officer was discourteous. These situations need to be reviewed in context to the scenario, environment, and other variables. In some cases, a loud verbal command may also startle a potential adversary by mentally stunning that individual's thinking processes and thus avoiding a use-of-force (Nowicki, 2001d). The final consideration is the stress factors involved in many police encounters. In accepting that the field is fraught with stress and the inexact nature of psychological and physiological responses to such highly-charged situations, the internal investigator and administrator must recognize that trained professionals can make infrequent sanctioned mistakes that should not carry a penalty, but are more appropriate for a remedial training or expectation setting session.

SICK LEAVE INVESTIGATIONS

Infrequently, the supervisor, internal investigator, and administrator may need to conduct an investigation into an employee's sick leave. Provisions of the *Americans with Disabilities Act* provide certain protections for those who are sick or disabled. In conducting these types of investigations, ADA consistent department sick leave policy is critical to resolving these situations. In addition, the investigation can only explore violations of legitimate policy and the behavior that prevents the terms and conditions of performance required to maintain the position. In addition, the organization should: (1) develop a clear ADA compliant policy regulating leave, (2) track employee sick use and taking corrective actions when abuse occurs, (3) have a set of steps in the policy to make sick claims, provide doctors excuses, supervisory home visits, (4) the maintenance of good records that are kept confidential based upon ADA standards, (5) contractual requirements that identify maximum excused time limits, (6) the ability to recognize patterns of abuse comparisons to unit sick leave, and (7) provisions to refer employees for professional assistance.

There are two other considerations for the investigation and monitoring of sick leave. The first is for the addition of sick leave as an indicator in early warning systems (Orrick, 2004a). Extreme care must be taken in how records are protected and used based upon union contracts, the ADA, and the *Family Medical Leave Act*. The second is that sick leave, either at the individual or organizational level may be an indicator of deeper problems in the organization. The National Institute of Ethics has found abuse of sick leave can be a symptom of a troubled employee (Orrick, 2004a). The internal investigator and administrator must maintain an open mind in these incidents and work to resolve these problems in the most positive of manners.

OFF-DUTY JOBS

Off-duty jobs represent an administrative and civil litigation problem (Weinblatt, 1999). Policy should be developed and enforced in regulating off-duty assignments. Policy should also be consistent with law wherein certain types of part-time employment are forbidden for law enforcement personnel. Care should also be taken in the review and approval of requests where the organization may incur some type of liability in cross-over responsibilities such as security-type roles.

When developing policy, the following issues should be addressed: (1) Uniform/nonuniform use, (2) duty equipment/vehicle restrictions, (3) process serving type positions where no law enforcement responsibility is required, (4) burglar alarm systems installation and monitoring, (5) types of employment (bars) and work hours restricted, (6) provisions in policy for denying/revoking/suspending off-duty employment, (7) restrictions on officers who are on probationary periods, and (8) advising department/communications when working such assignments as security where a police contact may be possible.

In the investigation of these types of incidents where a complaint is filed or civil claim made, the internal investigator will need to establish the actions of the employee and their authority to act. Part-time employment such as security should bring clear delineation that the employee is not a member of the department when so employed. Other types of employment will depend upon the employee's cross-over responsibilities and if the conduct was in violation of department standards.

FITNESS FOR DUTY EVALUATIONS

There are many factors that may impact a law enforcement officer's ability to perform their normal duties. While prescreening measures of background, physical ability, and psychological health are used prior to employment, most agencies have no substantive follow-up procedures for in-service personnel. When behavior is observed in an employee that indicates that they are having substantial difficulty in performing their assigned functions, then a Fitness For Duty Evaluation (FFDE) may be appropriate.

Fitness for Duty Evaluations are defined as:

> A specialized inquiry conducted by a specifically qualified mental health professional in response to complaints of an officer's reported inability to perform official duties in a safe and effective manner because of impaired behavior. It is generally conducted for purposes of estimating the risk that an officer's reportedly abnormal behavior represents to his department and to the community in general. (Rostow & Davis, 2002)

The purpose of the FFDE is to notify the police executive and department of information that touches upon behavioral, mental illness, or personality issues that diminish an officer's performance of his or her official role (Rostow & Davis, 2002). The FFDE is different than a medical evaluation where the performance issue is related to a medical rather than a behavioral or psychological condition.

Legal Issues

Ignoring inappropriate behaviors by personnel can likely incur significant liability on a department as the argument could be made in civil court that the department had a policy, pattern, or practice in place of failing to act on and remedy such conduct. Cases that have been decided in this are *McKenna v. Fargo* (1978), as well as others wherein the courts have generally maintained that a department has an overriding right to inquire into the mental stability of an officer and that other presumed rights, such as the right of privacy, are superseded by such concerns when a police officer is involved. Contrasting this, in a number of cases involving the *Family Medical Leave Act,* such as *Albert v. Runyon* (1998), the courts have held that the employer cannot require a fitness for duty examination if the employee has been certified by a physician or psychologist to be able to return to work. This rule is not absolute as behavior demonstrated upon return to work may continue to reveal indications of impairment or dysfunction (Rostow & Davis, 2002).

While ADA may place some limits on an employer's right to secure common medical information, particularly if it is not job-related, it allows that some forms of illness may interfere with the "business necessity." Personality or social interaction problems are usually not covered under the ADA, while mental illness is covered. As these actions may be subject to court review, the department should use a qualified and licensed psychologist who is able to offer expert testimony in the case. In addition, with respect to ADA and FMLA, in many states, no doctor-patient relationship is said to exist when the doctor (FFDE provider) is paid by the employer to examine the employee (Rostow & Davis, 2002).

Procedural Issues

Police executives face four options when confronting identified conduct on behalf of an officer that is inappropriate: (1) ignoring or taking no action, (2) discipline and/or termination, (3) referral to an employee assistance program, and (4) a Fitness for Duty Evaluation (Rostow & Davis, 2002). A policy should be in place that delineates the actions that will be taken when an FFDE is warranted based upon the actions of the officer. Cary D. Rostow and Robert D. Davis (2002) present a series of considerations for the internal investigator and administrator to consider when administering the FFDE:

1. In developing contracts with psychological service providers, the department should be identified as the "client," not the examinee.
2. FFDE files should be separate from internal affairs files.
3. Officers should be advised of the FFDE in writing and should not be required to disclose, or even discuss, the nature of his potential disability to the supervisor or other agency personnel.
4. The officer should be informed that the examination may touch upon a broad range of issues in many parts of their life, and while there is an expectation for consent to the testing, they may discontinue testing, evaluation, or the transmission of the report, and elect instead to submit to the prescribed administrative procedure. The refusal to submit to the FFDE may result in the loss of protections available to impaired or disabled officers.
5. The officer should be told to not report for the examination accompanied by his attorney, union representative, family members, or friends.
6. The FFDE provider should avoid creating reports that contain intrusive clinical or personal information beyond that needed to address the fitness questions.
7. All medical, psychological and mental health issues, work history, behavioral, legal, military, disciplinary history, should be forwarded directly to the examiner and not delivered by the involved officer.

Officer Considerations

A nationwide study by police psychologists revealed statistically that some 16% of police officers examined manifested personality disorders that were chronic in nature such as anti-social, narcissistic, paranoid, or abusive tendencies (Arnold, 2001). The immediate supervisor, internal investigator, and administrator should recognize that these will be difficult situations for both the department and employee. As such, all involved should not lose sight of the ultimate goal in identifying the presence of a psychological problem and provide proper intervention and treatment in order to save the officer.

Protocol and Policy Development

Protocol and policy development will enhance a department's ability to effectively respond to situations of this nature. A psychological FFDE is appropriate when an officer's behavior calls into questions his stability, emotional control, judgment, or psychological functions that create a reasonable doubt as to his psychological suitability to continue carrying out essential job functions in a safe and effective manner (Trompetter, 1998).

All attempts at remediation, training, counseling, and close supervision should be exhausted prior to exercising the FFDE (Trompetter, 1998). This is a severe step in the process that will have significant implications for all involved. Exhausting all lower level remedies in an effort to resolve the problem is the recommended strategy. However, when aberrant behavior is severe or of a nature that may endanger the officer or others, then the FFDE should be immediate. The FFDE should also be done by a police psychologist familiar with the field of policing and contemporary literature, its related personnel and civil rights issues, accompanied by standardized and published psychological testing (Rostow & Davis, 2002). In addition, a standardized evaluation should link psychological constructs to essential job functions (Trompetter, 1998).

The internal investigator and administrator should have some familiarity with the terminology and constructs of the evaluation that will be presented to the organization. Such terminology includes the domains of psychological fitness that should be examined and are identified as: (1) emotional control/anger management, (2) stress and threat tolerance, (3) acceptance of criticism, (4) impulse/risk control, (5) positive attitude, (6) assertiveness/tenacity, (7) command presence/persuasiveness, (8) integrity, (9) dependability/reliability, (10) initiative/achievement motivation, (11) conformance to rules and regulations, (12) adaptability/flexibility, (13) vigilance/attention to detail, (14) interpersonal sensitivity, (15) social concern, (16) teamwork, (17) practical intelligence/decision-making ability, and (17) objectivity/tolerance (Trompetter, 1998).

The FFDE should culminate in a final written report that is forwarded directly to the chief or designated administrator and kept confidential within the department. Psychological FFDE reports should include only the functional job limitations of the officer as well as the information necessary for the agency to make a determination of fitness or unfitness. If deemed unfit, or if the officer is likely to have emotional, psychological, or mental problems that would interfere with their ability to perform essential job functions of a peace officer in a safe and effective manner (Trompetter, 1998). The FFDE provider should offer written conclusions that contain one of four major outcome recommendations:

1. The officer is unfit and unlikely to become fit through any foreseeable short-term treatment process.
2. The officer is currently unfit, but there is a fair possibility of resolution with treatment.
3. The officer shows no discernible mental health or suspected physical problem either detailed or by self-report.
4. The lack of cooperation, honesty, effort, or openness by the officer has resulted in a failure by the examiner to reach reasonable clinical conclusions. (Rostow & Davis, 2002)

FREE SPEECH ISSUES

The issue of free speech with law enforcement personnel arises when they decide to make public statements concerning opinions and facts about the agency. The internal investigator and administrator must be aware that public employees do not relinquish their First Amendment rights to comment on matters of public interest by virtue of government employment as a state cannot condition public employment on a basis that infringes the employee's constitutionally protected interest in freedom of expression (Newbold, 2003).

There are certain limits placed on free speech and public employees. Public employees are not given free rein to say whatever they want as a person's constitutional rights must be balanced against any legitimate government interests. In determining if the speech was actionable by an agency, the *Pickering/Connick* analysis is conducted which consists of two steps: (1) the court determines whether the officer was speaking "as a citizen on matters of public concern and (2) then if it deems the speech a matter of public concern, the court must balance the individual's interest against the government right as employer "in promoting the efficiency of the public services it performs through its employees." In applying the balancing test, consideration is given to "whether the statement impairs discipline by superiors or harmony among co-workers, has a detrimental impact on close working relationships for which personal loyalty and confidence are necessary, or impedes the performance of the speaker's duties or interferes with the regular operation of the enterprise" (Newbold, 2003).

FEDERAL OVERSIGHT AND CONSENT DECREES

Enacted through federal legislation, the Civil Rights Division of the United States Department of Justice has been given the authority to investigate, and initiate civil litigation to eliminate, a "pattern or practice" of misconduct by law enforcement. The United States Supreme Court has decided that a pattern or practice violation exists when police misconduct in the agency's "standard operating procedure–the regular–rather than the unusual practice" is found to exist. The Justice Department has committed to litigate pattern or practice claims only when it is unable to negotiate a consensual resolution of the problems identified (Ferrell, 2003). Consent decrees have been utilized in places such as Montgomery County, Maryland, the New Jersey State Police, the Pittsburgh Police Bureau, the City of Steubenville, Ohio, and the City of Highland Park, Illinois (*Law and Order,* 2001a). The concepts within the decrees simply reflect policy reform, accountability, and increased disciplinary measures from a proactive managerial approach (Martinelli, 2002).

In order to prevent the control of a federal consent decree, a law enforcement agency should be aware of the common requirements in the agreements. One suggestion is to keep abreast of consent decrees and requirements in order to implement contemporary change in the department (Meyer, 2001). Reviewing those consent decrees that are available on the Department of Justice website (www.usdoj.gov) can give an agency invaluable guidance into operational and administrative requirements, monitoring of use-of-force issues, early warning systems, and the like.

When faced with the control of a consent decree, agencies should designate high-ranking lead officials in the agency as the liaison. These officials should have designated authority to make change in response to the requirements that will be placed upon the agency. Some agencies make the mistake of delegating this task to lower rank supervisory or command officers and this may impede real time change that will prevent agency turnaround.

One interesting speculative note is that if the federal government assumes authority and control, will there be a commensurate level of responsibility assigned? In other words, legally, if the federal government assumes total control of a local police department, do they assume their liabilities as well? (Cameron, 2000). This will only be discovered through time and court review.

GENERAL EMPLOYEE TYPE ACTIONS

With respect to general employee type actions, this subsection discusses such issues as the *Americans with Disabilities Act,* workers compensation claims, and arbitration in employee claims.

Americans with Disabilities Act

The *Americans with Disabilities Act* was formed to ensure that organizations did not engage in discriminatory practices based upon physical disabilities. As such, organizations must comply with the various standards set forth in the act and provide a reasonable accommodation where necessary to assist the employee in maintaining employment. Joseph E. Scuro (2001) recommends the following issues to consider as practical suggestions when dealing with employee complaints of ADA disabilities requiring affirmative steps on the employer's part to be in compliance with the act:

1. The condition claimed to be a "disability" by the employee should be reviewed carefully to determine if that condition-impairment rises to the level of a disability as defined under ADA.
2. If on the surface, the impairment-condition raised appears to be a "disability," that may in fact fit the ADA definition of "disability," is this condition specifically excluded from protection by the act? For example, individuals currently engaged in illegal drug use, those with psychoactive substance use disorders resulting from the current illegal use of drugs, compulsive gamblers, pyromaniacs, kleptomaniacs, etc., are specifically excluded from ADA legal protections.
3. If the impairment-condition does meet the ADA definition of "disability," will reasonable accommodation impose an undue hardship on the employer and its business operations?
4. Is the employee "an otherwise qualified individual with a disability"? ADA gives consideration to an employer's judgment as to what functions of a job are essential and if the employer has prepared a written (job) description . . . this description shall be considered evidence of the essential functions of the job.

Worker's Compensation Claims

Worker's compensation claims emerge from on-duty type injuries. The internal investigator as well as the line supervisor investigating such injuries has a tremendous responsibility to accurately and thoroughly investigate any injury that may lead to this type of claim. This responsibility is to the agency as well as the individual injured in the line of duty. Witness statements, photographs, diagrams, medical records, and the like will all be important to supporting an employee's claim of the extent of injury or supporting the agency when refuting a false claim. The initial and follow-up investigation may also require monitoring of claims for designated periods of time such as one year intervals is recommended (Close, 2001).

One such issue that often leads to these types of claims is the inordinate number of officers injured during the course of foot chases. Departments should implement a policy concerning when a foot chase will transpire balancing risk of injury against type of incident/crime (Close, 2001; Grossi, 2004). This may help in preventing unnecessary injuries and cost prohibitive claims filed with the agency. As an aside, officers and policy need to also consider the legal risk of injuring a suspect during a foot pursuit when the only incriminating factor is flight (Milazzo, 2000). This is an excellent example of a risk v. benefits analysis and developing practical policies that protect the officer, public, and the agency.

Arbitration in Employee Claims

In arbitration of employee claims, the courts have ruled that a distinction exists in the applicable collective bargaining agreement prior to filing a petition in a higher court. In the United States Supreme Court case of *Wright v. Universal Maritime Service Corporation* (1998), the Court examined the use of collective bargaining agreements and the use of arbitration in claims attached to such employee claims under the *Americans with Disabilities Act of 1990* (ADA), the *Age Discrimination in Employment Act of 1967* (ADEA),

Title VII of the *Civil Rights Act of 1964* (Title VII), the *Family Medical Leave Act of 1993* (FMLA), and other statutory claims. The issues in the Wright case encompassed the language in the collective bargaining agreement that must be "clear and unmistakable" as there should be a clause that employees must first seek relief through a grievance process prior to filing a separate employee claim under the aforementioned acts. In addition, the collective bargaining agreement is precluded from lowering the federally protected standards that exist with respect to employee rights, also included under the aforementioned acts (Eack & McGath, 1999; Higginbotham, 1999).

Figure 11-4. Law enforcement personnel confiscate legitimate and illicit property on a daily basis. Organizations must have a policy in place that ensures proper protection, care, storage, and release procedures to protect the community, department, and seizing officer (Photo courtesy of the Brockport, New York Police Department).

PROPERTY SEIZURES

Property seizures are fairly common place in the law enforcement realm, from a forged identification, to suspended license plates, to illicit drugs. The internal investigator will need to be concerned with two issues when a claim of improper seizure is made: (1) the location and condition of the property as well as (2) the right to seize the property.

Proper accounting systems should be in place and supported by policy that mandates any property seized must be kept in a secure evidence facility. Many times these allegations can be countered by locating the property in a Property Clerk's Office and providing the complainant with a receipt. Specific state laws can be referenced for reasons that property can be seized (e.g., evidence, safe keeping, contraband, etc.) and the time allowed for the maintenance of the property prior to final disposition (e.g., destruction, return, auction, etc.).

The more important concern in the investigation will be the legality or right to seize the property. This will be obvious in cases of illicit narcotics, stolen property, and the like. However, the justification becomes ambiguous when cash or other items are seized where a relationship to the laws must be established. In *Lathan v. City of St. Louis* (2001), the United States Court of Appeals of the Eighth Circuit held that failure to return property can amount to a due process violation and give the owner of the property a right to file a civil rights claim (Close, 2001).

CONSIDERATIONS IN POLICY DEVELOPMENT

Agency policy and procedure is the template for determining culpability issues of personnel who are the target of an internal investigation. While agency or organizational policy will most likely be the main reference for determining whether or not an edict was adhered to or violated, care must be taken in the original development of policy. This section discusses such issues as the legality, need for policy development, and issues related to the failure to develop policy in a law enforcement organization.

Court Opinions on Policy

The courts have provided guidance in policy development, albeit after the fact in most cases. The existing cases should be viewed with an eye for developing contemporary policy while fostering an understanding of the thought process of the judiciary. The courts have consistently held that local governments are liable for damages by public employees whose actions are governed by wrongful policy or no policy at all (Dahlinger, 2001). The court's intervention will be in determining such issues as if there was gross negligence cited on behalf of the agency in the presence of poor policy, or absence of policy altogether that should guide police actions and response to critical incidents. The courts also have the ability to make decisions in significant as well as insignificant cases in mandating law enforcement policy and procedure. For example, in *Smith v. Monsanto Chemical Company* (1985) the court held that an employer can develop arbitrary, ridiculous, and irrational rules, but must apply them evenhandedly. In a similar, lower level policy issue, The United States Supreme Court decided in *Atwater v. City of Lago Vista* (2001), the relationship between the need for police policy and effecting minor arrests (Ferrell, 2001). Cases such as these are a wakeup call for agencies that have insufficient or no policy and procedural guidelines since if the rule does not exist in the agency, during a subsequent litigation, it will most likely be imposed by the court.

Care must also be taken in policy development as plaintiff's attorneys often use a department's more restrictive policies to attempt to hold the agency to higher standards than required by the constitutionally correct standard of objective reasonableness (Martin, 2002). Policies that reflect higher and more restrictive standards than are required by the courts can produce a haunting theme for the department in civil litigation. As such, when a policy is codified, Chief Robert E. Cansler (1998) states that: "It is critical that adopted guidelines be followed. No lawyer can convince a judge or jury that you and your employees should not be required to follow your own guidelines. . . . A department's failure to follow its own guidelines will provide some of the best evidence of negligence" (p. 55).

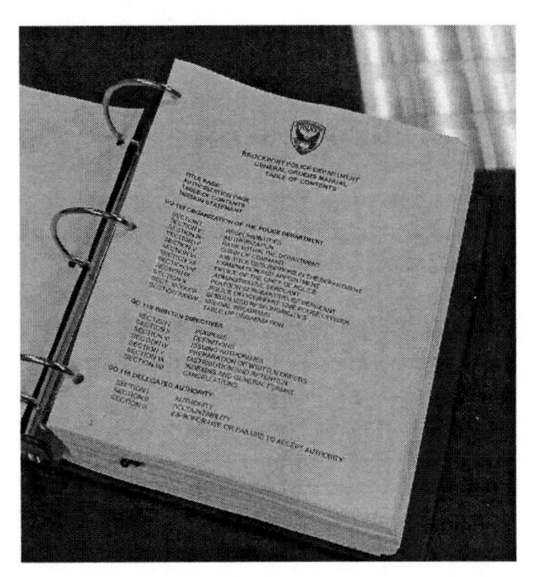

Figure 11-5. Policy research, formation, and dissemination are key components of an efficient and effective law enforcement operation (Photo courtesy of the Brockport, New York Police Department).

The Need for Contemporary Policy

The need for contemporary policy is self-evident. Policy and procedural manuals should be living documents. One of the goals of accreditation is to have departments continually review and update their policy and procedure to keep pace with the evolving needs of the organization and society. Departmental policy must reflect reality, practicality, and the underlying philosophy that accomplishing the departmental mission is more important than detail-oriented rules (Martin, 2002). A contemporary model of policy development is recommended in progressive police organizations and implementation involves three components: (1) cognitive adequacy which includes accuracy, simplicity, clarity, and inclusiveness, (2) communicability which includes that they are credible, durable, and cognizable, and (3) trajectory of improvement which includes systematically reviewing orders, revising orders to remain contemporary, and involving officers, command, attorneys, and all other stakeholders in the development and implementation process (Grattet, 2004).

Javier Soto (1998) succinctly states, "If the policy must be bent, it is time to change policy." Policies are violated in part because of their outdated or unworkable nature. Policies should be consistently reviewed for outdated language, terminology, all-encompassing policy, and ensure ease of comprehension and compliance (Martin, 2002).

Purpose, Research, Structure, and Implementation of Policy

The purpose of policy and procedure is to offer guidance and uniformity of response to routine and unusual incidents. To be effective, policies, procedures, rules, and regulations must reflect the desired conduct that is sought from personnel (Forsyth, 2003). In addition, officers should not have to guess what is and what is not official action (Soto, 1998).

Written policies should have two goals: (1) to keep everyone informed about operations, and (2) to support the supervisors in enforcing practices and procedures (Ellman, 1999). Those goals should be consistent with prevailing law and the needs of the community policed. Policies can be in most any form, from general orders, to special orders, written and verbal commands, and unwritten edicts. Dr. Ryken Grattet (2004) states that:

> General orders represent a central mechanism available to law enforcement leadership who confront recurring and potentially problematic enforcement issues, and nearly every American department relies on them to some degree. The implicit hope is that by formalizing a department policy on a particular issue, officer conduct will be consistent and appropriate. (p. 63)

The purpose of policy in most cases is to provide guiding principles and recommendations. Care must be taken in not making policies all encompassing or too restrictive. An example of this is in the policy of Salt Lake City, which was in fear of illegal aliens not reporting crimes, reacted by adopting a written departmental policy that officers not ask about the immigration status of either witnesses of victims (Law and Order, 2000d). Was this prudent policy even in the pre-9/11 era?

Policies must be intensely researched to match the needs of the affected organization. Many agencies, due to limited resources will adopt "verbatim" policies in order to satisfy requirements from a legal or accreditation orientation. Using other agency policies as guides is a prudent practice provided that the policy is researched and properly adapted to the affected agency. Policy should be developed for legal, operational, and administrative needs of the organization with the ultimate goal to support the service provided. The development of critical liability and subsequent training requires the use of legal, operational, and subject matter experts to formulate guidelines that will be legal, proper, justified, and have utility. Developing such policies as firearms use and deployment requires intensive research and testing. For example, the issue of flashlight attachment to weapons and accidental discharges when using the flashlight, and constructively, the gun muzzle to conduct searches (Aveni, 2002a).

Structure and implementation of policy is as important as policy research and development. Policies should be structured as concisely and cogently as possible. Those that are not can be difficult for employees to inculcate and operationalize (Field & Meloni, 1999). Such issues should be considered as a logical progression, simple language, checklists, diagrams, and varied mediums for review such as hard copy and electronic access through CD and a department intranet. The structure should also include contemporary resources; however, those resources that are automatically updated should be referenced rather than included to ensure greater accuracy of the information (Martin, 2002). Training and supervision are also required to implement policy effectively. Thomas Aveni (2002a) states that, "Training is the enabling tool of policy implementation" (p. 75).

The Danger of Unwritten Rules

There is a danger in the use of unwritten rules in a law enforcement organization. While it is inconceivable for every policy, practice, or rule to be documented, those that are not documented must be limited in scope and reach within the organization. Policy and practice violations are based upon the notion that illegal practices are spread through the organization and thus advocated by the organization. Some measure of unwritten rules will exist in all organizations. This occurs due to size, fragmentation, individuality, and various levels of experience and attitudes with supervisory and command staff. Many are valid and needed in the daily course of business operations. They can also be detrimental if they are incongruous with the legal and procedural edicts of the field and organization. Line personnel, supervisory, and command staff should be allowed a level of latitude in developing unwritten policy and practice as long as they do not conflict with the letter and spirit of the effective and efficient policies and practices of the organization.

CONSIDERATIONS IN TRAINING PROGRAM DEVELOPMENT

The internal investigation process must be an integral part of the training process. Law enforcement organizations must be learning organizations. The static approach to training in an organization can compromise such areas as liability, officer safety, and community expectations. During the internal investigation process, an impact on training can be made in two areas: (1) in identifying and recommending changes in outdated or inappropriate policies, practices, or activities that are being demonstrated in the field and subsequently brought to the attention of internal affairs staff and (2) a medium for validation of organizational training practices as the measure of organizational effectiveness is through compliance to contemporary policy and practice. As the compliance monitor, internal affairs can also report the positive activities of the organization and thus develop a validation and defense mechanism when the organization is called to task in its practices. Therefore, a relationship must be developed between these two entities or functions in pursuit of the best practices possible. This section addresses the legal and liability issues, training as an organizational priority, realistic training, and defensive tactics and firearms training.

Legal and Liability Issues

Training, like everything else that is done in the field must have a basis in the legal and liability issues. Many times these principles can be guiding or overriding. When the court becomes involved, the outcome can result in overriding principles that limit or wholly obviate law enforcement discretion in policy development and actions. The courts have clearly advised that consistent, periodic, realistic, and relevant in-service training, with standards and testing to acknowledge understanding is required (Soto, 1998; G. T. Williams, 2001a). The lead case in training issues is *Canton v. Harris* (1989) wherein a federal court ruled that a municipality is civilly liable for the failure to train its police force, where the plaintiff proves that the lack of training was so reckless or grossly negligent that it deprived a person of their constitutional rights. In general, it has to demonstrate that training does not currently meet acceptable standards within the law enforcement training community–it omits important aspects, is not satisfactorily documented, is not properly taught, or contains inadequate standards (Dahlinger, 2001). In addition, if the deliberate indifference to training led to an injury, it can form the basis for municipal liability only where the failure to train amounts to deliberate indifference to the rights of persons with whom the police come into contact with (Newbold, 2002).

In addition, in *Canton v. Harris* (1989), if there is a reasonable expectation that officers will be required to perform a particular task on a regular basis, and the court specifically mentioned attempting to arrest persons who flee from them, then the need to train the officers is "so obvious" that a failure to do so could be properly characterized as "deliberate indifference" by the department, leaving the agency open to civil litigation (Schembra, 2002).

Most case law in this area has been developed in the wake of civil rights and excessive force or wrongful death claims. The constructive effect has been to take the court's interpretation of the lead cases and make them a matter of more stringent departmental policy and training standards. Those stricter standards have also transcended lower level policy issues. The courts, while setting some minimum guidelines, have also postured that training must be contemporary and comprehensive enough to address the majority of situations facing the line level officer.

Two additional cases that have impacted law enforcement training policy from a liability perspective are *Whitney v. Warden* and *Young v. City of Providence.* In the case of *Whitney v. Warden* (410 U.S. 560), the court determined that training is not enough to avoid liability. The court held that if the training that is provided by the department is not documented, it did not occur (Hill, 2003). Training records can also produce fear in police administrators from a perspective of creating liability where none may exist. Discoverable records are only a negative issue if they indicate a performance that is inadequate or does not improve, thus indicating an issue of negligent retention (Oberlander, 2004).

With respect to firearms training, documented training in the use of "shoot-don't shoot" scenarios or judgmental shooting may diminish or eliminate an agency's liability in a failure to train case as was determined in *Young v. City of Providence* (Ryan, 2004). This type of mindset should transcend training programs that impact not only firearms policy, but also defensive tactics policy, search and seizure, arrest policy, and others that are high liability areas.

More vanguard court rulings are concerned with not only training standards, documentation, and critical skills development, but also with the qualifications of the instructors delivering and certifying the training. Steven J. Hill (2003) states that:

> Presently, courts are giving more scrutiny to the quality of specific training. They are giv-

> ing more credence to the qualifications of the instructor, his level of certification and whether the training provided was within acceptable professional standards. Courts now routinely study the instructor's resume, course lesson plans, and any examinations that may have been given to students during the training course administered. (p. 86)

Organizations are thus well-advised to engage in constant training, retraining, and update training required to defend against liability (Martinelli, 2002).

Training as an Organizational Priority

As Aviv Bar (2003) poignantly states, "While training law enforcement officers on a regular basis is the catalyst for promoting safety and reducing organizational liability, training is frequently overshadowed by other priorities" (p. 116). Law enforcement organizations often fail to act on training initiatives until forced to through some legal or political mandate. This often comes from organizations that are restricted in funds and resources in addressing any issue beyond the day-to-day catastrophes in administering a law enforcement organization. Accreditation has some impact beyond liability minimums, however, true innovation is conspicuously absent in most law enforcement organizations. Another exacerbating factor is that no national standards exist to determine what training is adequate or how often it should be offered (McKee, 2000). The cumulative effect is that training usually goes from the "freezer to the front burner" when a politically or legally sensitive issue arises. Operating in this orientation prevents organizations from planning, researching, and addressing current and future trends in law enforcement training needs. Therefore, law enforcement administrators should set the edict of training as an organizational priority in order to meet the contemporary and future needs of their organizations and communities they serve.

Realistic Training

As cited, all training must incorporate real life situations in order to simulate street level situations (see *Popow v. City of Margate,* 1979). In keeping with the court's decisions, many organizations have moved to developing simulations that mirror those situations faced in the field. In addition, progressive instructors have also moved to challenge the sterile classroom environment in such critical skills areas as defensive tactics and firearms training by rejecting standards that are beyond the minimum standards of the courts in assessment of liability issues. Instructors are comparing what are natural cognitive and psychomotor skills development to the standards of reasonableness and gross negligence imposed by the courts and aligning training program philosophy to meet these needs.

A contemporary concept in this ideology is the Recognition Primed Decision-making model. Aviv Bar (2003) cites the concept of the Recognition Primed Decision-making model (RPD) which:

> Suggests that individuals who are faced with critical decision-making tasks will quickly and sometimes unconsciously compare their situation to previous experiences and preplanned responses. By recognizing situational features that are analogous to plans stored in the brain, individuals are then able to form intuit courses of action. (p. 116)

Utilizing such concepts can increase the likelihood that personnel will respond to critical incidents in a trained and acceptable manner. Realistic training scenarios can be incorporated into basic, in-service, and advanced training sessions wherein the department will be better able to defend the actions of its personnel in these types of situations.

Combining Defensive Tactics, Firearms, and Tactical Communications Training

There should be a symbiotic relationship between defensive tactics and firearms training program development. These conceptual entities should be combined in the organizational training context in order to teach personnel options for force deployment and strengthen decision making skills. As Richard Oberlander (2004) states with respect to firearms training, "Judgment is a perishable skill" (p. 31). This has an equal affect on defensive tactics training as most law enforcement organizations train to the minimum required standards. In addition, combining defensive tactics, firearms training, and tactical communications in training scenarios can lead to a systematic approach to not only the training processes, but the resultant behaviors should assist in shaping officers who can properly assess the perceived threat and transition to the appropriate level of force to control the subject and situation. Therefore, a multifaceted approach is the recommended method for defense of the officer and agency in these types of situations.

Contemporary research and empirical data should always have a place in developing training programs, especially in the defensive tactics and firearms venues. For example, a majority of assaults on police officers are spontaneous or are attempts to resist arrest or escape custody. Therefore, training should be based in effecting an arrest with proper control in searching, handcuffing, and transportation techniques. In developing training programs, it is critical to gather data that demonstrates the needs of training officers and then integrate that data into program development, such as practical firearms training scenarios. All training should include a practical performance imperative as the

Figure 11-6. Communications training should be an integral component of any defensive tactics program (Photo courtesy of the Brockport, New York Police Department).

intended result of the session or lesson plan (Baratta, 1998).

Another consideration is that while training will most often concentrate on psychomotor skills, cognitive ability, and critical decision-making skill development, the reality is that instinctive behaviors also play a role in the response of the officer in a threatening or deadly situation. Psychomotor skills are defined as a muscular movement resulting from mental processes. There is a motor component, the movement itself, as well as a mental (cognitive) component. The cognitive component has to do with decision-making, when to perform the skill. A psychomotor skill is also an acquired ability to perform tasks in response to sensory stimuli (McKee, 2000).

Michael T. Rayburn (2000) states that, "No amount of training will override the instinct to survive. If the tactic taught is complicated and not intuitive, a person's brain will instinctively override it for one that is simpler, easier, and quicker to use" (p. 103). Rick Baratta (1998) explores this concept further as he defines the personal capabilities of an officer to meet a threat and survive into the categories of cognitive skills that are considered intellectual or thinking processes, such as planning tactics and decision-making. Affective or psychological skills are the ability to control ones emotions, and in managing fear and a will to survive, and motor or physiological skills that are defensive tactics and the use of weapons. All three are used when a lethal threat is encountered (p. 188). This must also be considered in training program development, and more importantly, in the investigative process.

One final point in training program development is the issue of equipment selection. Training program development includes equipment selection, such as firearms. In developing firearms policy and during equipment acquisition, a department forcing officers with small hands to use overly large frame pistols is a major safety violation and has been interpreted negatively by some courts (Blakely, 2004). While standards need to be in place, due to the courts forcing organizations to relax many requirements with respect to height, weight, gender, and other discriminatory factors, law enforcement organizations must respond with an acceptable range as opposed to a set standard that may in effect create more liability than the set standard.

Figure 11-7. Handcuffing situations can many times create tenuous situations, however, the internal investigator must err on the side of the officer when the matter is open for any interpretation (Photo courtesy of the Brockport, New York Police Department).

HANDCUFFING

Handcuffing is a matter of edict with defensive tactics instructors, a matter of policy with most police organizations, and a matter of preference with many police officers. Handcuffing should be a matter of legal, procedural, and safety issues rather than individual preference. Consequently, law enforcement organizations should look to the prevailing case law, accepted standards, and safety as tantamount issues rather than overriding issues. For example, when the internal investigator is examining a complaint of handcuffing, the investigator should balance all three of these concerns rather than merely relying on policy. This section reviews the legal issues, procedural issues, safety issues, and investigative issues of handcuffing.

Legal Issues

The handcuffing issue is far more discernable in arrest and custody situations than it is in investigative stops. However, the Supreme Court in such cases as *Terry v. Ohio* (1968) has recognized that officer safety is a valid and legal reason for securing suspects even when no probable cause to arrest exists. With this in mind, Carl Milazzo (1998) states that:

> Officers must understand the entire body of case law governing their safety, because tac-

tical training is less effective if an officer hesitates out of legal ignorance. . . . Some officers dangerously learn to hold themselves to a higher standard on the street because of ignorance or negative reinforcement in the courtroom. Fortunately, the law allows an officer to take reasonable steps to ensure safety. (p. 151)

The Supreme Court has recognized that officers are entitled to protect themselves during an investigative stop and are not required to ignore an articulable threat to their safety (Milazzo, 1998). Nine of 12 federal courts have approved the use of handcuffs during investigative detention, even absent probable cause to arrest. The only requirement is that the officer can articulate their belief that the subject was armed or dangerous. The officer may also use reasonable force to effectuate the detention in alignment with the requirements of *Graham v. Connor* (1989) (Milazzo, 1998).

The rule becomes much more lucid when a warrant or probable cause to effect an arrest exists. In these cases, the search can be automatic and extensive, in contrast to a *Terry Frisk* wherein only a patdown for weapons or dangerous instruments is permitted. Carl Milazzo (1998) also states that:

> Officers may automatically search a person incident to a lawful custodial arrest–limited to the area within the immediate control of the arrestee regardless of how minor the offense is or how unlikely it is that a weapon will be found. This rule is justified (1) to prevent the arrestee from obtaining a concealed weapon that could be used to harm an officer or effect escape; and (2) to prevent the destruction of evidence. (p. 151)

Complaints of this nature should be reviewed in light of the court's opinions on search and seizure and used as a balancing and not deciding factor when rendering a finding in an internal investigation.

Procedural Issues

A law enforcement organization should also have in force a policy for handcuffing procedures. This type of policy should be strict enough to mandate handcuffing procedures, however, it must also be broad enough to allow for latitude in the myriad situations that will be encountered by field personnel. These types of edicts must emanate from those in charge of the law enforcement organization who champion the advocacy of officer safety issues. Chief Gerald W. Garner (2002) states that, "All those in a position of leadership must make it clear through policies, procedures, rules, and most importantly, their own actions that a mandate for safe conduct exists throughout the agency" (p. 116).

Policies should refer to legal issues, training mandates, and the need for the officer's articulation in documenting these incidents in order to justify handcuffing in all situations. Policies should also include such techniques as double-locking in order to refute claims of injury. The double-locking technique should be documented every time it is used by the arresting or detaining officer (Nowicki, 2002b).

Safety Issues

Safety issues seem to be murky waters for officers and internal investigators to navigate. Legal issues, false confidence in suspect reactions and techniques, as well as the specter of a personnel complaint all come to bear when safety issues for handcuffing are cited as justification. The bottom line is that suspects can still be dangerous even when handcuffed (Nowicki, 2002b). False confidence in suspect detention comes from mere handcuffing as well as other trained techniques as Robert Black (2001) states that, "Too many officers

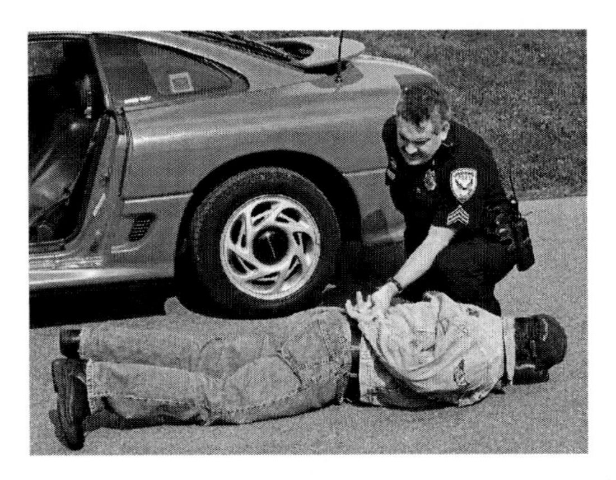

Figure 11-8. Handcuffing incidents should be examined from the legal, procedural, and safety issues involved prior to any consideration for complainant or community perceptions (Photo courtesy of the Brockport, New York Police Department).

fool themselves into believing that grounding a suspect eliminates the potential for effective resistance" (p. 92). The controversy will most certainly surround those incidents of an investigative detention, non-arrest, or unarrest situations. The controversy on when and how to handcuff will also surround arrest situations as well. For example, two Tampa, Florida police detectives were the tragic victims of a handcuffing mishap. Injuries, prosthetics, and investigators who are involved in custodial and non-custodial interrogation, all impact an issue that is intended to be black and white. While the safety issues in handcuffing a suspect in the front are self-evident, when the practice of handcuffing in the rear is precluded, then creative handcuffing methods need to be used (Albrecht, 2000). Safety is an equal and not overshadowed consideration in handcuffing those encountered as arrestees or suspects of potential criminal activity.

Investigative Issues

The internal investigator should include an examination of: (1) the circumstances of the stop or handcuffing as measured against the legal issues involved, (2) the nature of the restraint technique, (3) the reasonableness of the restraint technique, and (4) the actions of the subject in order to render a fair and impartial finding with respect to the officer's actions. Most justifiable actions stem from a combination of factors such as: (1) a crime under investigation, (2) knowledge that the suspect is armed and dangerous, (3) the behavior of the person being frisked, (4) a bulge or the actual observation of an object, and (5) the suspect's prior criminal record or history of violence, as known to the officer (Milazzo, 1998). Other considerations for the investigation should be any injury that is medically diagnosed or complained of. For example, soft tissue and nerve damage to the radial nerve on the inside of the wrist and the ulna on the outside of the wrist are legitimate concerns. It is still possible for injuries to occur even if the handcuffs are applied properly. A subject can violently struggle and cause injuries to himself in the struggle (Nowicki, 2002b). Thus, the onus is then placed on the subject rather than the involved officer.

One-on-one contacts will always carry with them an inherent danger and that fact should never be ignored by the internal investigator or law enforcement administrator in determining the fairest finding in an internal investigation. Chief Gerald W. Garner (2002) supports this as he states that, "The law enforcement leader who expects his people to practice what he preaches in the name of officer safety will unfailingly support them when their proper application of officer safety practices has confused or offended someone" (p. 118).

STOPPING PEOPLE AND VEHICLES

Many complaints arise from field stops of individuals as well as traffic stops. Citizens

Figure 11-9. Investigating complaints of field and traffic stops requires the internal investigator to examine all of the circumstances of the encounter including the reason, all current and historical information, department and supervisory edicts, and the level of intrusion and restraint (Photo courtesy of the Brockport, New York Police Department).

complain of officer tactics, stance, and a feeling of intimidation. Many of these complaints can be handled as a field conciliation, avoiding the need for a formal complaint and actually presenting an opportunity to educate the public. The internal investigator must exercise an immense amount of tact in these cases as they are most often justified stops, but have the potential for causing immense damage to the image of the law enforcement organization, despite the fact that the stops are justified.

From the perspective of legal justification, the United States Supreme Court in the case of *United States v. Arvizu* (2002) affirmed the Court's position of ruling that policing is an inexact science and decisions should be based upon a totality of circumstances, but also underscored the need to teach officers the importance of documenting all of the facts leading to their decision to make a stop or conduct a search (Whalen, 2002; Wood, 2002).

Conducting field interviews and traffic stops is a proven method for increasing visibility and reducing crime rates in communities across the country. One problem is that enforcement is most often concentrated in high crime areas such as urban environments. For many members of the minority community, mistaken involvement stops reinforce suspicions that the police use race or other personal characteristics as the basis for police action. The result may be a community-wide perception that police officers are biased and use pretextual stops to justify arrests. More importantly, although the actual number of incidents may be a very small percentage of all police-citizen enforcement contacts, there is clearly a disproportionate impact on the community's perception of the police. What also must be recognized is the fact that the vast majority of citizen contacts by police officers are not mistaken involvement stops. To address these concerns, internal investigators and law enforcement administrators should consider training as a component of the investigative process when a proliferation of these types of complaints becomes apparent. One proposed training model acronym is entitled DEAL: De-escalate and defuse, Empathize and explain, Apologize, and Leave them in control (Rappoport, 2003). Such measures of enforcement combined with a sensitivity to community concerns will go far to balance enforcement and crime control strategies with increasing an understanding in the communities policed.

The internal investigator should also consider the officer's training and experience when a formal complaint of this type is filed. For example, accepted and trained techniques for at risk vehicle stops and extraction should be included in the investigative package. Other accepted and trained techniques such as officer stance should provide the interviewing officer with an image of control and confidence, the proper reaction distance from the suspect if the encounter becomes violent, and the ability to escalate the use-of-force continuum. In addition, the officer must be prepared to use strong verbal commands and direction to the subject if warning signs are observed from the subject (White, 2000). While these techniques and actions may be offensive to the subject of a field or traffic stop, they are justified and should be the deciding factors of the investigation, not the perception of the complaining party.

SEARCHING PEOPLE, VEHICLES, AND LOCATIONS

Justification, reasonableness, technique, and documentation are all salient factors in the search process. While searches are regulated by the Fourth Amendment as well as individual state constitutions and case law, in many cases they are also regulated to an even higher degree by departmental policies. What's important to consider is that there is no "Bright Line Rule" that requires an officer to perform only in line with his or her training (McKee, 2000). An officer's actions in gaining compliance to a search must be deemed reasonable under the circumstances, for example, an officer who engages a suspect who is not compliant, while the officer is attempting to determine if the suspect is armed may justify higher levels of force until the subject complies (G. T. Williams, 2003b). Many complaints are filed based upon searches and violations of an individual's Fourth Amendment rights to be secure in their person. The United States Supreme Court however, has recognized the need for officer safety and has extended the ability to take reasonable steps to ensure that safety is a matter of protection under the law (Ferrell, 1999; Milazzo, 1998). The Court noted in the

Figure 11-10. Stops and searches are guided by the Fourth Amendment, state laws, and departmental policy as much as they are guided by the safety of the officer (Photo courtesy of the Brockport, New York Police Department).

incidence of vehicle searches under most circumstances that officers may:

1. Order both the driver and any passengers out of a vehicle as ruled in *Pennsylvania v. Mimms* (1997).
2. Perform a "patdown" of a driver and any passengers, upon a reasonable suspicion that they may be armed and dangerous as ruled in *Terry v. Ohio* (1968).
3. Conduct a "*Terry* patdown" of the passenger compartment of a vehicle, upon a reasonable suspicion that an occupant is dangerous and may gain immediate control of a weapon as ruled in *Michigan v. Long* (1983).
4. Conduct a full search of the passenger compartment, including any containers therein, pursuant to a custodial arrest as ruled in *New*

York v. Belton (1981). (Ferrell, 1999; also see Milazzo, 1998; Milazzo, 1999; Papenfuhs, 2003)

Searching an individual or location such as a private residence carries with it higher responsibilities as the level of Constitutional rights and protections are in effect lower for a vehicle than they are for a person or a residence. In searching a location, warrants, permission, exigent circumstances and other factors can justify a search. In the use of Protective Sweeps, incident to an arrest of a suspect in a home or other enclosed quarters, officers may check closets or other spaces where an attacker may be hiding (Milazzo, 1998). In searching a person, not only do legal issues impact the search, but also other factors. For example, mitigating factors must be considered when a suspect is searched such as realistic circumstances as weather, unusual situations, physical locations, the suspect's demeanor being disorderly or resistive, physically and verbally abusive, or covered with bodily fluids (Crotty, 1998). Additionally, the use of anonymous tips in conducting field stops and patdowns has been treated with more scrutiny by the courts. For *Terry* stops based upon anonymous informants, the following information should be documented:

1. Document the personal observations of the officer at the scene that confirm information provided by the anonymous informant.
2. Connect the criminal activity suspected with the officer's experience.
3. Establish by personal observation of the suspect's conduct, body language, and demeanor that there is potential criminal activity and that the suspect may be armed and dangerous.
4. Identify yourself as a police officer and initiate preliminary conversations with the suspect that will tend to support or disprove the officer's initial suspicion of the presence of a weapon or criminal activity. (Scuro, 2000b)

In all cases, officers need to be able to explain training and experience and how that training and experience allowed them to recognize the incriminating nature of the item seized (Milazzo, 1998). One method of minimizing complaints may involve the use of technology, such as portable handheld metal scanners issued to officers who are in the field. A handheld scanner would be equivalent to or less intrusive than a *Terry* stop and frisk (Rossi, 2001). In the investigation of these types of complaints, the internal investigator must consider: (1) the law, (2) the reasonableness of the search procedures, (3) the safety of all involved, including the officer, innocent third parties, and the subject of the search, and (4) prevailing departmental policies.

LINE OF DUTY DEATHS

In the United States alone, more than 15,000 officers have died in the line of duty (Berger, 2002). While most law enforcement agencies in the country may never face the tragedy of having an officer from their agency fall in the line of duty, the greater tragedy is those agencies that are not prepared to deal with this eventuality. Agency heads must develop plans and policy to properly and sensitively deal with the needs of the family of a lost member of the department. The internal investigations unit and staff should be involved in this process as they will most likely be tasked with conducting an administrative investigation into the incident depending upon the circumstances. How the investigation and follow-up activities are conducted will be the measure of the care, professionalism, and humanity of the agency heads and its members. In keeping with this philosophy, the organization and its staff must be prepared through policy development in order to respond to the needs of survivors (Berger, 2002).

Law enforcement officers include, but are not limited to, police, corrections, probation, parole and judicial officers. Line of duty is defined as any action that a public safety officer whose primary function is crime control or reduction, enforcement of the criminal law or suppression of fires is authorized or obligated by law, rule, regulation, or condition of employment or service to perform (Flemmings, 1999).

During the investigation, facts may come to the attention of the internal investigator that may need to be explored or clarified with family members. Factors that have been identified as germane to the investigation and a family member may have some intimate or personal knowledge of that will be substantive to the investigation at hand. The internal investigator must take great care in assessing the needs of the family as well as the appropriate time and place to conduct the interview in order to cause the least amount of damage or pain to the family members. The investigator should make every attempt to arrange interviews in advance as opposed to impromptu or surprise visits and at the outset offer any and all department services available to the family. The investigator should also offer to contact or allow for a close friend, other family members, clergy, or if requested, an attorney to be present during the interview. The progression of the interview should be narrowly focused and only explore the needed information to continue the investigation. The internal investigator should explain the purpose of the interview at the beginning of the contact, not leaving any guesswork on behalf of the family member or others present. The internal investigator should not venture into unnecessary areas in the interview that would be offensive or cause any more pain to the family than is necessary. The internal investigator should also end the interview with providing future contact information and to keep the family updated as to the progress of the case.

Policy also needs to be developed by the organization in making benefits programs available to the survivors of law enforcement personnel who have lost their lives in the line of duty. The Bureau of Justice Assistance administers the Public Safety Officers' Benefits (PSOB) program that awards death, disability, and education assistance benefits to survivors of law enforcement officers killed or permanently and totally disabled in the line of duty as a result of a traumatic injury (Flemmings, 1999). In addition, departments should develop contacts and protocol for use of support organizations such as Concerns of Police Survivors Inc. (COPS) in order to have a cadre of services available to survivors (Sawyer, 2002).

The organization should prepare for these incidents by establishing the steps in the following list as policy and practice:

1. Develop an emergency contact form to include the identity of a department liaison, clergy and religious affiliation, all family members by relationship, name, address, and telephone number.
2. Identify who will conduct the death notifies.
3. Preparation at area hospitals for family, friends, and the media to provide separate and private areas to wait.
4. Develop policy and procedure for assessing and dealing with the impact on coworkers and provide debriefing by a department approved psychologist, psychiatrist, or licensed counselor.
5. Identify and assign a funeral liaison to provide department escorts, honor guards, etc.
6. Identify and assign a benefits coordinator to provide family members with immediate assistance in filing claims, counseling and advice on department benefits and family support services.
7. Develop additional policies to deal with deaths that are the result of an accident, negligence, or suicide.

The department's impact on the recovery of the family can be immensely therapeutic if handled properly and expeditiously. The internal investigations unit and its staff can support this noble cause by their demonstrated care for the memory of the fallen officer and the continuing lives of those who must now deal with the great loss of a loved one.

CIVIL CLAIMS INVESTIGATION

Civil claims are a very real part of the everyday affairs of a law enforcement organization. Police officers today have a one in 30 chance of being sued in civil court. Of those lawsuits, 45 percent allege excessive force. Additionally, some 80 percent of those lawsuits are won before trial and of those that go to trial, 90 percent are won (Sanow, 2001b). Civil juries are also awarding record claims to those who are successful in their pursuit of alleged and realized damages. The internal investigations unit should be an integral part of this process in: (1) assisting department counsel in case investigation and representing the organization and targeted personnel, (2) identifying and correcting substandard or litigious behavior on behalf of the targeted personnel, (3) identifying and correcting similar substandard or litigious behaviors of other members of the organization that could lead to increased liability, and (4) offering recommendations in policy and training that is identified as lacking, incorrect, or substandard in order to protect the organization from future claims.

The internal investigator should have an understanding of civil case law and the various types of claims and torts that can be filed against the agency. A review of these types of claims is presented in this text, but the internal investigator will need to understand the federal, state, and local laws and issues in order to more effectively address these incidents. The internal investigator will also need to adhere to the guidance of the assigned attorney in order to provide a supportive role to the defense of the officer and agency. A list of steps to adhere to is provided for guidance in the internal investigators actions when a claim is filed directly with the agency or when notified of the claim by the organization's defense counsel:

1. A notice of claim is filed with the department/municipality generally listing the specific reasons for the claim along with the date(s) and location(s) of the alleged incident(s).
2. All notices of claim should be investigated thoroughly in order to effectively defend the involved personnel and the organization/municipality.
3. Collect all evidentiary documents related to the incident including photographs, diagrams, statements, and the location of any evidence.
4. Review and prepare a summary (Incident Review) of the case particulars if directed by defense counsel.
5. Consult with your insurance carrier's attorney, municipal attorney, or Corporation Counsel in order to determine the need for any additional investigation into the incident.
6. Always operate within the scope of the defense counsel's advice and direction.
7. Do not release any documents, evidence, or statements unless first cleared through defense counsel.

SUMMARY

This chapter discussed the numerous issues in administrative and civil claims investigations that the internal investigator may be involved in conducting. Some of the most common are insubordination, untruthfulness, and discourtesy complaints. The chapter then progressed through other limited opportunity but critical investigations such as fitness for duty assessments, policy, and training program development. The chapter then reviewed such issues as high complaint areas as stops, searches, and seizures and the areas of investigation the internal investigator should concentrate on. The chapter closed with a review of the needs of civil claims investigations and the requirements of the internal investigator in defending the organization and the officer in these types of claims.

Chapter 12

EVIDENCE IDENTIFICATION, EVALUATION, AND COLLECTION

INTRODUCTION

The identification, evaluation, and collection of evidence in an internal investigation is one of the most overlooked areas in the process. Evidence is most often considered a hard science and not necessarily considered of great importance in an administrative investigation. Quite the opposite is true though as evidence, properly identified and evaluated, can provide no better account of the circumstances of an event as it is not open to perception or bias. Evidence may exonerate an officer in the most serious to the most minor of allegations. Therefore, the level severity of the case should not affect the level of investigation when dealing with the internal complaint process. The fair and unbiased outcome could affect an officer's freedom, financial livelihood, or professional career. All of these outcomes should carry equal and not stratified importance in the eyes of the internal investigator and should be acted on appropriately. This chapter discusses the various types, collection techniques, and assessment of identified evidence in the internal investigations process.

EVIDENCE DEFINED

Charles E. O'Hara (1981) defines evidence as, "All the means by which an alleged fact, the truth of which is submitted to scrutiny, is established or disproved. The purpose of evidence is the discovery of the truth of the charge" (p. 621). Nowhere in the investigative realm is the latter statement more important than in the internal investigation. The discovery of the truth should be the only goal of the internal investigator as the position encompasses such roles as investigator, prosecutor, defense counsel, jury, and judge. The internal investigator must properly and fairly balance all of these responsibilities against the diligent and objective search for and evaluation of evidence. Frank Morn (2000) classifies evidence into five types as follows:

1. *Real Evidence:* These are physical, hard, or tangible objects of the crime that can be produced for an administrative or court proceeding.
2. *Direct Evidence:* This is evidence such as eye witness accounts and firsthand knowledge of the incident by complainant's and witnesses to the incident.

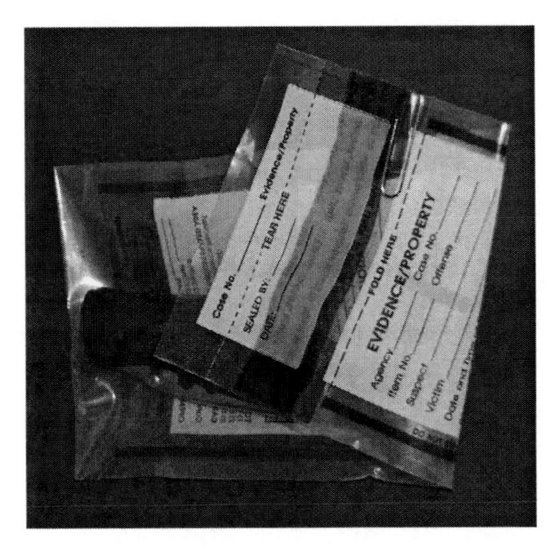

Figure 12-1. Evidence identification and collection is a critical aspect to most internal investigations (Photo courtesy of the Brockport, New York Police Department).

3. *Demonstrative Evidence:* This is evidence that is illustrative of specific points or aspects of the incident such as sketches, maps, photographs, charts, etc.
5. *Opinion Evidence:* This is evidence that may be offered by those who are court recognized experts in a specific field that are allowed to interpret information that would otherwise be too difficult for the lay person to understand.
6. *Circumstantial Evidence:* This is a type of indirect evidence that leads the reviewer to draw an inference. The essence of this type of evidence is the possibility of coincidence in connecting facts of the case in a chain of events. (p. 163)

THE ADMISSABILITY OF EVIDENCE

Frank Morn (2000) also discusses the foundational principles of the admissibility of criminal evidence in a legal proceeding. The concept is to prevent a reviewing individual or body from hearing improper evidence or misleading information. The concept of admissibility involves four aspects: (1) relevance, (2) materiality, (3) competence, and (4) privilege. The concepts are delineated below:

1. *Relevance:* Relevance is the issue of information obtained or used must have some type of relevance and connection to the issue at question.
2. *Materiality:* Materiality is the issue of information needing to be important to the issue or question at hand. Another issue is that material may be relevant but insignificant to the outcome of the case and should not be given more weight in the examination than is appropriate.
3. *Competence:* Competence is the issue of laying a proper foundation for other evidence in the investigation. This can be exemplified through the inappropriate techniques or methodology of the investigator in case investigation may obviate the use of such evidence at the review stage.
4. *Privilege:* Privilege is the admissibility rule that allows certain evidence to be excluded from the review stage. The theory holds that certain evidence that is developed through confidential relationships must be sacrificed in order to preserve the relationship. This deals with such relationships as matrimony, attorney-client privilege, doctor-patient, and priest-penitent to name a few. (p. 161)

These principles are crucial for the internal investigator to understand to prevent prejudicing the outcome of a case. Technical rules of evidence are sometimes relaxed due to these proceedings being in the administrative or civil realm. However, these concepts are more presented for the spirit of the law than the letter of the law. The internal investigator exercises an immense amount of power in the process that should be balanced with an even greater amount of discretion. The internal investigator must do what is legal, proper, justified, fair, ethical, and support the premise that this process is the ultimate search for the truth.

WITNESS CLASSIFICATION

Witness classification in an internal investigation is different than that of a criminal or civil case. Witnesses fall into several different classifications dependent upon their relationship or lack of relationship to the target officer, complainant, or case. The following list is a series of witness classifications and their definitions. These classifications and their definitions should be used in the documentation and evaluation of testimonial evidence in an internal investigation.

Involved Witnesses: The subject and witness officers, the complainant, and those witnesses known to the complainant or who enjoy a relationship with the complainant or any of the involved officers.

Independent Witnesses: Those witnesses who enjoy no relationship with either the involved personnel, the complainant, or other witnesses when the other witness has such a relationship to the officer or complainant. These could also be lay witnesses who have a perceptual or subjective opinion, however, it is not based upon a relationship to any of the parties in the case.

Expert Witnesses: Those witnesses whose expertise qualify them to render an informed opinion on the case facts such as assistant district attorneys, medical and technical experts, etc.

Witness classification weighs heavily with respect to the merits of the evidence presented. For example, involved witnesses most often carry equal weight unless some mitigating circumstances exist, such as their stakeholder status or any benefit to be gained. An involved officer, complainant, or witness who has a relationship to any of the parties could be perceived as having some type of benefit to be gained in offering a tainted version of an incident. Independent witnesses on the other hand, carry a higher weight in the process as they can be presumed to have no stake in the process and it is hoped that their version is more accurate given the confines of their individual perceptions. Expert witnesses are somewhat of a paradox as care must be taken that the opinion doesn't go to the highest bidder. Such experts as assistant district attorneys and medical personnel are often a prime example of experts who will offer qualified and untainted opinions in a case.

Independent witnesses as well as physical evidence can be used to confirm or refute involved witness statements in case evaluation. In weighing the evidence, a preponderance of the evidence is the prevailing rule, however, that scale is intended to work in both directions. The following is an example of how witness classification as well as content and context may affect the outcome of a case.

An officer stops a violator for a passing a red light. A ticket is issued and the violator pleads innocent and asks for a trial. During the trial, the officer testifies to observing the red light violation and issuing the ticket. The violator, during an examination of the officer states, "Why did you ask me about my speeding?" The officer, on the record states that he did not ask such a question and his notes of the event do not indicate that the officer observed any such violation. The violator is found guilty of the violation and is ordered to pay a fine.

Subsequent to the conviction, the violator files a personnel complaint alleging that the officer was untruthful in court through false testimony of stating he did not inquire about the violator's speeding. The officer is questioned during the internal investigation about the alleged lie and denies that the question was ever asked of the violator. On its face, both of the witnesses can be classified as involved in the incident and in effect, carry equal weight. Since there is no independent witness or physical evidence such as a tape of the conversation, the prima facie case would indicate that the finding should be not sustained as not enough evidence exists on one side or the other to prove or disprove the allegation. To end the case at this juncture would be an injustice to all of the involved parties, especially the officer and the court.

Like the peeling of an onion, several layers need to be revealed to fully examine the nature of the case and provide a more informed understanding of the motivations of both parties. These cases must be measured against the totality of circumstances standard to be thorough and fair. The available evidence as well as the seminal issues of the investigation must all work to provide the fairest finding possible:

1. The complaint was made after the conviction in court, not before.
2. The violator was convicted of the violation.
3. The officer is responsible for traffic enforcement in this agency.
4. The officer did not charge the complainant with a speeding violation.
5. The officer's notes did not reflect any indication that the violator was observed speeding.
6. The court did not make an issue of the alleged questioning.
7. The court did not call into question the officer's integrity when the issue was raised.
8. Even if such a question had been asked, it may have been part of the officer's investigation and thus justified.
9. What benefit or gain would the officer receive from lying to the court in this case?
10. The officer was sworn in the court setting to tell the entire truth as he knew it.
11. The officer was questioned during an internal investigation under threat of discipline or termination and maintained that such a question was not asked.

Viewed in this light, there is no malicious or deceptive reason for the officer to lie. At most, it would be an honest mistake that was viewed by the court as insignificant to the final outcome of the case. The cumulative effect of this examination thus changes the finding from a not sustained to an unfounded. This is important to the credibility of the agency and the fairness of the investigative process as well as the officer, the officer's career and ability to competently and credibly testify in court in future proceedings. Additional evidence may include the complainant's history with respect to any previous complaints filed and their dispositions. The officer's personnel record could also be reviewed to ascertain if any previous complaints of this nature have been lodged and their disposition as well. This measure may also enhance the ability of the reviewer to make a determination that is aligned with the principle of a proper and complete investigation into the allegation.

TESTIMONIAL EVIDENCE

Testimonial evidence in the criminal and civil realms involves some type of interchange during a question and answer session or an interrogatory. In the criminal realm it can be through depositions, grand jury, and court testimony. In the civil realm, it can be through formal depositions, examinations before trial (EBT's), and during court proceedings.

To provide some working definitions, interrogatories are written questions submitted by one party in a lawsuit to another party which must be answered under oath. The purpose of the interrogatories is to gain further insight into the incident and to tie the officer down to certain answers (Smith, 1998). A deposition, on the other hand, is oral testimony given under oath by a party to a lawsuit or a witness, prior to trial (Smith, 1998). An additional working definition of testimonial evidence that is documented in the internal investigation is the supporting deposition or affidavit, which is completed by the internal investigator and carries more weight in the internal investigation than a basic deposition which is taken in many criminal cases in an effort to develop or support probable cause to arrest, not provide sufficient evidence to convict in and of itself.

Testimonial evidence can be captured in many ways and added to the investigative package. Such instruments can be: (1) supporting depositions and affidavits, (2) stenographic statements, (3) transcribed video and audio taped interviews, (4) intra-departmental or special reports completed by involved or witnessing personnel under the auspices of a departmental investigation, (5) examinations before trial or EBT's, and (6) court/trial records and transcripts.

EVIDENTIARY DOCUMENTS

Because of the latitude in evidentiary rules in internal investigations, which somewhat mirror those of civil claims investigations, the range of evidentiary documents runs the gamut. A rule of thumb is that documents can be deemed relevant if they are not unduly prejudicial to any of the parties to the complaint and shed light on the issue or allegation involved. There are several methods of recording evidentiary statements that include: (1) video-recording, (2) audio recording, (3) paraphrased written statements, and (4) verbatim written statements (M. J. Sullivan, 1998). These can be turned into evidentiary documents that can be made part and parcel to the case package. Another test for evidentiary documents is if they are used as a part of the normal course of business for the enterprise. For example, business records in law enforcement are crime reports, depositions, transcripts, and the like.

In obtaining written statements that will be deemed as evidentiary documents, the investigator should: (1) review case reports, documents, and evidence, (2) choose a proper or tactical location for the interview, (3) match corroborative evidence to the persons statement, (4) include date and time at the start of the interview, subject's educational background, the subject's ability to read and write, whether or not they are under the influence of drugs or alcohol, and if so, the substance, and (5) if the subject has eaten recently and provide refreshments if needed or requested (M. J. Sullivan, 1998). Several examples of evidentiary documents that are developed through investigative interview or are collected from within and outside of the agency are:

1. All correspondence from the complainant and/or any witness.
2. All investigative reports.
3. All administrative reports.
4. All legal and court records if applicable. One note in these documents is that they may be voluminous and unmanageable for the inclusion in the investigative package. The internal investigator should only include the relevant areas of the court record, document, or statement. The cover page of the original document should also be included for validation.
5. Medical records and transcripts that are not protected information. For example, during an interview of medical personnel, the interviewee discloses such things as carrier status like the complainant having AIDS or HIV status. This type of information must be redacted from the official record.
6. All other agency documents (e.g., dispatch records, log sheets, etc.).

7. Any and all relevant reports/documents. Examples would be: (1) a complaint of an illegal street or vehicle stop when intelligence information or report exist or (2) copies of reports of police action when complainant documents the contrary (Crime Report/Field Interview/Contact Form, etc.).
8. Mechanical, electronic, and hand drawn sketches of the scene completed by investigating officers, technicians, etc.
9. Maps of the general area of the incident. Maps and diagrams add another dimension to the case to aid comprehension and perspective.
10. Record checks on the complainant and witnesses only when the investigator can show a direct relationship to the case. Most often these types of records are precluded from addition to the case package as officer personnel files should not be added. Such information could unduly influence case outcome.

Records such as officer personnel files should be excluded unless some direct relationship exists. The officer's complaint history should be excluded so as not to taint the review process, however, records deemed as germane to the issue being investigated should be included. For example, an officer is involved in a chase where in an innocent third party is killed. Records of the lack of a motor vehicle accident history, basic and specialized driver training, experience of the officer in operating a police vehicle in pursuits and emergency situations would all be relevant to the case.

EXPERT TESTIMONY

Expert testimony can be extremely valuable in the internal investigations process. An expert opinion can be rendered by a defensive tactics instructor with respect to a specific tactic or by a firearms instructor concerning the training an officer has received or the efficacy of a tactic. Expert witness testimony has often been a dominant factor in determining liability or lack thereof in civil lawsuits. Its value in the internal investigation process should not go unnoticed. The following section discusses the legal and procedural issues in the use of expert witnesses.

Legal Issues

Several cases have impacted the admissibility of expert witness testimony. For example, in *Frye v. United States* (1923), the court defined the rule of "general acceptance" of scientific theory and expertise of a witness to offer opinion based evidence. This was a landmark case predicated on the admission of polygraph results to the court as a science that could translate to trial based evidence. Several other cases have impacted the use of expert testimony in the federal courts. Such cases as *Daubert v. Merrell Dow Chemicals, Inc.* (1993), *Kumho Tire Co. v. Carmichael* (1999), and *General Electric Co. v. Joiner* (1997) have shaped the federal courts opinions on expert testimony. The *Federal Rules of Evidence* have also been modified to narrow the evidence admissible from witnesses called as experts as well as to apply more stringent tests as to those opinions offered as expert testimony.

Under the *Federal Rules of Evidence* and the court ruling in *Kuhmo Tire Co., Ltd. v. Carmichael* (1999), an expert can testify only to scientific or technical evidence that is based on a sound methodology and can be shown to be reliable and relevant to the questions involved in the case (Rostow & Davis, 2002). In the Ninth Circuit Court in the case of *Reynolds v. County of San Diego* (1996), the Court stated that the fact that an expert disagrees with an officer's actions does not render the officer's actions unreasonable. In the Seventh Circuit Court in the case of *Maltby v. Winston* (1994), the Court excluded the plaintiff's expert on general police procedure as incompetent to testify on undercover drug operations. Also in the Seventh Circuit in the decision of *Berry v. City of Detroit* (1994), the Court rejected the notion that there exists a "field" of expertise in the non-specific area of "police policies and practices" and disapproving of an expert testifying that a police department was "deliberately indifferent" to the welfare of its citizens (MacLatchie, 2000). Under the *U.S. v. Whitted* (1993) ruling decided in the Eighth Circuit Court, it is inappropriate for an expert to testify as to the lack of candor or untruthfulness of an officer as it is highly inappropriate and constitutes legal error (MacLatchie, 2000).

In *Jaffee v. Redmond* (1996), the United States Supreme Court concluded that, pursuant to the *Federal Rules of Evidence* Section 501, communications by a law enforcement officer to a licensed psychologist, social worker, therapist or psychiatrist was deemed to be exclusively confidential and free from both pre-trial discovery efforts and admissibility at trial except when the patient's privacy is outweighed by the evidentiary need for disclosure (see Inset). *Federal Rules of Evidence* Section 702 also specifically governs the admissibility of expert witness testimony, in that it provides for the presentation of scientific, technical, or other specialized knowledge to assist the trier of fact (judge/jury) in understanding the evidence or to determine a fact in issue, a witness who is qualified as an expert by knowledge, skill, experience, training, or education may offer the opinion to the court.

As a general guide, these lead cases are presented to the internal investigator and administrator in order to develop an understanding that in the criminal and civil arenas, certain standards are necessary to qualify witnesses as subject matter experts. Such rules should be mirrored in the internal investigation process when an expert is used to render an opinion in a case.

Inset

Jaffee v. Redmond, 518 U.S. 1
Brief Filed: 1/96
Court: Supreme Court of the United States
Year of Decision: 1996

Issue: Whether a psychotherapist-patient privilege was recognized under Rule 501 of the Federal Rules of Evidence. The US Supreme Court granted certiorari to review a decision of the Seventh Circuit that recognized the existence of a psychotherapist-patient privilege and held that confidential communications of a police officer with a licensed social worker were protected from compelled disclosure.

Index Topics: Confidentiality/Psychotherapist-Patient Privilege

Facts: The defendant police officer shot and killed an individual to prevent the stabbing of another person. The decedent's family brought suit against the officer alleging constitutional violations and seeking damages for wrongful death. After the shooting, the officer sought counseling from a licensed clinical social worker. Plaintiffs sought to obtain information regarding the contents of the counseling sessions. The defendant refused, citing psychotherapist-patient privilege. The trial court found that the Federal Rules of Evidence did not provide for a psychotherapist-patient privilege. When the defendant continued to refuse to comply, the trial court instructed the jury that it could draw an adverse inference from this refusal and could presume that the contents of these communications would be unfavorable to the defendant. The jury awarded the plaintiffs $545,000 in damages. The Seventh Circuit reversed, finding that the Federal Rules of Evidence did, indirectly, recognize a psychotherapist-patient privilege because all fifty states recognized some sort of psychotherapist-patient privilege. The court reasoned that recognition of the privilege would serve to encourage troubled individuals, as well as those who witness, participate in, and are intimately affected by acts of violence in today's stressful, crime ridden environment, to seek the necessary professional counseling and to assist mental health professionals to succeed in their endeavors. The plaintiffs sought review in the US Supreme Court.

APA's Position: APA submitted an amicus brief arguing that: (1) Federal Rule of Evidence 501 authorizes the federal courts to recognize a psychotherapist-patient privilege; (2) common law principles, applied in the light of reason and experience, strongly support recognition of a psychotherapist-patient privilege in that (a) psychotherapeutic clients have a strong expectation of confidentiality, (b) confidentiality is essential to the success of psychotherapy, (c) society has a strong interest in fostering the psychotherapeutic relationship and in protecting client privacy, and (d) the benefits of the psychotherapist-patient privilege outweigh its costs; and (3) applying the psychotherapist-patient privilege using a case-by-case balancing approach would substantially undermine the value of the privilege.

Result: The US Supreme Court affirmed the Seventh Circuit decision. The Court decision supported the arguments presented in the APA brief.

Identifying and Managing Expert Witnesses

The organization must first have an understanding of qualifications and standards for validating an expert's opinion. In addition, the organization must also have a methodology for identifying and managing the selected experts. The primary job of an expert witness is to educate the jury, prosecutor, and/or the attorney they are working for (Badger, 1999). Experts in the internal investigation perform relatively the same function, educating the investigator, administrator, civilian review board or board of commissioners, and legal counsel.

When selecting the expert witness, obtain a resume or portfolio in addition to the written opinion that can be added to the case package. If the expert's portfolio includes publications, ensure the expert has published in the area of expertise. When preparing the expert, do not hide any facts that are germane to the case so that they do not become a damaging factor in any subsequent review or proceedings (Badger, 1999). Chances are that the expert's testimony will consist of a subjective impression rather than an articulable objective standard (MacLatchie, 2000). When rendering an expert opinion, the expert should not hypothesize as to what the right tactic would have been, rather limiting their opinion as to the efficacy of the deployed tactic given the totality of the circumstances involved. The expert should also sign a confidentiality agreement concerning the information learned in the internal investigation. The expert should be admonished in the need for privacy of personnel records and only be allowed to disclose such information with permission of the organization or through proper court proceedings.

If an expert is called to provide a deposition or testify in a court proceeding, some additional issues must be considered. An expert witness will attempt to limit the information provided during the pre-trial interrogatory in order to prevent attacks on the witness stand. Some guidance in testimony can be garnered in the advice of experts such as a general rule that there are seven answers to most deposition questions: "yes, no, green, I don't know, I don't remember, I don't understand the question, and I need a break" (Badger, 1999). In addition, when an expert is called to testify the jury will be instructed concerning several factors to be considered in the credibility and believability of the witness. The jury will be instructed that when weighing the strength of expert testimony, they are also to consider the expert's bias, prejudice, qualifications, relationship to the party and–most important in the case–the accuracy upon which the opinion is based and the inherent probability or improbability of the testimony (Knight & Callanan, 2003). For the latter, these same concerns should be addressed in the opinions offered by an expert in an internal investigation so that undue weight is not given that will prejudice a case finding.

Types and Examples of Expert Witnesses in Internal Investigations

Expert witnesses can be an immense asset as well as detriment to an internal investigation. For example, civil suits against departments are successful because experts testify to national patterns of secrecy and cover-up (Martinelli & Pollock, 2000). Experts will most often be able to add clarity to an investigation as well as justify the actions of the involved personnel. An expert should be used as often as needed and resources should not be an excuse as the initial investment in the use of an expert may ward off any future claims of liability, bias, and others that have become a matter of convention in the internal investigation process.

Legal Advice: Legal advice is the most common area in an internal investigation. This advice can be for both criminal and civil matters. In the criminal realm, the issue may be a field stop, search, or probable cause for arrest to name a few. District attorneys and their assistants are an excellent resource for this review. They will offer an expert opinion on the legality or justification for matters in the criminal realm. For civil litigation, usually a municipal or corporation counsel attorney can be consulted to offer their qualified insight. The civil litigation side of this equation is much more complicated and requires the review of someone who is versed in this area. A review on the attorney's letterhead will suffice for the case package.

Medical Personnel: In the case of an alleged or claimed injury, medical evaluations from the diagnosing or treating medical personnel are appropriate. Most often, after a records release form is signed and the records obtained, they will need to be translated from the medical terminology and abbreviations to lay terms. These can be translated by the actual doctor or other medical personnel such as a physician's assistant or nurse. The internal investigator can either complete a supporting deposition or tape record the interview for later transcription. A report on the doctor's or hospital's letterhead is also acceptable, however, these may take more time than allowed in the case and will most likely require follow-up to have completed. Therefore, the personal interview is the recommended technique in order to obtain these records.

Certified Firearms and Defensive Tactics Instructors: Firearms and defensive tactics instructors can be used to review techniques and tactics, equipment, validity of options that were used, and training given to the involved employee by the department. These types of experts should provide a copy of their certification or resume of their qualifications to validate their opinions. A written intra-departmental report for the review is also acceptable for the investigative package. The firearms or defensive tactics instructor should review only the validity of the tactics used and refrain from offering an opinion as to what options or tactics that could have or should have been used. The firearms or defensive tactics instructor is reviewing what somebody has done based upon that individual's experience, training, and perception, not what the expert "may" have done in a similar set of circumstances.

Accident Reconstructionists: Accident reconstructionists can be used in fleet vehicle accident investigations that involve death, or injury, high speed pursuits that result in an accident, and any other incident involving the motion of a vehicle that may be the cause for criminal or civil liability. These investigations can be highly involved and technical and need the qualified review of an expert in order to render a valid and informed finding as to the actions of the involved personnel. Experts of this type can be found in many agencies internally, or through collaborative agreements with large agencies such as sheriff's departments and state police agencies. Accident reconstructionist reports will be highly technical and will need translation to laymen's terms for the final package. Maintain a close liaison with the reconstructionist and assist in developing the final internal investigation report with them to ensure that all who will review the case will have an understanding of the circumstances and analysis that is sufficient to render a fair and equitable finding. Reconstructionists will also speak in range terms, such as minimum and maximum speeds. Such opinions should be limited to the absolute minimums as those can be proven in a court or civil setting.

Evidence Technicians: Evidence technicians develop an expertise in evidence identification, scene reconstruction, and evidence collection. This expertise is developed through formal training and education as well as tacit or experiential skills. They can perform certain scientific types of tests, comparisons such as fingerprints and the like, visual comparisons of items such as broken automobile parts, and firearms processing. Evidence technicians through their official reports and supplemental reports can offer expert opinions in their area of acumen and should be used whenever the need arises.

Laboratory Analysis: Police laboratory analysis is another option for expert review of evidence. Physical evidence can be exposed to a host of analyses that are appropriate to the investigation. One example is a complaint of excessive force wherein the subject alleges to have been pistol whipped or struck with a flashlight. The instrument can be secured and submitted to the police laboratory for analysis of trace evidence, skin, bodily fluids, and the like in order to prove or disprove the allegation.

Fingerprint Identification: Fingerprints can also be used in the internal investigation process. For example, an officer alleges that a suspect struggled with him for his weapon, thus resulting in a police involved shooting. The weapon can be processed for operation, number of live ammunition left in the weapon, GSR testing of the officer and suspect, and any fingerprints on the weapon. While the absence of fingerprints may not prove the officer was being untruthful as handguns have a low rate of fingerprint retention, the presence of fingerprints may shed light on the statement of the officer.

Fraud and Forgery Examiners: Fraud and forgery examiners can be used in cases where officers are alleged to have misappropriated funds and there is a paper trail to follow. Forgery examiners can be used in the scientific analysis of such claims as forged signatures on confession forms.

Polygraph/VSA Operators: Polygraph and voice stress analysis are also effective tools in the internal investigation process. Polygraphs can be used in assessing the veracity of a complainant's allegations of such issues as stolen drugs or money. Most polygraph operators will only administer the polygraph to a voluntary examinee. Offering the polygraph to a complainant may lead to the truth of the matter. In addition, if a complainant refuses to take a polygraph or fails to appear for the polygraph after agreeing to take it, this fact can be used as evidence to support the officer's account. While failing to take a polygraph or failing to make the appointment are not in and of themselves indicative of untruthfulness, they are circumstantial pieces of evidence that can be presented in the case as a component of the totality of the circumstances.

All experts who review an internal investigation should sign a confidentiality agreement stating that they will not release any information from the case unless by approval of the agency or under proper court order. As a closing note, the expert should be prepared ahead of the review to only offer an opinion of the actions taken in the incident by the involved personnel. The expert should also be reminded that the review must be based upon the standards that the Supreme Court has set in the concepts of reasonableness of actions, the viewpoint and mindset of the officer at the time of the incident, and if the actions rose to the level of gross negligence, or were they acceptable given the totality of the circumstances facing the officer at the time and place of the incident. The expert's review is not the place for conjecture and hyperbole.

MEDICAL RECORDS

Medical records are an essential component of the investigation into complaints of excessive force as well as other injuries sustained by a person who is subjected to police actions or in police custody at the time of the alleged injury. Cases like *Canton* were predicated on a claim of physical injury and the lack of medical treatment. Any injury or potential injury should then be evaluated and treated medically, or at the very least, the offer of treatment made at a medical facility.

Medical records should then be obtained and translated as a part of the internal investigation in order to completely address the allegations and protect the officer and organization from unfounded claims of injury. While medical records have historically been a matter of confidentiality, the advent of the *Health Insurance Portability and Accountability Act of 1996* (HIPPA) added several additional restrictions. A complainant can however, waive those privacy rights and allow the internal investigator to retrieve the relevant records.

The internal investigator should have the complainant sign a medical records release waiver in order to retrieve all records that are associated with the evaluation and medical services rendered in relation to the incident being investigated. The records release form should contain the following information:

1. Complainant's name and any alternate names the complainant uses.
2. The complainant's full address and telephone number.
3. The date or dates of evaluation and treatment.
4. A statement for the release of all medical records, diagnoses, and treatments, to any and all medical personnel involved in the complainant's evaluation and convalescence.
5. A statement that releases the department, internal investigator, and all medical personnel and treatment facilities of any civil or criminal liability for the use of the records in the investigative process.
6. A place for the complainant to sign and affirm.
7. A place for a notary public to affirm the statement and signature of the complainant.

A draft of the form should be developed and reviewed by the law enforcement organization's legal counsel as well as area hospitals or medical consortium in order to ensure that the form meets the requirements for medical records release. The complainant should also be given a copy of the release form as a part of the complaint.

When the medical records are obtained by the internal investigator, an appointment should be made with either the attending physician or an assisting medical professional such as the nurse or physician's assistant involved in the evaluation of the complainant. Personally interview the physician or medical staff member who conducted the evaluation and/or treatment. Show photographs of the complainant for identification and verification of the presence or lack of injuries. Have the interviewee explain the evaluation and treatment in laymen's terms. Ask for their qualified opinions as to the permanence of any diagnosed injuries and if the alleged force that was applied would have appeared excessive given the circumstances. The internal investigator can either take a supporting deposition or taperecord the interview for transcription by a stenographer.

The internal investigator should also explore any previous similar injuries if at all possible. During the interview of the complainant, the investigator should ask if the complainant has any preexisting injury or condition that may have been the precursor for the injury claimed. This may prove that the injury was sustained prior to the incident or that if proven, the actions of the officer may have merely aggravated an existing medical condition rather than being the primary cause of the injury claim. For example, a complainant may allege that a shoulder or wrist injury occurred during handcuffing or the placement in the police vehicle. These types of claims are common as are such preexisting injuries to shoulders and wrists during normal work or a previous accident or altercation. This information would then rightly minimize the resultant actions of the officer involved in the arrest.

PHYSICAL EVIDENCE

Physical evidence in the internal investigation can be from the three main categories, direct, indirect, and circumstantial. Physical evidence includes tangible evidence such as weapons, samples, and trace evidence. In major cases such as an in-custody death or police involved shooting, the concurrent criminal investigation will commence and most likely an evidence technician will be assigned to process the scene. The internal investigator should not be lulled into a false sense of security that all the tasks for the internal will be completed. A criminal investigation will be focused on the penal and procedural laws and may overlook the needs of the internal investigation. With this in mind, the internal investigator should be involved in reviewing the criminal investigation as it progresses while also conducting their own investigation. That investigation should also include the search for physical evidence.

In the most serious of cases, all available investigative and scientific techniques should be deployed. For example, there are numerous tests and procedures that can be done at these scenes as avenues of investigation that may not be used because of the low success rates, however, they should be used in these cases as a method to rule out aspects of the investigation and ensure a comprehensive case protocol.

The internal investigator should be versed in the emerging technologies in the areas of physical evidence. For example, testing for gunshot residue (GSR) is a residue that is often deposited on the hands, face, and clothing of the shooter with the most prevalent ingredients as lead, barium, and antimony. Substances such as urine, fertilizer, and cosmetics can provide a false-positive in some cases. Residue can also be removed by washing or inadvertently rubbing it off. The technique yields a low rate of positive results and is useless if the primer does not contain both barium and antimony. New systems such as the ASPEX GSR system can now determine the dimensions as well as chemical structure of residue and this is more accurate than previous technologies (Lundrigan, 2004). In police involved shootings, these tests should be administered to all involved, officers and suspects alike. Other technologies such as the advancements of ballistic testing of rifling, which is not possible in shotguns, can reveal evidence under such advancements as the Duke Projectile Recovery System, wherein the powder residue that remains on the recovered round is significant for chemical matching purposes (Wallace, 2004).

The internal investigator should receive training in the identification, processing, and collection of physical evidence as a part of their training in order to ensure that all aspects of the investigation are effectively completed.

The next consideration in the issue of physical evidence is that of search and seizure laws and restrictions. The internal investigator must operate from an orientation of the legal allowances in evidence recovery. Seizing physical evidence falls under the Fourth Amendment of the United States Constitution and qualified exemptions exist for plain view observations, exigent circumstances, vehicle exceptions, and the like. In general, the internal investigator can search and seize in areas of company property and company vehicles as there exists no right of the employee to be secure from such intrusions. Care must be taken though, in searching lockers, desks, briefcases, bags, and other items or areas that may be under the exclusive control of the employee. In these cases, the internal investigator should seek voluntary and knowing consent from the employee or obtain a search warrant prior to proceeding. The internal investigator should also consider court orders for such documents and records as financial and telephone records when the employee refuses to give permission for the records.

There is both the criminal and disciplinary side to be considered. For example, the criminal side should always prevail in lieu of the internal. If the matter is potentially or obviously a criminal matter, then all protections should be afforded to the suspected employee and precautions taken to ensure a criminal conviction. If the case is strictly an internal, some latitude exists for the internal investigator, however, taking the safest route may be prudent if the employee is to be disciplined and terminated so that a wrongful termination challenge can be defended successfully.

An example of this can be found in the review of the *Matter of Boyd v. Constantine* (1993) wherein the City of Buffalo, New York police charged an off duty New York State trooper with illegal possession of marijuana. One key point was that the Buffalo police did not know the defendant was a police officer nor were they acting as agents of the New York State Police. The Court of Appeals in New York State affirmed the use of the evidence in the termination proceeding stating that, "only negligible deterrence would result from the exclusion of the evidence' and 'the suppression of the evidence would have a significant adverse impact upon the truth-finding process in administrative proceedings concerning police officers involved in drug related incidents" (J. J. Sullivan, 1999). This case accentuates how a disciplinary or termination proceeding can be challenged and the need for following the rules of evidence when investigating allegations of criminal conduct as well as the need to effectively discipline in a law enforcement organization.

PHOTOGRAPHIC EVIDENCE

Photographic evidence in an internal investigation should follow the same rules as those for court presentation. They must be authenticated by the photographer or investigator, depict a fair and accurate representation of the scene, subject, or item in view, and must not be unduly prejudicial towards the case. The value of photographic evidence is immeasurable in the internal investigation. Photographs can allow for the reviewer to examine the scene or incident in a panoramic view as well as in detail. This next section discusses all of the aspects of photographic evidence that the internal investigator may be exposed to.

Figure 12-2. Many different options present themselves to the intuitive internal investigator. Booking video and photographs, security cameras, and the passerby all can provide photographic and video documentation of incidents under investigation (Photo courtesy of the Brockport, New York Police Department).

Types of Photography

Photography can be from basic and specialized equipment based upon availability and need. The most predominant is the standard 35 mm camera in point and shoot versions or with some advanced equipment such as manual adjustments, telephoto lenses, and the like. Polaroid® or instant photographs are another option, but are limited in reproductive value.

Digital cameras are the next level and are an excellent resource for the investigation because of the ability to manipulate and enhance the photograph for review and investigative purposes. Some concerns exist with digital photography in the ability to alter the evidential value or perspective. Advanced digital cameras have security features built in that can be used to defend such claims in court challenges.

Many scenes will need to be photographed at night and several options should be considered. Alternate light sources can be brought to the scene when standard flash photography will not suffice. Such alternate light sources can be obtained by the department or obtained from such entities as highway or road departments, fire departments, and others who routinely work during the evening hours. Time exposures are also an excellent option for dark scenes and can be presented in court and other proceedings for authentication in their fair and accurate representation of scenes with respect to lighting conditions and perspectives. Another concept called "painting with light" can be used for large scenes with available flash photography. A final technique is aerial photographs of the scene to provide perspective to horizontal photography techniques and diagrams. Aerial photographs can be taken from a plane, building tops, and the booms of fire or bucket trucks.

Existing Photographs and Videotape

Existing photographs of scenes can be found through bystanders who photograph or videotape an incident. Some examples can be found through such high profile incidents as the Rodney King incident or the Philadelphia incident. In the age of technology and closed circuit television, photographs and videotape can also be located in banks, businesses, parking facilities, and city streets just to name a few. The responding and investigating officers in the initial incident may have also taken photographs of the scene or subject that should be obtained for the investigation. The internal investigator may also seek the assistance of the media in obtaining raw footage and photographs of a scene in order to make these a part of the investigation. Another source of existing photographs may be those presented by the complainant or their attorney. These should be added to the case package if copies can be obtained. The presentation of these photographs should also be placed in perspective of where they came from and the timing of the photographs if this fact can be credibly established.

Subject Photography

Subject photography should be taken contemporaneously to the incident and after the incident whenever possible. Subject photography should include: (1) identification photographs of both the face and profile views, (2) from all four sides, (3) specific injuries, and (4) lack of injuries. Photographs of the involved officer should also be taken at the scene and post incident to document any injuries sustained during the use-of-force. Photographs of the officer should depict the same points as in the aforementioned subject photography including if the officer was in uniform or obviously an officer by display of a lettered jacket or badge if the officer was in plainclothes at the time of the incident. The condition of the officer's clothing should also be documented through photographs at the scene. Photographs of the subject and officers should also be taken at the scene if at all possible in order to replicate the lighting conditions and perspective of the officer at the time and place of the incident.

Scene Photography

Scene photography should be done close in time to the incident as well as when it is well lit with alternate light sources and daylight. Time exposures should add perspective to flash and well lit photographs of scenes. When photographing a scene, the standard location, panoramic, and specific views should be considered. In addition, photographs should be taken with consideration for the perspective of the officer, complainant, and any witnesses. If the perspective is from a window, a vehicle, or other location, photographs should also be taken from these angles and heights in order to accurately and fairly represent the views of the respective witness. Photographs should be taken from every possible angle and view as comparing the cost of film to the irreplaceable cost of the loss of evidence cannot be compared.

New and Follow-Up Photography

The internal investigator may also need to conduct some new or follow-up photography. This may be because certain points were missed in the original investigation or new information has come to light in the continued investigation. The internal investigator should make every effort at the follow-up activities, even if the information or task may seem unproductive. This type of follow-up only proves that the investigation has not overlooked any matters and is thorough in addressing the allegations.

Booking Photographs and Mugshots

The internal investigator should also secure prints of booking photographs and mugshots. These could reveal information concerning previous injuries and the lack of injuries when entering the booking office for processing. Any related reports or documentation of this may also be helpful to the investigation.

Medical Photography

Medical photography refers to the efforts of technicians, medical doctors, and medical examiners or coroners to document physical trauma. This can also include photographs taken of injuries by officers, supervisors, and internal investigators. Trauma such as injuries and wounds should be documented photographically and in as much detail as possible. Basic, advanced, and specialized equipment should be used for these purposes.

The internal investigator should also take great care in the need for photographs that depict private parts or genitalia of the complainant or involved officer. Injuries in such areas may be documented by the evaluating and treating medical personnel and can be described in the medical records and subsequent statement. If photographs are necessary, they should be taken by a technician, investigator, or medical personnel of the same gender to minimize embarrassment. Photographs should also be strictly framed and limited to the affected area of the injury in order to further limit the depiction of the genitalia. The investigator can include a standard body diagram to indicate the area the photograph was taken in relation to the body if that perspective can't be gained from the photograph.

During photography, a sheet or gown can be used to cover these areas when the photograph is taken. The same technique can be used post mortem in the autopsy stage. If photographs have been taken that display such areas, then the internal investigator should occlude these bodily areas with tape or some other barrier. These photographs can also be enhanced electronically to show only the area of injury or cover/delete an area.

Videotaping Scenes and Subjects

Another method of documenting scenes and subjects is through the use of videotaping. Analog and digital systems are both acceptable forms of video documentation. Some considerations for videotape are that the tape should have some logical progression through the scene. This can be planned ahead of the actual taping by means of a scripted progression. The script should be a seamless flow of information whenever possible. A general panoramic view to the identification of specific pieces of evidence is one method. Another method is to take the viewer through the discovery of each piece of evidence as it was discovered, or the progression of the incident from witness statements. The key to scripting is a consistent and logical flow for the viewer. It must make sense at the outset as it most likely will not after it is recorded.

Other considerations are proper lighting conditions. Video needs consistent and adequate lighting in order to be effective and properly represent the scene as it was found and viewed by the investigators. Ensure that the scene is well lit by camera-mounted lighting as well as alternate lighting sources when daylight conditions do not exist. The investigator should also consider muting the videotape as extraneous noise and comments may detract from the presentation of the tape in a court proceeding or internal hearing on the matter. The investigator should make at least two copies of the original. This will allow for the original to be immediately secured into property while additional copies are available for review, presentation, and possible processing for still photographs.

Authenticating Photographic Evidence

Authenticating photographic evidence usually comes from court testimony during a direct examination. In the internal investigation process, this process is less formal, but no less important. Photographs should be authenticated by means of investigative reports, written statements, or on-the-record interviews. If a photograph or series of photographs is submitted for case review and there is no police, investigative, or technician's report that authenticates them, then some type of statement or deposition should be attached that attests to the content of the photographs, date, time, and location of the photographs, identity of the photographer, and identity of the individual submitting the photographs, if different from the photographer. Photographs submitted during a stenographic, audiotaped, or videotaped interview can be validated on the record by the interviewee. This may occur from the complainant submitting photographs of injuries or other information they feel is relevant to the case, involved officers, union representatives, and the like.

Photographic Arrays of Personnel

Often times when a complaint is filed, it is usually removed in time from the incident and may require an identification procedure. Whenever the officer's name is known or unknown, a photographic array should be viewed by the complainant in order to attempt an identification. Any witnesses should also view the photo array separately from the complainant and any other witnesses present. The internal investigator should adhere to the same procedures as a criminal photographic array identification procedure. The internal investigator should also refrain from showing the complainant or witnesses to the incident a single photograph such as in a confirmatory identification, as this may be viewed as highly prejudicial to the case. There are series of recommended steps that internal investigator should follow when assembling the array and conducting the procedure:

1. Five (5) additional photographs of police personnel of like or similar appearance that do not have identifying characteristics such as name, rank, etc. should be included in the array. Like a criminal array, they do not have to match exactly, but must be similar so as not to be unduly suggestive. If the agency does not have enough photographs due to size, then other photographs can be used of similar appearance as long as either they all have similar clothing/uniforms visible or the clothing is occluded through computer alteration or physical means. Other agency photographs can be used with permission as long as the visible portion of the uniform is similar or occluded. The internal investigator should also document who assembled the array and the names of the other personnel who were used in the array.
2. Assemble separate photo-arrays for each involved or subject officer separately. Do not include more than one officer in the array that was at the scene or involved in the complaint.

3. When showing the photo-array, do not be suggestive in words, actions, or mannerisms. Advise the complainant or witness that they will be viewing a series of photographs and that they can take as much time as needed during the viewing. The complainant or witness should then be asked to independently identify anyone they recognize in the photograph, and if so, under what circumstances?
4. The internal investigator should never release any identifying information concerning the officer than is already known to the complainant or witness. For example, if the complainant can only describe the officer or provide a badge or car number and the photographic array is based upon this. The complainant or witness should only refer to the officer in any subsequent interview or statement as the number assigned within the photographic array (e.g., "Number 4 was the officer who was discourteous to me").
5. The internal investigator must always remember that they are protecting the complainant's as well as the officer's rights to due process.
6. Document the specific responses (e.g., identification or lack of identification) in the appropriate form (e.g., supporting deposition, stenographic statement, taped statement, etc.).
7. Preserve the photographic array as evidence per your department's evidence procedure or internal investigations unit policy.

MEASURING, SKETCHING, AND DIAGRAMMING SCENES

Measuring, sketching, and diagramming scenes is usually left to the most serious of incidents in the investigative process. While this step is somewhat laborious and requires some level of technical drawing ability, the efforts expended will undoubtedly enhance the quality of the internal investigation. The diagram will add an additional perspective to the photographs and other reports of the specific incident. With the benefits involved and the skill required for making a diagram, the internal investigator may find this time to be a wise investment in the investigative process. A small investment in training, a set of tape measures, and some simple mechanical drawing tools can bring the investigation to an entirely new level.

There are several purposes for taking measurements and completing a diagram. They include: (1) developing a permanent record of the event, (2) can be used as a supplement to photographs of the scene, (3) can aid in the interview process with complainants, witnesses, and involved personnel, (4) can aid in the reconstruction of the event at a later time, and (5) can aid in testimony and presentation of evidence in departmental and court proceedings.

Measurements should be taken of everything that is relevant to the scene. In some cases, horizontal measurements may need to be augmented by vertical measurements such as the height of a vehicle, window, street light, etc. A good example is provided through crash scene diagrams which should contain any nearby buildings, utility poles, and any other objects that could create a view block for the drivers and witnesses involved in the collision, and should be measured for height as well as location to provide an accurate representation of a scene (Warren & Meyers, 2004). This same ideology should be brought to all scene measurements and diagrams as anything at the scene that may have had an impact or some relevance should be documented.

The next step after identifying everything that needs to be measured is to identify a permanent reference point to work from and then decide on the type of measurement technique. There are different types of reference points, such as those that are: (1) tangible where a physical object can be located, (2) semi-tangible where a mark or second reference point is made that is located a certain difference from a tangible reference point, and (3) an intangible reference point wherein a reference point is created where two reference lines meet.

One measurement is not enough to locate a point as two are needed to plot a location on a diagram. Therefore, every point must be located by a measurement from at least two separate points or lines. For example, in using the coordinate measurement technique, the first tape should be stretched in a northerly direction from a permanent reference point that is located at the furthest southwest point of the scene to be measured. The measurements will all then have two reference points to plot on the diagram (e.g., North 7'2" and East 10'5"). The tape measures should be held at a right angle or 90 degrees so as the diagram can be accurate with respect to placement of the relevant references on the diagram. The triangulation method requires two reference points to work from where the location is plotted on the diagram where both measurements intersect.

In the measurement of items, they can be measured with one point such as small items like a weapon or shell casing, two points for mid-size objects such as bodies or cars, and three or more points, such as large pools of fluid, large vehicles, buildings, etc.

The final considerations in completing the hand drawn diagram are that the internal investigator should indicate the compass direction, date, time, location, case number, and names of personnel who assisted in the measurements or completion of the diagram. The diagram should also indicate that it is "Not drawn to scale" to avoid any court challenges on certification or precision accuracy.

For critical incident scenes such as police involved shootings and fatal accidents involving police pursuits and the like, the internal investigator should also consider the use of electronic diagramming such as a total station. These are far more accurate and can produce mapping of the scene in a scale format. These programs can also be designed to provide for complete scene representation of layering when certain points may need to be excluded at a later time. Many police organizations are purchasing this equipment and may be available within the investigator's organization or a neighboring agency that can be requested for assistance.

POLYGRAPH PROTECTION ACT AND VOICE STRESS ANALYZATION

Use of the polygraph and voice stress analyzer (VSA) can be an effective method of investigation in the internal investigations process. Serious allegations with respect to such issues as bribery, missing or stolen money, and drugs, as well as others are lodged against law enforcement personnel with consistency. The majority of allegations have no basis and are unfounded after investigation. Some however, are questionable and require additional means of investigation to continue the search for the truth. The polygraph and VSA are such tools that can be used to guide the internal investigator on this path.

The polygraph and VSA are effective investigative tools if used sparingly. The internal investigator should limit their use to the most serious allegations such as missing or stolen money and property, drug allegations, and bribery claims. Polygraph and VSA use are strictly regulated by the *Polygraph Protection Act* (1988), state laws, and collective bargaining agreements. There are three groups that the investigator will encounter in the use of the polygraph: (1) complainants, (2) witnesses, and (3) involved personnel. They are addressed separately as:

Complainants: Complainants who allege serious violations can be requested to take a polygraph or VSA examination. The internal investigator can minimize the impact by explaining to the complainant that the procedure is needed to attempt to verify their allegations. The complainant must volunteer for the test and arrangements can be made for the examination to be administered. The polygraph or VSA operator should sign a confidentiality agreement in the case review and be afforded access to the entire case to prepare for the test. The results of the test can be used as indirect or circumstantial evidence in the internal investigation. More often though, the complainant will fail to make the polygraph or VSA appointment to complete the test. This fact can also be presented in the internal investigation as evidence on behalf of the involved officer.

Another consideration is the allegation of sex crimes. Infrequently, law enforcement personnel are accused of sex crimes and these investigations are not only serious, but must exercise the highest discretion. The use of the polygraph or VSA is not a recommended technique with alleged victims of these crimes. More importantly, some states have passed legislation that forbids the use of the polygraph or VSA with victims of sex crimes. For example, the *New York State Criminal Procedure Law* Section 160.45 expressly forbids district attorneys and law enforcement personnel from requiring or even requesting the victim of a sex crime to submit to the test. In the related decision of *Sarro v. City of Sacramento* (1999), the court found that a police department's overly intrusive internal investigation of a sexual harassment complainant's personal life may lead to liability (Americans for Effective Law Enforcement, 2005).

Witnesses: Witnesses, like complainants carry all of the same requirements in requesting and administering the polygraph or VSA. There will be fewer opportunities to request this procedure with witnesses. These limited opportunities may present themselves, but the internal investigator must carefully consider the use of resources towards this end. Several issues such as involvement in the incident, involvement with any of the principals in the incident, availability of the polygraph operator, and voluntariness will all have an impact on this decision in the investigation.

Involved Personnel: Involved personnel present a few issues. Protections under the law and collective bargaining agreements may wholly preclude the use of the polygraph with an employee. Most states allow a polygraph only if suggested by the employee (Thurnauer, 2002). Even if provisions existed, a polygraph or VSA operator will most likely refuse to administer the examination on an involuntary subject. Other issues such as the possibility of the release of such results through a civil or federal discovery proceeding all impact the decision to use the polygraph or VSA on personnel involved in an internal investigation.

The internal investigator must remember that the purpose of the process is to find the truth, not convict or exonerate the officer. Evidence and not attitude will be the deciding factor in a case. In the use of the polygraph or VSA, the internal investigator should endeavor to not assume that every complainant nor every officer is untruthful and develop a policy, whether written or unwritten, that subjects every one involved in an internal investigation to a truth verification test. To reiterate, the findings can be introduced in the internal investigation process and administrative hearings, however, the procedure should be used in moderation as it is an option in the process of internal investigation and should not define the process of internal investigation.

SUMMARY

This chapter discussed the numerous issues in evidence identification, evaluation, and collection. The need for the internal investigator to recognize that evidence, whether testimonial or physical is a salient component of the internal investigations process. The chapter reviewed the merits of physical evidence, testimonial evidence, and the various types of documents that can be used in the progression of the case. The chapter then reviewed such issues as expert testimony, scene investigation, and an in-depth review of the photography options available to the internal investigator. The chapter closed with a review of the requirements and practical uses of the polygraph and voice stress analyzer in an internal investigation.

Chapter 13

CASE INVESTIGATION SUMMARY AND PACKAGE

INTRODUCTION

The case investigative summary is where the entire investigation comes together. The case summary is where the internal investigator documents not only the results of the investigation, but also, the recommended investigative findings for each respective allegation. This chapter addresses the form, function, and presentation of the investigative case summary.

CASE INVESTIGATIVE SUMMARY

The case investigative summary serves as a type of executive summary of the allegations and evidence uncovered during the investigation. The investigative summary is analogous to a court information or bill of particulars as beyond its use internally, it may also be used for presentation in an administrative hearing or judicial setting. Therefore, it should meet the requirements of all of these purposes in order to be effective. The final case investigative report is authored by the internal investigator and outlines three major components: (1) the specific allegations, (2) the evidence that supports or refutes the allegations, and (3) the recommended findings for each allegation.

Any information that is extraneous or that does not have an impact on the allegations or specific evidence should not be included in the case investigative summary. Unless information has a specific purpose, it does not belong in the investigative summary (Arnold, 1999). Many specific investigative steps may not reveal any probative information. The case investigative summary should include only those probative or substantive pieces of evidence that either confirm or refute the allegations of the complainant. The internal investigator will not exclude or redact any information from the case package unless required by law or policy, however, there are other reports that will be attached that will be more appropriate for the documentation of those investigative steps.

Recommended Format

The investigative case summary should follow a specific format in the organization. The format can be tailored for the organization's needs as well as the investigator's needs. Specific examples are provided throughout the chapter as well as in the

Figure 13-1. A police supervisor completing the internal investigation summary (Photo courtesy of the Brockport, New York Police Department).

Appendix at the end of this chapter. The following is a recommended format for the case investigative summary:

1. Introductory Paragraph
2. Findings Section for the Specific Allegations
3. Incident Synopsis
4. Evidence to Support the Specific Allegations
5. Evidence to Refute the Specific Allegations
6. Identify, Separate, and Explain Each Allegation Along with the Recommended Findings
7. Miscellaneous Section for any Ancillary or Satellite Issues

Introductory Paragraph

The introductory paragraph should set out the basic particulars of the investigation. This paragraph is intended to prepare the reviewer by identifying the purpose of the report. The paragraph should include: (1) the complainant's name, (2) the involved officer's name or names, (3) where and how the complaint was received, (4) the case number, (5) a direction to the reviewer to remove themselves from the investigation if they have any relationship with the complainant, witnesses, or involved personnel beyond that of a professional and work based relationship, and (6) a statement to admonish the reviewer from sharing any information in the case as it is a strictly confidential investigation.

Findings Section for Specific Allegations

The Findings Section for the specific allegations should include a finding for each of the allegations. For example, "Allegation 1 is unfounded, Allegations 2 and 3 are exonerated, and Allegation 4 is not sustained." This also prepares the reviewer for the internal investigator's recommended findings in the case. As the reviewer progresses through the case, they will be able to understand the logic of each finding as opposed to the risk of being surprised after review of the individual allegations. This section sets the tone for what the reviewer will be examining in the completed investigation.

Incident Synopsis

An incident synopsis is another integral part of the case investigative summary. The synopsis should be included for all investigations. The reviewer will most often not gain a clear and concise picture of the event if only the allegations are addressed. As such, the internal investigator should develop a synopsis or executive summary of the event from beginning to end. The synopsis should take the reviewer on the journey from the first contact to the last contact with the complainant. The internal investigator should give the reviewer a picture of the entire incident so that the review of the specific allegations will be clear and unequivocal.

Evidence to Support the Allegations

In the section for Evidence to Support the Allegations, the internal investigator should provide a list of the evidence, documents, and information included in the package that supports the allegation from the complainant. Each allegation should be separated and a specific reference to supportive evidence should be made by attachment number. For example, "Allegation 1 is supported by Attachment 1, the complaint form, Attachment 2, the statement of the complainant, and Attachment 3, the involved witness statement." This section as well as the next assists in part, in weighting the evidence available in order to render a finding based upon a preponderance of the evidence.

Evidence to Refute the Allegations

In the section for Evidence to Refute the Allegations, the internal investigator should provide a list of the evidence, documents, and information included in the package that refutes the allegation from the complainant. In this section, as in the aforementioned section, each allegation should be separated and a specific reference to refuting evidence should be made by attachment number. For example, "Allegation 1 is refuted by Attachment 4, the involved officer's statement, and Attachment 5, the independent witness statement." A critical concern in completing these sections is that the evidence is properly evaluated as to its credibility. If the evidence carries merit and credibility, then the next issue is that it is properly classified.

In addition, an evidentiary attachment may be listed in both the supporting and refuting sections depending upon the nature of the allegation. For example, a complainant may allege that they were struck with an impact instrument and thus subjected to excessive force. The involved officer then admits to the use of the PR24 in an active countermeasure against a resisting suspect. The subject resistance report also verifies the officer's account. In this scenario, the officer's statement and subject resistance report can both be listed in partially supporting the allegation, however, the allegation may still be unfounded if the officer was justified in the actions taken. In contrast, if the complainant alleges that they were struck with an impact instrument and the officer denies the allegation, only the complainant's statement would be listed as supporting information. The officer's statement of denial would then only be listed in the refuting section of the report.

Identify and Address Each Allegation

In this section, each allegation should be identified and addressed separately. This ensures that each allegation of the complainant is investigated and dealt with thoroughly and objectively. Each allegation should begin with a heading for its corresponding number. For example, Allegation 1: Complainant Alleges the Officer Was Discourteous. The allegation should then be addressed with a series of at least five paragraphs. Each paragraph should include verbatim quotes and statements that apply to the allegation. The individual titles and structure should be completed as follows:

The Complainant and Involved Witness Statements: The first paragraph should begin with the complainant's specific allegation and verbatim quotes such as, "The officer was discourteous as he referred to me as a (expletive)." This paragraph should be a cogent review of the complainant's single allegation. Each statement or reference should include where the information can be found in the investigative package (e.g.,

Attachment 1). Also included in this paragraph will be any involved or non-independent witnesses to the incident. This is done because the complainant and involved witnesses both carry the same evidential weight in the investigative process. The internal investigator should also note if no involved or non-independent witnesses exist in the case.

The Subject and Involved Personnel Statements: A second paragraph should include the subject officer's statement and any involved witnessing officers. This paragraph should address the subject officer's responses to questions regarding the single specific allegation. Each statement or reference should include where the information can be found in the investigative package (e.g., Attachment 1). Also included in this paragraph will be any other personnel who were witnesses to the incident. This is done because the subject of the complaint and witnessing personnel both carry the same evidential weight in the investigative process. The internal investigator should also note if no additional involved or witnessing personnel exist in the case.

Independent and Expert Witness Statements: A third paragraph should document any independent and uninvolved witness statements as well as expert testimony or opinions. This paragraph should address the observations of the independent witness regarding the single specific allegation. This paragraph should also include any expert witness statements or opinions that are relevant to the specific allegation. Each statement or reference should include where the information can be found in the investigative package (e.g., Attachment 1). This is done because the independent witnesses and expert witnesses both carry higher or more evidential weight in the investigative process than the complainant, involved witnesses, or involved personnel. The internal investigator should also note if no independent or expert witnesses exist in the case.

One exception to this is the inclusion of the statement of an involved officer who corroborates a complainant's, involved witnesses, or subject officer's admission to culpability in the allegation. If a witnessing officer verifies such information the weight of the statement is increased and it is included as being more independent and valid than a witnessing employee.

Relevant Law, Policy, and Procedure: A fourth paragraph should cite all relevant laws, policies, procedures, training, etc. relating to this specific allegation. These references should be copied, included, and referred to as attachments to the investigative package as previously mentioned. The internal investigator should include only the relevant section or pages of the reference rather than the entire reference in the case. The internal investigator should also delineate the differences between legal, liability, and department procedural issues in this section. For example, an allegation of excessive force results in exoneration with respect to tactics. In addition, the officer failed to file a department report, which is a department procedural issue, then this should be clear to defend the officer and agency against a criminal complaint or civil suit, while allowing for proper departmental actions to remediate the substandard behavior.

Recommended Finding: A fifth paragraph should include the recommended finding of the internal investigator. This should be a critical review of the aforementioned building block process of the investigative findings. The review should specifically state if the culmination of the investigative information indicates a preponderance of the evidence that the allegation fits within any of the listed recommended case findings (see chapter 5: Definitions and Terminology–Case Findings). The exception is that if not enough evidence exists to render a fair and impartial finding, then the allegation should be disposed of as not sustained.

Grouping Allegations: A final note for consideration is the use of grouping of allegations that have the same classification and the same findings. For example, a case may have three excessive force allegations: (1) Pepper spray, (2) straight punch, and (3) kick. The allegations have determined findings through investigation as: (1) Pepper spray and (2) straight punch are exonerated, while (3) kick is unfounded. The internal investigator may choose to combine Allegations (1) and (2) as a single allegation into: (1) Pepper spray and straight punch and (2) kick. This method ensures that each allegation is properly investigated and addressed while also limiting the total number of allegations against the involved officer. The investigation should not be a quantitative examination or numbers game, but rather a qualitative examination of the facts.

Miscellaneous Section for any Ancillary or Satellite Issues

After all of the allegations have been individually addressed, the final section of the case investigative summary is dedicated to any satellite or ancillary issues that were discovered during the investigation. This section can also include any information that is relevant to the case, but not included in the allegations section. The internal investigator can cite any policy or training program recommendations or needed changes, low level matters of oral counseling that may have already been addressed prior to or during the investigation and any formal training, counseling, or discipline that was administered as a result of the investigation. Any related documentation should also be included in the investigative package and referenced as described above.

The internal investigator must realize that this is not the time to find something wrong when no untoward actions were cited in the original investigation. Ancillary or satellite issues should have some significance before they are formally addressed in this manner. As a main theme of this text, these are not witch hunts. Therefore, such low level matters may be more appropriately addressed through informal counseling and training as opposed to formal addition to the case file. An immense amount of integrity is lost when a satellite issue is used as a last ditch effort to find an officer guilty of "something" in a case.

WORD USAGE AND TERMINOLOGY

Word usage and terminology are the measure or the professionalism and tact of the internal investigator. The internal investigator must choose unbiased language and base findings on the evidence presented, not conjecture and innuendo. The internal investigator should always write in an objective tone in consideration of all types and levels of audiences that may be involved in the review of the case. The internal investigator should never use derogatory comments or remarks towards the complainant, witnesses, or the involved personnel. Terms and phrases need to be appropriate to the communication medium of a professional investigator. The findings should always be based upon verifiable facts and accepted levels of evidential proof in an administrative or civil setting. The findings should also be based upon qualified opinion that can be defended to attorneys, arbitrators, judges, civilians, administrators as well as the subjects involved in the investigation.

EXPERT AND LAY OPINIONS

In chapter 12: "Evidence Identification, Evaluation, and Collection," in the sections entitled "Witness Classification" and "Expert Testimony," expert witnesses are defined and an example of how an opinion should be handled in the internal investigation. The issue of including an unqualified opinion in the investigation is a precarious one at times. Some believe that any opinions or comments of the officer's personal feelings or motivations for the incident should be omitted from the investigation (Arnold, 1999). In the previous example offered, an opinion such as speculation of officer motivation may be included if it is a component of a series of factual issues, events, or statements rather than a stand alone affirmation.

In the matter of lay opinions, the internal investigator should consider the adopted standards of the courts with regard to offering opinions as to height, weight, speed, and the like. However, these opinions should be given no weight unless some independent factor such as an independent witness, officer verification, or other evidence exists to confirm it. An unqualified opinion can be damaging and unduly prejudicial to the investigation. Unless the aforementioned circumstances exist, opinion based conclusions should be limited in scope to experts such as those listed in chapter 12: "Evidence Identification, Evaluation, and Collection."

Reference to these experts should also be clear in the case investigative summary citing the attachment that qualifies their ability to offer an expert opinion (e.g., a resume or documentation of certification) and the attachment that includes the opinion (e.g., summary or investigative/technical report). This may be a single attachment wherein the expert provides a statement of their qualifications at the outset of the report and then completes the report with their rationale for their finding or opinion. A district attorney, municipal attorney, or medical doctor will not require the resume or statement of qualification unless the opinion is in a specific area of expertise. Other experts such as defensive tactics instructors, firearms instructors, and accident reconstructionists will need such a statement in order to validate their conclusions and opinion.

REFERENCE MATERIALS

The inclusion of reference materials is an additional method of case validation. In chapter 7: "Investigative Techniques and Procedures"–the section entitled "Reference Materials," discusses the use of reference materials conceptually with respect to the internal investigation. This section discusses the practical applications of these materials. Reference materials should include every item referenced in the case investigative summary. An additional example is provided in the investigative case package template included in Appendix A. The reviewer should not have to search beyond the investigative package for answers or to be able to draw an informed conclusion.

Copies of all of the reference materials should be indexed and included in the table of contents in the investigative case package. These references should include, but not be limited to: (1) relevant law sections (e.g., penal law, criminal procedure law, municipal codes, case law, etc.), (2) departmental policy and procedure (e.g., general orders, special orders, rules and regulations, individual memos or directives, etc.), (3) relevant training and specialized training (e.g., firearms, defensive tactics, driver training, etc.), (4) specialized unit policies and training (e.g., SWAT, K-9, Bomb, etc.), (5) historical records (e.g., policies, procedures, or training, and law that were in effect at the time of the incident, but have since changed), and (6) perishable materials (i.e., any information or documentation that may be lost or episodic in nature).

The internal investigator should also limit the attachments to the most relevant of sections. For example, if the case involves an excessive force complaint, the internal investigator need only include the particular defense of justification section of the penal or criminal laws. The entire law book does not need to be included. Other reference materials such as policy and procedure can be included in there entirety if they are limited in pages or several separate sections of a policy that applies to the investigation that would be confusing if broken up or separated.

CASE PREPARATION AND PRESENTATION

All of the best investigation may very well be lost in a poorly prepared or presented final product. The more work that an internal investigator invests in the preparation and presentation of the investigation will demonstrate the level of professionalism as well as the level of care about the particular case. This section addresses some simple tips for accomplishing this objective.

Case Preparation

As the internal investigator begins the investigation, a process should be in place to maintain a consistent structure and format. Organization and planning are the proverbial keys to success. At the outset, the internal investigator should use two, three-ring binders for the investigation. The first three ring binder should include all of the original documents and be kept in a secure and safe place. The second - three ring binder should include copies of all documents in the original case binder so that it can be taken with the investigator to on-site interviews, the scene of the incident, and also used to highlight and make notes concerning key aspects of the investigation. The documents can be separated by three-ring dividers in the working package or by stick on notes on a temporary basis until the assembly of the final case package.

None of the attachments should be numbered until the investigation is completed and the case investigative summary is being authored. This prevents any confusion later caused if attachments need to be re-arranged in the case package. The final table of contents should be similar to the example provided in Appendix A. The only items that should be numbered should be evidence or photographs that may need to be referred to in the interview process. One example is for photographs to be in chronological order or identified by an alpha character if the number of photographs is limited and manageable. For example, photographs can be identified by the letters A through Z so they can be referred to in the interviews as "Photograph A." The subsequent reference in the case investigative summary would be (Attachment 6, Photograph A). If the photographs are numbered, they can be referred to in the interview process as "Photograph 1," with a subsequent reference in the case investigative summary as (Attachment 6, Photograph 1). Physical evidence should be photographed and included in the package in the same manner.

Case Package Assembly

The following is a set of recommendations for assembling the final case package. An investigative case package template is included in Appendix A.

Using a Three-Ring Binder: The final case package should be packaged in a formal three-ring binder. A window binder for the cover is preferable as it should include a cover page with the basic information of the case. A hard or soft cover is acceptable. Using a binder as opposed to stapling or a permanent binding method allows for the addition of post investigation documents such as extended command remarks, civilian review comments, and final letters to the officer and complainant. If the package is stapled or permanently bound, the addition of these post-investigation documents will be difficult. If the case is merely left in a manila folder or envelope, the documents can be lost, misplaced, or out of order and will cause problems later in the review process.

An appropriate sized three-ring binder should be provided for the particular case volume. Some may need merely a one-inch binder, while others may need several four-inch binders. In the incidence of several binders, the original table of contents should be copied and placed in the subsequent binders in order for the reviewer to have this reference in the subsequent binder as well rather than having to refer back to the first binder in the series.

Cover Page: The case should include a formal cover page that is marked in bold print "CONFIDENTIAL." The information included on the front of the package should be on an as needed basis to prevent inadvertent disclosure of information if a case is carried about or on the investigator's desk. The cover page should include only: (1) the law enforcement organization's name and logo (logo is optional), (2) the section or unit responsible for the management and filing of the investigation (e.g., Internal Affairs Unit, Professional Standards Unit, etc.), (3) that the case is a personnel complaint investigation, (4) that the package is the investigative summary, (5) the case number, and (6) that the case is confidential and may be reviewed only by authorized personnel as designated by the chief, sheriff, superintendent or other chief executive officer of the organization. Any other information regarding complainant's name, witnesses, officer names, location, date, crime report or event numbers should not be included on the cover page.

Confidentiality Statement: Include a confidentiality statement as the first page of the package. This statement should be authored by the chief executive of the organization such as the chief of police, sheriff, superintendent, or a designee. The designee could be the commander of the internal investigations unit or the internal investigator. The designee must indicate in the confidentiality statement that the order is being issued under the auspices of the chief executive of the organization. The confidentiality statement should include: (1) a warning that internal investigations are confidential matters of the organization, (2) the case number, (3) a statement that cites the particular law and departmental rule or regulation that forbids disclosure of the information under penalty of law (e.g., *New York State Civil Rights Law* Section 50a), (4) a location for all designated reviewers to sign and date that they have read and understand the requirements and restrictions for the review. The issue of case confidentiality is discussed in depth in chapter 14: "Case Review Process" in the section entitled "Record Confidentiality and Storage." The internal investigator and administrator should embrace this concept from an ethical as well as legal perspective. Ethically, cases should not be available for review that disclose personnel and personal information of department employees as well as witnesses, complainants, and the like. This is also a critical factor should a plaintiff challenge the method of case confidential review, access, and storage. A department may lose such a claim in court if the process has minimal restrictions for access or are left in places where they can reviewed by unauthorized personnel or people.

Table of Contents: Provide a table of contents for both investigative and administrative attachments. This should be inclusive of every attachment in the investigation so the items included should be numbered appropriately. The case should follow a logical progression in the hierarchy of the process. An example is provided in Appendix A of this progression.

Attachment Numbering and Dividers: The case package should be separated as attachments and each attachment should be designated by a numbered divider that corresponds to the table of contents. This provides for ease of review as when the investigative case summary is reviewed, the attachments can be referred to as supporting evidence for the findings and the reviewer can easily locate the referenced information if needed.

Photographs and Photographic Arrays: These pieces of the package will be thicker than the other attachments and should be included at the very end of the package. One recommendation is to have photographs printed in a 5" x 7" format so that two can be included on each page. The photographs can then be numbered, or lettered, depending upon the internal investigator's preference. The photographs should also be attached to a heavier paper such as card stock and placed in page protectors to protect the image. Unless it is absolutely necessary, photographs should not be enlarged beyond an 8" x 10" print as everything should be included in the original package and not a separate entity. This provides for the ability to refer to the evidence or photographs in the case investigative summary and prevents the loss of evidence or the mistake of not providing all evidence for the review process.

Photographs can also be scanned electronically and digital photographs are also acceptable. These attachments can be manipulated to several copies on one 8 1/2" x 11" page and numbered or lettered electronically. They should also be placed in page protectors to protect the images during review.

Case Presentation

Internal investigation case presentation can happen by paper review as well as formal oral review and defense to a command board, civilian panel, legal counsel, or a combination of these bodies. The internal investigator should be not only prepared to present and defend the investigative findings in both internal and external proceedings, but more importantly, should be comfortable with the idea. The following is a set of recommendations for preparing for the formal presentation of the internal investigation.

Know the Facts of the Investigation: The internal investigator should not try to present the case with a limited knowledge of the case facts. The internal investigator should know the case intimately and prepare separate notes if necessary to address key points that may be brought out during the presentation.

Know the Audience: The internal investigator should know the audience being presented to and the needs of these bodies as well as the types of questions that will be asked. A command board is different from a civilian review board. Legal counsel will also be different from a police commission. Therefore, the internal investigator will need to know the types of information that can and cannot be released in these environments that are regulated by law or collective bargaining agreement. The internal investigator should also consider having the confidentiality agreement signed by all those who are present for the review. These should be added to the investigative package.

Prepare Handouts: Handouts should be prepared ahead of time that are specific to the audience. The entire case package, the investigative summary, a bulleted handout, executive summary, or a combination of these may be considered for this purpose. The internal investigator should also include a written confidentiality statement in the handouts and decide if they will be collected at the end of the review and destroyed. If the records will be maintained by members of the audience, a timeline for retention, secure storage, and a method of destruction should be determined prior to or at this meeting. The internal investigator should not leave this issue to the design of the audience or to chance.

Use a Lesson Plan: These presentations are in essence, educational sessions. They are designed to transfer knowledge pertaining to the incident that is unbiased and relevant. As such, they should be treated as educational rather than judicial settings. The difference is that in a judicial setting, there will be opposing sides and arguments for or against the findings. In these types of settings, they are informational in nature and are the presentation of facts and evidence for the audience to draw conclusions from. The internal investigator is not the judge, jury, defense, or prosecutor in these settings, but rather a conduit for qualitative investigative process in this specific case. The internal investigator is there to defend the investigation not the parties of the investigation.

Synopsize and Direct: The facts of the case should be synopsized and the presentation should be directed towards the key points. These types of presentations will most likely need to be completed within a small window of time. The internal investigator should also determine the time frame allowed and how much information can be presented in that time frame.

Prepare for Tough Questions and Feedback: Anticipate and plan for tough questions that will be presented by the audience. One reality is that everyone believes that they are an expert at something. Some believe they are experts at everything. Police command, attorneys, and civilians will most often feel the need to offer some type of question that will attempt to put the internal investigator in a position of feeling that the investigation was somehow inadequate or lacking. Others will attempt to bring their own perceived level of acumen in a particular area to the review process. Some do this with a genuine desire to offer qualitative feedback to the process, some feel the need to justify their role in the process despite how thorough the case is, some suffer from personality or psychological disorders that feed a desire to place others in tenuous positions, while still others will simply feel that they are the boss and nothing is good enough! That being said, the internal investigator will need to demonstrate a level of composure and tact that is beyond normal expectations. The measure of the character of the internal investigator is how effectively they are able to handle such legitimate and illegitimate feedback on their investigative skill or the quality of their particular case. The internal investigator should always be open to feedback in order to increase future case quality and unfounded attacks.

CASE REVIEW

In chapter 14: "Case Review Process," the options and reviewing bodies are discussed in depth. The addition in this chapter is to present the chronology within the case investigative summary completion. Case review should not commence until such time that the investigation is completed. There should be no tasks left to be done nor questions unanswered prior to the review process. Failing to adhere to this principle devalues the internal investigator's work and necessitates adding needless time and steps to an already cumbersome process.

The review process should be a strict policy that is written and practiced in the organization. The policy should be sanctioned by the law and chief executive of the agency and limited to only those responsible to supervise the investigation, review the quality, or render a finding. Allowing needless or additional non-essential personnel or people in the investigative process is unethical and may also be damaging to the organization, internal investigator, and the involved personnel.

CASE COMPLETION

After the case is completely reviewed and all investigative and administrative tasks have been completed, the case must be finalized by the several remaining tasks. The following set of tasks is recommended for completion prior to the case being finally filed.

Final Letter to the Complainant: A final letter should be sent to the complainant by certified mail advising them of the case disposition for each allegation made. A formal department letterhead should be used. The letter should be written directly and personally to the complainant and be a professional and courteous reflection of the investigation and the department's position on welcoming legitimate complaints and praise for department personnel. The letter should only generically state the specific allegation (e.g., Unnecessary Force–Struck With a PR24) and the finding (e.g., Exonerated) supported by the evidence revealed during the investigation. In addition, the letter should not include any identity information not already known to the complainant. This should be handled in all letters as a generic statement to the effect that a "complaint was filed against personnel or members of the organization." The letter should be authored by the internal investigations unit or investigating supervisor and signed by the chief executive or his designee. The letter should also provide the complainant with a designated contact person or unit should they have any questions concerning the investigation or findings. This could be the investigating supervisor, ranking officer within the subject officer's command, the internal investigations unit, a member or designee of the chief executive officer, or the chief executive officer if so desired. A copy of the letter may be sent to the complainant's attorney if the attorney had any involvement in the case, however, this is at the discretion of the chief executive of the organization as the final letter to the complainant is suffice to close the case.

No notice is required for any witnesses in the investigation. Neither the investigation nor the findings should be shared with any unnecessary individuals. Witnesses to the incident have no rights to disclosure other than their original statement. This can be offered and a copy made at the time of the statement or at the conclusion of the investigation if requested.

In cases where a sustained finding or charge was supported, indicate only that the allegation was sustained. The letter must not indicate the officer's identity if unknown to the complainant or the penalty imposed. The letter should again, only state that a complaint was filed against a member of the organization and that the specific allegation was sustained. Penalty disposition is strictly a matter for privileged internal review. This is no time for public displays as they are not public matters. This information will most likely be protected by law and contractual bargaining agreement. All information concerning a satellite ancillary issue discovered during the investigation must also be omitted from the final letter to the complainant. These are most often minor issues or deal with larger departmental issues rather than the complainant's concerns. A poor tactic is to find an officer guilty of a satellite issue in order to send an obligatory letter to the complainant indicating that the officer was found guilty of some wrongdoing, even if not originally alleged.

The internal investigator should document any follow-up contact from the complainant, others involved in the case, the inability to deliver the letter, the signed mail receipt, and any other supportive documentation should be added to the package. Dependent upon the nature of the contact, appropriate chain of command notifications may also be in order.

Final Letter to the Involved Officer: A final letter should be sent to the involved personnel either by personal service of a supervisor or certified mail advising them of the case disposition for each allegation made. This correspondence can be an intra-departmental correspondence and should also only include the specific allegation and related finding. This letter is no less important than the letter to the complainant. If the letter to the complainant is generated by the chief executive officer, then the latter to the involved officer should also come from the same individual. Utilizing lower ranking personnel for this task minimizes the importance of the involved personnel in the investigation as well as the organization. If the chief executive officer delegates the task of the complainant's final letter to a designee, then the same individual should complete the final letter to the officer.

As in the issue of civilian witnesses, witnessing personnel also have no right to notification concerning case disposition. The rights of witnessing personnel only extend to disclosure of their original reports and any statements they may have provided in the investigation. Copies of these statements can be provided to the witnessing personnel by request or by policy.

Loose and Extra Documentation: Any loose documentation in the case should be disposed of properly. For example, the recommendation for making an additional package for field use and to highlight for the purposes of interviews should be destroyed so as any inadvertent case disclosure is obviated. Any additional copies or documents that would be considered as evidence or may be requested during any discovery procedure such as the examples provided in the Rosario decision (see chapter 6: "Legal and Labor Issues") should be maintained as part and parcel to the original case package.

Storage in a Safe and Secure Location: This information is discussed in depth in chapter 14: "Case Review Process–Record Confidentiality and Storage."

SUMMARY

This chapter discussed the numerous steps involved in the completion of the investigative case summary and package. The chapter also discussed the recommended format of the case investigative summary and the stratified process of evidence presentation and the recommendation protocol for each allegation presented. The chapter then progressed through such issues as word usage and terminology and the need for the internal investigator to be need for professional and neutral language in the final investigative report. The chapter then reviewed the use of expert and lay opinions, reference materials, and professional case preparation and presentation techniques. The chapter closed with a review of a set of additional steps in case review and completion. As a part of this chapter, the addition of an Appendix includes an investigative case package template for the internal investigator to use as a guide in the process.

Chapter 14

CASE REVIEW PROCESS

INTRODUCTION

The case review process is the capstone procedure for the internal investigator's work. The case review process offers a measure of quality control while also validating the internal investigator's work. This process will most likely involve an internal chain of command review as the first line of demarcation followed by other reviews such as civilian and legal. The investigation must always must be treated with the highest confidentiality and only those necessary to the investigative process, such as the investigators and respective command should have access or even knowledge of the case (Field & Meloni, 1999). Any review beyond these entities must include a strict agreement and process for investigative confidentiality. This chapter discusses the various entities and recommended procedures for the different levels of review.

INVESTIGATIVE PEER REVIEW

One highly overlooked area of review is the use of peers in the process. Investigative case review should begin with the internal investigator scrutinizing their own work in their preliminary review. The next phase should involve the use of other internal investigators or law enforcement supervisors to review the case thoroughness, quality, and support for any recommendations for final disposition. The internal investigator should seek out those who can objectively and constructively offer feedback on the merits of the investigation. Those who have political agendas, personal connections to any of the involved parties, or are biased towards the internal investigator's work should not be used. This can be a valuable quality control measure and should be considered whenever the internal investigator completes an investigation.

COMMAND REVIEW

Command review is an integral part of every internal investigation. Command review can be as simple as forwarding the case from the investigating supervisor directly to the chief executive officer or any other linear or stratified process as long as all other recommended requirements are met. The chief executive officer should not only have strict controls over the review process but the manner and attitudes of those in the reviewing chain. For the process to be valid, every reviewer must maintain the highest levels of integrity and objectivity. There is literally no room for personal agendas and pernicious acts that will undermine the involved officer, complainant, internal investigator, or the subordinate reviewing supervisors and command personnel.

The chief executive officer should set forth a mission statement and general set of guidelines for the review. This message can be delivered through a training session with all supervisory and command staff of the law enforcement organization wherein the chief executive officer affirmatively states that the review process is one of quality control and an opportunity for learning, not scrutiny or discipline. The difficulty of these types of investigations cannot be overstated and adding an insidious or micromanaging opinion to an internal investigator's work only adds to the burden. The chief executive officer should set the tone and be firm in their beliefs, policies, and practices that this process is thorough and impartial. Any deviation by any reviewing command personnel is a direct reflection on the chief executive officer's character, integrity, and reputation.

The command review process itself should involve competent personnel as well as a delineated and trained process of review. The reviewing command personnel should review the case for quality, thoroughness, accuracy, and proper support of the recommended findings. A separate report should be written by each reviewing supervisory and command officer that addresses these four areas as well as any additional areas required by the chief executive officer.

If the review involves a recommendation for additional investigative work, the case should be forwarded through the entire internal chain of command and these recommendations should be approved by the chief executive officer. If an external review is included, then any issues as identified as incomplete should be done prior to this stage. This is done to keep the process from being micromanaged and to assess whether or not the reviewer is objectively reviewing the case or infusing a personal agenda. The cumulative affects of the comments are what the chief executive officer should review, not an individual opinion that may be biased.

With respect to the review of recommended findings of the internal investigator, these reviewing command personnel should never force the reviewing supervisor to alter or change a recommended finding. While these recommendations can be a topic of intelligent discussion with the internal investigator or any subsequent level of command, the finding should be born from the internal investigator's perspective and knowledge of the case. If there is a discrepancy or disagreement, then the reviewing supervisor, command officer, or chief can invoke executive privilege and complete a review report that documents the rationale for their disagreement with the recommended findings.

In smaller organizations where there are limited levels in the process, the chief executive officer should have at least two opinions to base their final opinion on. If a law enforcement agency has two sergeants and one has completed the investigation, then the chief executive officer should engage the second supervisor in the review. If a sergeant and lieutenant or officer of higher rank are assigned to the agency, then those additional reviews can occur as necessary but should not be predicated on each other. They should emerge as equal and independent reviews absent of the influence of the other.

The command review process is the first and hopefully, final step in the internal investigation assessment process. This critical step lays the proper foundation for any and all subsequent reviews including, civilian, legal counsel, the court system, and criminal or civil juries. With respect to federal oversight, the organization must not only demonstrate that there exists a valid complaint intake and investigation process, but also the command review process provides a system of checks and balances to prevent and address claims of police abuse.

LEGAL AND LABOR ISSUES REVIEW

The legal and labor issues review are interrelated and interdependent concepts. Liability and disciplinary matters are weighted equally with following the edicts of maintaining the proper function of the law enforcement organization. One should not eclipse the others. The internal investigator and administrator should decide what level of review is appropriate and at what stage the review should be conducted or is mandated.

Legal issues review should involve both criminal and civil issues. This review should take place during the investigative process and prior to the completion of the investigation. These types of reviews will lend credibility and guidance to many internal investigations. This will also answer any questions of this type that would arise in subsequent command and civilian reviews.

The labor issues review should be through the prevailing legislative and case law as well as a comparison to the organization's collective bargaining agreement. For lower level issues, this can be accomplished by the internal investigator and addressed in the investigation with copies of supporting documentation. For issues of consequence, the internal investigator may seek the guidance and opinion of the organization's collective bargaining team or municipal counsel. This can be communicated through a written opinion that is made a part of the case.

A consideration for the law enforcement organization is to involve the collective bargaining group in the review process. Realistically, the organization should have nothing to hide from the union. So much animosity is created when a law enforcement organization decides to shroud the process in secrecy from the union while sharing the information with command staff, civilians, legal counsel, and others. The administrator must ask themselves that if the records of the investigation are shared with so many others and will ultimately have to be released if subpoenaed by the target officer's attorney in any adverse personnel action, then why are they excluded from release to the union? Part of a collective bargaining agreement can be their review of an internal investigation. This can involve a single designated union representative or team. These individuals would be held to the same level of confidentiality that others in the review process are held to. These individuals can offer a written opinion on the merits of the case and make reasonable recommendations for any changes in the findings or additional investigative tasks which may need to be completed. This can also lead to the union conceding in cases where there exists sufficient probative evidence to convict the officer and force a plea. This can also lead to an objective review of the evidence where the department may not have a strong case and thus waste valuable resources in pursuing a disciplinary action that may ultimately be lost by the agency. The law enforcement administrator should think in these terms; if the internal investigations unit represents a fasces or symbol of authority, that fasces should be surrounded by an olive branch.

CITIZEN REVIEW

The issue of citizen review is fraught with controversy. From all perspectives, civilian review is viewed as problematic in its design, management, and credibility. As a stop gap measure to control police practices, civilian review has had some positive and negative repercussions. This section discusses the options and programs in civilian review systems.

The Concept of Civilian Review

The inception of civilian review was intended to provide an independent control process for allegations of police abuses. In the history of the law enforcement world, concerns have been founded in limited incidents wherein police overstep their authority and act not only beyond the scope of employment, but worse yet, commit criminal acts under the color of law. Civilian review was brought about during very troubling times in the law enforcement field and has been in existence for many years. While civilian review may add yet another level of scrutiny, the opportunity to shape the process should be taken by a police department (Boatman, 2001). Civilian review should also be seen as an opportunity to institutionalize long lasting reform in agencies that have experienced these issues with their personnel (Monahan, 2000).

Several variations of civilian review can be observed in jurisdictions throughout the country. For example, Portland uses a Police Internal Investigations Auditing Committee that handles appeals of internal affairs investigations; Cincinnati uses the Office of Municipal Investigation which handles complaints of serious misconduct by any city employee; Rochester, New York uses a group of civilian mediators to review completed investigations and make recommendations to the Chief of Police; and San Jose uses the Office of Independent Police Auditor to accomplish this same result (Boatman, 2001). The Minneapolis Civilian Review Authority investigates citizen complaints and refers appropriate mediation cases to the Minneapolis Mediation Program (Finn, 2000a). All have positive and negative implications for the investigative review process. There are four main types of civilian oversight systems:

1. Citizens investigate allegations of police misconduct and recommend a finding to the head of the agency.
2. Officers investigate allegations and develop findings. Then, citizens review and recommend that the head of the agency approve or reject the findings.
3. Complainants may appeal findings established by the agency to the citizens who review them and make recommendations to the head of the agency.
4. An auditor investigates the process the agency uses to accept and investigate complaints and reports to the agency and the community the thoroughness and fairness of the process. (Finn, 2000b)

The concept of civilian review is an important issue given the present state of law enforcement as well as its future in the United States. The concept of civilian review, while carrying merit, must also be seen as an evolving discipline. Civilian review must be tempered with the practical application of law enforcement services in a free society. Deputy Commissioner Joe Farrow (2003) eloquently makes this point as he states that:

> The crux of the law enforcement officer's problem is weighing the individual's liberty against the social and legal necessities of regulation. The most basic balance that a review system must strike is this: It must allow law enforcement great latitude and flexibility and yet require that it adhere strictly to the dictates of the formal legal system. It is neither an easy nor a particularly clear balance to maintain. (p. 24)

Civilian Review Programs

Civilian review programs have been implemented for positive and negative reasons. From a developmental perspective, civilian review programs can make a needed connection to the community in law enforcement operations. Civilian review programs, given the right make up of staff can provide developmental opportunities in the review of internal investigations as well as the formation of policy and procedure, and the validation of the efficacy and integrity of a department's internal investigation process. As many as three-fourths of the largest cities in the United States have established some form of citizen law enforcement review (Farrow, 2003). Smaller agencies should also consider the implementation of such a process as this seems to be the wave of the future.

Concerns exist on behalf of the police as they perceive oversight procedures represent outside interference, oversight staff lack experience with and understanding of police work, and oversight processes are unfair (Finn, 2000b). These concerns are echoed on the civilian side as they perceive the process as lacking the influence to change the system. Both sides should be considered when developing a system within a law enforcement organization. In addition, the system must still be workable within the unique needs and responsibilities of contemporary law enforcement personnel. Deputy Commissioner Joe Farrow (2003) argues very convincingly for such a balance as he states that:

> The ideal compromise system should essentially leave complaint investigations to law enforcement professionals, subject to ultimate citizen review as needed. The system should allow great latitude to the law enforcement professional and subcultural structure for dealing with complaints. The final implementation of discipline should be left to the chief; that is his or her job, and it should remain so. (p. 29)

Mediation Programs

Mediation is defined as, "A process of negotiation, usually invoked to resolve an impasse. It brings together two or more interested parties to reconcile differences and to reach a voluntary agreement or settlement" (Finn, 2000a, p. 67). Mediation involves a neutral third party that assists the officer and complainant in reaching a resolution to the issue absent the offering of solutions or decisions. The parties involved make their own decisions through the facilitation skills of the mediator to resolve their dispute (Coletta, 2003). Peter Finn (2000a) also states that, "Mediation benefits are most likely to occur when misunderstandings, miscommunication, or lack of communication are the primary factors in the dispute between an officer and a citizen" (p. 74). Mediation is an excellent method for law enforcement organizations to effectively dispose of complaints in a manner that is satisfactory to the community while developing stronger community relations. Mediation is also an opportunity for the involved personnel to have a one-on-one contact with a complainant to hear their concerns in a non-disciplinary setting. The officer is also afforded the opportunity to explain the reason for their actions and come to some resolution without the matter being formally investigated.

Statistically, about 85 percent of cases that go to mediation reach some sort of resolution. An example of successful outcomes of mediation can be cited in the Washington, DC police department where the department referred 42 cases in which citizens filed language or conduct complaints against officers to mediation. Thirty-one of those cases resulted in mediated agreements that led citizens to drop their complaints and reconcile with the officers (Coletta, 2003). Police departments in general are finding that mediation of certain types of complaints can work to satisfy all parties involved (Finn, 2000a). Some great successes can be found in the Minneapolis Mediation Program which reaches an agreement in approximately 90 percent of complaints referred (Finn, 2000a).

Another example of a mediation or conciliation program exists in the Rochester New York Police Department. In this agency, eight types of complaints are eligible for conciliation, ranging from failure to take what a complainant perceives was appropriate action (e.g., not making an arrest) to discourtesy to damaged property (e.g., during the execution of a search warrant). Cases involving allegations of excessive force are not eligible for conciliation. The conciliator requires no signed agreement from the parties, merely a letter is sent to all involved, including Internal Affairs indicating if the matter was resolved or not resolved. In addition, if the complainant is not satisfied, they can re-file their complaint with Internal Affairs (Finn, 2000a).

Some concerns are raised concerning the confidentiality of this process. Mediation is confidential as mandated by statutes in most states. Mediation communications are considered privileged and not subject to court discovery (Coletta, 2003; Finn, 2000a). The parties involved must be made aware through a signed agreement that all communications will be confidential. If as complainant opts to continue with the complaint process should the mediation be unsuccessful, they should not be allowed to share any information concerning the conversations that took place between the officer, complainant, and mediator. If this information makes it to a formal record, such as through a video, stenographic statement, or recording, it must be redacted prior to inclusion in the case file and review process.

In addition, officers should not be sent to the mediation without some preparation as to the process, requirements, and expectations of their conduct. Officers need to be made aware of the process prior to entry into a mediation or conciliation. That may take training on behalf of the organization in making officers aware of their personal communication and presentation skills so that the mediation can be productive and not debilitate into a situation that is worse than the original complaint.

The Ombudsman Concept

The Boise Police Department has implemented a unique variation to civilian review by using a civilian ombudsman. Creating the office to deal with personnel complaints, provide a civilian liaison between police and community members, and make recommendations on policy, the ombudsman was seen as a viable alternative to the civilian review process. The office uses a methodology of the power to initiate civilian investigations while an independent auditor (ombudsman) reviews the investigations and makes recommendations to the mayor and police chief (Boatman, 2001).

Program Development Considerations

Legal Considerations: Legal considerations of mediation programs center on prevailing law and the extent to which the law allows empowerment of these commissions. In most cases, civilian review commissions should not and cannot be empowered to make disciplinary decisions. Criminal juries are precluded from making sentencing decisions as they are a matter of law and within the purview of the judge. Most states preclude the imposing of discipline to any other entity than the chief executive officer of the agency. Therefore, the civilian review board's input should be strictly limited to the merits of the case and the level of evidence that either acquits or convicts the involved officer.

Policy Considerations: Extreme care needs to be taken in the development and implementation of civilian review authority through policy. While there are benefits that may be enjoyed through their recommendations on suggestions and training (Finn, 2000b), they also will most likely not have the experience, background, or legal acumen to effectively set policy and procedure that can be operationalized in a police organization. In developing policy and procedure for the use of mediation programs, the department should:

1. Identify the types of cases that should be referred to mediation.
2. Establish policies and procedures on when and how referrals will be made.
3. Train officers to explain to explain the mediation process, its intent, and its value to disputing parties.
4. Develop a system for putting disputants in contact with the mediation center.
5. Develop a means of tracking case outcomes and their impact on time and resources. (Coletta, 2003)

Training Considerations: Extensive training should be afforded for civilian members of review boards, mediators/conciliators, administrators, and civilian complaint intake personnel. A curriculum that involves departmental policy, procedure, trained techniques, and practical experiences such as mandatory ride-alongs should be used to edify the board members in the procedural as well as practical implications of the delivery of law enforcement services.

Investigative Considerations: Two issues are raised in investigative considerations: (1) investigative powers of the board and (2) their oversight responsibilities in ensuring a quality investigation by the law enforcement organization. With respect to the investigative powers of the board, care must be taken in how these powers can impact the rights of the involved personnel when the proceeding is removed to an external body of investigation and review. Interview and subpoena powers may be limited by law, collective bargaining agreement, and the knowledge, skills, and abilities of the board. In ensuring quality in the investigative process, they must be trained and versed in contemporary investigative techniques rather than anecdotal information that leads to failed rhetorical attempts to improve the process. In contrast, properly trained and guided civilian oversight systems may also have a positive impact on the quality and thoroughness of a department's internal investigations (Finn, 2000b).

Another important factor in civilian review board reviews of an investigation is the inclusion of an officer's training record that is germane to the allegations of the case. For example, previous employment, such as lateral transfers, may have been trained in a manner that does not meet the current department's training standard, and if not retrained, the information needs to be considered not only in the case, but also by the civilians. A classic case in Orange County Florida involved a lateral transfer wherein the deputy was fired for using pepper spray to wake an unconscious subject. Previous training allowed deputies to use ammonia capsules to revive unconscious and unresponsive subjects. The civilian review board concluded that the sheriff's office had a poor pepper spray policy because it required automatic termination for misuse regardless of mitigating circumstances (Finn, 2000b).

REVIEWING THE EMPLOYEE'S DISCIPLINARY RECORD

The employee's disciplinary record should never be a part of the review process until such time as the case is completed and a finding applied by all of the reviewing bodies. Some organizations will include the disciplinary record in the command review portion as a part of the case review process. In theory, this practice saves time and allows for a method of early warning or intervention for the command structure. However, significant and irreparable damage may be caused to the case if the previous record is considered as a part of the current case.

The proper convention of case reviews should wholly exclude any previous disciplinary history of the employee. The case should pass through the normal review chain and a recommended finding for each allegation should be applied without being tainted by the implications of any previous complaints or sustained acts of misconduct by the employee. Such inclusion could unduly influence a reviewer into sustaining a finding that may not reach the necessary level of evidence in the case under review. This will lead to serious issues in any subsequent disciplinary action. The chief executive or designated administrator who must defend the actions of the organization will have to defend the case on its own merits. As such, the case should be as thorough and unbiased as possible.

Once a case has been properly reviewed and the level of evidence properly and sufficiently supports a sustained finding of misconduct, then the previous disciplinary record should be reviewed by command to determine the proper discipline under the concept of progressive discipline. If the case reveals a finding that is favorable to the officer, or a finding of not sustained, the record can then also be reviewed in an attempt to identify any patterns of conduct or to determine if some early intervention strategy may be appropriate.

This should also be a matter of strict policy in the case review process. Having this type of policy can be used to bring a sense of fairness to the process. This policy can also be used to defend the administrator from allegations of bias in the process. Acts such as this build credibility in the organization's processes and prove to the adjudication body that the organization protects the rights of all of the involved parties equally.

THE SUSTAINED FINDING

Also a part of the review process is the incidence of a sustained finding in an internal investigation. Recognizing that this occurs on average in five percent to 10 percent of the investigations, the internal investigator and administrator must be prepared to effectively, efficiently, and humanely deal with such occurrences. Most internal investigations that result in a sustained finding of misconduct involve mistakes of judgment (Serpas, Olson, & Jones, 2003). Only a fraction of cases involve wanton disregard of policy or law, therefore only a fraction should be treated as egregious in nature and deserve a strict punitive response. For the most part, these cases are an inadvertent error rather than an intentional act.

The internal investigation must be based upon a solid investigative foundation in order to justify a sustained finding. Supervisors who conduct internal investigations, as well as administrators who review them must understand that they are responsible for ensuring that all of the facts have been gathered, that a thorough and objective review is completed with respect to the available evidence, not anecdotal or suppositional, and base their decisions and recommendations on the facts only (Harris & Gilmartin, 2000). This should not only be a moral and procedural imperative, but may be a matter of law in most states. For example, Police Officer Bill of Rights requirements in affected states include such language as "no discipline without just cause" (Thurnauer, 2002). Once this level of evidence is reached and the understanding of the intent of the act, then several other issues must be considered.

When reaching this point, the disciplinary threshold must be crossed. While this phase can be handled in several positive and negative ways, the process must be internally supported. Support of supervisors from mid and executive level management in the disciplinary process is considered a critical component to the process of imparting and maintaining discipline in effective law enforcement operations (Harris & Gilmartin, 2000). John J. Harris and Dr. Kevin M. Gilmartin (2000) also cite the number of obstacles standing in the way of disciplinary actions as: (1) lack of administrative support, (2) arbitrators and other review boards, (3) inadequate documentation, (4) civil service, unions, and labor organizations, (5) time consuming disciplinary process, (6) fear of reprisal, and (7) insufficient training on how and when to discipline employees (p. 20). Once these obstacles have been effectively dealt with then, appropriate penalties should be meted out, especially when ethical breaches are sustained that the chief administrator has explicitly stressed (Bergner, 1998).

DETERMINING THE APPROPRIATE PENALTY

At the conclusion of a case wherein a sustained misconduct finding is revealed, the next decision making process involves determining the appropriate penalty. Invoking discipline is a complex process of balancing the legal, procedural, and humanistic aspects of resolving a problem or issue. The punitive side of discipline is seldom needed in the process of correcting substandard behavior.

The Concept of Discipline

Discipline is a process of achieving and maintaining conformity to standards established by an employer. The maintenance of discipline is accomplished or implemented through both positive and negative feedback on observed substandard behaviors. Discipline can also be equated as control, regulation, authority, obedience, and punishment (Trautman, 2003a). There are two types of discipline: (1) positive discipline, which involves counseling and training and (2) negative discipline which involves punitive measures or punishment.

The precept of discipline is to correct behavior. The nature of the act, egregious nature of the act, and previous conduct of the employee are determining factors in the disciplinary methodology, such as positive or negative approaches. Other factors such as the level of evidence available, the strength of the case, the employee's acknowledgement, atonement, and cooperation in the case also may impact the decision making process in invoking discipline. Correcting substandard behavior must be accomplished by maintaining the dignity of the involved personnel through an impartial process that prevents future acts of transgression (Field & Meloni, 1999).

Disciplinary actions must also be based upon the concept of progressive discipline. Progressive discipline involves the use of progressively stricter sanctions for similar violations of policy and procedure. Some of the most common incidents of this nature are chargeable or at fault fleet vehicle accidents. For example, the first at fault accident may involve a simple training memorandum or driving school. A second accident in a finite period of time may involve discipline such as a formal letter of reprimand, while a third accident in a finite period of time may involve an unpaid suspension from duty. The officer's previous record is important in determining the progressive disciplinary sanctions, however, the officer's record should not be reviewed as a part of the case until the entire case is completed and a finding attached by all involved.

The Affects of Discipline

Disciplinary processes have affects on both human resources and organizational systems. From a human resource perspective, a survey conducted in 1995 concerning morale issues with respect to disciplinary processes revealed that 48 percent of the 2,708 respondents believed that internal investigations and discipline lacked objectivity and fairness (Field & Meloni, 1999). This belief system permeates most law enforcement organizations and has an equally debilitating affect on performance. In addition, the cumulative affect significantly impacts organizational effectiveness in law enforcement operations.

Additional human resource issues deal with perceptions of discipline as an effective leadership model. Discipline as a leadership technique is intended to promote ethical behavior, however, it sometimes destroys the unity and teamwork so essential for integrity. Unfair discipline will also cause dissention among the ranks and will ultimately fail to prevent bad behavior (Trautman, 2003a). Discipline must be a tempered and last resort of case resolution.

Aside from the human resource issues are organizational systems issues. Most law enforcement organizations deserve the restrictions placed upon them by collective bargaining agreements and case law as they either take an unnecessarily harsh position in invoking discipline or moving forward with weak cases that not only violate the due process rights of the employee but fail to prove their argument in front of a regulatory body such as an arbitrator or court. Chief Mark W. Field and Deputy Chief Thomas E. Meloni (1999) state that:

> Civil service systems, merit boards or commissions are essential to protect officers from abuse of politics or misuse of administrative power. The history of political interference and systematic or individual corruption practices created the need for civil service protection and police officers' bills of rights enacted in many states. (p. 87)

Therefore, administrators must be ever mindful of the quality of the case, the rights of the involved personnel, and the issue of progressive discipline when considering any such adverse employee actions. The administrator must endeavor to be perceived as equally fair in the eyes of the courts, community, and the human resources of their organizations.

Mitigating Factors in Imposing Discipline

Since so much of police work involves making decisions in complex and rapidly evolving situations many times based upon internal instincts, latitude should be afforded in the disciplinary process concerning officers. Contemporary thought in discipline process suggests that police organizations implement a progressive or caring-based model as opposed to simple complaint investigation and levying penalties in resolving issues of identified employee misconduct (Field & Meloni, 1999).

To take this perspective, the administrator must exercise an immense amount of circumspection in not only reviewing the facts of the case, but also must look behind the facts to determine the appropriate action that will resolve the identified problem. Very few incidents of sustained substandard behavior or misconduct are the result of malice, animus, or strict intent. The administrator should infuse a process that is likened to a pre-sentence hearing in a criminal case wherein these factors are reviewed and considered prior to invoking the discipline. Some foundational causes of substandard behavior are: (1) lack of, poor, or forgotten training, (2) momentary lapses in judgment, (3) the interference of personal life crises, (4) organizational barriers or pressures, or (5) fundamental character flaws.

Lack of, Poor, or Forgotten Training: Budgets, resources, and politics all impact organizational training. Other issues are changes in the law and needs of the community served. With respect to budgets and resources, most law enforcement organizations operate in fiscally constrained times and training most often is administered as a matter of last resort rather than as an organizational edict. Often times when training programs are delivered, they are not designed to increase capacity, but rather a rudimentary review to somehow inform while releasing the organization of liability. Compounding the issue of the absence of training or poor training is the issue of forgotten training. Many of the skills required for the delivery of law enforcement services are diminishing skills. Cognitive skills such as the understanding of contemporary laws and policies as well as psychomotor skills in defensive tactics and firearms use all need frequent refreshers to maintain acceptable levels of capacity.

Momentary Lapses in Judgment: One forgotten aspect of law enforcement services is that they are delivered by people. Beyond the arguments of advanced training, experience, and heightened responsibility, decisions and actions are delivered by people; people who are fallible, make mistakes, and have no ill intent other than they have misjudged the moment. While reasonableness is a measure there are also subtle levels of reasonableness that must be recognized and dealt with appropriately. Administrators must never lose their humanity in correcting substandard behavior. The loss of this quality makes us no better than tyrant rulers in history who also failed at the attempts to command.

The Interference of Personal Life Crises: This is one of the most overlooked areas as law enforcement officers are expected to rise above all else in order to effectively perform their roles. The opposite is true though as marital and family problems, substance abuse, financial problems, child care, and a host of others may severely impact the employee's ability to perform in the work environment. These types of incidents should not be treated as excuses, but rather as bona fide mitigating condition that may require professional intervention in order to save the employee.

Organizational Barriers or Pressures: This is perhaps the most treacherous and controversial of mitigating factors that the internal investigator must champion the fight against and the law enforcement administrator must admit and respond appropriately to. Organizational barriers, policy failures, poor or malevolent supervision and management, and the influence of external political forces all fit in this category and are all inappropriate as deciding factors for the imposition of discipline. This is also no time for the codification of retroactive rules.

Fundamental Character Flaws: While the three previous issues are salient to the determination of mitigating circumstances that are in part to wholly beyond the control of the law enforcement officer, fundamental character flaws speak directly to the personal responsibility of the individual law enforcement officer. These types of violations are directly related to the officer's specific intent and run the range of minor violations to criminal acts. These types of acts must be dealt with appropriately as well as decisively. Additional records that can be reviewed in assisting the internal investigator in recommending the appropriate penalty or remediation can include their pre-employment background investigation, personnel files, and training records.

Alternative Methods of Discipline

Discipline was previously defined as having options of negative and positive consequences. Negative discipline is most often a matter of law, precedence, and collective bargaining agreement. The law enforcement administrator must also consider the use of positive disciplinary methods to resolve cases of sustained substandard behavior or misconduct. Very simply stated, punishment should be appropriate to the violation (Forsyth, 2003). As such, an array of appropriate resolution type actions must be considered such as coaching, retraining, verbal warnings, counseling, and disciplinary action (Harris & Gilmartin, 2000). Counseling, remedial training, and referrals to professional services should be the first consideration in any imposition of discipline and only the strongest and most validated arguments for tempered punitive discipline should be used to correct such substandard behaviors.

To invoke positive disciplinary type measures such as counseling, training, and the like, the employee may also be afforded the right to union representation. In *Lewis v. National Labor Relations Board* (1978), a federal appeals court reaffirmed the *Weingarten* holding and extended it to counseling sessions about the employee's job performance, which was the "preliminary stage in the imposition of discipline" (Americans for Effective Law Enforcement, 2005). Therefore, the law enforcement organization should consider policy that affords the collective bargaining unit the opportunity to be present at such sessions by an official notification process.

The Discipline Coordinator/Advocate

The imposition of discipline will bring with it questions of fairness and equity. To ensure that a fair process is in place, organizations should consider the appointment of a disciplinary coordinator to recommend discipline that is fair, adequate, and meets legal and procedural requirements. This is beyond the scope of an internal affairs unit and command staff and is a third party who is an unbiased advocate for both the agency and the accused officer. This position should be free from political, investigative, or organizational influence. The selection of this individual should garner with it an agreement with the current department command that no repercussions will be realized for decisions that are against the recommendations of the internal investigations unit, department command, or its executive leadership team.

End of Review Stage Procedures in Contemplating Discipline

If the final outcome of the case is that a sustained finding of substandard behavior, misconduct, or corruption warrants the use of negative or punitive based discipline, then the internal investigator or internal affairs unit, under the auspices of the chief executive officer must follow an additional set of procedures:

1. Review any contemplation of charges with the municipal attorney or corporation counsel who will be responsible to defend the organization in any subsequent hearing. The internal investigator and chief executive officer should be prepared to follow any recommendations the legal advisor may have, including any recommendations to reinvestigate certain aspects or not proceed because of the lack of strength of a case or prevailing case law and union agreement.
2. If legal counsel approves the case to move forward to a disciplinary process, and there is a civilian complainant involved, then the complainant should be sent a letter advising of the charges to be contemplated. The internal investigator should also make a follow-up contact in order to determine if the complainant

will cooperate with any future proceeding.

3. The involved officer should also be advised in writing of the charges contemplated. The involved officer should also be provided with an "Opportunity to be Heard."
4. The collective bargaining group should also be advised in writing of the contemplation of charges.

THE OPPORTUNITY TO BE HEARD

In chapter 6: Legal and Labor Issues–Due Process Rights of Public Employees the case of the *Cleveland Board of Education v. Loudermill* (1985) is discussed. This Supreme Court decision mandated the element of due process in disciplinary cases involving employees who are entitled to respond to proposed discipline prior to a dismissal proceeding. The court decision provides the employee an opportunity to present reasons why the proposed action should not be taken. This process is the "Opportunity to be Heard."

The process affords the involved employee the opportunity to offer an independent and unsolicited statement to the chief executive of the law enforcement organization. The purpose of the statement is an attempt to mitigate the circumstances or have the charges wholly rescinded. The statement is based upon the employee's offer of information or evidence through a verbal or written statement. The process can be administered by the employee: (1) giving the statement directly to the internal investigations unit, (2) giving the statement directly to an immediate or designated supervisor of higher rank than the accused employee, or (3) the employee delivering a written or recorded statement to the person or unit charged with the disciplinary process.

The process should be set up as a standard statement being issued by hard copy to the officer and also read into the formal record if the proceeding is recorded by stenographer, audio, or videotape. The designated supervisor who is assigned to administer the process should not ask questions or engage in any interchange with respect to the employee's statement. This is to ensure that the employee is allowed full control over their offer of any additional evidence or a rationale for the actions alleged. There should also be no plea offer or reprieve of any kind delivered during this process. This type of action should be wholly separate from the Opportunity to be Heard as this process has a specific and independent purpose in the disciplinary proceeding. The involved officer also has the right to have representation present (Union representative or attorney) at this proceeding and their name and identity should be made a part of the official record.

This record then is delivered as a part of the disciplinary package to the chief executive officer for consideration in levying the final discipline. The chief executive officer should consider any information brought forward in this statement in order to maintain that the process is fair and thorough should any information be brought out that requires further investigation.

The employee can also opt to not exercise the Opportunity to Be Heard and remain silent. The offer and refusal should also be documented in the disciplinary package. The verification can be documented in several ways, such as delivering a hard copy of the Opportunity to Be Heard to the employee that offers them the opportunity to refuse the proceeding. The documentation can include a statement wherein the employee must verbally or in a separate writing, refuse to exercise this option, or the hearing can be scheduled and unless the employee asks for a rescheduled proceeding, their failure to appear can also be deemed as their refusal to exercise this option.

SERVING THE FORMAL CHARGES AND PLEA AGREEMENTS

Serving the formal charges has legal, procedural, and human implications. The legal issues will have to be based upon state law, case law, and collective bargaining agreement. Procedural issues deal directly with the system set up for handling the preferment of charges in the organization. The final issue is the human implications due to the traumatic experiences of the employee when being served charges. All three are of equal importance in the process.

Some primary considerations are that charges should be reviewed by legal counsel prior to service. Copies of all related documentation should also be given to the legal counsel as the process moves forward. The charges should also be served in person by a ranking officer. If this is not possible, then they should be served by certified or registered mail with a return receipt. Some type of affidavit should be completed for the service. If in person, then the affidavit should be completed by the supervisor or commanding officer serving the charges. If by certified or registered mail, the affidavit should be completed as such and attachment of the mail receipt to the original affidavit should be completed by the internal investigations unit staff or chief executive officer's designee. The adherence to any mandated timelines should also be considered in offering a plea agreement to the employee prior to the continuance of the process. For example, the *New York State Civil Service Law* affords the involved officer eight (8) calendar days to enter a plea in writing directly to the chief executive officer of the agency.

The complainant and all witnesses should be notified of the impending contemplation of charges and the need for their assistance at any subsequent departmental or legal proceeding. It is critical to solicit their cooperation and appearance at the proceedings. Each witness should also be personally served with the proper request for appearance at the proceeding. For example, in New York State, police chiefs are empowered to issue a Chief's Subpoena under the provisions of the *New York State Civil Practice Law and Rules* Section 2308.

The employee may have several options at this point depending upon the aforementioned laws and protections. The employee may plead guilty or be able to opt for a department command board hearing, an independent arbitrator, or may be subject to the strict authority of the chief executive's purview in the disciplinary process. This process will lead to the final culpability of the employee in the incident.

The employee may also be offered a plea agreement. This can be done in order to end the process wherein the employee acknowledges culpability and will plead guilty to a lesser offense or lesser penalty in order to satisfy any charges that have been brought. Plea agreements should be considered in most incidents where misconduct is sustained. This disposition is a method for the employee to save face and for the organization to dispose of the case without any further monetary or human resource investments. In moving forward in a case when the employee is willing to plead guilty for a lesser penalty may prove counterproductive for the organization. Such actions when considered in the context of a weak case or the thought of an independent arbitrator finding the employee not guilty can unnecessarily waste organizational resources.

After a final disposition had been rendered or if the employee opts to accept a plea agreement, a determination of the penalty must also follow guidelines that include the concept of progressive discipline, precedent setting cases in the organization of similar incidents, consideration for the complainant, the act, and the involved employee. The chief executive officer should review the involved employee's personnel record to determine the level of progressive discipline in the case. A notice of final determination must then be sent to the involved employee specifying the particular aspects of the offense, any previous discipline, and the penalty levied. The employee should be allowed to submit a letter of response prior to invoking the determined discipline. Another recommendation is that if not provided by collective bargaining agreement, such documentation should also be provided to the collective bargaining unit.

The immediate command, internal investigations unit staff, and chief executive officer should also understand that this may be an extremely traumatic experience for the employee. The potential for the employee acting out in a manner that may hurt themselves or others has a very high potential at this point. The employee should be provided with support or counseling services contemporaneously to the serving of charges. A collaborative relationship with the collective bargaining unit can assist in this process. While it will be necessary to serve charges in these types of cases, working with a collective bargaining unit member who can be on site to immediately monitor the employee and provide assistance can be a very prudent practice.

HEARINGS AND ARBITRATIONS

Hearings and arbitrations should be the last resort in the disciplinary process. They are employed when no viable means of case resolution can be had. Conceptually, their use is in ensuring the maintenance of discipline in a law enforcement organization. With respect to police organizations, police chiefs believe that it is crucial to have control over the disciplinary process in order to maintain police effectiveness and integrity. Studies in both Chicago and Houston have revealed that arbitrators find in favor of these respective police departments in approximately 50% of the cases that are brought to a hearing (Ferrell & Iris, 1999). With such a risky endeavor for an agency to participate in the arbitration or hearing process, discretion and the use of other methods should be exhausted well before a hearing or arbitration is considered.

POST-DISCIPLINARY ACTION MONITORING

After the imposition of discipline, the organization should also have a finite process in place for monitoring the employee's behaviors and actions in order to minimize any negative repercussions. Employee's may act out or act in a manner to sabotage the agency's operations. This should be conducted by the immediate supervisor with progress reports for a defined period of time.

RECORD CONFIDENTIALITY AND STORAGE

Record confidentiality and storage should be maintained throughout the progression of the investigation as well as any subsequent proceedings. Employees, complainants, and witnesses should be afforded the right to privacy by law as well as moral imperative. This section discusses the legal and procedural issues of record confidentiality and storage.

Legal Issues

The first consideration is the legal issues involved in records confidentiality and requests for release. Much discussion and controversy surrounded the codification of the *Freedom of Information Law.* Enacted to assist the American public in access to official records, the law however, is not a carte blanche rule for release. Several exclusions are included concerning sensitive information, access to continuing investigations, and an individuals right to access records that they may not have a significant interest in viewing are all a part of the law. There are also exclusions to the rule that are provided by superseding laws. For example, the *New York State Civil Rights Law* precludes the release of police personnel records. This law supersedes the provisions of the *Freedom of Information Law.*

The test in many cases will be the level of interest a person may have in access to the records. For example, motor vehicle accident reports kept by police authorities are to be opened to the inspection of persons who have an interest in the contents of the records. Based upon this, it is clear that not everyone or anyone has a right to such records, only a party that has an interest to the information contained in such documents. This interest or right may be derived by one of the participants in the accident or an insurance company defending such accident, or someone who can demonstrate a clear interest in having a right to such inspection of these records. So, not everyone can have access to a motor vehicle accident report. The same holds true for other types of reports filed in police organizations such as crime reports, technician's reports, evidence, and the like.

Three additional legal issues must be considered when questions concerning the handling of employee records are raised: (1) information added to the personnel file, (2) information released from the personnel file, and (3) the promise of confidentiality.

Information Added to the Personnel File: There are also limits as to the additions that can be made to the employee's personnel file. Case law is leaning towards adding protections concerning what the employer may legally add to the employee's work record. Therefore, care must be taken in what information is added to a personnel file. For example, in the case of *Watson v. Sexton* (1991), a termination letter that was added to the officer's personnel file that included allegations impugning the employee's good name, reputation, honor, or integrity may be sufficient to raise a liberty interest. Additionally, the Eleventh Circuit Court has held that placing stigmatizing information in a terminated police officer's personnel file and internal affairs file was sufficient to meet the publication test and thus required a pretermination hearing (Unkelbach, 2003).

Information Released from the Personnel File: Releasing information from the file can bring not only criminal but also civil sanctions. In New York State, releasing such information is a misdemeanor. Another example in releasing officer personal information such as home address and contact information may raise a liberty interest. Under the *Freedom of Information Act,* requests are filed for information surrounding cases. In *Kallstrom v. City of Columbus* (1998), personal information of undercover officers was released during criminal discovery to violent gang members. As such, the United States Court of Appeals of the Sixth District ruled that the City's actions placed the officers and their family members in special danger by substantially increasing the likelihood that a private actor would deprive them of their liberty interest in personal security (Zoufal, 2000).

The Promise of Confidentiality: Law enforcement organizations and internal investigations units must exercise an immense amount of caution when promising principles in an internal investigation any level of confidentiality. Donald R. Zoufal (2001) states that:

> The right to privacy occurs irrespective of the person's status as a witness, victim, or suspect. Even persons not involved in the investigation may have a privacy interest. Unless some compelling government interest justifies dissemination, the release of such information would likely expose municipalities to liability under 42 U.S.C. Section 1983.

Therefore, promising witnesses and complainants confidentiality in an internal investigation and a subsequent release of information occurs that leads to harm of the subject may result in significant liability to the department (Zoufal, 2000; Zoufal, 2001).

Procedural Issues

Records confidentiality must garner strict procedures in access and release. They are governed by state and federal laws as well as in collective bargaining agreements. There are a set of basic recommendations in records confidentiality that should be a part of policy and practice in the law enforcement organization so that intentional and inadvertent releases are prevented. A law enforcement organization should enact the following rules and procedures:

1. Personnel records should be kept securely locked away and only in the police chief's or designee's control (Thurnauer, 2002).
2. All access should be strictly controlled and records only viewed by those who have the authority and proper reason for viewing, removing, or copying.
3. All records should be kept in a secure location and should be signed for using a log or other means including the date and time of access and if the files were removed, where they were taken, if they were copied, and when they were returned.
4. Electronic copies of packages should be on a secure PC or network. Protections such as firewalls, anti-hacking, and password protections should be used to protect the records and to defend against any court actions or challenges.

Rethinking Traditional Wisdom

The internal investigations process is one of a strict confidential nature. As such, numerous protections from a legal and procedural perspective must be in place to protect all of the involved parties as well as the affected law enforcement organization. This shroud of secrecy however, brings with it a level of animosity from the rank and file. The need for changing employee attitudes towards the process will not occur until law enforcement administrators rethink the traditional wisdom of keeping all records confidential from the employee. The law enforcement administrator should consider the boundaries that can be pushed in discussing the details of completed cases with employees if the employee desires.

If a case is found in favor of the employee or if the case finds sustained conduct and the case is resolved through positive methods of discipline, the law enforcement administrator should consider a process of sharing information from the investigation with the employee. The law enforcement administrator can mandate procedures that prevent the release of information such as witness names, identifying evidence, require the employee to sign a confidentiality agreement, limit the time of the meeting if the employee begins to demand information beyond the scope of release, and other methods in order to facilitate this process. This measure would go far in building trust in the investigative process, the administration, and the internal investigations unit.

EMPLOYEE ACCESS TO PERSONNEL FILES

Employee access to personnel files should be a matter of policy and practice in a law enforcement organization. Fairness and due process should be the guiding principles in this area. While standards vary from state to state, the general rule is that officers are allowed reasonable access to their personnel files as a matter of correcting or challenging inaccuracies in the records of the department. A case the Fourth Appellate District, Division Two answered this question very definitively. In *County of Riverside v. Superior Court* (Madrigal) (2001), the court ruled that an officer has an absolute right to view, comment upon, and challenge documents and entries in their "personnel records." This case came about as a challenge to exercise due process rights that were guaranteed under the California Public Safety Officers Procedural Bill of Rights (POBRA) (Stone, 2001).

As a matter of law and as a matter of fairness, employees should be allowed limited access to their personnel records. This viewing should be controlled and limited in scope to demographic information on cases as well as specific discipline issued to the employee. The employee shouldn't be allowed to review the details of each case, however, should be allowed to formally challenge any entry in their file. This should be followed up with an administrative review and response from the chief executive of the law enforcement organization.

SUMMARY

This chapter discussed the numerous steps involved in the completion of the investigative case review process. The chapter discussed the various methods of a stratified process of investigative case review. The chapter then progressed through the process and issues related to civilian review. The chapter then reviewed the issues of disciplinary hearings and determining the appropriate discipline for sustained acts of misconduct based upon the principle of progressive discipline. The chapter closed with a review of a set of additional steps in personnel record confidentiality and employee access to personnel files.

Chapter 15

RISK MANAGEMENT

INTRODUCTION

Risk management is a vanguard process used by the private sector to measure risk and develop appropriate techniques to effectively protect the organization from the types of risks that are inherent to the particular business. Risk management used in the private sector to prevent such ominous issues as shrinkage and civil exposure involve the implementation of security measures, insurance policies, and self-insurance just to name a few. This chapter addresses the methods and models of risk management in the law enforcement realm.

LAW ENFORCEMENT RISK MANAGEMENT

The concept of risk management is entering the law enforcement realm in an effort to minimize those inherent risks associated with the delivery of police type services. Not unlike large scale businesses in the service production field, an agency must review its most costly litigation and analyze the alleged officer misconduct, the policy or custom challenged, and draft reform measures needed in order to reduce agency liability (Martinelli, 2002). A precipitating factor for this has been the shocking increase in high profile misconduct investigations across the country (Arnold, 2001). Dale H. Close (2001) states that, "Risk management is now critical for every police agency, regardless of size" (p. 16).

Greg Meyer (2000) states that, "The essence of risk management in a law enforcement organization is to review the work histories of police employees for officer-involved shootings, other uses of force, vehicular pursuits, traffic accidents, and on-duty and off-duty misconduct, all with an eye toward identifying patterns and trends that ideally result in early intervention and training to reduce the number of incidents that subject the organization to liability" (p. 58).

There have been numerous high profile cases of police misconduct across the country. Several have been so egregious as to shock the conscience of the community, courts, and law enforcement with equal disgust, pain, and fear. With respect to the Abner Louima case and the concept of an "unaccountable work ethic," risk managers must ask themselves how uniformed police officers could believe they were immune from discovery or discipline, so much so that they could sodomize a citizen with a plunger in their own precinct restroom? (Martinelli, 2002). In another high profile case, the Rampart Board of Inquiry

Figures 15-1 and 15-2. Risk management systems should be considered in organizations where the use of cumulative information could lead to the early identification of officers with potential problems. The implications of such a system may thwart the escalation to egregious acts such as those observed in the L.A.P.D. Rampart Division by former officer's Rafael Perez and Nino Durden (CNN).

Figure 15-3. Abner Louima received an $8.75 million settlement in his brutality case (CNN).

Report revealed such deficiencies on behalf of the department in identifying problem officers as: (1) failure to review reports, (2) failure to provide effective oversight, (3) failure to develop proactive auditing procedures, and (4) failure to examine events closely to identify patterns (Monahan, 2000). Risk management has thus been identified by such entities as the federal government as a method of preventing such corrupt and sinister acts.

NEEDS ASSESSMENT

Prior to implementing a system or purchasing a software package, the law enforcement organization should conduct a needs assessment. These systems are generically based however, must also be unique to the organization. In general, operations and personnel issues that carry greater legal risks for police departments fall into nine categories: (1) racial profiling, (2) use-of-force, (3) police pursuits, (4) crashes involving police vehicles, (5) workers' compensation injuries, (6) employee claims, (7) unemployment claims, (8) property seizures, and (9) response to catastrophic events. Any risk management system development should also include four steps in review: (1) analysis of any possible risks, (2) an evaluation of police department policies that might be called into play or be applicable to any potential risk situations,

(3) an analysis of the practices of the department in connection with a particular type of risk identifying what practices are followed in areas where no specific written policy applies, and (4) establishment of goals for the department in dealing with potential risks (Close, 2001).

Needs assessment should be conducted for any endeavor the law enforcement organization decides to pursue, especially those involving early warning systems. These systems cannot be administered with a cookie cutter approach or solely on the word of a salesman. They must emerge from the organization's true and concerted efforts in identifying a system that addresses the unique legal, procedural, and community-based needs for the department to continue to conduct effective and efficient operations.

EARLY WARNING/EARLY INTERVENTION SYSTEMS

Most efforts to deal with misconduct have been from a reactive posture rather than proactive (Arnold, 2001). The resultant damage has proven devastating to law enforcement officers and their organizations alike. Early warning, or more appropriately termed, early intervention systems, have been proposed as a method of minimizing risk to the officer, agency, and their respective community.

The advent of early intervention systems can lead to identifying problems before they reach an acute stage and allow for positive intervention strategies. However, predicting future behavior involving police misconduct can only occur when specific actions are known to lead to misconduct for which this concept has been referred to as behavioral profiling (Arnold, 2001). These parameters are discussed in the subsection entitled *Nice to Know v. Need to Know* of this chapter. Therefore, early warning systems based upon this type of criteria have allowed managers and supervisors to discover officer performance that has exceeded organizational expectations (Rhyons & Brewster, 2002). The purpose of the early warning system then, is to engage in non-disciplinary corrective action when it's needed (Rosenbaum, 2001).

Proactive measures must then be implemented for an early intervention system to work effectively. Early intervention systems must not only be proactive, but be conducive for use within the organization. Early warning systems can be as simple as an individual supervisor who keeps copious records of all employee issues, even those that seem innocuous, but may later lead to larger issues (Green, 2002). Departments may have separate systems that can be reviewed collectively in order to identify emerging problem situations or a software package that encompasses all of the systems and information needed to begin the process. In the development and use of information technology based systems, Tim Dees (2003) states that there are several approaches to developing a system, "But all of them involve creating a relational database of personnel and complaint information, and then mining that database to identify relationships that might not otherwise be immediately evident" (p. 89).

The immediate supervisor, internal investigations unit staff, and law enforcement administrator must also recognize that these systems are only the precursor for a more in-depth examination of the issues. Charts and graphs are not the deciding factor for intervention, but rather an informed examination of issues that are brought to the attention of these reviewing entities by means of a system designed to identify possible aberrant behavior. These systems should never be the end all for a very sensitive and crucial decision-making process.

INDICATORS AND PERFORMANCE THRESHOLDS

Indicators and performance thresholds are parameters built within a system or procedure that identify possible aberrations in behavior. The notion of this type of system was born from several incidents of police abuses that led to independent commission review. Additional influence has been brought to the field by the federal government and accreditation processes. An example is found in the Christopher Commission findings of the Los Angeles Police Department. The Commission found that a significantly large number of problem officers posed a much higher risk of excessive force than other officers. During the period of 1986 and 1990, 18,000 officers faced allegations of using excessive force or improper tactics. Of those, 183 were generated for four or more complaints. Forty-four officers were responsible for six or more complaints, 16 had eight or more, and one officer was responsible for 16 complaints. The top five percent of officers, as ranked by the number of reported incidents, accounted for more than 20 percent of all reported use-of-force incidents (Monahan, 2000).

Other such information has come to light concerning the use-of-force by police personnel. For example, according to a study on use-of-force conducted by the International Association of Chiefs of Police with respect to officer education and age, some 73 percent of all reported police uses of force were attributed to officers with 12 years of education or less. Sixty percent of all police uses of force were attributed to officers between 20 and 30 years of age, and 36 percent were committed by officers between the ages of 31 and 40 years of age (Henriquez, 1999).

Thresholds and parameters can also be defined as behavioral markers which have been discovered through independent research. Identifying problem behavior through "markers" revealed from the research data were poor performance, hostility and anger, unnecessary risk-taking, increases in use-of-force and insubordinate conduct (Arnold, 2001). Early warning systems are used to detect a significant event in an officer's statistics, such as a high number of use-of-force incidents, sick days, or vehicular pursuits, or a low number of arrests and citizen contacts. Most often, supervisors find that there is a satisfactory explanation for the irregularity identified (Rhyons & Brewster, 2002). Some reviews reveal the need for further inquiry and in fewer cases, an intervention strategy.

If a review is warranted, then the chief executive or his designee should examine patterns of behavior as well as the nature of complaints as compared the demographics. Comparative data must be reviewed in the context of the employee's work environment. Unfair comparisons will be the undoing of any system. For example, some departments compare such statistical data in the context of the entire department. One example is use-of-force. The following discussion is of a hypothetical agency. The agency has 100 personnel assigned, however, only 60 are actual patrol officers. The remainder are investigative and command staff. Further compounding the issue is that 10 officers are assigned to administrative assignments. The agency records 200 uses of force per year. To develop a threshold, the agency divides the number of uses of force by different parameters. The following table is a simple example of how many variations can be used in calculating the base threshold and the mistakes as well as proper method for this calculation.

This hypothetical exercise is designed to add clarity rather than confusion. The clarity is derived from the understanding that the process of developing thresholds and the preliminary identification of aberrant behavior is a far more complex issue than the police

Table 1. Developing Early Intervention System Thresholds

Reference	Uses of Force	Number of Officers	Threshold Point
1. By Department of 100	200	100	2
2. By Patrol Force of 50	200	50	4
3. By Section/Zone and Patrol Force of 50			
Section A	100	18	5.6
Section B	50	16	3.1
Section C	50	16	3.1
4. By Car Beat/Geographic Area			
Car Beat A	20	1095	0.018
Car Beat B	5	1095	0.005
Car Beat C	0	1095	0
5. By Shift Assignment and Patrol Force of 50			
Shift A (Midnights)	70	12	5.8
Shift B (Days)	40	18	2.2
Shift C (Afternoons)	90	20	4.5
6. By Unit and Patrol Force of 50			
Unit A (Tactical)	50	5	10
Unit B (Patrol)	150	40	3.75
Unit C (Traffic)	0	5	0
7. By Individual Officer			
Department Average of Patrol Force of 50	200	50	4
Officer A	20		20
Officer B	7		7
Officer C	0		0

administrator may be led to believe. Each of these areas is examined individually below:

1. *By Department of 100:* This is perhaps the simplest calculation and by far, the most deceiving. This is done to attempt to minimize the number of uses of force by the agency by spreading them out amongst the entire population. This unfairly and dangerously develops thresholds that hold officers who are on the front line to unachievable standards.
2. *By Patrol Force of 50:* This type of evaluation more fairly captures the department average, however, as are provided in subsequent examples is still not the best measure of actual incidents of use-of-force. While this example increases the base average number by 100 percent it also more fairly measures the actual incidents of use-of-force.
3. *By Section/Zone and Patrol Force of 50:* This example provides an opportunity for the administrator to compare particular sections/zones/districts of the area of responsibility. This example shows that Section A has statistics for use-of-force that are 80 percent higher than Section B and Section C. Before the administrator assumes that there is a problem, much more analysis must take place such as the crime rates, age of the officers assigned, demographics, command policies for aggressive policing, types of properties in

the area such as residential compared to liquor establishments, and many others that may explain why there is this disparity.

4. *By Car Beat/Geographic Area:* Another method is by car beat or geographic area. In this example, the use-of-force by car beat ranges from 20 to 0. However, the calculation by car beat is by the number of officers assigned by the number of days in the year (e.g., 3 x 365 = 1095). This example may seem insignificant, however this needs to also be measured against shift assignment, the consistency or inconsistency of officers assigned to this particular car beat as well as the issues raised in those covered in *By Section and Zone.*
5. *By Shift Assignment and Patrol Force of 50:* This example provides an equitable assessment when comparing similar criteria. In this example the evaluation is by temporal period. Similar calls for service and crime patterns occur across time periods and can thus be compared more fairly from this perspective. Note that Shift A has a rate of use-of-force that is 160 percent higher than Shift B (5.8 to 2.2). Remember though that the department average in Example 2 above was four per officer per year. This only demonstrates a 45 percent increase over the average. And this increase may be justified dependent upon the review of the actual incidents. These types of variations may be unique to shift assignment or may be anomalies. Consider a bar fight on midnights where the officer pepper sprays 20 brawling patrons and must by policy complete a use-of-force report for each. This would inordinately inflate both the shift statistics as well the individual officer's statistics.
6. *By Unit and Patrol Force of 50:* This next example examines statistics by patrol units. Unit B has an average use-of-force rate that is below the department's average (3.75 to 4) while Unit A, a tactical deployment has a rate that is 150 percent higher than the department's average (10 to 4). This could be attributed to their assignment to the worst areas and times where crime and violence is at its highest thus drawing a sympathetic response in the statistics. This could also be a product of poor supervision, inflated camaraderie, unwritten unit policy on protecting the unit's reputation through a high arrest policy, and the like. Therefore, there could be positive or negative reasons for the spike in these numbers.
7. *By Individual Officer:* The individual officer is one of the most common measures, however, the administrator should consider the previous examples. These as well as many other variations in data analysis exist to develop qualitative information to lead to informed decisions. For example, Officer A has a rate of use-of-force some 400 percent higher than the department average. Officer B has a rate of use-of-force that is 75 percent beyond the department average. Both are well beyond the department average, but will they be treated the same or differently in the review? Will these officers be judged on an informed review such as determining if they are brutal officers? If the statistics represent anomalies? Or if they are assigned to very violent or docile areas patrol? More importantly, Officer C has no uses of force for the evaluation period. Does this mean that the officer is lazy? A better communicator? Or, assigned to a non violent area of patrol?

The number of variations is endless, however, contrary to what may be stated or believed, these systems will not provide answers. They only provide a system of data collection that leads to further investigation. The onus is upon the administrator to develop an all inclusive system of data collection and to properly as well as fairly evaluate that data in order to protect the community, department, and the involved officer. With this in mind, early intervention systems should collect data concerning work history with respect to such issues as complaints and discipline. Data should be drawn from such sources as personnel files, payroll systems, off-duty work files, records management systems such as arrest and crime reports, internal affairs files, award and decoration records, and industrial injury reports, among others (Rhyons & Brewster, 2002). After identifying these thresholds the administrator must then put steps into place for follow-up such as further investigation, training, counseling, and possibly corrective disciplinary action (Martinelli, 2002; Rhyons & Brewster, 2002).

NICE TO KNOW V. NEED TO KNOW

The administrator must also consider the types of information that will be needed to make such decisions. Ignorance and morbid curiosity can lead to erosion of the system's intent as well as a significant liability to the organization and officer if this is not properly handled. Prior to requesting an analysis the administrator should have a keen understanding of the types of analysis as well as the meaning of an analysis. Department's that have decided to design and implement a system use all information, both positive and negative, to assess the potential for aberrant behavior on behalf of the employee. These criteria are fairly consistent dependent upon agency standards. The Phoenix Police Department system is an excellent example of this concept and has the following criteria for assessment in place:

1. Awards
2. Employee-requested notes
3. Overtime use
4. Sick leave use
5. Use-of-force by officer
6. Use-of-force against officer
7. Pursuits
8. Arrests
9. Discipline
10. Involvement in significant events (such as officer-involved shootings)
11. Commendations
12. Industrial injuries and exposures
13. Off-duty work
14. Police-involved accidents
15. Citations
16. Police involved shootings
17. Training (Rhyons & Brewster, 2002)

The Phoenix Police Department system is also designed to purge data that is more than five years old (Rhyons & Brewster, 2002). This should be designed so as not to lose a five-year-window, but to have the oldest year's information deleted as the newest information is entered. This will offer consistent information to the agency for the identification of patterns in not only individual officers, but trends in the department and the community served. The organization must first review any records retention rules or laws that exist prior to destroying any information that is gathered as a part of the department's business records.

TACIT SKILLS AND KNOWLEDGE OF SUPERVISORS

What early intervention systems do not do is replicate the tacit skills and knowledge of immediate supervisors. If anything, they work against this concept by circumventing or usurping the authority of police supervisors through a centralized system and may cause more harm than good. The administrator must invest in this aspect of the early intervention system as the immediate supervisor will most likely know that there is a problem long before system thresholds are met and recognized. In essence, the early intervention system is not a substitute for good supervision. Supervisors can use the early intervention system as a statistical tool to assess officer performance, provided the performance assessed is placed into a relevant context and the entire performance realm is reviewed (Rhyons & Brewster, 2002).

Beyond the early intervention system data is the need for supervisor training in the behavioral and psychological aspects of at risk employees. For example, officers may develop "marker" behaviors that signify problem behaviors (Arnold, 2001). These types of behaviors are reflected in the majority of an officer's use-of-force requiring medical treatment for a significant injury. Therefore, the administrator should develop systems where psychologists train police supervisors to detect precursors of problem behavior and how to act upon them through intervention support before the accrual of official complaints (Arnold, 2001).

THE RISK MANAGER POSITION

The administrator should also consider adding the position of risk manager to the organization. The position of risk manager is one that analyzes dangers, hazards, and potential losses associated with liability, damage or pain suffered by either their employees or by those considered to be benefactors of their businesses' product (Martinelli, 2002). These positions can be filled by a trained individual in the organization that can work directly with agency or municipal counsel, insurance carriers, and others to assess and manage risk in the organization. This comes from reactive and proactive measures such as responding to an incident to minimize the damage to the organization as well as developing contemporary policy in light of law or procedural changes in order to avert future risk. Training, circumspect, and authority are the three characteristics needed in filling this position for the benefit of the organization.

PROACTIVE RISK MANAGEMENT STRATEGIES

There are several different strategies that can be employed in risk management techniques. Thomas J. Martinelli (2002) recommends the following series of proactive risk management strategies for a law enforcement organization:

1. Establish a goal oriented service philosophy.
2. Draft an individual unit or division mission statement.
3. Conduct an annual review of causes of action resulting in settlements or judgments.
4. Establish an early warning system:
   - Tracking rules infractions.
   - Tracking citizen complaints.
   - Tracking "unfounded" complaints.
   - Tracking misdemeanor dismissals by judges/prosecutors.
5. Develop a "think tank" unit to collect cutting edge police training tools.
6. Support training and re-training:
   - Ethics awareness training.
   - "Setting in motion"/conflict avoidance training.
   - Whistleblowing duties of public servants.
   - Discussion/analysis of departmental/legal purpose behind policies. (p. 18)

To build upon the training aspects of early intervention systems, several theorists believe that this is a foundational concept. For example, academies need to add emphasis to developing programs that teach excessive force intervention techniques that teach officers how to properly intervene in tense and controversial situations (Miraglia, 1999). A greater emphasis on teaching interpersonal communication skills and conflict resolution skills may be one of the best methods to avoid using force at all (Nowicki, 2000b). Additional methods of reducing liability and risk can many times focus in the wrong areas. While training in firearms and impact weapons takes place, many departments rarely train in handcuffing, laws of arrest, search and seizure, warrantless entry to residences, and so on (Nowicki, 2004). In response to this, departments must develop a structured tracking system that addresses and utilizes the academic side of police training (Martinelli, 2002).

Additional methods of reducing liability and risk involve such proactive measures as used by the Phoenix Police Department. A unique component of their system is that when performance thresholds are exceeded, a committee review is put into motion. The committee is made up of department managers, labor representatives, a peer representative, and a mental health care professional. The committee also has several options to the disposition of the review, including revising department policy, mandating individual or department-wide training, requiring counseling or intervention, and ordering a temporary or even permanent transfer of an individual. This review is not a part of the disciplinary process (Rhyons & Brewster, 2002). Using such proactive measures validates the department's decision making processes and defense in the internal hearing and court systems review.

SUMMARY

This chapter discussed the numerous steps involved in the process of risk management. The chapter discussed the various types of risk management systems. The chapter then progressed through the process developing performance and behavioral thresholds specific to the law enforcement organization. The chapter then reviewed the issues of liability and proactive strategies for risk management. The administrator must bear in mind that risk management is a double-edged sword; techniques to avert risk may in and of themselves create risk. Care must be employed when developing thresholds, reviewing the information in context, and validating responses to identified patterns of aberrant behavior.

Chapter 16

TRAINING AND MANAGING INTERNAL INVESTIGATORS

INTRODUCTION

Training and managing internal investigators are interrelated and interdependent concepts. Managers must recognize that this work requires a level of training and mentoring far beyond that needed to be a supervisor or manager in a law enforcement organization. For the manager to ignore this will only bring many of the problems discussed throughout this entire text. To ensure that internal investigations are conducted with the highest standards requires commensurate training. To maintain those standards requires strong leadership and managerial skills. This chapter addresses the various methods of training and management of the internal investigations unit and its staff.

CURRICULUM DEVELOPMENT

Curriculum development is based upon the needs of the position, discipline, and organization. From the position perspective, training should encompass every aspect of potential investigations that the position will be responsible to conduct. Training can be offered in varying levels to match responsibility in the investigative process. For example, a line supervisor should be trained in complaint conciliation, the types of complaints they would formally investigate, and first response priorities and responsibilities at a critical incident scene. Managers would receive more extensive training in the rights of employees, rights of the organization, and continual incident management. Internal investigations unit staff would receive the entire training regimen in order to advise on and manage the entire investigative process.

The Washington DC Police Department conducted an impressive needs assessment and follow-up by providing the training to ensure that their police involved shooting team was properly trained and prepared to handle their responsibilities. Their program includes training in: (1) homicide investigation, (2) interview and interrogation, (3) crime scene processing, (4) deadly-force investigation, (5) civil rights investigations, (6) hate crimes, (7) legal issues, (8) police psychological training and week at local hospital in psych training, (9) case strategic planning, (10) leadership, (11) communication, (12) teamwork, (13) commitment, (14) the FBI Behavioral Science Unit, (15) suicide-by-cop investigations, (16) evolution of training through critical comments of community and others, (17) presentation skills, (18) research skills, (19) union contracts, (20) labor law, (21) reenactments of deadly force incidents using video and digital photography, (22) less than lethal investigations, (23) post deadly force roundtable discussions with command staff, and (24) the development of a regional force investigation consortium (Ederheimer, 2000). Additional training should include completion of an evidence technician school as much evidence may be lost due to the lack of recognizing the importance as well as having the ability to process and secure such evidence.

The unit and organization should also adopt an orientation of continuous improvement. Using such concepts as the learning organization can build upon this concept of continuous improvement through training. As investigations are completed and information as well as techniques are learned as well as discarded, these new pieces to the proverbial puzzle should be included in such items as training bulletins, in-service trainings, and specialized schools.

Curriculum development should be the focal point of the program and not be an afterthought. One idea or training module should not be the focus of a program that is intended to prepare personnel to conduct such critical and sensitive investigations. Therefore, inclusive curriculum development using systems theory and thought processes will help to deliver the needed information to this student population.

COMMON TRAINING NEEDS

Some universal needs of internal investigations staff should be blended into all training programs. While many are listed in the curriculum development subsection of this chapter, two areas, those of communication and conflict resolutions skills and ethical awareness should be included as a matter of convention.

Communication and Conflict Resolution Skills

So much of what the internal investigator does on a daily basis involves communication and conflict resolution skills. This type of training is far beyond that of a course in interview and interrogation. While interview and interrogation programs teach methods to elicit information, communication and conflict resolutions skills teach the internal investigator the ability to identify and reframe their words in order to assist irate citizens with their understanding of law enforcement policy and procedure. Handling complaints and resolving conflict requires a different set of skills than those needed in investigating crimes and the interview of victims and suspects.

Communication is a perishable skill and without practice will deteriorate over time (Lewis, 2001). This compounds the infrequency that some supervisors may have in receiving and handling personnel complaints. Many can be handled with the simple attention of a concerned law enforcement supervisor. Most complaints handled at this level can be to the benefit of the citizen, department, and involved officer. Therefore, this set of skills needs continuous refreshment.

Communication and conflict resolutions skills may also have other aggravating factors that keep the interaction from resolution. Experiences of the supervisor, constant complaints from the same citizen, the perception of the insignificance of a citizen complaint and the notion of cultural differences or "cultural baggage" all play a part in complaint resolution. Cultural baggage is experiences, upbringing, and education which in sum, creates an individual; to ignore cultural baggage risks inflaming the passions of the citizens.

Perception is a mix of assumptions and inferences translated through different cultural bags; an assumption is a fact mixed with an emotional question mark. A simple technique to overcome perceptions is to make them explicit, bring them out in the open by checking them (Lewis, 2001). The supervisor must experience a level of introspect prior to their ability to effectively overcome such aggravating factors.

Three techniques are recommended for conflict resolution through communication: (1) build rapport though building on perceptions, try to develop a commonality, and desire to understand the issues that confront the individual, (2) fact finding through mutual understanding of facts that affect relationships, providing feedback, listening without interruption or defensiveness, and (3) problem solving by getting people to see the answer for themselves and taking ownership of the solution and work to solve it (Lewis, 2001).

The first stumbling block is to recognize that these skills are perishable and necessary. The second stumbling block is to incorporate a meaningful training session that develops these skills in the trainee so as they can be demonstrated effectively in the real world.

Ethical Awareness

Ethical awareness training is a quagmire for inclusion in any training program. While this will always be a difficult topic to broach, this should not be the deciding factor for exclusion from a training program. For internal investigations unit staff and department command staff, the issue becomes a predominant one. Ethical violations are more pronounced and destructive at these levels and overshadow any issue that may have been identified in the original investigation. Therefore, these types of programs should be included in any internal investigations training offered at all levels in the organization.

Likened to the need for officer ethics training, internal investigators should also undergo a specifically tailored and rigorous program of ethical awareness training. Recommendations for training models include a case law approach and disciplinary rulings that were supported after a hearing rather than one that depends solely on philosophical rationales for ethical decision making. There is a great need to specify and personalize the abstract concept of "doing the right thing" (Martinelli & Pollock, 2000). This concept should also be extended to the command ranks as a part of promotional systems to inculcate these attitudes at the outset of assignment. Ethics training is a moral imperative as well as a viable method of reducing liability. Agencies have expanded the level and role of ethics training at all levels of the organization. One example exists in the Chandler Arizona Police Department which has redesigned its sergeants and lieutenants training programs to emphasize ethics in all aspects of their operations by creating a mandatory 80 hour school for new sergeant's and 120-hour school for new lieutenant's (McNeff, 2001).

Ethical awareness training can be by name, or more effectively, by design. Another alternative is to fold ethics training into other training topics. Ethics should be integrated into every training module so as it is not a stand alone ideology (McCarthy, 2000; McNeff, 2001). This method allows for the issue of ethics to be brought into play in everything the internal investigator does on a daily basis as opposed to a separate topic.

MANAGING THE UNIT

A recognized fact is that internal investigations units and systems have universal problems, politically, operationally, and ethically.

With these conflicting entities at work, it is no wonder that internal investigations units are considered extremely dysfunctional systems for all who are involved in the process. This section briefly discusses the unique management needs of the internal investigations process, the unit, and its staff.

The internal investigations process must be designed and managed to equitably support personnel investigations. This should be the mission of the process. This support should also be garnered from the highest levels of the organization transcending the organization to its lowest ranks. Other support types of entities should also have a complete understanding of the process such as the community, politicians, and collective bargaining units. Managing the process really takes place at the organizational level as any discrepancy or shortcoming in the system reflects poorly on the entire system.

Managing the internal investigations unit requires a supervisor or manager who understands the pressures of politics, personalities, and bias and is able to effectively defend against these insidious influences in order to keep the process on track. The supervisor or manager must be strong enough to take a stand against any injustices that befall not only complainants, but also the involved officers and champion the role of the defender of the process.

Managing the internal investigations staff will also be a test of stamina and character. When the internal investigations staff have conducted the proper investigation that does not take a popular stance, then this will be the supervisor's or manager's opportunity to prove their worth and belief in the system. That system of support should also come from the entire command staff in the organization. When the staff comes to believe they will be supported in the process, the turning point for the staff to support the organizational mission in the internal investigations process will be met. It is also critical that internal investigators see themselves as part of the chief's management team and a process of shared values and philosophies be put into practice in the unit (McCarthy, 2000).

As these entities develop and grow in the organization so shall the understanding of the need for this process. The internal investigations supervisor or manager must recognize the need for improvement in the system and take the appropriate measures to correct the process. These may be human resource, policy, or organizational imperatives for change and work to make those changes possible. In contemporary workforce applications, police administrators must create commitment on the part of followers through leadership and the development of individual capacity (McCarthy, 2000). The internal investigations unit supervisor or manager position will be one of the most taxing and yet one of the most rewarding positions in the organization if administered properly with only the process in mind.

UNIT POLICY

As in other areas of policing, developing specific policies and procedures for an internal investigations unit is important to the unit's function and success. Therefore, the establishment of appropriate policies, in written form such as policy and procedure manuals, development of a mission statement, core values, and proper administrative guidance. Administrative manuals must be complete but need not be voluminous. Continuous evaluation of citizen complaints should also take place to determine if policy guidance and operating procedures are adequate for the organization to properly function (McCarthy, 2000).

BROCKPORT POLICE DEPARTMENT
GENERAL ORDER

General Order: 305	Effective Date: 10/01/03
Subject: Professional Standards / Internal Affairs	
Reference Standards: 14.4, 25.1, 25.2, 25.6, 25.8	
Rescinds: General Order 305 Dated 10/28/02	
Page 1 of 4	Appendix

I. PROFESSIONAL STANDARDS / INTERNAL AFFAIRS FUNCTION

To ensure the integrity of the Brockport Police Department and its members, it is the policy of the department to document, investigate and properly adjudicate all allegations of misconduct by department members.

II. DEFINITIONS:

A. Platoon / Unit Complaint: Include but are not limited to any alleged violation of department administrative procedure, rule, order, abusive or discourteous behavior, unprofessional demeanor or action by a member of the department.

Figure 16-1. Examples of Unit policies can be found through the IACP and other police departments that are accredited or have been proactive in their efforts to service their respective communities (Photo courtesy of the Brockport, New York Police Department).

PERFORMANCE EVALUATIONS

Performance evaluations are a part of most all human resource driven organizations. They may be either formal or informal systems of providing feedback to an employee on their individual performance for a defined period of time. Their application in law enforcement was as much a part of accreditation than as a means of improving performance. Their importance as a developmental tool should not be understated as they provide a validated means for providing qualitative feedback to the employee on the expectations of the organization and its supervisory staff.

In developing and administering a performance evaluation system the organization must distinguish between roles and design a system that is based upon job task analyses. In patrol and administrative functions there will exist common and starkly different functions to be performed. Performance evaluations need to be diverse enough to encompass basic job tasks while being specific enough to provide an evaluation tool for those jobs that have specific functions. The internal investigations process is one such need in an organization as it is critical to set the proper expectations as well as provide qualitative feedback to maintain and increase personal and professional capacity.

Since the internal investigator serves a separate and distinct function, a separate and distinct evaluation process should be employed. Internal investigations unit managers should also view these evaluations as opportunities to teach investigators how to make ethical decisions in the investigative process as well as hold them accountable for their investigations (McCarthy, 2000; McNeff, 2001).

For a performance evaluation system to be effective in this realm, the administrator must conduct a job task analysis that measures such behaviors as administrative ability, investigative ability, interview and interrogations skills, conflict resolution and communication skills, just to name a few that would be considered for an evaluation. Other considerations would be caseload, case quality, administrator feedback on case findings, complainant and community feedback on relational skills and resolution strategies. Use of a specific system can go far in developing employees in a positive manner to conduct the highest quality investigations.

SUMMARY

This chapter discussed the numerous issues involved in training and managing internal investigators. The chapter discussed the various methods of curriculum development and common training needs. The chapter closed with the issues of managing an internal investigations unit, developing unit policy, and the use of a separate performance evaluation system for internal investigations unit staff.

Chapter 17

FUTURE TRENDS IN INTERNAL INVESTIGATIONS

INTRODUCTION

The future of the internal investigations process may hold some very complex issues that administrators must begin to prepare for now. The process must be an evolutionary system that is continually prepared for the impending challenges of the field. This chapter addresses the implications of those future trends.

LITIGATION INVOLVING INTERNAL INVESTIGATORS AND CHIEFS

A future trend in the internal investigations process may be an increase in litigations involving internal investigators and chief executives of law enforcement organizations. Employees are more likely to seek redress for adverse or incompetent actions of their employers in employment actions. Complaints of this nature can be filed internally, with the Equal Employment Opportunity Commission, Public Employee Relations Board, and the courts in state and federal actions. Employees are becoming less likely to sit idle in the face of these types of actions. Transferring the onus to the investigator or the chief is a method to minimize culpability, especially when procedural errors or a case for bias can be made.

The internal investigator and administrator must begin to think in terms of such issues that have been raised in the science of fingerprints. Fingerprints have withstood seventy odd years of scrutiny until the *Daubert* decision. Previous to that point, attorneys experienced great difficulty in attacking an officer testifying to the identification of fingerprints. Defense attorneys then subsequently chose to attack the science of fingerprints. The *Daubert* decision allowed for the review at the federal level of the purported imperfections in the science of fingerprint identification. DNA, on the contrary, is based in a hard science and at the moment cannot be effectively attacked. Defense attorney tactics have switched to attacking the collection and analyzation processes rather than the science of DNA. As such, unions and defense attorneys may be researching methods to attack the internal investigations processes in specific agencies as well as the entire discipline.

Several lawsuits challenging adverse actions against chiefs and city administrators have prevailed in favor of the employee. An extension of the *Canton* decision can be drawn in the failure to train internal investigators and their subsequent acts that violate the civil rights of employees. Departments are also being held strictly accountable for such issues as wrongful terminations. For example, a California jury found the City of Inglewood California liable in a reverse discrimination suit that resulted from disciplinary action and the termination of a police officer. Officer Jeremy Morse was fired and his partner was suspended due to a use-of-force incident. The jury decided in favor of the officers and awarded them the sum of $2.4 million in the case (Cable News Network, January 19, 2005). Such cases arise from poor or biased investigative practices, severe actions that fail to employ a progressive discipline mindset, or disciplinary action that is purely for political reasons.

Figure 17-1. Inglewood Officer Jeremy Morse and his partner prevailed in a lawsuit brought against the municipality alleging that disciplinary actions taken against them were unfair and biased (CNN).

TRAINING PRIORITIES

In general, case law states that the lack of a training budget is no excuse for failing to provide training (Oberlander, 2004). Many states only provide basic academy training to officers, minimal to no training to immediate supervisors, and in-service training that barely meets state standards. Given the potential for claims of adverse employee actions, the issue of training is also held in the limelight as proper training may have avoided arbitrary actions or allowed for the internal investigator to properly defend their actions to a hearing board, independent arbitration body, or the courts. Most internal investigators, supervisors, and law enforcement administrators for that matter, receive no training in the internal investigations process. As delineated in this text, the internal investigations process is very complex and unique requiring a different skill set than those needed of the average law enforcement investigator, supervisor, or manager. Administrators should take the lead in this concept as mandated by such federal decisions as *Canton* in order to prepare their agencies for the multifaceted and intricate needs of these critical investigations.

A NATIONAL MODEL OF INTERNAL INVESTIGATION

The proliferation of federal oversight and public outcry for monitoring systems as well as the integrity of the investigative process may lead to a trend towards a national model of internal investigation. This philosophy may be embraced by such organizations as the International Association of Chiefs of Police, the National Sheriffs Association, or be mandated by the federal government by legislative act. Individual police corruption investigative commissions such as the Knapp Commission, the Christopher Commission, the Crimi Commission, and others have taken an agency level approach, however, whether real or perceived, the problem still exists. As such, the federal government may be forced into mandating a national model of internal investigation that agencies will have no latitude in designing unless they begin to recognize the need and prepare early. Speculation of the inception of federal oversight as a step towards the eventual restructuring of this nation's law enforcement into the federalization that is common around the rest of the world may not be out of the realm of possibility (Cameron, 2000). While the federal government is researching the efficacy of policies on evidence protocol, moves such as federal oversight, the mandate of early warning systems for departments that meet certain thresholds, and other measures may be the precursor for this type of move.

CERTIFICATION

Certification at the local, state, and federal levels may also be in the future. Basic police certification and recertification have been in place for eons. Basic supervision was the next move in this field. Some states have now opted to mandate the certification of investigative staff. In this realm, a mandate may be felt by a governmental entity or by state and federal accreditation processes as a move to improve the ability of law enforcement to respond to the reality and perception of poorly conducted internal investigations.

REACHING THE POINT OF TRUST

The concept, while somewhat counterintuitive may be a move in the right direction before any substantive change may take place. While the officer may never completely trust the internal investigations process, much improvement can be made in the system. This type of change in attitude must be built over time and must come from the organization, not the officer. Because of decades of abuse, poor publicity, and some unforgiving case law, agencies will need to bring this notion forward on their own and be consistent in its stated mission as well as actions. This element of trust must be built one supervisor at a time through one agency at a time. Only then will the problems of the Blue Wall of Silence and untruthfulness begin to wane.

SUMMARY

This chapter discussed the future trends of the internal investigations process. Such issues as litigation, training, certification, and others will have an individual as well as collective impact on the field and the process of investigation. The conduct of the internal investigation is a critical issue in the context of law enforcement organizational operations. A law enforcement agency must maintain an efficient and effective operation of community service in light of the need to be ethical and responsive. When transgressions are reported, they threaten the very fabric of this requirement and the safety and service that are provided to the community. In response, the law enforcement agency must take aggressive action by means of the conduct of thorough and fair internal investigations. Police work is one of the more noble and selfless occupations in society (International Association of Chiefs of Police, 1998a). That altruistic and nobility of orientation is not without weakness, error, and proper intent. The internal investigation requires fortitude, integrity, and most importantly, courage to do what is right, legal, proper, and justified under the spirit and letter of the law.

This monumental task carries with it a burden of balance in allowing law enforcement personnel enough latitude to work in an environment that encourages rather than discourages legitimate police work in the inexact world of policing. Several noted individuals have recognized the near impossibility of this task. One such person is Dr. Dennis J. Stevens (2001) who states with respect to officers who hesitate to act based upon fear of complaints and litigation that:

> Professionally trained police officers need to conduct their duty in a proficient and legal manner in keeping with an advanced democratic society. But crime control includes a host of hard answers and dedicated officers. One of those answers is centered in the thought that when a civilized society cannot stand the horrors of crime and willingly becomes its victim by not dealing competently with it, then that society will surely be enslaved by the uncivilized. (p. 107)

The most difficult times are assuredly ahead of us!

Appendix

INVESTIGATIVE SUMMARY TEMPLATE

(Package Cover Page)

"CONFIDENTIAL INVESTIGATION"

Police/Sheriff's Department

Section/Unit Responsible for the Investigation (e.g., I.A.)

Personnel Complaint Investigation

Investigative Summary

Case Number

This case is confidential and may be reviewed only by authorized personnel as designated by the chief, sheriff, superintendent, or other chief executive officer of the organization.

POLICE/SHERIFF'S DEPARTMENT

Internal Investigation Case Package Index

Case # 06-0001

1. Command Remarks/Recommendation Form
2. Final Letter to Complainant
3. Notice of Finding to Subject Officer
4. Disciplinary/Remedial Training Attachments (if applicable)
5. Investigative Summary of Investigating Sergeant/Lieutenant
6. Investigative Action Report (case notes) of Investigating Sergeant/Lieutenant
7. Relevant Law Sections (NYS Penal Law, NYS Criminal Procedure Law, NYS PL Article 35.00, Municipal and Town Codes, Other laws, excerpts, etc.)
8. Relevant Departmental Policies & Procedures (Subject Management, Courtesy, Tow Policy, etc.)
9. Relevant Police Manual Excerpts (Accident Investigation, Investigative Techniques, Handling of Special Situations Such as Domestics or Emotionally Disturbed Persons, Orders of Protections, etc.)
10. Relevant In-Service & Specialized Training Materials (Defensive Tactics, Firearms, SWAT, etc.)
11. Complaint Form
12. Statement of Complainant Including the Advisement Form (Steno, Supporting Deposition, Synopsis of Taped Interview, etc.)
13. Involved Witness Statement(s)
14. Independent Witness Statement(s)
15. Expert Witness Statement(s) (A.D.A., Municipal Attorney, Defensive Tactics Instructor(s), Firearms Instructor(s), Crash Management Experts, Polygraph Expert, Forgery & Fraud Examiner, Lab Analyses, etc.)
16. Subject Officer(s) Statements including a Copy of the Right to Representation Advisement's (Steno, Special Report(s), Synopsis of Taped Interviews, etc.)
17. Witness Officer Statements (Steno, Special Report(s), Synopses of Taped Interviews, Supporting Depositions, etc.)
18. All Relevant Criminal Police Reports & Packages (Crime, Incident, FIF, Prisoner Data, Court Accusatory Instruments, Grand Jury Packages, Evidence Technician Reports, etc.)
19. Any and All Supporting Information that is Germane to the Case (e.g., Roll Call Information that Identifies the Subject of the Complaint as a Drug Dealer when the Complaint is of an Illegal/Inappropriate Street Stop, etc.)
20. All Relevant Administrative Police Reports & Packages (Subject Management/Use-of-force, Officer Injured, Post-Pursuit, etc.)
21. Medical Reports/Transcripts & Medical Testimony (Steno, Taped Interview, Supporting Deposition, etc.)

22. Any Photographic Line-Up Used
23. Daily Activity Report(s) of All Subject(s) and Witness Officer(s)
24. O.E.C. Event Summary & Copy of Tape
25. Scene Diagram(s) & Area Map
26. All Scene & Subject Photographs with a Separate Index for Same

NOTE: Each attachment should be marked at the bottom of every page for easy referencing.

COMMAND REVIEW REMARKS FORM

Lieutenant's Remarks & Recommendations:
Signature ______________________ Date ____________
Captain's Remarks & Recommendations:
Signature ______________________ Date ____________
Major's Remarks & Recommendations:
Signature ______________________ Date ____________
Deputy Chief's Remarks & Recommendations:
Signature ______________________ Date ____________
Chief's Remarks & Recommendations:
Signature ______________________ Date ____________

NOTE: This form should be modified and added to include only those Chain of Command personnel who are responsible for case review. The investigator's recommendations are already included in the Investigative Summary.

POLICE/SHERIFF'S DEPARTMENT

Special Report

To: Chief/Sheriff, via the Chain of Command
From: Sergeant/Lieutenant (Assignment)
Date: (Date Investigation Completed)
Subject: Internal Investigation # 99-0001

Introductory Paragraph

"On the above date, the Complainant (Name) filed a personnel complaint with the Department alleging misconduct on behalf of (Department members) concerning an incident that occurred on (Date) at (Location)."

Findings Section for the Specific Allegation

"The Complainant (Name) alleged that Officer/Deputy (Name) was (1) Discourteous, (2) Used excessive force by striking him with a PR-24 and spraying him with Pepper spray, (3) Failed to secure the Complainant's personal property, to wit, his drivers' license per Departmental directives, and (4) Had no basis for the traffic stop. The facts of the investigation support the findings of (1) Unfounded, (2) Exonerated, (3) Sustained, and (4) Exonerated for the respective allegations."

Incident Synopsis

"Briefly, on (Date & Time), Officer/Deputy observed a (Vehicle Description) being operated in a westerly direction on West Ridge Road near the intersection of Elmgrove Road in the Town of Greece, New York. The vehicle was being operated by the Complainant, of whom, is the registered owner. At this time, the Complainant passed an internationally recognized traffic control device, to wit, a steady red light that controls the flow of westbound traffic, and continued westbound on West Ridge Road. Officer/Deputy engaged his emergency equipment on his marked patrol vehicle and attempted to conduct a traffic stop. The Complainant failed to stop until he reached West Ridge Road at North Union Street in the town of Parma, New York. The Complainant immediately exited his vehicle and challenged Officer/Deputy while standing in the roadway. Officer/Deputy issued several verbal commands to the Complainant, who ignored the Officer/Deputy's lawful orders and continued to advance in a threatening manner, attempting to punch the Officer/Deputy with both fists. The Officer/Deputy first utilized Pepper spray, but it was ineffective due to the high winds. The Officer/Deputy then utilized his Department issued PR-24 and delivered a jab to the Complainant's lower abdominal area. The Complainant responded by falling to the pavement. The Complainant was then handcuffed without further incident and placed in the right rear of the Officer/Deputy's marked patrol vehicle. The Complainant was issued the attached summonses for Passing a Red Light and for Operating an Unregistered Motor Vehicle with No Insurance. The Complainant was also charged with harassment and resisting arrest. The Complainant was transported to Park Ridge Hospital by the Officer/Deputy for medical examination and treatment. The Complainant was treated and released and was issued an appearance ticket."

Evidence to Support the Specific Allegations

(1) Discourtesy:

Attachment 11, the Complaint Form, Attachment 12, the Stenographic Statement of the Complainant (etc.)

(2) Used excessive force by striking him with a PR-24 and spraying him with Pepper spray:

(3) Failed to secure the Complainant's personal property, to wit, his drivers' license per Departmental directives:

(4) Had no basis for the traffic stop:

Evidence to Refute the Specific Allegations

(1) Discourtesy:

Attachment 14, the Statement of the Independent Witness, Attachment 16, the Statement of the Subject/Involved Officer (etc.)

(2) Used excessive force by striking him with a PR-24 and spraying him with Pepper spray:

(3) Failed to secure the Complainant's personal property, to wit, his drivers' license per Departmental directives:

(4) Had no basis for the traffic stop:

Identify, Separate, & Explain Each Allegation Along with the Recommended Finding(s)

Discourtesy:

Complainant & Involved Witnesses

The Complainant states that Officer/Deputy yelled at him, "Get back in the f------ car" (Attachment's 11 & 14). There is no additional involved witness to support the Complainant's allegation.

Officer/Deputy & Involved Personnel

Officer/Deputy states that he/she did not make any discourteous remarks to the Complainant (Attachment 16).

Independent Witnesses

The Independent Witness states that at no time did the Officer/Deputy ever act in a discourteous manner towards the Complainant.

Recommended Finding

Therefore, a preponderance of evidence exists to support the finding of UNFOUNDED for this allegation, as the act complained of apparently did not occur.

(2) **Used excessive force by striking him with a PR-24 and spraying him with Pepper spray:**

In addition to the above witness information include the following:

Defensive Tactics Techniques

The supporting documentation and statements were reviewed by Officer/Sergeant (Name), a New York State Bureau for Municipal Police Certified Defensive Tactics Instructor. In his/her expert opinion, the tactics that were used, to wit, the use of Pepper spray and the use of a PR-24 Jab, were legal, proper, and justified based upon the circumstances, the level of force/resistance demonstrated by the Complainant, New York State Law, Departmental policy, and trained defensive tactics techniques (Attachment 15).

Medical Evaluation & Treatment

A review of the statement of Dr. (Name) has revealed that the complainant did not suffer any significant or permanent injuries, nor any that would have appeared to be the use of excessive or unnecessary force on behalf of the involved Officer/Deputy (Attachment 21).

(3) **Failed to secure the Complainant's personal property, to wit, his drivers' license per Departmental directives:**

In addition to the above witness information include the following:

If any remedial training is conducted for sustained allegations, include the type of training as well as who conducted it in this section.

(4) **Had no basis for the traffic stop:**

Remember, in allegations of a legal nature seek the opinion of the experts, the District Attorney's Office.

Miscellaneous Section for any Ancillary/Satellite Issues

No ancillary or satellite issues were developed during the course of the investigation.

This investigation is being submitted through the chain of command for review, recommendations, and determination of final disposition.

POLICE/SHERIFF'S DEPARTMENT

Intradepartmental Correspondence

To: Case File
From: Sergeant/Lieutenant (Assignment)
Date: (Date Follow-Up Completed)
Subject: Investigative Action Report (Case Notes) # 99-0001

This report should be a step-by-step account of the investigative steps you completed in the case from the time it was issued to you to the time the case investigation (not administrative review) is completed.

Neighborhood Canvas

(Date Completed)

Address Checked	Name/Business	Telephone	Info (W/PK/NO/NI)

Witness Interviews

Document witness interviews of those who have knowledge in two manners as follows:

Interview – John Q. Citizen (Date/Time/Location)

Mr. Citizen was identified as a passer-by and observed the entire incident. Mr. Citizen gave the attached supporting deposition of his account of the incident.

Interview – Jane Doe (Date/Time/Location)

Ms. Doe was identified as a person with knowledge. Ms. Doe observed the original traffic stop and the Complainant exit his vehicle and advance on the Officer/Deputy in a threatening manner by waving his fists. Ms. Doe left to find a telephone to call police over her observations. Ms. Doe did not observe any additional contact between the Officer/Deputy and the Complainant. Ms. Doe refused to give a written statement at the time of her interview.

Scene & Subject Photography

A log sheet should be completed with the following information:

Location/Description	**Direction**
Photographs taken of the Complainant by Sergeant at complaint intake at Section/Zone on (Date & Time)	
1) Subject Identification	N/A
2) Subject Front	N/A
3) Subject Back	N/A
Photographs taken of the subject by involved Officer/Deputy at Park Ridge Hospital on (Date & Time)	
4) Subject Identification	N/A
5) Subject Front	N/A
6) Subject Back	N/A
Photographs taken of the scene by Sergeant on West Ridge Road on (Date & Time)	
7) Traffic Control Device for Westbound traffic on Ridge Road west at Elmgrove Road (Cycle Red)	W
8) Traffic Control Device for Westbound traffic on Ridge Road west at Elmgrove Road (Cycle Yellow)	W
9) Traffic Control Device for Westbound traffic on Ridge Road west at Elmgrove Road (Cycle Green)	W
10) Scene Photographs – West Ridge Road at North Union Street	N
11) Scene Photographs – West Ridge Road at North Union Street	S
12) Scene Photographs – West Ridge Road at North Union Street	E
13) Scene Photographs – West Ridge Road at North Union Street	W
14) Photograph from the location of Independent Witnesses observations	S/W

Use this section as your index cover for your photographs of the incident/complaint.

Photographic Array

The attached photographic array was assembled by Sergeant (Name) on (Date):

Photographic Array 1

(1) Officer (Name)
(2) Officer (Name)
(3) Subject Officer (Name)

(4) Officer (Name)
(5) Officer (Name)
(6) Officer (Name)

NOTE: Any identification, or lack of identification should be documented only in the statement of the viewing complainant/witness. Do not repeat the information here.

Medical Records

All efforts and dates/times to retrieve medical records should be documented here. Don't repeat the interview of medical personnel, that information should be complete in the interview.

Polygraph/VSA Examinations

This section should document if the Complainant/Witnesses were offered the opportunity for a polygraph, and if the technique was used. Don't document the results of the polygraph if used as they should be in a formal report from the examiner.

Scene Sketch(es) & Diagram(s)

This section should identify what scene diagrams were completed and by whom. The legend can also be included in this section with the actual measurements, or also, attached to the diagram in the attachments section (e.g., # 25 on the example index)

Additional Information

Any additional information should be documented here that is germane to the case such as a record check on the complainant if you can demonstrate relevance, etc.

Attachments

Attach all additional correspondences that do not fall under other categories to this report, e.g., letters to complainant's and witnesses, return postal receipts, etc.

BIBLIOGRAPHY

Adcox, Ken: Doing bad things for good reasons. *The Police Chief, 67:* 16–27, 2000.

Albrecht, Steve: The pros and cons of creative handcuffing. *Law and Order Magazine, 48:* 19–20, 2000.

Alexander Hamilton Institute: *Effective Interviews for Every Situation.* Maywood, Modern Business Reports, 1991.

Americans for Effective Law Enforcement: Disciplinary interviews and compelled reports. *AELE Law Library of Case Summaries: Employment and Labor Law for Public Safety Agencies.* Retrieved from the World Wide Web on July 21, 2005 at http://www.aele.org/discsample.html.

American Psychological Association: *Jaffee v. Redmond 518 U.S. 1,* Retrieved from the World Wide Web on February 17, 2006 at http://www.apa.org/psyclaw/jaffee.html.

American Society of Law Enforcement Trainers: ABE: Evaluating LTL technology. *The Law Enforcement Trainer, 18:* 21–23, 2003.

Anderson, Aimee B.: Profiling claims based on equal protection: Decisions signal move away from high plaintiffs' burden. *The Police Chief, 67:* 12–14, 2000.

Anderson, Jonathan L.: Iron discipline: Then and now. *Law and Order Magazine, 49:* 77–78, 2001.

Armon, Rick: Ex-cop, a convicted molester, blames training, may sue city. *The Democrat and Chronicle,* 2003, July 3.

Armstrong, Hunter, & Nibler, Nick: Law enforcement training and evolutionary combative behavior. *The Law Enforcement Trainer, 14:* 16–38, 1999.

Arnold, Jon: Internal affairs investigation guidelines. *Law and Order Magazine, 47:* 43–46, 1999.

Arnold, Jon: Early misconduct detection. *Law and Order Magazine, 49:* 80–86, 2001.

Arnold, Jon: Accountability. *Law and Order Magazine, 50:* 122–123, 2002.

Artwohl, Alexis, & Christensen, Loren W.: *Deadly Force Encounters.* Boulder, Paladin, 1997.

Atkinson-Tovar, Lynn: Impact of repeated exposure to trauma. *Law and Order Magazine, 51:* 118–123, 2003.

Aveni, Thomas: The persistence of questionable shootings. *Law and Order Magazine, 50:* 70–75, 2002a.

Aveni, Thomas: The facts, fictions and liabilities of handgun qualification. *Law and Order Magazine, 50:* 40–45, 2002b.

Aveni, Thomas: Following standard procedure: A long-term analysis of gunfights and their effects on policy and training. *Law and Order Magazine, 51:* 78–87, 2003a.

Aveni, Thomas: The force continuum conundrum. *Law and Order Magazine, 51:* 74–77, 2003b.

Badger, Joe: Rules for 'experts.' *Law and Order Magazine, 47:* 22–23, 1999.

Badger, Joe: Crash investigation and physical evidence. *Law and Order Magazine, 50:* 26, 2002a.

Badger, Joe: Human factors in accident investigation. *Law and Order Magazine, 50:* 12, 2002b.

Badger, Joe: First 10 things to do at an accident scene. *Law and Order Magazine, 51:* 18–20, 2003a.

Badger, Joe: First 10 things to do at an accident scene: Part II. *Law and Order Magazine, 51:* 14–16, 2003b.

Badger, Joe: First 10 things to do at an accident scene: Part III. *Law and Order Magazine, 51:* 10, 2003c.

Badger, Joe: First 10 things to do at an accident scene: Part IV. *Law and Order Magazine, 51:* 10–12, 2003d.

Badger, Joe: Malfeasance of office. *Law and Order Magazine, 51:* 16–18, 2003e.

Bar, Aviv: Incident debriefings for patrol. *Law and Order Magazine, 51:* 116–117, 2003.

Baratta, Rick: Understanding critical skills training. *Law and Order Magazine, 46:* 188–193, 1998.

Baratta, Rick: Firearms training: It's not what it used to be. *Law and Order Magazine, 47:* 65–71, 1999.

Barker, Thomas, & Carter, David L. *Police Deviance* (3rd ed.). Cincinnati, Anderson, 1994.

Bartlett, Derrick D.: Tactical disarmament: Most dangerous option. *Law and Order Magazine, 48:* 84–88, 2000.

Beasley, Norman, & Holmberg, Carl: Justice Department's civil disorder initiative addresses police training gap. *The Police Chief, 67:* 113–122, 2000.

Berger, William B.: Agency response to line of duty deaths. *The Police Chief, 69:* 6, 2002.

Bergner, Laurie L.: Changing departmental ethics: Tips from chiefs for chiefs. *Law and Order Magazine, 46:* 87–89, 1998.

Bir, Cynthia: Less-lethal impact modeling. *Law and Order Magazine, 50:* 94–99, 2002.

Black, Robert: Handcuffing dangerous persons. *Law and Order Magazine, 49:* 91–94, 2001.

Blakely, Tim: Teaching, learning, and believing. *The Law Enforcement Trainer, 19:* 46–49, 2004.

Boatman, Robert: Monitoring the police: The civilian ombudsman as a community liaison. *Law and Order Magazine, 49:* 219–220, 2001.

Boddy, James E.: Labor board reverses field on non-union disciplinary interviews. *FindLaw for Legal Professionals:* Retrieved from the World Wide Web on July 2, 2005 at http://library.findlaw.com/2004/Sep/27/133583.html.

Boertien, Robert: Hostile workplace. *Law and Order Magazine, 50:* 70–73, 2002.

Borelli, Frank: 21 feet is way too close. *The Law Enforcement Trainer, 16:* 12–15, 2001.

Borrello, Andrew: Police impact weapons: A foundation for proper selection. *Law and Order Magazine, 47:* 65–71, 1999.

Borrello, Andrew: The terminology trap: Non-lethal, less-than-lethal, less-lethal or lethal? *Law Enforcement Trainer, 15:* 60–65, 2000.

Borrello, Andrew: Felony car stops: A comparison of two widely used methodologies. *Law and Order Magazine, 49:* 49–52, 2001.

Borrello, Andrew: The terminology trap II. *Law Enforcement Trainer, 17:* 34–35, 2002a.

Borrello, Andrew: In search of the safest stop: Introducing the felony hybrid stop method. *Law Enforcement Trainer, 17:* 37–40, 2002b.

Bragg, Robert. M.: OC spray and science: One good study is worth a hundred opinions. *Law Enforcement Trainer, 15:* 18–19, 2000.

Brooks, Michael E.: Using a racial characteristic in a criminal investigation. *The Police Chief, 67:* 10, 2000.

Brown, Ed: Transitioning the role of police psychologists. *Law and Order Magazine, 48:* 89–90, 2000.

Buice, Ed: The seven i's and big c of police news. *Law and Order Magazine, 50:* 8, 2002a.

Buice, Ed: The nighmare-in-Noble wakeup call. *Law and Order Magazine, 50:* 16, 2002b.

Buice, Ed: Character: The core of crisis communication. *Law and Order Magazine, 50:* 12, 2002c.

Buice, Ed: This is a recording. *Law and Order Magazine, 50:* 22, 2002d.

Buice, Ed: When the world is watching. *Law and Order Magazine, 51:* 24–26, 2003a.

Buice, Ed: When SWAT hits the fan. *Law and Order Magazine, 51:* 12, 2003b.

Buice, Ed: Keys to successful media interviews. *Law and Order Magazine, 51:* 26, 2003c.

Burke, Tod, & Rigsby, Rhonda: Suicide by cop revisited. *Law and Order Magazine, 47:* 97–102, 1999.

Byrd, Edwin H.: Title VII and employer liability: Study Supreme Court rulings, but don't forget everything you've learned. *The Police Chief, 65:* 145–150, 1998.

Byrd, Edwin H.: Do "maximal restraints" violate clearly established law? *The Police Chief, 67:* 10–12, 2000.

Byrnes, John D.: Measuring human aggression. *Law Enforcement Trainer, 18:* 24–29, 2003.

Cable News Network: $8.75 million settlement over police brutality. *Cable News Network,* July 13, 2001.

Cable News Network: American morning transcripts. *Cable News Network aired January 19, 2005.*

Retrieved from the World Wide Web on 02/17/2006 at http://transcripts.cnn.com/TRANSCRIPTS/0501/19/ltm.02.html.

Cable News Network: Bailey, Fuhrman discuss polygraph test on "Larry King Live." *Cable News Network,* March 21, 1997.

Cable News Network: Beating captured on police video. *Cable News Network,* December 1, 2003.

Cable News Network: Boston police accept "full responsibility" in death of Red Sox fan. *Cable News Network,* October 22, 2004.

Cable News Network: Ex-L.A. cop gets two years in shooting. *Cable News Network,* May 6, 2002.

Cable News Network: Ex-LAPD officer pleads guilty to federal charges. *Cable News Network,* December 17, 2001.

Cable News Network: Mark Fuhrman's perjury probation ends. *Cable News Network,* April 24, 1998.

Cable News Network: He did it his way–Giuliani reflects on trials, success in City Hall. *Cable News Network,* December 30, 2001.

Cable News Network: How to stop false confessions such as in the Central Park jogger case. *Cable News Network,* December 17, 2002.

Cable News Network: Inglewood cops post bail, remain on leave. *Cable News Network,* July 19, 2002.

Cable News Network: New Orleans police fired for roles in beating. *Cable News Network,* December 22, 2005.

Cable News Network: N.J. troopers charged in 'racial profile' case. *Cable News Network,* September 9, 1999.

Cable News Network: N.Y. policeman sentenced to 30 years for torture of Haitian immigrant. *Cable News Network,* December 13, 1999.

Cable News Network: Officer breaks LAPD's 'code of silence.' *Cable News Network,* September 21, 2000.

Cable News Network: Police won't be prosecuted in death after beating–Cincinnati prosecutor: No evidence of crime. *Cable News Network,* May 6, 2004.

Cable News Network: Rodney King reluctant symbol of police brutality. *Cable News Network,* March 3, 2001.

Cable News Network: Second LAPD officer enters plea agreement in corruption scandal. *Cable News Network,* March 30, 2001.

Cable News Network: Serpico resurrects his decades-old criticism of NYPD. *Cable News Network,* September 23, 1997.

Cameron, Bruce W.: Could there be a fed in your future? *Law and Order Magazine, 48:* 4, 2000.

Cansler, Robert E.: Technology liability considerations. *The Police Chief, 65:* 53–55, 1998.

Carlan, Philip E.: Managing sexual harassment liability: A guide for police administrators. *The Police Chief, 67:* 124–129, 2000.

Carrick, Grady: Could A police response to racial profiling. *Law and Order Magazine, 49:* 79–82, 2001.

Cataldo, Anthony M.: The fallacy of aerosol subject restraints–pepper spray. *Law Enforcement Trainer, 18:* 12–15, 2003.

Chudwin, Jeff: Officer survival and after action issues. *The Law Enforcement Trainer, 14:* 16–17, 1999.

Clede, Bill: Recognizing mental illness. *Law and Order Magazine, 46:* 121–126, 1998.

Close, Dale H.: How chiefs should prepare for nine liability risks. *The Police Chief, 68:* 16–27, 2001.

Colaprete, Frank A.: The necessary evil of IA. *Law and Order Magazine, 51:* 96–100, 2003.

Coletta, Craig: How police departments can benefit from referral to community mediation programs. *The Police Chief, 70:* 72–77, 2003.

Collins, John M.: Discipline for insubordination. *The Police Chief, 66:* 12–14, 1999.

Cope, Curtis J.: Report writing review: A supervisor's mandate. *The Law Enforcement Trainer, 17:* 32–35, 2002.

Cox, Stephen M.: Racial profiling: Refuting concerns about collecting race data on traffic stops. *Law and Order Magazine, 49:* 60–65, 2001.

Crotty, Jim: Searching suspects. *Law and Order Magazine, 46:* 79–82, 1998.

Cuadros, Jaime: Beanbags as an affective alternative. *Law and Order Magazine, 50:* 100–101, 2002.

Culp, Margaret H.: Officer-involved orders of protection: A management challenge. *The Police Chief, 67:* 10–12, 2000.

Czarnecki, Fabrice, Kasanof, Adam, & Trautman, Neal: Preventing police suicide: What you can do to help. *The Law Enforcement Trainer, 17:* 22–25, 2002.

Dahlinger, Charles: The consequences of not adequately training or reviewing departmental policy. *Law and Order Magazine, 49:* 53–54, 2001.

Dailey, Danny J.: No response may be preferred. *Law and Order Magazine, 46:* 94, 1998.

Dallett, Kevin: Training and aerosol subject restraints. *The Law Enforcement Trainer, 19:* 8–11, 2004.

Daniels, Wayne H.: Training for pursuit driving. *Law and Order Magazine, 50:* 80–83, 2002.

Daniels, Wayne H., & Spratley, Lynnette: Lawsuit defense: Protecting the department from litigation. *Law and Order Magazine, 51:* 54–59, 2003a.

Daniels, Wayne H., & Spratley, Lynnette: Brainpower not horsepower: Teaching officers when and how to end pursuits. *Law and Order Magazine, 51:* 85–89, 2003b.

Dees, Tim: Internal affairs management software. *Law and Order Magazine, 51:* 88–95, 2003.

Demetriou, George: Within arm's reach: Winning in the "forbidden" zone. *The Law Enforcement Trainer, 17:* 32–35, 2002.

Democrat and Chronicle: Police "flash-bang" injures woman, 18, in drug raid aimed at someone else. *The Democrat and Chronicle,* 5B, January 22, 2005.

Devanney, Joseph: Excessive force claim. *Law and Order Magazine, 50:* 12–13, 2002.

Devanney, Joseph: Pepper spray ruling against the police. *Law and Order Magazine, 51:* 14–121, 2003.

Devanney, Joseph, & Summers-Devanney, Diane: Civil rights policy. *Law and Order Magazine, 51:* 10, 2003a.

Devanney, Joseph, & Summers-Devanney, Diane: Canine case law. *Law and Order Magazine, 51:* 12–14, 2003b.

Dorsch, Donald: Opened door for lawyers, burden for officers. *Law and Order Magazine, 49:* 102, 2001.

Eack, Kevin D., & McGath, Daniel R.: Mandating arbitration in statutory discrimination claims: A new option for law enforcement agencies? *The Police Chief, 66:* 10, 1999.

Ederheimer, Joshua A.: How one department improved deadly-force investigations through leadership models and business theories. *The Police Chief, 67:* 22–34, 2000.

Edwards, Jennifer: Evendale leaders shrug at report. *The Cincinnati Enquirer:* Retrieved from the World Wide Web on February 20, 2006 at http://www.enquirer.com/editions/2002/03/20/loc_evendale_leaders.html.

Eisenberg, Clyde B.: Pursuit management. *Law and Order Magazine, 47:* 73–77, 1999.

Ellman, Edgar S.: Put your policies in writing. *Law and Order Magazine, 47:* 146–147, 1999.

Fantin, Linda: The police car of choice has a deadly record. *The Salt Lake Tribune,* 2003: Retrieved from the World Wide Web on February 14, 2006 at http://www.firepanel.net/images/07-28-03%20Police%20Car%20History.pdf.

Farrow, Joe: Citizen oversight of law enforcement: Challenge and opportunity. *The Police Chief, 70:* 22–29, 2003.

Ferrell, Craig E.: The department's right to question vs. the officer's right to avoid self-incrimination. *The Police Chief, 64:*10–12, 1997.

Ferrell, Craig E.: U.S. Supreme Court: Don't base car search only on traffic violation. *The Police Chief, 66:* 10, 1999.

Ferrell, Craig E., & Iris, Mark: The arbitration experience: Splitting the baby, or justice? *The Police Chief, 66:* 11–13, 1999.

Ferrell, Craig E.: Atwater underscores the need for carefully crafted departmental policies. *The Police Chief, 68:* 10–12, 2001.

Ferrell, Craig E.: Code of silence: Fact or fiction? *The Police Chief, 70:* 9–11, 2003.

Field, Mark W., & Meloni, Thomas E.: Constructive police discipline: Resurrecting the police spirit. *Law and Order Magazine, 47:* 85–91, 1999.

Findlaw.com: *Cleveland Board of Education v. Loudermill,* 470 U.S. 532 (1985). Findlaw.com. Sunnyvale, CA: Retrieved from the World Wide Web on February 17, 2006 at http://caselaw.lp.findlaw.com/cgi-bin/getcase.pl?court=us&vol=470&invol=532.

Finn, Peter: Two mediation systems help manage citizen complaints. *The Police Chief, 67:* 67–80, 2000a.

Finn, Peter: Getting along with citizen oversight. *The FBI Law Enforcement Bulletin, 69:* 22–27, 2000b.

Flemmings, Ashton E.: Responding to line of duty deaths: Understanding the PSOB. *The Police Chief, 66:* 40–42, 1999.

Forsyth, Richard: Increase ethical conduct. *Law and Order Magazine, 51:* 101–105, 2003.

Franscell, George J., & Maurer, Ann M.: Court decisions provide guidance on use of canine units. *The Police Chief, 67:* 138–147, 2000.

Fuller, John: Cultural diversity? Don't forget the disabled! *Law and Order Magazine, 48:* 84–85, 2000.

Fuller, John J.: Street cop ethics. *The Law Enforcement Trainer, 16:* 6–8, 2001.

Fuss, Timothy L., & Snowden, Lynne L.: Surveying sexual harassment in the law enforcement workplace. *The Police Chief, 67:* 65–72, 2000.

Gallo, Frank J.: Profiling v. racial profiling: Making sense of it all. *The Law Enforcement Trainer, 18:* 18–21, 2003.

Garmire, Bernie L. (Ed.): *Local Government Police Management* (2nd ed.). Washington, International City Management Association, 1982.

Garner, Gerald W.: Leading officers to safety. *The Police Chief, 69:* 116–119, 2002.

Gelber, Christopher: LAPD bureau psychologists hit the streets. *The Police Chief, 70:* 29–31, 2003.

Gilmartin, Kevin M., & Harris, John J.: The continuum of compromise. *The Police Chief, 65:* 25–27, 1998.

Ginn, Beverly A.: Due process issues in employment: A brief overview. *The Police Chief, 70:* 10–11, 2003.

Goldfarb, Daniel A.: In search of the silly thought: An addition to the debriefing process. *The Police Chief, 65:* 121–123, 1998.

Grattet, Ryken: Making the most of general orders. *The Police Chief, 71:* 63–66, 2004.

Graves, Alex: Law enforcement involved domestic abuse. *Law and Order Magazine, 52:* 108–111, 2004.

Gravesen, Gregory W.: Sun considerations for crash reconstruction. *Law and Order Magazine, 51:* 14–16, 2003.

Green, Don: Problem employees in smaller agencies. *Law and Order Magazine, 50:* 96–99, 2002.

Grimes, Dick: How to reduce the potential of workplace violence. *The Police Chief, 70:* 32–34, 2003.

Grossi, Dave: Use-of-force policy and procedure: Tactically sound, administratively feasible? *The Law Enforcement Trainer, 17:* 20–21, 2002a.

Grossi, Dave: Laser sights. *Law and Order Magazine, 50:* 96–100, 2002b.

Grossi, Dave: Surviving foot pursuits. *The Law Enforcement Trainer, 19:* 50–51, 2004.

Gundy, Jess: The complexities of use-of-force. *Law and Order Magazine, 51:* 60–65, 2003.

Hall, Dennis: Corruption report fails to raise ire among IACP chiefs. *Police Magazine, 22:* 20–22, 1998.

Harris, John J., & Gilmartin, Kevin M.: Malcontent and disgruntled employees: What is a supervisor to do? *The Police Chief, 67:* 19–24, 2000.

Harrison, Bob: Policy and procedure: What new sergeants need to know. *Law and Order Magazine, 49:* 151–153, 2001.

Heal, Sid: The push for less-lethal. *The Law Enforcement Technology, *:* 72, 2000.

Heal, Sid: An evaluation of less-lethal munitions. *Law and Order Magazine, 49:* 88–93, 2001.

Henriquez, Mark: The IACP national police use-of-force database project. *The Police Chief, 66:* 154–159, 1999.

Herman, Susan: Law enforcement and victim services: Rebuilding lives, together. *The Police Chief, 69:* 34–37, 2002.

Higginbotham, Jeffrey: Arbitration of federal statutory claims. *The Police Chief, 66:* 10–12, 1999.

Hill, Rodney, & Logan, Joan: Civil liability and mental illness: A proactive model to mitigate claims. *The Police Chief, 68:* 29–32, 2001.

Hill, Steven J.: Racial profiling: A challenge for American policing. *Law and Order Magazine, 47:* 94, 1999.

Hill, Steven J.: Firearms instructors under fire. *Law and Order Magazine, 51:* 84–87, 2003.

Holcomb, Jayme W.: Search and seizure issues in United States v. Drayton. *The Police Chief, 69:* 10–11, 2002.

Honig, Audrey L.: Police assisted suicide: Identification, intervention, and investigation. *The Police Chief, 68:* 89–93, 2001.

Honig, Audrey L., & Roland, Jocelyn E.: "Shots fired; Officer involved." *The Police Chief, 65:* 116–120, 1998.

Hoofnagle, Laura: Recognizing depression and raising awareness among law enforcement professionals. *The Police Chief, 69:* 84–89, 2002.

Hopper, Joan A.: Less-lethal litigation departments and the courts react to less-lethal standards. *Law and Order Magazine, 49:* 87–91, 2001a.

Hopper, Joan A.: Firearms training: Court's divergent rulings. *Law and Order Magazine, 49:* 39–43, 2001b.

Hopper, Joan A.: Every second counts to the U.S. Supreme Court. *Law and Order Magazine, 52:* 22–24, 2004.

Horne, Jennifer: Congress considers new measures to ban alleged profiling. *The Police Chief, 68:* 8, 2001.

Hughes, Johnny: Drug interdiction profiling. *Law and Order Magazine, 49:* 24, 2001.

Hurley, James: Officer survival: Officers need to be educated and trained to win. *Law and Order Magazine, 48:* 112–113, 2000.

Ijames, Steve: Engagements: Tactics and training for unconventional encounters. *The Law Enforcement Trainer, 14:* 8–11, 1999.

Ijames, Steve: Impact projectiles: Ten things a chief needs to know. *Law and Order Magazine, 50:* 86–93, 2002.

Institute for Labor Studies and Research: Defending disciplinary cases. *Institute for Labor Studies and Research,* Retrieved from the World Wide Web on 06/30/2005 at www.rilaborisntitute.org/grievance8.htm.

International Association of Chiefs of Police: Ethics training in law enforcement. *The Police Chief, 65:* 14–24, 1998a.

International Association of Chiefs of Police: IACP report shows police rarely use force. *The Police Chief, 65:* 18–22, 1998b.

International Association of Chiefs of Police: Officer-involved shooting guidelines. *The Police Chief, 65:* 108–109, 1998c.

International Association of Chiefs of Police: The importance of the advisor's role. *The Police Chief, 65:* 138–144, 1998d.

International Association of Chiefs of Police: Clarification of federal domestic violence-firearms legislation. *The Police Chief, 67:* 12, 2000a.

International Association of Chiefs of Police: Model policy offers guidance on investigating officer misconduct. *The Police Chief, 67:* 44–50, 2000b.

International Brotherhood of Teamsters: Weingarten: Three decades of union representation. *International Brotherhood of Teamsters,* Retrieved from the World Wide Web on 02/11/2006 at http://edu.teamster.org/hottopics/weingarten30.htm.

Kester, Don: Less lethal technology expands: Options increasing for law enforcement officers. *The Law Enforcement Trainer, 17:* 12–13, 2002.

Kinchin, David: The trauma of police work. *Law and Order Magazine, 48:* 63–65, 2000.

Kirschman, Ellen: Organizational stress: Looking for love in all the wrong places. *The Police Chief, 65:* 127–135, 1998.

Klotter, John C., & Ingram, Jefferson L. *Criminal Evidence* (8th ed.). Anderson Publishing, 2004.

Knight, Susan, & Callanan, Joe: Police expert malpractice. *The Law Enforcement Trainer, 18:* 10–17, 2003.

Korte, Gregory: Police inquiry scorches Roach. *The Cincinnati Enquirer:* Retrieved from the World Wide Web on Date, 2006 at http://www.enquirer.com/editions/2002/03/20/loc_1police_inquiry.html.

Kruger, Karen J.: New U.S. Supreme Court decision further illuminates the two rights to counsel. *The Police Chief, 71:* 11–12, 2003.

Laur, Darren: The anatomy of fear and how it relates to survival skills training. *The Law Enforcement Trainer, 17:*20–28, 2002.

Law and Order: Aggressive policing model not inherently racist. *Law and Order Magazine, 46:* 4, 1998.

Law and Order: NYPD tests officer integrity. *Law and Order Magazine, 47:* 6, 1999.

Law and Order: LAPD report calls for change. *Law and Order Magazine, 48:* 6, 2000a.

Law and Order: Trooper fired for refusing gambling. *Law and Order Magazine, 48:* 6, 2000b.

Law and Order: Officer files $10 million in discrimination claims. *Law and Order Magazine, 48:* 6, 2000c.

Law and Order: Mayor prohibits INS from accompanying police. *Law and Order Magazine, 48:* 6, 2000d.

Law and Order: Council fires officer who shot in direction of dogs. *Law and Order Magazine, 48:* 6, 2000e.

Law and Order: Fighting corruption. *Law and Order Magazine, 48:* 6, 2000f.

Law and Order: Overcoming the perception of racial profiling. *Law and Order Magazine, 49:* 94–101, 2001a.

Law and Order: IACP's less lethal force options course. *Law and Order Magazine, 49:* 95–99, 2001b.

Law and Order: Confronting biased enforcement claims. *Law and Order Magazine, 49:* 91–94, 2001c.

Law and Order: Phoenix patrols with tasers. *Law and Order Magazine, 51:* 6, 2003a.

Law and Order: Phoenix PD purchases Taser X26s. *Law and Order Magazine, 51:* 6, 2003b.

Law and Order: Pepperball's new 12 gauge impact plus. *Law and Order Magazine, 51:* 18–20, 2003c.

Lawrence, Chris, & Mohr, Wanda K.: Investigator protocol: Sudden in-custody death. *The Police Chief, 71:* 44–52, 2004.

Leibig, Mike: The rights of police officers threatened with termination: Loudermill's neglected protection. *The Virginia Coalition of Police and Deputy Sheriffs,* 2001, September: Retrieved from the World Wide Web on July 2, 2005 at http://www.virginiacops.org/Articles/Loudermill/Loudermill.htm.

Lesh, David N.: The duty to warn. *The Law Enforcement Trainer, 18:* 16–18, 2003.

Lewis, Scott: Conflict resolution: Communication as the ultimate problem solving tool. *Law and Order Magazine, 49:* 243–245, 2001.

Litchford, Jody M.: ADA decisions provide guidance for enforcement activities. *The Police Chief, 68:* 15–17, 2000.

Lober, Richard E.: Value-based leadership and the role of internal affairs. *The Police Chief, 69:* 54–57, 2002.

Lonsway, Kim, & Conis, Pete: Officer domestic violence. *Law and Order Magazine, 51:* 132–140, 2003.

Lonsway, Kim, & Harrington, Penny: Model policy for officer domestic violence. *Law and Order Magazine, 51:* 141–149, 2003.

Lundrigan, Nicole: Gunshot residue technology. *Law and Order Magazine, 52:* 66–68, 2004.

MacLatchie, Scott D.: Defending police shootings: Some helpful case law against trigger-happy lawsuits. *Law and Order Magazine, 48:* 109–113, 2000.

Makholm, John A.: Legal lights. *The Law Enforcement Trainer, 15,* 2000a.

Makholm, John A.: Legal lights. *The Law Enforcement Trainer, 15,* 2000b.

Makholm, John A.: Legal lights. *The Law Enforcement Trainer, 16:* 57, 2001.

Makholm, John A.: Legal lights. *The Law Enforcement Trainer, 17:* 46–47, 2002a.

Makholm, John A.: Legal lights. *The Law Enforcement Trainer, 17:* 54–55, 2002b.

Makholm, John A.: Legal lights. *The Law Enforcement Trainer, 17:* 53–54, 2002c.

Makholm, John A.: Legal lights. *The Law Enforcement Trainer, 17:* 66–67, 2002d.

Makholm, John A.: Legal lights. *The Law Enforcement Trainer, 17:* 54–55, 2003a.

Makholm, John A.: Legal lights. *The Law Enforcement Trainer, 17:* 64–65, 2003b.

Makholm, John A.: Legal lights. *The Law Enforcement Trainer, 17:* 52–53, 2004.

Margolis, Jeremy: Proactive defense strategies can minimize risk. *The Police Chief, 67:* 18–23, 2000.

Martin, Jeff: Pursuit termination: A lifesaver? *Law and Order Magazine, 49:* 30–33, 2001a.

Martin, Jeff: 3QFC pursuit decision making model. *Law and Order Magazine, 49:* 16–17, 2001b.

Martin, Jeff: Revising departmental policy and procedural manuals. *Law and Order Magazine, 50:* 114–116, 2002.

Martinelli, Thomas J.: Proactively managing risk the old fashioned way: Getting back to the basics of police service. *The Law Enforcement Trainer, 17:* 12–19, 2002.

Martinelli, Thomas J., & Pollock, Joycelyn M.: Law enforcement ethics, lawsuits, and liability: Defusing deliberate indifference. *The Police Chief, 67:* 52–67, 2000.

Massine, Mike: Integration of use-of-force training. *The Law Enforcement Trainer, 17:* 44–46, 2002.

Mayer, Martin J., & Coble, Paul R.: Utilizing the department's legal counsel at major incidents. *The Police Chief, 65:* 8, 1998.

McBride, Mike: Fighting talk. *The Law Enforcement Trainer, 16:* 10–11, 2001.

McCarthy, Robert: Steps chiefs can take to prevent unethical behavior. *The Police Chief, 67:* 36–43, 2000.

McKee, Frank: Psychomotor skill retention. *The Law Enforcement Trainer, 15:* 22–24, 2000.

McKenna, Brian: When bullets don't work. *The Police Marksman, 26:* 6–11, 2001.

McNeff, Michael: One agency's effort to reduce liability risk through emphasis on ethics. *The Police Chief, 68:* 10, 2001.

Means, Randy: The history and dynamics of section 1983. *The Police Chief, 71:* 10, 2004.

Meek, James G.: Racial profiling and traffic stops conference. *Law and Order Magazine, 49:* 95–96, 2001.

Meissner, Craig S.: Response to a bribe offer. *Law and Order Magazine, 46:* 87–88, 1998.

Messina, Phil: Dissecting the Diallo shooting: Four seconds to Hell. *The Law Enforcement Trainer, 15:* 8–46, 2000.

Meyer, Greg: Current use-of-force issues. *The Law Enforcement Trainer, 14:* 26–32, 1999.

Meyer, Greg: Risk management at the front line: The basics. *The Law Enforcement Trainer, 15:* 58–59, 2000.

Meyer, Greg: Overcoming reluctance to use legitimate force. *The Law Enforcement Trainer, 16:* 36–37, 2001.

Milazzo, Carl: Supreme Court emphasizes significance of officer safety. *The Police Chief, 65:* 151–156, 1998.

Milazzo, Carl: Searching containers inside vehicles. *The Police Chief, 66:* 10, 1999.

Milazzo, Carl: Stopping and chasing, or is it the other way around? *The Police Chief, 67:* 11, 2000.

Milazzo, Carl, & McNaught, Claire: SWAT team liability. *Law and Order Magazine, 50:* 97–100, 2002.

Miller, R. K.: Diversionary devices. *Law and Order Magazine, 50:* 62–66, 2002.

Miller, Tim: ALERT pursuit seminars. *Law and Order Magazine, 50:* 12, 2002.

Miraglia, Greg: Teaching the tactics of intervention. *The Police Chief, 66:* 30–33, 1999.

Monahan, Francis J.: Investigative commissions: Implemented reforms prove ephemeral. The *Police Chief, 67:* 79–84, 2000.

Moody, Bobby D.: Professional traffic stops vs. biased traffic stops. *The Police Chief, 65:* 6, 1998.

Morn, Frank: *Foundations of criminal investigation.* Durham, Carolina Academic Press, 2000.

Morrell, Alan: Deputy faces child porn charges. *The Democrat and Chronicle,* 1A, 2004, September, 16.

Morrison, Gregory B., & Shave, Phillip L.: Firearms training and the smaller department. *The Police Chief, 69:* 17–24, 2002.

Mueck, Robert B.: Probable signs of submission. *The Law Enforcement Trainer, 14:* 22–67, 1999.

Mueck, Robert B.: Racial epithets by police officers: Why they have no place in law enforcement. *Law and Order Magazine, 48:* 28–32, 2000.

Mulroy, Darrell E.: Stress: How it contributes to poor performance. *Law and Order Magazine, 48:* 67–68, 2000.

Mulroy, Darrell E., & Santiago, Julio: Warning shots revisited. *Law and Order Magazine, 46:* 96–99, 1998.

Myers, Mary E.: Waiting in the dark. *Law and Order Magazine, 46:* 69–72, 1998.

Neubauer, Ronald S.: Police use-of-force in America: An IACP update. *The Police Chief, 67:* 6, 1999.

New York State Department of State: Freedom of Information Law. *NYS DOS Committee on Open Government, Freedom of Information Law:* Retrieved from the World Wide Web on December 2, 2002 at http://www.dos.state.ny.us/coog/foil.html.

New York Times: *Ex-Trooper lectured and is sent to prison.* Retrieved from the World Wide Web on February 21, 2006 at http://query.nytimes.com/gst/fullpage.html?res=9E0CE6D7123BF934A25751C1A964958260. 1992, December 17.

Newbold, Mark: Officer liability for failure to disclose exculpatory evidence. *The Police Chief, 68:* 10–13, 2001.

Newbold, Mark: Conducted energy weapons and police liability. *The Police Chief, 69:* 11–12, 2002.

Newbold, Mark: Free expression and the public safety employee. *The Police Chief, 70:* 10–11, 2003.

Nielsen, Eugene: Cap-stun OC certification program. *Law and Order Magazine, 51:* 62–64, 2003a.

Nielsen, Eugene: Lasers helping firearms training. *Law and Order Magazine, 51:* 80–83, 2003b.

Noble, Jeff: Police officer truthfulness and the Brady decision. *The Police Chief, 70:* 92–101, 2003.

Nowicki, Ed: More to the Philly incident than media has shown. *Law and Order Magazine, 48:* 128, 2000a.

Nowicki, Ed: Comprehensive use-of-force training. *Law and Order Magazine, 48:* 72–77, 2000b.

Nowicki, Ed: The instructor. *Law and Order Magazine, 49:* 20–22, 2001a.

Nowicki, Ed: Use-of-force options. *Law and Order Magazine, 49:* 35–37, 2001b.

Nowicki, Ed: Dealing with litigation. *Law and Order Magazine, 49:* 29–31, 2001c.

Nowicki, Ed: Language and voice commands. *Law and Order Magazine, 49:* 21–22, 2001d.

Nowicki, Ed: OC spray update. *Law and Order Magazine, 49:* 28–29, 2001e.

Nowicki, Ed: Developing good reports. *Law and Order Magazine, 49:* 23–24, 2001f.

Nowicki, Ed: Body language. *Law and Order Magazine, 49:* 27–28, 2001g.

Nowicki, Ed: Lethal force options. *Law and Order Magazine, 49:* 18–20, 2001h.

Nowicki, Ed: Seven things every chief should know. *Law and Order Magazine, 49:* 33–34, 2001i.

Nowicki, Ed: The taser. *Law and Order Magazine, 49:* 24–25, 2001j.

Nowicki, Ed: Expandable batons. *Law and Order Magazine, 49:* 26–27, 2001k.

Nowicki, Ed: Latest lethal force training. *Law and Order Magazine, 50:* 8–10, 2002a.

Nowicki, Ed: Handcuffing. *Law and Order Magazine, 50:* 14–15, 2002b.

Nowicki, Ed: How not to fight. *Law and Order Magazine, 50:* 26–27, 2002c.

Nowicki, Ed: Weapon retention: Training and equipment. *Law and Order Magazine, 50:* 20, 2002d.

Nowicki, Ed: Total use-of-force training. *Law and Order Magazine, 50:* 24, 2002e.

Nowicki, Ed: Pepper with power. *Law and Order Magazine, 50:* 12–14, 2002f.

Nowicki, Ed: Racial profiling problems and solutions. *Law and Order Magazine, 50:* 16–18, 2002g.

Nowicki, Ed: Language of force. *Law and Order Magazine, 50:* 26–27, 2002h.

Nowicki, Ed: Deadly force: More than firearms. *Law and Order Magazine, 51:* 24–26, 2003.

Nowicki, Ed: Reducing liability through training. *Law and Order Magazine, 52:* 28–29, 2004.

Oberlander, Richard: Judgment evaluation and force option training simulators: Providing real world critical incident experiences. *The Law Enforcement Trainer, 19:* 31–35, 2004.

O'Hara, Charles E.: *Fundamentals of Criminal Investigation* (5th ed.). Springfield, Charles C. Thomas, 1981.

Oliver, Jerry A.: Lessons learned: Collecting data on officer traffic stops. *The Police Chief, 68:* 23–34, 2001.

Onder, James J.: Tips for conducting professional traffic stops. *The Police Chief, 68:* 26–30, 2001.

Orrick, Dwayne: Controlling abuse of sick leave. *The Police Chief, 71:* 39–42, 2004a.

Orrick, Dwayne: Practical pepper spray training. *Law and Order Magazine, 52:* 100–103, 2004b.

Papenfuhs, Steve: Subject control: Multiple officer takedowns. *Law and Order Magazine, 47:* 65–67, 1999.

Papenfuhs, Steve: Combating the skilled fighter: Recognizing and defending against this threat. *Law and Order Magazine, 48:* 131–134, 2000.

Papenfuhs, Steve: Tactically sound vehicle stops: A shift in mind-sets can save lives. *Law and Order Magazine, 51:* 80–84, 2003.

Parent, Richard B.: Suicide by cop: Victim precipitated homicide. *The Police Chief, 65:* 111–114, 1998.

Parent, Richard B.: Surviving a lethal threat: The aftermath. *Law and Order Magazine, 47:* 155–158, 1999.

Parent, Richard B.: Police shootings: Reducing the risks. *Law and Order Magazine, 48:* 82–84, 2000.

Parker and Waichman, L.L.P.: Ford Crown Victoria fires. *Parker and Waichman, L.L.P.* website, 2006: Retrieved from the World Wide Web on February 17, 2006 at http://www.yourlawyer.com/topics/overview/Ford_Crown_Victoria/.

Parks, Bernard C.: Ombuds office provides simpler method of reducing conflict among employees. *The Police Chief, 67:* 83–89, 2000.

Paynter, Ronnie L.: Suicide by cop. *The Law Enforcement Technology, *:* 40–44, 2000.

Paziotopoulos, Pamela A.: Workplace domestic violence. *Law and Order Magazine, 51:* 104–109, 2003.

Pedersen, Dorothy: Sleepy heads on patrol. *The Law Enforcement Technology, *:* 130–138, 2001.

Perry, Frank L.: Repairing broken windows: Preventing corruption within our ranks. *The FBI Law Enforcement Bulletin, 70:* 23–25, 2001, February.

Pinizzotto, Anthony J., & Davis, Edward F.: Suicide by cop: Implications for law enforcement management. *Law and Order Magazine, 47:* 95–98, 1999.

Pommerville, Paul A.: The Balkan war, diversity and police misconduct. *The Police Chief, 66:* 126–131, 1999.

Prabhu, Sandy, & Turner, Nancy: Rising to the challenge: Preventing police officer domestic violence. *The Police Chief, 67:* 43–55, 2000.

Praet, Bruce D.: Suicide by cop or death by indifference? *The Police Chief, 69:* 14, 2002.

Rappoport, Richard J.: Effective management of mistaken involvement stops. *The Police Chief, 70:* 35–41, 2003.

Rayburn, Michael T.: Instinctive tactics for low light shooting. *Law and Order Magazine, 48:* 103–106, 2000.

Rayburn, Michael T.: The shove and shoot drill revisited. *Law and Order Magazine, 49:* 53–55, 2001.

Reak, Kevin P.: Positional asphyxia revisited. *The Police Chief, 65:* 11, 1998a.

Reak, Kevin P.: Does releasing information violate the Constitution. *The Police Chief, 65:* 10, 1998b.

Reak, Kevin P.: Recent court cases shed light on how to deal with anonymous tips. *The Police Chief, 68:* 10, 2001.

Reilly, Christopher A.: The science of pepper spray. *Law and Order Magazine, 51:* 124–130, 2003.

Rhyons, Lori, & Brewster, David C.: Employee early warning systems: Helping supervisors protect citizens, officers, and agencies. *The Police Chief, 69:* 32–36, 2002.

Rohr, Carol Ann: Training for managing crowds and responding to civil disobedience. *The Police Chief, 68:* 10, 2001.

Rosenbaum, Steven H.: Patterns and practices of police misconduct. *Law and Order Magazine, 49:* 67–71, 2001.

Rosenthal, Rick: Media do's and don't's: Guidelines help media stay within limits covering crisis. *Law and Order Magazine, 48:* 19–20, 2000.

Rosenthal, Rick: More winning strategies. *Law and Order Magazine, 49:* 16–17, 2001a.

Rosenthal, Rick: Your critical incident. *Law and Order Magazine, 49:* 16–17, 2001b.

Rosenthal, Rick: Tips from the best in the business. *Law and Order Magazine, 49:* 21, 2001c.

Rossi, Guy: Metal-Tec 1400 handheld metal scanner. *Law and Order Magazine, 49:* 165–168, 2001.

Rostow, Cary D., & Davis, Robert D.: Psychological fitness for duty evaluations in law enforcement. *The Police Chief, 69:* 58–66, 2002.

Ryan, Jack: Training liability in the use of deadly force. *The Law Enforcement Trainer, 19:* 25–28, 2004.

Safety Forum: *Ford's Crown Victoria: Police car inferno.* Retrieved from the World Wide Web on February 20, 2006 at http://www.safetyforum.com/cvpi/.

Sanow, Edwin: Controlled force: Easy to remember defensive tactics. *Law and Order Magazine, 49:* 70–73, 2001a.

Sanow, Edwin: Survival force seminar. *Law and Order Magazine, 49:* 64–68, 2001b.

Sanow, Edwin: Satisfaction with the police. *Law and Order Magazine, 51:* 4, 2003.

Sawyer, Suzie: Strength through support: COPS program help victims become survivors. *The Police Chief, 69:* 38–39, 2002.

Scanlon, James: Ownership theory. *Law and Order Magazine, 52:* 104, 2004.

Schafer, John R.: Color of law investigations. *The FBI Law Enforcement Bulletin, 69:* 15–20, 2000.

Schembra, John: The mental aspect of emergency driving. *Law and Order Magazine, 50:* 88–90, 2002.

Scuro, Joseph E.: Federal civil rights update: Recent significant decisions by the U.S. Supreme Court. *Law and Order Magazine, 46:* 98–101, 1998.

Scuro, Joseph E.: Court expands prosecutions for false statements. *Law and Order Magazine, 48:* 29–30, 2000a.

Scuro, Joseph E.: Supreme Court reviews "stop and frisk" conduct. *Law and Order Magazine, 48:* 12–14, 2000b.

Scuro, Joseph E.: The Americans with Disabilities Act in the 21st century. *Law and Order Magazine, 49:* 31–33, 2001.

Serpas, Ronald W., Olson, Joseph W., & Jones, Brian D.: An employee disciplinary system that makes sense. *The Police Chief, 70:* 22–28, 2003.

Siegel, Paul J.: Nonunion employees gain right to representation during investigatory interviews, 2000, August: *International Risk Management Institute.* Retrieved from the World Wide Web on July 2, 2005 at http://www.irmi.com/Expert/Articles/2000/Siegel08.aspx.

Sifling-Aardema, Pattiann D.: Use of less-lethal alternatives not required when use of deadly force justified. *The Police Chief, 67:* 56–60, 2000.

Smith, Brad: Preparing K-9 operations for meritless lawsuits. *Law and Order Magazine, 46:* 101–106, 1998.

Smotzer, Andrew A.: Critical incident stress. *The Law Enforcement Trainer, 18:* 32–35, 2003.

Soto, Javier: Avoiding the teeth of liability. *Law and Order Magazine, 46:* 99–104, 1998.

Spaulding, Dave: Operating in reduced light. *Law and Order Magazine, 49:* 17–18, 2001.

Spector, Elliot B.: Liability for failure to disclose exculpatory information. *The Police Chief, 65:* 12–14, 1998.

Spector, Elliot B.: Stopping suspects based on racial and ethnic descriptions. *The Police Chief, 69:* 10–12, 2002a.

Spector, Elliot B.: Improper tactics and use-of-force liability. *The Police Chief, 69:* 13–14, 2002b.

Stevens, Dennis J.: Police officer stress. *Law and Order Magazine, 47:* 77–81, 1999.

Stevens, Dennis J.: Civil liability and selective enforcement. *Law and Order Magazine, 49:* 105–107, 2001.

Stine, Joseph J.: A ballistic vest against lawsuits: Protecting yourself and your department against civil liability. *The Police Chief, 68:* 44–47, 2001.

Stone, Michael P.: Supreme Court grants review of Court of Appeal holding that "waivers" of peace officers' rights are void. *The Law Enforcement Trainer, 16:* 32–35, 2001.

Strong, Paul: Ethics. *Law and Order Magazine, 52:* 65, 2004.

Sullivan, John J.: *Civil Liabilities of N.Y. Law Enforcement Officers* (3rd ed.). Flushing, NY: Looseleaf, 1999.

Sullivan, Michael J.: Obtaining and recording out of court statements. *Law and Order Magazine, 46:* 105–108, 1998.

Swope, Ross E.: The core-virtue bell curve. *The Police Chief, 65:* 37–38, 1998.

Swope, Ross E.: The ethical gatekeeper. *Law and Order Magazine, 50:* 132–135, 2002.

Thurnauer, Beau: Internal affairs: Practice and policy review for smaller departments. *The Police Chief, 69:* 73–82, 2002.

Trautman, Neal: Truth about police code of silence. *Law and Order Magazine, 49:* 68–76, 2001.

Trautman, Neal: The code of silence antidote. *The Law Enforcement Trainer, 17:* 18–21, 2002.

Trautman, Neal: Self-accountability: The ultimate integrity tool. *Law and Order Magazine, 51:* 52–58, 2003a.

Trautman, Neal: Stopping political interference. *Law and Order Magazine, 51:* 104–110, 2003b.

Trompetter, Philip S.: Fitness-for-duty evaluations: What police agencies can expect. *The Police Chief, 65:* 97–107, 1998.

Uhrig, Steve: Police/martial neck restraints and why they are confusing to nearly everyone. *The Law Enforcement Trainer, 14:* 12–16, 1999.

University of the State of New York State Education Department: *Records retention and disposition schedule CO-2 for use by counties.* Albany, University of the State of New York State Education Department, 1993.

Unkelbach, L. Cary: Name-clearing hearings. *The Police Chief, 70:* 13–16, 2003.

Vila, Bryan, & Kenney, Dennis J.: Tired Cops: The prevalence and potential consequences of police fatigue. *NIJ Journal, 248:* 16–21, 2003.

Voegtlin, Gene: IACP opposes traffic stops legislation. *The Police Chief, 66:* 8, 1999.

Wallace, Ronald: Duke projectile recovery system. *Law and Order Magazine, 52:* 36–39, 2004.

Ward, William, Parsons, David, & Connor, Gregory: Contact-cover/command-control. *Law and Order Magazine, 48:* 245–246, 2000.

Warren, Joe, & Meyers, Duane: PowerPoint for crash scene. *Law and Order Magazine, 52:* 28–33, 2004.

Warren, Rocky, & Olsen, Mitchell: Large vehicle pursuits and attacks. *Law and Order Magazine, 50:* 26–30, 2002.

Weinblatt, Richard B.: Managing off-duty jobs. *Law and Order Magazine, 47:* 84–88, 1999.

Weiss, Jim, & Davis, Mickey: Deadly force decision-making. *Law and Order Magazine, 50:* 58–62, 2002.

Weiss, Jim, & Davis, Mickey: The latest Taser technology. *Law and Order Magazine, 51:* 108–112, 2003.

Weiss, Jim, & Dresser, Mary: Learning to survive: Making it realistic improves retention. *Law and Order Magazine, 48:* 113–116, 2000a.

Weiss, Jim, & Dresser, Mary: Reaching out to the mentally ill. *Law and Order Magazine, 48:* 133–136, 2000b.

Weissberg, Michael W.: The reactive/non-reactive training controversy. *The Law Enforcement Trainer, 14:* 10–47, 1999.

Wells, Jim: Law enforcement safety and stops. *Law and Order Magazine, 52:* 10–12, 2004.

Westrick, Aaron: The "Philly case" . . . reasonable officer lag time. *The Law Enforcement Trainer, 15:* 30, 2000.

Whalen, Michael J.: Supreme Court ruling: Officer has no constitutional right to lie. *The Police Chief, 65:* 10, 1998.

Whalen, Michael J.: Supreme Court rulings acknowledge practical considerations of law enforcement. *The Police Chief, 69:* 11, 2002.

WHEC-TV: *Former police officer takes plea deal in child porn case.* March 10, 2005. Retrieved from the World Wide Web on February 21, 2006 at http://www.10nbc.com/news.asp?template=item&story_id=14271.

White, Stanley I.: Interview stance. *Law and Order Magazine, 48:* 47–48, 2000.

Williams, George T.: Interviewing officers involved in a deadly force event. *Law and Order Magazine, 47:* 38–41, 1999a.

Williams, George T.: Preventing spray and pray. *Law and Order Magazine, 47:* 43–46, 1999b.

Williams, George T.: Re-thinking force policies. *Law and Order Magazine, 47:* 42–46, 1999c.

Williams, George T.: Use-of-force reporting: Separate reports not a good idea. *Law and Order Magazine, 48:* 71–75, 2000.

Williams, George T.: Outcome-based defensive tactics training. *Law and Order Magazine, 49:* 82–85, 2001a.

Williams, George T.: Death by indifference. *Law and Order Magazine, 51:* 66–69, 2003a.

Williams, George T.: What is compliance? *Law and Order Magazine, 51:* 70–73, 2003b.

Williams, Myrick: Anti-knife training: Contact defense and control. *Law and Order Magazine, 50:* 56–61, 2002.

Wood, Scott: Totality of the circumstances: Analysis for reasonable suspicion reaffirmed by the Supreme Court. *The Law Enforcement Trainer, 17:* 22–26, 2002.

Zeichner, Irving B.: Inside justice. *Law and Order Magazine, 46:* 10, 1998.

Zelig, Mark: Families as victims in post-incident trauma. *The Police Chief, 65:* 124–126, 1998.

Zoufal, Donald R.: Legal issues in law enforcement information sharing. *The Police Chief, 67:* 8–10, 2000.

Zoufal, Donald R.: Law enforcement information sharing raises privacy issues. *The Police Chief, 68:* 8–10, 2001.

CASE LAW INDEX

SUBJECT INDEX

D

E

J

K

L

M

S

V